THE CHRONICLES OF FERNÃO LOPES

View of Lisbon as on folio from the *Chronica del Rey D. Ioam I de Boa Memoria e dos reys de Portugal o decimo*, *Primeira parte*, 1644. The city and people of Lisbon are main characters in this chronicle as they support the Portuguese faction defending the Master of Avis's right to the Crown. (Image by courtesy of Arquivo Nacional Torre do Tombo, Lisbon, Portugal)

THE CHRONICLES OF FERNÃO LOPES

VOLUME 3

THE CHRONICLE OF KING JOÃO I OF PORTUGAL, PART I

Edited by
Amélia P. Hutchinson
Juliet Perkins
Philip Krummrich
† Teresa Amado

Translated by
† R. C. Willis
Philip Krummrich
Juliet Perkins
Iona McCleery
Francisco Fernandes
† Shirley Clarke

Principal Consultant
Patricia Anne Odber de Baubeta

With an Introduction by
Josiah Blackmore

TAMESIS

First published 2023
By Tamesis (Serie B: TEXTOS)

ISBN 978 1 85566 398 5

Tamesis is an imprint of Boydell & Brewer Ltd
PO Box 9, Woodbridge, Suffolk IP12 3DF, UK
and of Boydell & Brewer Inc.
668 Mt Hope Avenue, Rochester, NY 14620, USA
www.boydellandbrewer.com

The publisher has no responsibility for the continued existence or accuracy
of URLs for external or third-party internet websites referred to in this book,
and does not guarantee that any content on such websites is, or will remain,
accurate or appropriate

A CIP record for this title is available from the British Library

To medievalists of all ages who preserve and share the knowledge and understanding of times past to illuminate the future, especially the colleagues, collaborators, and friends we sadly lost in the course of this project:

Teresa Amado
R. C. Willis
Shirley Clarke
Nicholas G. Round

CONTENTS

LIST OF ILLUSTRATIONS

Frontispiece: View of Lisbon as on 1644 folio from the *Chronica del Rey D. Ioam I de Boa Memoria e dos reys de Portugal o decimo, Primeira parte*. Image by courtesy of Arquivo Nacional Torre do Tombo, Lisbon. Crónicas n.° 8, PT/TT/CRN/8, 'Imagem cedida pelo ANTT'.   ii

The editors, contributors and publisher are grateful to all the institutions and persons listed for permission to reproduce the materials in which they hold copyright. Every effort has been made to trace the copyright holders; apologies are offered for any omission, and the publisher will be pleased to add any necessary acknowledgement in subsequent editions.

Sponsors

NATIONAL ENDOWMENT FOR THE HUMANITIES

The Fernão Lopes Translation Project, including the publication of Fernão Lopes's chronicles for the first time in English, has been made possible in part by the National Endowment for the Humanities: Exploring the human endeavor

REPÚBLICA PORTUGUESA
CULTURA
DIREÇÃO-GERAL DO LIVRO, DOS ARQUIVOS E DAS BIBLIOTECAS

Funded by the Direção-Geral do Livro, Dos Arquivos e das Bibliotecas / Portugal

REPÚBLICA PORTUGUESA
CULTURA

BNP BIBLIOTECA NACIONAL DE PORTUGAL

THE ANGLO-PORTUGUESE SOCIETY

MOSTEIRO DA BATALHA

PATRIMÓNIO CULTURAL
Direção-Geral do Património Cultural

CAMÕES INSTITUTO DA COOPERAÇÃO E DA LÍNGUA PORTUGAL
MINISTÉRIO DOS NEGÓCIOS ESTRANGEIROS

BATALHA DE ALJUBARROTA
CENTRO DE INTERPRETAÇÃO

IEM INSTITUTO DE ESTUDOS MEDIEVAIS
NOVA FCSH | FCT

FLAD
LUSO-AMERICAN DEVELOPMENT FOUNDATION

Franklin College of Arts and Sciences
UNIVERSITY OF GEORGIA

Willson Center for Humanities & Arts
UNIVERSITY OF GEORGIA

THE WALLACE COLLECTION

ABBREVIATIONS

The Portuguese Royal Family (with English and Castilian connections)

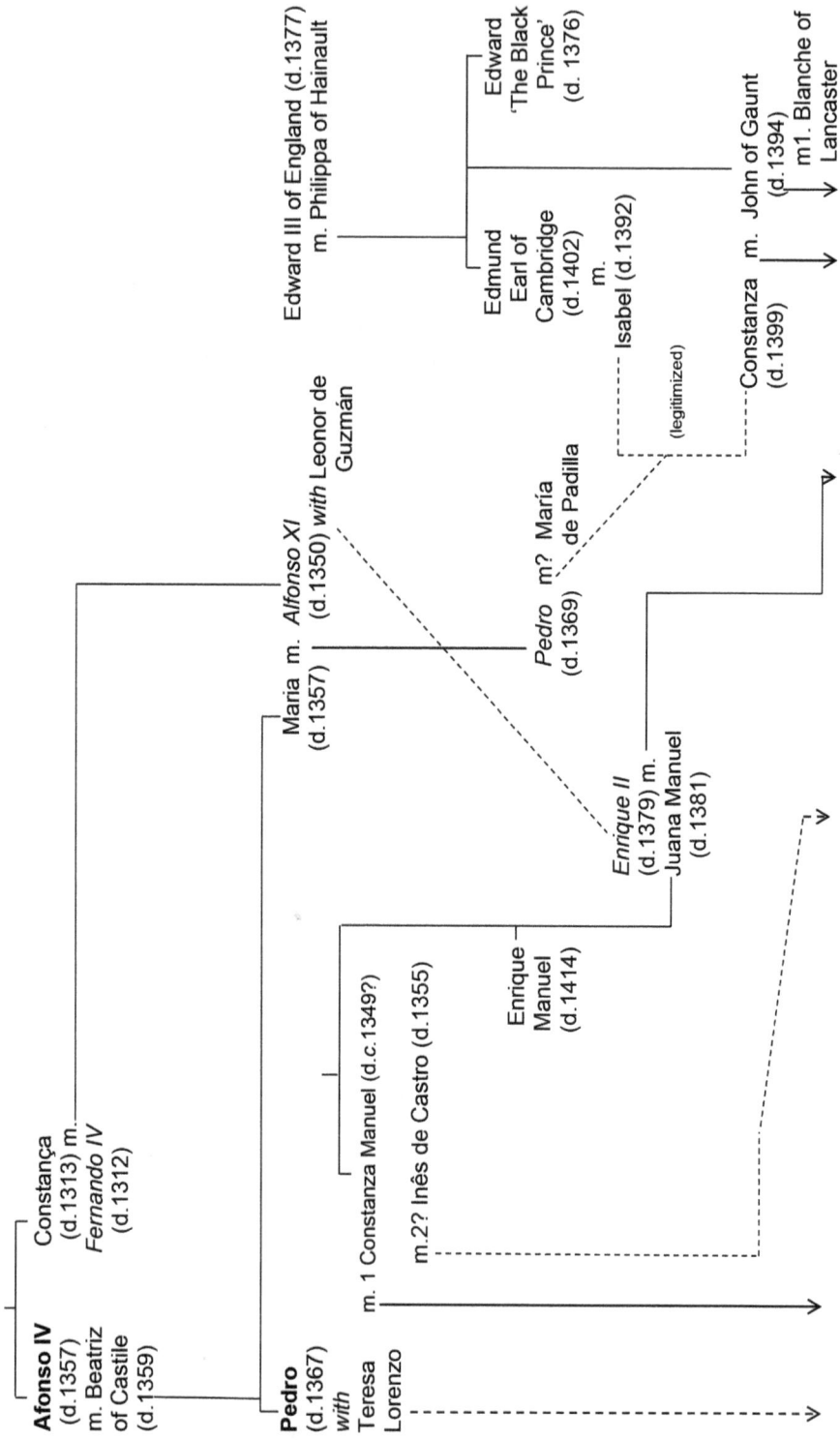

Afonso IV (d.1357) m. Beatriz of Castile (d.1359)

Constança (d.1313) m. Fernando IV (d.1312)

Pedro (d.1367) with Teresa Lorenzo

m. 1 Constanza Manuel (d.c.1349?)

m.2? Inês de Castro (d.1355)

Enrique Manuel (d.1414)

Maria m. Alfonso XI (d.1357) (d.1350) with Leonor de Guzmán

Pedro m? María (d.1369) de Padilla

Enrique II (d.1379) m. Juana Manuel (d.1381)

Edward III of England (d.1377) m. Philippa of Hainault

Edward 'The Black Prince' (d.1376)

Edmund Earl of Cambridge (d.1402) m. Isabel (d.1392)

(legitimized)

Constanza m. John of Gaunt (d.1399) (d.1394) m1. Blanche of Lancaster

Fernando (d.1383) **m.** Leonor Teles (d.1405x10?)

Maria Teles (d.c.1379) m. João (d.1397)

Beatriz (d.1381)

Dinis (d.1403)

Elizabeth m. Sir John Holland (d.1400)

Juan I (d.1390) m.1 Leonor of Aragon

m.2 Beatriz (d.c.1430)

Enrique III (d.1406) m. Catalina (d.1418)

Juan II (d.1454)

Fernando I of Aragon (d.1416)

João I (d.1433) m. Philippa (d.1415)

with Inês Peres

Branca (d.1390)

Afonso (d.c.1400)

Duarte (d.1438)

Pedro (d.1449)

Isabel (d.1471)

Henrique (d.1460)

João (d.1442)

Fernando (d.1443)

Nuno Álvares Pereira (d.1430) m. Leonor de Alvim

Beatriz (d.1415) **m.** Afonso (d.1461)

Beatriz (d.1439) m. Earl of Arundel

Key

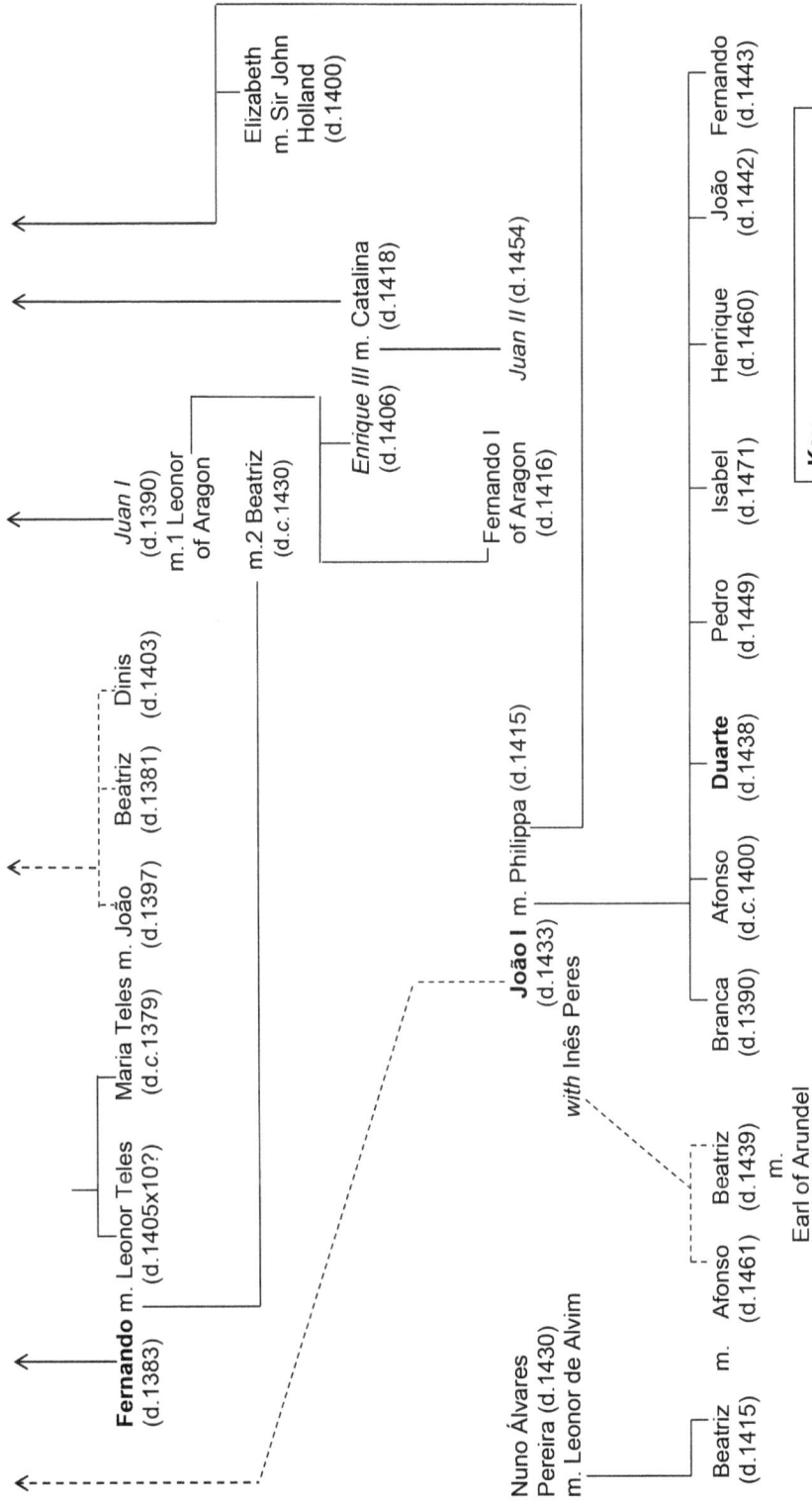

Name in **bold** = king of Portugal
Name in *italics* = king of Castile
--------- = illegitimacy

The Teles de Meneses family

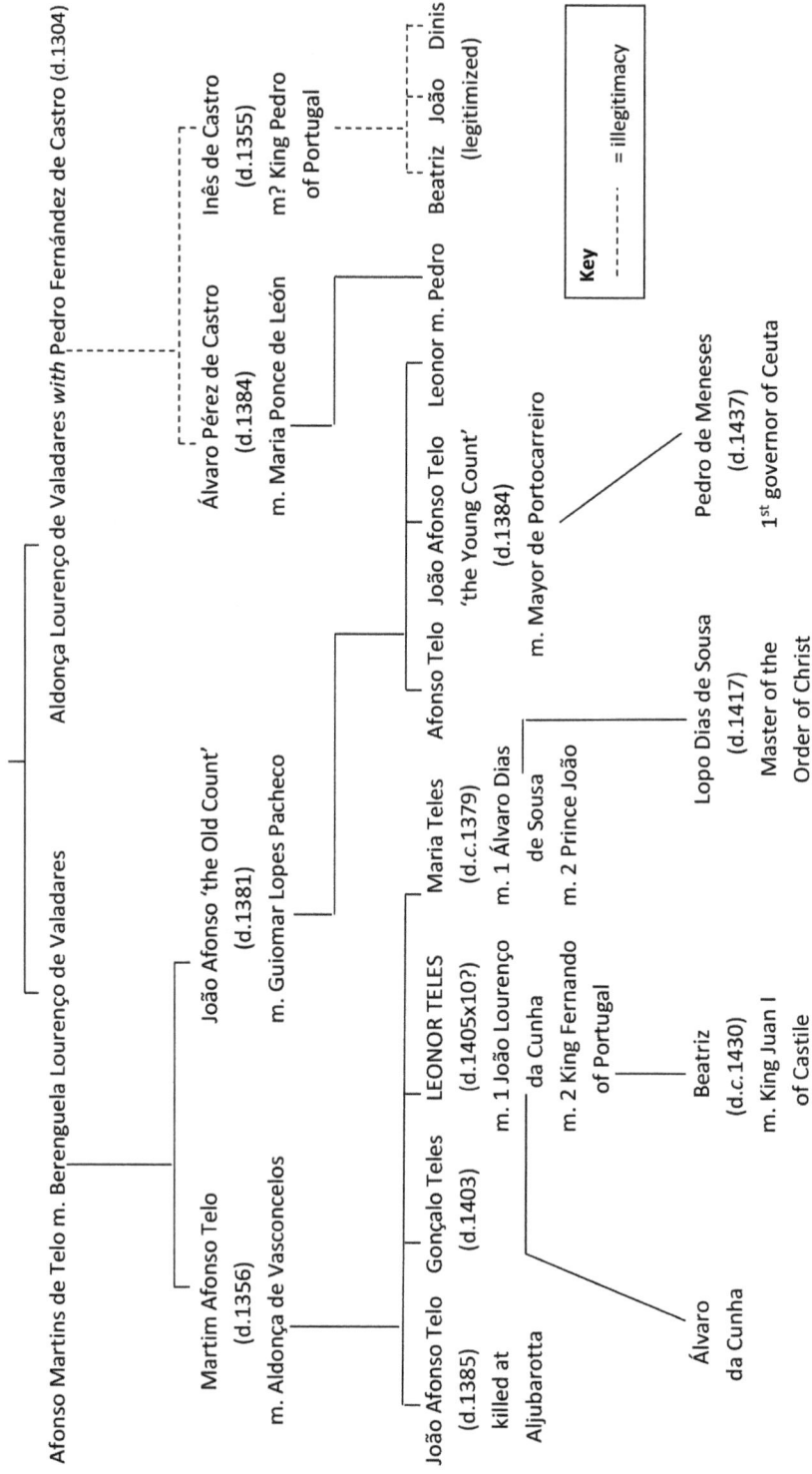

Afonso Martins de Telo m. Berenguela Lourenço de Valadares

Aldonça Lourenço de Valadares *with* Pedro Fernández de Castro (d.1304)

Martim Afonso Telo
(d.1356)
m. Aldonça de Vasconcelos

João Afonso 'the Old Count'
(d.1381)
m. Guiomar Lopes Pacheco

Álvaro Pérez de Castro
(d.1384)
m. Maria Ponce de León

Inês de Castro
(d.1355)
m? King Pedro
of Portugal

Beatriz   João   Dinis
(legitimized)

João Afonso Telo
(d.1385)
killed at
Aljubarotta

Gonçalo Teles
(d.1403)

LEONOR TELES
(d.1405x10?)
m. 1 João Lourenço
da Cunha
m. 2 King Fernando
of Portugal

Maria Teles
(d.c.1379)
m. 1 Álvaro Dias
de Sousa
m. 2 Prince João

Afonso Telo

João Afonso Telo
'the Young Count'
(d.1384)
m. Mayor de Portocarreiro

Leonor m. Pedro

Álvaro
da Cunha

Beatriz
(d.c.1430)
m. King Juan I
of Castile

Lopo Dias de Sousa
(d.1417)
Master of the
Order of Christ

Pedro de Meneses
(d.1437)
1st governor of Ceuta

Key

------- = illegitimacy

Introduction

The Chronicle of King João I of Portugal, Part I

JOSIAH BLACKMORE

The *Crónica de D. João I*, in two parts, is the final work of Fernão Lopes. It therefore is the chronicle that shows us Lopes working in full maturity, at the height of his skills as a writer of history. Lopes composed the chronicle sometime towards the middle of the 15th century. In 1454, D. Afonso V appointed Gomes Eanes de Zurara as successor to Lopes in the post of *cronista-mor*. Zurara's first task was to complete the *Crónica de D. João I* with a third and final part, commonly referred to as the *Crónica da tomada de Ceuta*.

The *Crónica de D. João I* is remarkable, not only because it can be considered Lopes's magnum opus but also because of the political history behind it. The text recounts the rise to power and the reign of João I (r. 1385–1433), founder of the Avis dynasty, and the first Portuguese monarch elected to the throne as opposed to genealogical succession. Fernão Lopes thus faced the job of detailing how this politically anomalous chapter in Portuguese history came to be, at the same time legitimating the newly-formed dynasty with the authoritative force of prose historiography. The result is a chronicle that is self-consciously cognisant of historiographic method and claims to truth and impartiality, while also an engaging narrative in its own right, a culminating moment in the Iberian tradition of chronistic writing in the vernacular that stretches back to the 13th century. Part I of the *Crónica* details João's rise to power between 1383 and 1385, while Part II recounts João's reign as king to 1411.

A brief summary of the political history that is the subject of the first part will provide a context to the narrative project Lopes undertook. The series of events that led to João's occupation of the throne began in 1383 with the death of King Fernando, after which, in A. R. Disney's words, there ensued 'the greatest dynastic crisis in Portugal since the kingdom had come into being.'¹ By legitimate succession, the son of Beatriz (Fernando's young heiress) and King Juan of Castile would inherit the crown; but if the marriage produced no children, then it would pass directly to Juan and Portugal and Castile would be united. Until such a time, Fernando's widow, Leonor Teles de Meneses, would serve as regent. This was problematic, since Leonor belonged to a faction favoured at court but that included many foreigners. João, bastard son of Pedro I and Teresa Lorenzo (Fernando's half-brother) and Master of the Order of Avis, was one of many who opposed Leonor's regency, especially on account of Leonor's Galician lover, Juan Fernández Andeiro, and her Castilian sympathies. João and a group of followers invaded the palace and murdered Andeiro, eventually gaining control of Lisbon. Juan of Castile opposed João on the basis of his legitimate claim to the crown. A few months after Fernando's death in 1383, due to João's growing support among Portuguese loyalist noblemen, the Master of Avis was proclaimed regent and protector of the realm.

King Juan of Castile was still nonetheless determined to overthrow João, and, throughout 1384, military confrontations between the Castilian king and the Portuguese pretender to the throne continued on Portuguese soil. Meanwhile, João's support grew. This included Nuno Álvares Pereira, a talented military leader who would soon be the constable of the new king's army and who emerged as one of the notable heroes in Portugal at this moment in the country's history. In the spring of 1385, a *Cortes* was convened at Lisbon, and the noted jurist João das Regras successfully advocated for João's candidacy for the throne. In April 1385 João was proclaimed as King João I of Portugal of the dynasty of Avis.

This is the story Fernão Lopes narrates in the first part of the *Crónica*. In addition to the political and military dimensions of the events of 1383–1385, Lopes also addresses the reality of a king brought to power by the support of popular sentiment, a fact that will work itself into the narrative fabric of the chronicle. Throughout both parts of the chronicle, Lopes incorporates references to a wide range of authors and genres: Cicero, Aristotle, Isidore of Seville, the venerable Bede, and the Grail cycle of Arthurian narrative are among the list of numerous, erudite citations the chronicler includes. Apart from these scholarly texts, Lopes's narrative is based on three major historical sources: the anonymous *Crónica do condestabre* (completed *c*. 1440) on Nuno Álvares Pereira, the Castilian chronicler Pero López de Ayala's *Crónica del Rey D. Juan I*, and the Latin writings of a certain Dr Christophorus which

¹ A. R. Disney, *A History of Portugal and the Portuguese Empire* (Cambridge: Cambridge University Press, 2009), vol. 1, p. 117. My schematic overview of political events is based on Disney, pp. 117–21, who should be consulted for fuller details.

have since disappeared.² While the use of archival sources and textual citations is common in medieval historiography, it nonetheless demonstrates Fernão Lopes's considerable reading and learning (despite his humble origins), and this incorporation of a web of learned writing into the chronicle itself confers a certain legitimacy and *gravitas* on the Avis dynasty, its first monarch, and its claims to power and legitimacy. Gabrielle M. Spiegel has shown how vernacular prose historiography in 13th-century France, for some members of the aristocracy, involved the search for ethical and ideological legitimacy;³ in a general sense, Lopes's *Crónica* also represents a use of historiography to lend the Avis dynasty a legitimacy in the context of its contentious and anomalous rise to power, although in using Portuguese as the language of history Lopes participates in an Iberian tradition of chronistic prose in the vernacular that traces back to the historiographic enterprise of Alfonso X, of Castile (1221–1284).

The first part of the *Crónica de D. João I* begins with a prologue in which Lopes addresses the problem of bias in historical writing and lays out the basis of his scholarly methodology. In essence, the prologue is a brief theoretical disquisition on historiographic textuality in terms of how history writers must overcome an inclination or disposition (*afeiçom*) to write favourably about the 'senhores em cuja mercee e terra viviam' [great lords whose dependents they were and on whose lands they lived] in order to produce an account which contains the 'clara certidom da verdade' [clear grasp of the truth].⁴ Lopes's postulation of the *afeiçom* [bonds of affection] (and its underlying cause, the *mumdanall afeiçom* [worldly bonds]) as a deterrent to historiographic impartiality draws on a number of medieval sources that treat of the problem of

---

²   The *Crónica de D. João I* circulated in manuscript form for almost two centuries before all three parts first appeared in print in 1644, when the Lisbon printer António Álvares issued the *Chronica del Rey D. Ioam I de boa memoria e dos reyes de Portugal o decimo.*

³   See *Romancing the Past: The Rise of Vernacular Prose Historiography in Thirteenth-Century France* (Berkeley: University of California Press, 1993), esp. pp. 1–10.

⁴   For more on this prologue, see Josiah Blackmore, '*Afeiçom* and History-Writing: the Prologue of the *Crónica de D. João I*', *Luso-Brazilian Review*, 34:2 (1997): 15–24. Teresa Amado provides a case-study analysis of historiographic narrative prior to Lopes in the important *Livro de linhagens* of the Conde D. Pedro in 'Belief in History', in Miguel Tamen and Helena C. Buescu (eds), *A Revisionary History of Portuguese Literature*, (New York: Garland, 1999), pp. 17–29. See also Amado's comments on Fernão Lopes in *Fernão Lopes, contador de história: sobre a Crónica de D. João I* (Lisbon: Estampa, 1991) and 'Fiction as Rhetoric: A Study of Fernão Lopes's *Crónica de D. João I*', *The Medieval Chronicle*, 5 (2008): 35–46.

judgment and the exercise of reason. Aware that his own chronicle or version
of events, in such a context, might be open to question, Lopes is prompted to
declare that his scholarly methodology, which included consultation of books
in a variety of languages, effectively removes any doubt about the veracity
of what he relates. In the tradition of medieval Iberian historical chronicles,
which characteristically include some sort of prologue or prefatory comments
in a way that presents the chronistic narrative as a more-or-less transparent
record of events, Lopes's prologue is noteworthy in that it addresses the status
of the writer, or the problematic relationship between writer, truth, and text in
historical narrative. As an arbiter who must mediate between differing accounts
of events, our chronicler, in a general sense, seeks to obviate the question
of the political legitimacy of the Avis dynasty and its first king by detailing
a scrupulous ethics of historiography and *modus operandi* of composing the
chronistic narrative.

The narrativisation of historical events is part of the story Lopes tells in
both parts of the *Crónica de D. João I*. How history becomes narrative, or
is rendered into textual genres, in part underlies Lopes's practice of historiographic discourse and is itself one of the themes of his chronicle. This
meta-narrative concern – that is, the story of how history becomes a story
– is testament to Lopes's scrutiny of the authorial process and the factors
that determine the shape of narrative. Throughout the chronicle, Lopes incorporates popular and orally-transmitted stories, rumours, and songs as part
of the web of historical voices that we hear and that all contribute to the
multifaceted, narrative landscape of medieval Portugal in the context of João
I's rise to kingship. Let us consider just two brief examples, both from the
first part. Chapters 60 and 61 present us with Leonor composing two sets of
letters in which she responds to the recent political upheaval: one set is to
be dispatched to authorities in Portugal, and the other to the King of Castile
in which Leonor invites him to invade Portugal. Leonor is in residence in
Alenquer after having fled Lisbon following the assassination of her lover,
Juan Fernández Andeiro, at the hands of the Master of Avis. Lopes points out
that the content of the letter she sends to the Portuguese is not the same as the
letter sent to the Castilian monarch. The former presents an attitude of peaceful
reconciliation and maintains that Leonor has every intention of preserving
Portuguese independence even though the Spanish king will soon be arriving,
and that the Master of Avis should present himself to her for the purposes
of 'fazer direito e justiça'.[5] The latter invites Juan to invade the country
and promises allyship so that Leonor may wrest control of the government.
Lopes refers to the reason Leonor wrote this second set of letters by citing an

---

[5]   *CKJ1*, Chapter 60: 'seeing that justice be done.'

anonymous historical text ('segumdo alguũs em seus livros assiinam'),[6] which holds that Leonor desired to exact vengeance on those who killed her lover, causing her to flee Lisbon. Her hatred is not only directed towards the elite group that actually carried out the assassination of Juan Fernández but also to the people of Lisbon who supported João: '[Leonor] vimgaria de todos, espeçiallmente dos homẽes e molheres de Lixboa … que numca avia de seer vimgada, ataa que tevesse huũ tonell cheo das linguas delles.'[7]

Here, as in other parts of the *Crónica*, Fernão Lopes narrates in detail events that surround the act of textual composition. The sending of the letters constitutes an act of textual dissemination, as we witness competing versions of stories relating to João being composed and circulated as text. We see the birth, in the form of the epistles, of documents that constitute historical evidence but that differ markedly in their representations of events and authorial disposition. Both sets of documents are by the same author and refer to the same facts, but in considerably different ways. It could be argued that Leonor has capitulated in the most flagrant way to the *afeiçom* of Lopes's prologue since her affections and inclinations have caused her deliberately to misrepresent her intentions in the letters to the Portuguese. These documents thus pose a problematic question concerning the relationship of events to the text(s) that narrate those events. In Leonor's case, behind a number of supposedly reliable documents – the letters, after all, carry court authority – lurks the insidious desire for personal revenge, and Leonor seeks to bring it about by manipulating the representation of her sentiments to two distinctly different readerships. The link between text and historical truth is thus highly tenuous.

The second case occurs later in the first part, in Chapters 157 and 158, which narrate an episode centred on Fernão Gonçalves de Sousa, who, as Lopes reports, was 'o mais saboroso homem que em Portugall avia', or 'the most entertaining man in Portugal.'[8] In 1384, Nuno Álvares Pereira is travelling the Portuguese countryside to rout out Castilian sympathisers. He arrives at the town of Portel and confronts Sousa, the town's mayor, who realises he must leave his castle and his position because he does not support João's cause. As he prepares to leave, he calls out to his wife and orders music to be played, and then sings the following song:

---

⁶ *Ibid*, Chapter 61: 'as some authors assert in their books'.

⁷ *Ibid*, '[Leonor] would inflict her vengeance on all of them, especially on the men and women of Lisbon… she would never be avenged upon the latter until she had filled a cask with their tongues.'

⁸ I summarise briefly here my longer essay, 'Singing the Scene of History in Fernão Lopes', in Michelle M. Hamilton and Núria Silleras-Fernández (eds), *In and of the Mediterranean*, (Nashville: Vanderbilt University Press, 2015), pp. 143–55.

> Pois Marina baillou,
> tome o que ganou;
> melhor era Portell e Villa Ruiva,
> que nom Çafra e Segura,
> tome o que ganou,
> dona puta velha.[9]

Lopes explains that the mayor lost Portel and Vila Ruiva but was given Zafra and Segura in Castile, and that he referred to his wife in this fashion because it was well-known that she had persuaded her husband to switch allegiance to Castile. Sousa's song is, in fact, a satiric song in the tradition of the Galician-Portuguese school of lyric, and this is noteworthy since scholars generally consider this poetic practice to have ended in the mid-14th century (*c.* 1340) according to the dating of when the last-known poems were composed.[10] Lopes's inclusion of Sousa's *cantiga* seems to suggest that Galician-Portuguese lyric culture was still being practised four decades after its presumed demise. Furthermore, the lyric insertion, much like the song included in Chapter 115 on the siege of Lisbon, which is sung by unnamed women, constitutes one of what could be termed the many historical voices Lopes incorporates into his text. Lopes's transcription of these forms of singing or speaking does not mean that he was necessarily 'less choosey about the rank of his informants'[11] because they are popular in nature but rather because these popular forms of discourse are part of a polyphonic culture that narrates the past. Since the Portuguese *povo* was supportive of João's claim to the throne, Lopes allows the people a voice in narrating their country's history.

---

[9]   See translation in Chapter 158 below.

[10]   Frede Jensen, *The Earliest Portuguese Lyrics* (Odense: Odense University Press, 1978), p. 18.

[11]   P. E. Russell, 'Archivists as Historians: The Case of the Portuguese Fifteenth-Century Royal Chroniclers', in Alan Deyermond (ed.), *Historical Literature in Medieval Iberia*: Papers of the Medieval Hispanic Research Seminar 2 (London: Dept. of Hispanic Studies, Queen Mary and Westfield College, 1996), pp. 68–83, at p. 70.

THE CHRONICLE OF
KING JOÃO I OF PORTUGAL, PART 1

Prologue

Bonds of affection have caused many writers, when charged with composing historical accounts, to take great liberties, particularly when writing about those great lords whose dependents they were and on whose lands they lived, and where their ancestors were born, for they wrote very favourable accounts about these men and their deeds. Such partiality derives from warm worldly bonds which are nothing but a perfect correspondence between something and our human understanding of it. Thus, from the land on which men have been reared and to which they have long grown accustomed, there springs up a bond between their understanding and the land itself, so that, when called upon to pass judgement on any aspect of it, whether to praise it or to criticise it, their account is never accurate: if they praise it, they always exaggerate, whereas, if they do the opposite, they neglect to describe its shortcomings in all their true reality.

Some maintain that this bond and natural inclination is also due to the fact that when hunger, which is life's great herald, is satisfied with food for the body, the blood and spirits deriving from such sustenance become so akin to it as to generate this bond. Others, however, have argued that the bond derives from the seed at the very moment of conception, thus creating this predisposition in what is generated from it and establishing the bond not only with a man's forebears, but also with the land on which he lives.

It seems that this is just what Tully[1] meant when he declared: 'We are not born for ourselves, because part of us belongs to our homeland and another part belongs to our kin.' Accordingly, a man's judgement always falters when relating the deeds pertaining to either the land to which he belongs or the people who inhabit it.

These natural bonds have caused some historians who have written about matters relating both to Castile and to Portugal, even though they were authoritative writers, to stray from the right path and to rush along obscure tracks, so that in certain passages the shortcomings of their countries should not be seen too clearly. This applies especially to the great conflict that the most virtuous King João of Happy Memory, whose regency and reign now follow,

[1] Marcus Tullius Cicero, *De Officiis*, transl. Walter Miller, The Loeb Classical Library 30 (Cambridge, Mass: Harvard University, 1913), Book 1, Part 7:22. <https://penelope.uchicago.edu/Thayer/E/Roman/Texts/Cicero/de_Officiis/1B*.html> [Accessed 25 February 2022]; compare to Duke Pedro's translation in his *Livro dos Ofícios de Marco Tullio Ciceram, o qual Tornou em Linguagem o Ifante D. Pedro, Duque De Coimbra*, ed. Joseph Maria Piel (Coimbra: Acta Universitatis Coimbrigensis, 1948), Book 1, Part 7, p. 18.

had with the noble and powerful King Juan of Castile. These historians failed to give some of his actions the praise which they merited, while embroidering others in a misleading way, and dared to publish these accounts during the lifetime of those who had been with him and who were well aware that the reverse was true.

We have adopted a different approach. Setting aside all personal bonds, which for the above reasons we could have clung to, in this work we have chosen to set down the unadulterated truth, leaving out all feigned praise as regards the good events, and simply revealing to the people in plain terms whatsoever adverse occurrences there were and the way in which they came about.

If God were to grant to us what He did not deny to other authors, namely a clear grasp of the truth in what they wrote, then without any doubt we would not only shun lying about what we know, but we would also avoid blundering into writing what is not true. That is because making mistakes is nothing other than believing what is false to be the truth. We too, convinced by the ignorance of old texts and sundry authors, could well make mistakes in what we set down, because when a man writes about something of which he is not certain, he will either make it briefer than it was or dwell on it longer than he should. However, to tell lies in this volume is very far from our intention. Just imagine how carefully and how diligently we have perused vast numbers of tomes in diverse tongues and from sundry countries, not to mention public documents from many archives and other places, through which, after long vigils and hard study, we could not be more certain than we are about the contents of this work.

If the opposite of what this text states is found in other books, you can be sure that what they are saying is based not on knowledge but on erroneous information. If, indeed, others happen to be looking in this chronicle for beauty and novelty of wording rather than for the truth of what we report, then our account can only prove disappointing; it may be very easy for them to listen to,[2] but it has been very arduous for us to compile it.

Nevertheless, not troubling ourselves with their reactions and setting aside the artificial and ornamented reasoning which gives great delight to those who listen to it, we prefer the simple truth to embellished falsehood. Do not

---

[2] An indication, perhaps, that Fernão Lopes had in mind an oral reception of his works. When used for administrative purposes (e.g. checking precedents or citing documents), we can assume that the chronicles were read, in much-handled working copies, by royal officials. But in other contexts – at court, for example – where a more general interest was involved, reading aloud for a listening public was a well-established practice.

conclude that we assert anything unless it has been confirmed by many people and ascertained by reliable documentation. Were this otherwise, we would prefer keeping silent to writing what is untrue.

How could there be any room left to us for beauty and elegance of expression, when all the diligent effort devoted to this work is not enough to enable us to write down the naked truth? Accordingly, we shall cling firmly to the truth and we shall set down the illustrious deeds, most worthy of remembrance, of the famous King João, when he was Master of Avis, relating the way in which he slew Count Juan Fernández and how the people of Lisbon were the first to adopt him as regent and defender, followed afterwards by others in the kingdom, and how thenceforth he reigned and in what period. We shall publish these things briefly and most properly in the order that now follows.

Chapter 1

How the count's death was planned on a number of occasions and yet was not carried out

When some people discuss the death of Count Juan Fernández, which is where the great deeds of the Master of Avis begin, they come out with an allegation which does not please us: they declare that fortune frequently postpones the death of certain men for a long time, in order to give them a more dishonourable end later on. This, they claim, is what fortune did in the case of the said Count Juan Fernández, in that it delayed many times the death which certain people planned for him, in order to leave him in the Master's hands so that he would kill him in a more dishonourable way. We are not happy with this assertion, because, both with regard to the person who killed him, as well as to the circumstances of his death, none of the others could have killed him without this being an occasion of far greater dishonour to him.

But we consider that God Most High, in Whose providence nothing ever fails, and Who had arranged that the Master should become king, so ordained matters that none other but he should kill the count; moreover, that he should do it at a particular time and subject to certain circumstances, even though he was quite capable of doing it in a different way. One thing is certain: for a considerable time, the count had continued to perpetrate the great evil which we have mentioned, namely of sleeping with the wife of his liege lord, from whom he had received so many favours and such increase in his status, and this fact could scarcely resound in the ears of great lords and noblemen without generating within them a particular and profound desire to avenge the dishonour that had befallen King Fernando.

But in order to bring this about, two great hindrances had to be overcome. The first one was that Count Juan Fernández was protected by many doughty noblemen, who constantly accompanied him by day and by night; the second was that anyone undertaking the task would put his own life in jeopardy and could be totally destroyed, a risk which most men are afraid of taking.

Others added that such action would lead to an even greater defamation of the king and would bring even greater dishonour on the queen's kinsfolk, namely the Counts of Barcelos and Arraiolos and other grandees of the realm. Therefore, on the occasions when they talked about the matter, they all agreed that they wanted to play a part in it, but no one dared to be the first to set about it. Indeed, Count Juan Fernández was well aware that he was not very safe from such people, though he gave no hint thereof. Rather, he was safeguarded from all of them by his lofty estate and by the protection which he received from so many who through him had received great and favourable judgements from both king and queen.

However, it happened that Count João Afonso, the queen's brother, returned from Castile, where he had been a prisoner in Saltes.[3] When he reached Lisbon, on hearing of the ill repute of his sister concerning her relationship with Count Juan Fernández, a repute which was now much worse than when he had left her, he was greatly angered at this news and resolved to kill Juan Fernández.[4] He spoke about this to some of the best men in the city, in particular Afonso Eanes Nogueira, as well as speaking to others, who were all his vassals.

Count João Afonso set out to see King Fernando in Rio Maior (where the king was at that time, after returning from Elvas, where he had been ready to do battle).[5] The count had the company of many others who had journeyed there with him. Once he had arrived, according to some accounts, he made preparations one night and with his men set a secret ambush in order to kill Juan Fernández. Unaccompanied, Count Juan Fernández emerged from the palace with merely a torch, but, when they saw its blaze, these other men moved too swiftly. On hearing them, and without knowing who they were, Count Juan Fernández was greatly frightened and turned back. Saved as he was on that occasion, no further steps were taken at that time.

---

[3]   According to Pero López de Ayala, the Battle of Saltes took place on 17 July 1381. See Pero López de Ayala, *Crónicas*, ed. José-Luis Martín (Barcelona: Planeta, 1991), *Crónica del Rey Don Juan I*, Year 3, Chapter 4, p. 533. See also *CKF*, Chapter 124, note 213, and Chapter 125, note 215.

[4]   See the *CKF*, Chapter 156.

[5]   See the *CKF*, Chapter 156.

Others give a different account, saying that the queen, who was a shrewd woman, before her brother arrived, in one way or another knew about his intentions towards Count Juan Fernández. When lodgings were sought for her brother, she gave orders that a chamber be sumptuously prepared for him in the palace where she was residing, saying that she wanted him to have lodgings where she was. Indeed, she made him most welcome. It was assumed that the queen had bestowed on her brother some great gift and had dissuaded him from proceeding with the matter, because he did not strive again to bring it about. That was how Count Juan Fernández escaped on that occasion.

Chapter 2

How certain people planned the count's death, and for what reason it was not carried out

The opportunity passed, not to be repeated, and the king departed, making his way to Santarém. At this juncture, the wife of the King of Castile, Queen Leonor,[6] passed away and Count Juan Fernández was dispatched on an embassy to Castile, as you have heard.[7] As the ill repute of the Queen of Portugal's relationship with him did not cease, the matter was discussed at very great length by certain lords of the realm, especially by those who were allied to the king, owing to their close association with him and to his elevation of their honour and rank. This they did because they were greatly disturbed at the dishonour to their liege lord which resulted from that relationship.

Among those who were greatly disturbed in this way was, as we have said, Count João Afonso, the queen's brother, since he was a major counsellor of the king, prominent in his Royal Council and a man for whom the king had a very great liking. By contrast, though she was his sister, he enjoyed far less the trust and love of the queen, because she felt that he was ill-disposed towards Count Juan Fernández, owing to the reputation which they both shared.

This brother, the Count of Barcelos, was deeply upset at the king's dishonour and realised that his sister, for as long as Count Juan Fernández remained alive, would not abandon her affair with him. Consequently, he decided once more to take steps to bring about his death, discussing the matter with the Master of Avis, with Dom Pedro Álvares, the Prior of the Hospitallers, and with Gonçalo Vasques de Azevedo.

---

[6] Leonor of Aragon.
[7] In *CKF,* Chapter 157.

They all agreed that it would be best if the deed were to be carried out by some man of little account in respect of any potential consequence, as it was preferable that a man of little standing should perish, rather than some honourable man of lofty station. Firstly they spoke about this with Fernando Álvares de Queirós, who was a *criado*[8] of the king, a man ready for anything and who was accompanied daily by four mounted men. But he uttered many excuses, declaring that in no way would he do anything to displease the queen, especially such an action as this, for which she would certainly feel particular grief.

They next spoke to Rodrigo Eanes de Buarcos, a squire of similar standing to Fernando Álvares, who constantly accompanied Gonçalo Vasques de Azevedo and was greatly devoted to him.

This man was happy to carry out the task, so they agreed that, when Count Juan Fernández came back from his embassy to Castile and re-entered Portugal, he would be ambushed by Rodrigo Eanes, along with five or six men on horseback: Rodrigo Eanes would kill him and then take safe refuge until they had resolved the situation. When this plan had been agreed, they heard that Count Juan Fernández had left Castile and was heading back to Portugal. Rodrigo Eanes set out at once and made his way via Alcobaça to Leiria, through which it was said that Count Juan Fernández was to pass. However, the count took the route through Espinhel and so he eluded Rodrigo Eanes on that occasion, thus escaping death.

Chapter 3

How the king ordered the death of Count Juan Fernández, and why it was decided not to do it

It would not be an unworthy question, if anyone reading or listening to this chronicle were to ask, 'As the affair between the queen and Count Juan Fernández had been bruited abroad for so long and had been so widely made public, had the king no suspicion of it? Did he know of the rumour?' The answer is as follows: among the features of love written about by those who have discussed it at length and have been reared in its court, it is true that, however much a person in love may wish to conceal the fact, it proves impossible, owing to a number of signs, remarks and other giveaway gestures,

---

[8]   Someone born and bred in the service of a great lord, usually someone of high standing, and of great trust.

to avoid offering some hint of the burning desire which constantly dwells in that person's heart. Besides, when people notice unaccustomed acts of fondness or attentiveness, where there is no established bond that prevents tongues from wagging, they easily presume the blunder to which such a person can fall victim.

Consequently, King Fernando noticed the many ways in which the queen showed an unseemly affection and fondness towards Count Juan Fernández and the great increase in his status which she sought for him in any way that she could. As a result, the king reached a firm conclusion in his own mind as to what the truth was, a truth which people at large were assuming, even though he was unaware of the rumours and public gossip about the queen and her dealings with the count. Indeed, despite their sincere sorrow for his dishonour, no daring soul had made so bold as to tell him, out of fear of some punishment as their reward or of some deadly hatred in return for their friendly gesture. That, indeed, had been the fate of a number of people for passing on information of such a kind, particularly when relating it to kings and great lords.

King Fernando, therefore, fully understood what the situation was but gave no hint that he did, for fear of revealing, through his doubts, something which rumours and public gossip had long been asserting. When the queen took their daughter to Elvas for her wedding to the King of Castile, and when King Fernando gave orders for his own transportation from Salvaterra [de Magos] to Almada, the king decided to kill the count in the following manner.

He ordered his private secretary [João Gonçalves] to compose a letter to the Master of Avis, his brother, in which he commanded and enjoined him that once he had seen the letter he should find some means of killing Count Juan Fernández, though he did not explain why. In the letter he also commanded Gonçalo Mendes de Vasconcelos, the Chief Governor of Coimbra, to give orders that the Master, his brother, should be made welcome in the city and that its castle be handed over to his keeping. To that purpose, he fully discharged Gonçalo Mendes from his oath of obedience towards himself three times over.[9] The secretary prepared the letter, fully understanding what it was about (some say it was composed by João Gonçalves). On completing the task, he went back to the king and said, 'Sire, you have commanded me to compose this letter,' and he summarised its content for him, 'if it is your wish to consider these matters closely, Your Grace cannot fail to grasp that on no account should you send it, because of the huge problems it could cause. You must be aware, Sire, that the Master, your brother, is well loved by everyone

[9]   This was the traditional formula used when a monarch released the governor of a castle from his allegiance in order to be allowed to transfer it to another.

in the land, and that if he held Coimbra, and you were to die, which God forfend, all forces would flock to him, and he would become the king of this country. In that way your daughter would be disinherited, with the result that she and any son whom she might have by her husband could only by some huge miracle recover that inheritance. For that reason it is my opinion that, subject to Your Grace's favour, you should waive such a command for the time being. Besides, if you are so furious with Count Juan Fernández that you think he deserves such a fate, then, later on, you will have plenty of time to have him killed at any moment you choose and by another means than this.'

The king pondered on these matters and decided that the arguments were valid. He tore up the letter, and so it was not sent. That is how Count Juan Fernández escaped being killed.

After this occurrence, when King Fernando was ill and badly stricken by that very ailment from which he died, in the course of the evening of the night on which he passed away, Count Juan Fernández was among those who were in attendance. When the count realised that the only outcome was the king's death, he greatly feared that his own actions would lead to someone accusing him at that very moment. Indeed, his fear was as great as any felt on banishment and caused him to rush out of the royal chamber at once and hurry away to his own county.

As he went out of the door, a squire of Count João Afonso, Pedro Eanes Lobato by name, knowing that he had wanted to kill him in Rio Maior, as we have explained,[10] asked the count whether he should kill Count Juan Fernández there and then, as he thought it a very suitable time to do so with impunity. But the Count of Barcelos, although he very much wished to see the count dead, forbade him, and that was how, on that evening, Count Juan Fernández escaped, because it seemed that his hour had not yet come.

Chapter 4

How it was planned that Count Juan Fernández was to be killed, and for what reason his death was averted

Once again plans were laid to bring about the count's death, and this is how it was to be done. When the queen wrote to all the noblemen in the land, urging them to attend the month's mind[11] which was due to be held

---

[10]   In Chapter 1 above.

[11]   The commemorative mass held to mark the passage of a month since a person's demise.

for King Fernando, she sent the message to Nuno Álvares, who was with his wife in the province of the Minho, requesting his presence at the ceremony.

Nuno Álvares, greatly disturbed at the king's death, made ready without delay, along with thirty squires, all well equipped with their arms, plus a number of foot soldiers. No one else went to the month's mind accompanied by soldiers other than he. In this way, he arrived in Lisbon, where the ceremony was due to be held.

After the obsequies and everything else had been completed, on a given day Nuno Álvares went to see Prior Pedro Álvares, his brother. Having talked to him and spent some time with certain noblemen who were present, he walked away in solitude through the palace, pondering on what would befall the realm, now that it had become bereft. He wondered who would defend it against those who might seek to attack it, especially as it was said that the King of Castile had arrested Prince João and his own brother Count Alfonso,[12] as soon as he had learned that King Fernando was dead, and was assembling his troops with a view to making a powerful incursion into the kingdom.

With all this on his mind, he reached the positive conclusion that there was nobody else who had greater reason to undertake the defence of the realm than the Master of Avis, the son of King Pedro. He knew that he was a valiant knight, for he had been closely acquainted with him for a very long time. He swiftly realised that the task had to begin with the death of Count Juan Fernández Andeiro, in whom the queen placed such high hopes. With his mind aflame with these thoughts, he looked around throughout the palace and came upon Rui Pereira his uncle, who happened to be there. Going up to him, he told him everything that was on his mind with regard to the defence of the realm, who ought to take charge of it, and all about killing Count Juan Fernández, adding that he would willingly participate in this, provided that the Master was also willing to go ahead with it.

Rui Pereira had already been greatly concerned about these matters and was overjoyed at what Nuno Álvares had told him. Indeed, he was so pleased that he could not help going straightaway to see the Master to tell him all about these things. The Master was also pleased at this and immediately sent for Nuno Álvares. He thanked him profusely for what he had told Rui Pereira. Nevertheless, he spoke to Rui Pereira as follows: 'I have the impression that I am not now hearing people complaining about the queen's actions quite so much as earlier, nor even talking about them as much as they were wont to do.'

---

[12]   Prince João was the elder son of King Pedro and Inês de Castro. Count Alfonso Enríquez was the Count of Noreña and Gijón, half-brother of Juan I of Castile. Married in 1379 with Dona Isabel, illegitimate daughter of King Fernando. See *CKF*, Chapter 95.

Rui Pereira said: 'My lord! Are you unaware of how this has come about? When I was preparing to marry my wife, everyone talked of how I wanted to marry Violante Lopes. But once we were married, nobody ever talked of our marriage again. Such are these two, my lord, that they have been committing their sinful deeds for so long that everyone considers them to be already married. That is why people don't talk about them as much as they did at the outset.'

The Master started to laugh at this and urged Nuno Álvares, for his part, to gather together as many men as he could, in order to bring about the death of Count Juan Fernández the very next day. Nuno Álvares was happy to do this and immediately left the Master, heading back to his residence in order to prepare himself and to make such arrangements as were necessary. Just as he was making preparations in great haste, the Master sent him a message telling him to abandon doing what he had said, because it was impossible for it to be carried out at that time.

Nuno Álvares was greatly displeased at this, because it delayed the matter even further, and went back to the Master, putting to him many good and relevant arguments as to why the process should be cut short and take immediate effect. Realising that he could not persuade him, he took his leave and hurried after the prior his brother, who had already left, bound for Santarém. He caught up with him in Ponteval, where he stayed for only a few days. In this way the death of Count Juan Fernández was yet again put off, as on other occasions, because, as we have said, it seems that his hour had not yet come.

Chapter 5

How the death of Count Juan Fernández was brought about, and who was the first to raise the matter

Sometimes great deeds tend to begin with people, through whom common folk could never imagine them to be possible. Hence it came to pass that in Lisbon there was a citizen named Álvaro Pais, an honourable and wealthy man, who had been King Pedro's chancellor of the great seal and afterwards King Fernando's. While Álvaro Pais was living in the royal household, he began to suffer greatly from gout and, therefore, begged the king to favour someone else with that office and to provide for him to retire and take up residence in Lisbon, where he already had houses and a settled place in which to dwell.

However, his discomfort was not as great as the huge vexation welling up in his heart at the king's dishonour which was brought about by the queen's ill repute. The king duly provided for him to retire and reside honourably in Lisbon. At the request of Álvaro Pais, the king commanded the city councillors to do nothing without the agreement of Álvaro Pais, and for that reason they sometimes went to his house to seek his advice as to how they should proceed, when, owing to his infirmity, he was unable to be present in their council chamber.

Nature, which obliges men to resort to the qualities with which they were born, bore down so much on Álvaro Pais that, as he could not lose his rancour and hatred for the dishonour which had been brought upon the king his liege lord, he wanted nothing more than to see Count Juan Fernández killed, given that he had not been killed while King Fernando was alive.

Taking the view that it was an appropriate time to discuss the matter, he spoke in secret with Dom João Afonso, the Count of Barcelos and brother of the queen, for he knew well that he too hated Count Juan Fernández and for the same reason, and said: 'Sir, you are well aware that I am a *criado* of King Fernando, whose soul be in God's keeping, and you know of the honour and increased status which he bestowed upon me, on account of which I and all his *criados* ought to be deeply aggrieved at the dishonour done to him and ought to avenge it in whatever way we are able, even though he is now dead, especially those who enjoy such honour and status as make it easy for them to do so. Indeed, sir, you know only too well for just how long the people have been speaking about the ill repute which the queen your sister has earned through her relationship with Count Juan Fernández. This was the case not only during the king's lifetime, but also even now her ill repute does not cease, nor will it do so as long as this man remains alive. Once he were to be killed, it would cease with the passage of time, and matters would be forgotten. Consequently, all worthy men should be aggrieved at the situation, especially you, who are her brother: on the one hand, because of the many favours and increased status which the king bestowed upon you, and, on the other hand, because she is your sister and, by dishonouring herself, she also brings shame on you and on all her house. Though I know that you understand the matter and that already you would have liked to take it into your hands, I nevertheless decided to speak to you about it. You may deal with this as you see fit, but for my part I have to tell you that, were I in your position and were I able to do something about it, as you can, then I would not allow such a thing to go on and would accept running any risk that God would wish to send me.'

The count declared that indeed he was fully aware of all these matters and that he was grateful to him for his good intentions, adding that there had been a time when he had wanted to take such steps, but that for the immediate future he could not see a good opportunity to set about it. After they had discussed the subject for a long time, he addressed him with the following words, 'Álvaro Pais, do you know to whom, in my opinion, you should speak about this? Speak to Dom João, the Master of Avis, for he has just as good a reason to be aggrieved at the dishonour brought upon the king as I do. Nor do I see anyone better suited to do this than him, nor better suited to tackle any unexpected challenge which may confront him.'

Álvaro Pais replied: 'It would give me great pleasure to discuss the matter with him, and, indeed, with anyone else who I might think could set about it. But when you decline to do it, you who are so much better placed to do so than anybody else, then I have great doubts as to whether he or any other man will wish to do so.'

The count answered: 'I shall tell the Master that you wish to speak to him about a matter affecting his honour, and that, as you are incapacitated by your pain and are unable to go and see him, then the next time he is passing through the town he should ride this way and speak to you. I do believe that he is man enough to wish to perform this task.'

So much they agreed, and the count took his leave. Álvaro Pais's new concern was now to speak to the Master.

Chapter 6

How Álvaro Pais spoke to the Master about the death of Count Juan Fernández, and concerning the agreement which they came to

The count spoke to the Master of Avis, telling him that Álvaro Pais would like to speak to him about a number of matters affecting his honour and service, and that he should go and see Álvaro Pais when next passing through the town, because, owing to his being incapacitated by his malady, he could not visit the Master in his residence.

The Master, in order to find out what this was all about, wasted no time in going to see Álvaro Pais and went to talk to him at his house. When they were both in a quiet spot, Álvaro Pais began to present the entire argument which he had put to the Count of Barcelos, mentioning as well the excuses which the count had made in his reply. Consequently, he had come to the conclusion that there was no one else in the entire kingdom who had better grounds for carrying out the task than the Master.

Álvaro Pais said: 'First of all, it is because you are the king's brother and the person to whom the king's dishonour must be more painful than to anyone else. The second reason is that, at the behest of the king and queen, as everybody knows, you were arrested and placed in great danger; if simply for no other reason than to safeguard your own life, for it never will be safe as long as Count Juan Fernández remains alive; for that reason alone you should do this deed, particularly as, with the king being dead, they will now commit acts of even greater evil. They fear you because they know only too well that you are bound to resent this situation more than anyone else and they will, therefore, constantly seek ways and means by which your own life can soon be terminated. Moreover, since more than all others, you are the one most suited to seek revenge for this situation by acting in the way which I have described, you will accomplish a great and noble deed which will be recalled by posterity, so much so that among men, at this time, no other praiseworthy action could be found fit to be its equal.'

On hearing these many powerful arguments, the Master greatly favoured the proposal and agreed to carry it out. However, he was assailed by a number of major doubts, as all the ways of his bringing it about were heavily obstructed. In particular, said the Master, anyone venturing to carry out this deed, especially in the city, needed to have some help from the people, owing to the possible misadventures which could arise.

So intent was Álvaro Pais that he demonstrated to the Master that every difficulty could be easily overcome when it came to accomplishing the deed, just as if it were a trivial action. As for help from the people, about which the Master spoke at length, his answer was that, if he chose to go ahead with the matter, he, Álvaro Pais, would offer the help of the whole city, because he believed he could arrange it.

Owing to his ardent nature and stout-heartedness and in his anxiety to gain more honour, the Master was encouraged by what Álvaro Pais had said and decided to go ahead. On hearing the Master declare his intention to proceed with the matter despite anything, the worthy man could not have been more overjoyed. Weeping with pleasure, he moved slightly away from the Master, glanced at him and asked, 'Is it true, then, my son and my lord, that you are willing to carry out this noble deed?'

'Yes, certainly', replied the Master, 'and I would not abandon it, come what might.'

Then Álvaro Pais went up to him, kissed him on the cheek and declared, 'My son, my lord, I can now see what makes the sons of kings different from those of other men.'

They then began to discuss in detail the best way in which the count's death could be brought about and in what circumstances. After they had discussed the matter for a considerable period of time, the Master took his leave and returned to his lodgings.

Chapter 7

How Count Juan Fernández attended the month's mind of the king, and how the Master was appointed officer of the marches for the Alentejo

We described how on the night of the king's passing Count Juan Fernández left for his county in great haste and in great fear at that hour of what harm might befall him for what he had done. For that reason, some might well wonder about how afterwards he had the audacity to attend the month's mind, since it was attended by many more great lords and noblemen than were present when the king died, and some of whom he greatly feared. Very few of them were in Lisbon at the time of the king's death, because, when they returned with the queen from the wedding [of Princess Beatriz and Juan of Castile],[13] each one made for his own territory or governorship, as was the case with Gonçalo Vasques de Azevedo, who went to Santarém, where he was the governor and had property, and as was similarly the case with many others.

You should understand that the count was quite terrified when he went [to the ceremony]. Moreover, when the queen wrote to all noblemen urging them to attend the month's mind, and when her letter was delivered to Count Juan Fernández, his wife vehemently advised him not to attend, imploring him to stay away, on the grounds that she believed it not to be in his best interests.

Not heeding her advice, the count set out for Lisbon and reached Santarém. There he sought lodging with Gonçalo Vasques de Azevedo, who in outward show was very much his friend. Gonçalo Vasques welcomed him but rebuked him for wearing black and not coarse brown cloth like the others and made him change into it. The count asked him whether he intended to be present at the month's mind, and he answered that he did not, dissembling in his excuses. But the truth was that Gonçalo Vasques suspected what later was to come about and did not wish to get embroiled in such an upheaval, being uncertain about what would ensue, and therefore advised the count not to attend.

Though the count was afraid of certain people, of none was he quite so afraid in his heart as of the Master of Avis, the king's brother. Yet his fear of him and of the others did not prevent him from speaking freely, for he conversed cheerfully and demonstrated friendliness.

Furthermore, if he had had some grounds for being afraid while King Fernando was alive, and much more so when he died, he now began to recover his confidence, believing that every single one [of his enemies] would be

---

[13] In *CKF*, Chapter 169.

distracted from such intent [to kill him], simply because of the many cares that increasingly beset everybody now that a new world was about to begin. With these bold thoughts he then left Santarém, without believing that any mishap could befall him. Besides, Dame Fortune let him think more confidently that such was the case, since she had already decided to bring about his early death. Thus he arrived in Lisbon where he encountered many others who were already there to attend the month's mind.

The count was well received by everybody and was given a close and warm welcome by the queen, who dispatched with him all the affairs of state. After the month's mind had been celebrated, the queen summoned the great lords of the realm to the Royal Council in order to discuss the treaties which existed between the two kings.[14] The news had spread that the King of Castile wanted to break these treaties and was gathering his forces with a view to invading the realm.

It was agreed by the queen and all those present that the realm should be defended, were the King of Castile to advance against it. Nor should his demands be met in any respect, save in those aspects contained in the treaties. As all the great lords were assembled, it was also agreed that the border regions should at once be made ready [for war], and it was decided which lords should be in charge of them and how many lances each lord should have at his disposal. This was done, and all the districts were immediately distributed among them.

The Master [of Avis] was appointed to watch over the lands pertaining to his Mastership, along with certain towns and castles in the adjoining area. He also received an immediate written statement listing all those who were to be on guard with him, as well as the order of payment to them.

Chapter 8

How the death of Count Juan Fernández was arranged, and how the Master left Lisbon with no intention of killing him

When we look up the accounts provided by those who have written books on these matters and who have drawn on the evidence provided by those who were present at the time, then, according to what most of those witnesses

---

[14] Juan I of Castile and Fernando of Portugal.

say, the Master, having agreed with Álvaro Pais to kill Count Juan Fernández, immediately communicated this secret to the Count of Barcelos, Dom João Afonso, as well as to Rui Pereira and others. They all assured him that they would be with him in readiness when once he chose to set his hand to the task.

While the queen was busy with the governance and provisioning of the realm, matters in which the Master was nevertheless constantly involved, he frequently made his way to the house of Álvaro Pais, sometimes accompanied by the count, sometimes on his own, in order to discuss bringing about the death of Count Juan Fernández. They particularly discussed how they could turn to the people to assist them in this matter. Álvaro Pais, who was very eager to see the deed carried out, assured him that in all certainty the people would help. It was not that he would reveal their secret intention to anybody, but rather that he believed it to be certain that the lack of goodwill felt by ordinary folk towards the queen and Count Juan Fernández would cause them to react against them, once they realised that the time and the place were appropriate.

They agreed that, in order to do things in the best way possible, as soon as the Master reached the palace and began to set his hand to the task, Gomes Freire, his page, mounted on his horse, would at once gallop through the city to the house of Álvaro Pais, yelling out at the top of his voice that people should go to the aid of the Master of Avis, because he was about to be killed.

Álvaro Pais would then rush forth with his men as if in a rescue party, calling out to any people he came across in the streets, who would willingly accompany him once they heard his appeals, and in that way the whole city would come together to help the Master. Once the matter had been discussed in this way and agreement reached that this was how it was to be done, the Master was provided with everything he needed, all the required documents were duly handed over to him, and he took his leave of the queen in readiness for his departure.

As regards the Master's departure, a number of authors differ and relate matters as follows: some say that he pretended to be leaving that day, as leave in fact he did, in order that Count Juan Fernández should be more confident about him, if he had any fear of him; the Master would then return next day and find the count to be less wary and less accompanied by others; meanwhile, for his part, Álvaro Pais would make ready.

Others present his departure in a different way, and this version we find more satisfactory, for they state that, although the Master agreed with Álvaro Pais to set about his task in the way that you have heard, he was, however, greatly fearful of the consequences and for the following reasons.

One reason is that certain people to whom the Master spoke found excuses when he was on the point of setting matters in train, for they were afraid of the queen, who had the support of the King of Castile and could later bring about their dishonour and death. However, these were certainly not Rui Pereira and some of the Master's men, to whom he passed on this information. Moreover, the Master was now deep in thought, as he was very doubtful whether the people's help, predicted by Álvaro Pais, would actually ensue or would only ensue too late.

However, the main reason, more important than all others, was the powerful protection provided by a large number of valiant nobles who constantly accompanied Count Juan Fernández. They included Martim Gonçalves de Ataíde, João Afonso Pimentel, Pero Rodrigues da Fonseca, Fernando Afonso de Miranda and others, as well as a good thirty squires drawn from the count's men every day.

Consequently, having carefully considered these factors, despite his immense courage and sturdy resolve, he harboured great doubts about setting matters in train. He left the city after he had eaten at midday and went to spend the night in Santo António, a village 3 leagues away, by then having set aside his intention of killing the count.

While he was there, the Master thought once more about the fact that this affair had been discussed with so many people, among whom some who, in order to win favour from the queen and Count Juan Fernández, either at that point or later, could perchance reveal it to each one of them. After such a disclosure both he and his followers would be subject to the direst consequences, which would also be the fate of everybody involved in the conspiracy. Once he had given careful thought to all this, there began to arise within him a powerful urge and firm intent to kill the count the following day, laying himself open to whatever outcome fortune might bring.

In order to allay suspicions about his return, he at once summoned Fernando Álvares de Almeida, a knight of his Order and comptroller of his household, instructing him as follows: 'Go back at once and sleep in Lisbon. In the morning make preparations for me to dine there. Inform the queen that I intend to go back, because I believe I've not been properly provided with everything I need.' Fernando Álvares left at once and arrived in the city late in the evening, but still in time to inform the queen and Count Juan Fernández of the reason for his visit and that the Master was intent on coming back the following day, because he thought that he had not been properly provided with everything he needed. The queen and the count replied that he would be welcome on his return and that he would duly receive everything he needed when once he arrived.

Chapter 9

How the Master [of Avis] returned to Lisbon, and the manner in which he slew Count Juan Fernández

On the morning of the next day the Master left the village where he had slept and began to set off without any unusual urgency. It is said that on the way he revealed this affair to some of his men, namely to the commander of Juromenha,[15] as well as to Fernando Álvares, Lourenço Martins de Leiria, Vasco Lourenço (who later became a bailiff), Lopo Vasques (who later became a grand commander) and Rui Pereira, who went out to meet him. The Master addressed one of them as follows: 'Go on ahead as fast as you can and tell Álvaro Pais to get ready, because I'm about to do the deed that he knows about.'

The squire went off in haste, gave Álvaro Pais the message and went back to the Master, who was approaching. The Master was wearing a haubergeon and came accompanied by some twenty men all wearing haubergeons, vambraces and swords hanging from their waists as if on a journey. He reached the palace at the hour of tierce[16] or just after, without stopping anywhere else. When he dismounted and they began to ascend to the upper floor, they whispered among themselves, 'All be ready, because the Master intends to kill Count Juan Fernández.'

The queen was in her chamber with some of her ladies-in-waiting, all seated on the dais. Her brother the Count of Barcelos, Count Álvaro Pérez, Fernando Alfonso de Zamora, Vasco Peres de Camões and others were sitting on a bench. Count Juan Fernández, who had previously been at their head, was now standing in front of her and starting to speak to her in a leisurely manner. As he was talking, there was a knocking at the door and the doorman, as the Master entered, sought to close the door so that none of his men could enter, saying that he would ask the queen, not because he held any of them in suspicion, but because she was in mourning, and it was not customary for anyone to enter, except those lords [with her], without first informing her. The Master replied to the doorman, 'What gives you the right to say that?' and entered in such a way that all his men went in with him. He advanced slowly towards where the queen was. She stood up, as also did everyone else present.

After he had bowed low to the queen and greeted all the others, and they in turn had greeted him, the queen told them all to be seated and addressed

---

[15] Fernão Rodrigues de Sequeira.

[16] Around nine o'clock in the morning.

the Master as follows: 'What is this, brother? What brings you back from your journey?'

He said: 'I have returned, my lady, because it seemed to me that I had not been properly provided with everything I needed. You commanded that I should take charge of the district of the Alentejo, lest the King of Castile should seek to invade the realm and break the treaty that exists between you and him. As that frontier is replete with troops and great lords, for example the Master of Santiago, the Master of Alcántara and other valiant noblemen, and as those whom you have allocated to guard it with me seem to be so few, I have accordingly come back to request that you provide me with more vassals, so that I can serve you in a manner befitting both my honour and your service.'

The queen answered that this was well reasoned and at once sent for João Gonçalves, her private secretary, so that he should consult the book of vassals for that district, in order to grant to the Master as many as he required of his own choice and so that he should at once be properly provided with everything he needed. João Gonçalves was summoned in haste and went off to sit with his assistant secretaries to consult the books and provide the Master with all he duly required.

Thereupon the Counts of Barcelos and Arraiolos, each in turn, began to issue invitations to the Master, and Count Juan Fernández, more insistently than the others, urged him to eat with him. The Master refused to accept any of their invitations, excusing himself by saying that he had his food already prepared, having given instructions to his steward. Nevertheless, they say that he spoke to the Count of Barcelos in great secret, so that nobody else could hear him: 'Count, leave this place, as I intend to kill Count Juan Fernández.' They add that the count answered that he would not leave but would remain there with him to help him. 'No, do not stay', said the Master. 'Rather, I beg you to leave this place and wait for my arrival at dinner. God willing, as soon as the deed is done, I shall join you at the meal.'

Fortune, in order to better prepare the path to Count Juan Fernández's demise, now made him fearful of the Master's arrival and so put it in his mind to send all his men to arm themselves and hurry back to his side. In whatever way it happened, all his men left the palace, both the noblemen who accompanied him and the others, and they went off to arm themselves in order to return to his side. That was the reason why he remained alone without them, and not one of them was present when he died.

Likewise, the queen now focused her attention on the Master's men and, noticing that they were all armed, became so distressed that she addressed them all as follows: 'Holy Mary, help me! What an excellent custom the English have, that in peacetime they don't bear arms or care about doing so but wear good clothes and gloves on their hands, as young women do. Yet, when they are at war, then they bear arms and make due use of them, as everyone knows.'

The Master declared: 'That is indeed very true, my lady, but they do so because they so often have wars and are seldom at peace. Therefore, it makes very good sense to have that custom. But the opposite applies to us, for we are often at peace and rarely at war. In fact, if we did not bear arms in peacetime, then, when war came, we would not be able to handle them.'

They discussed this and other matters until the time came to eat, whereupon the Count of Barcelos and the others took their leave, as most of them could well foresee what was done afterwards. Count Juan Fernández remained behind, and his heart sank. Again he invited the Master: 'My lord, you must eat with me.' 'No, no', said the Master, 'my meal is already prepared.'

'But you must eat with me', replied the count. 'While you're here talking, I'll go and order the meal to be prepared.'

'No, don't go', said the Master, 'I've a matter to raise with you before I leave and then I must be off, because it's time to eat.'

The Master then took his leave of the queen and led the count by the hand. They both made their way out of the chamber and went to a great room that was in front of it. All the Master's men went with him, with Rui Pereira and Lourenço Martins the closest at hand. As the Master and the count approached a window, his men heard the Master speaking quietly to him and they all became very still. The words that they exchanged were so few and uttered in such a low voice that no one at the time understood what they were. It is, however, stated that they were as follows: 'Count, I'm astonished that you're a man whom I held in high esteem, yet you strive to bring about my dishonour and death.'

'I, my lord?' he said, 'whoever told you that was a very great liar.'

The Master, who was more interested in killing him than in arguing, drew out a long knife and smote him with it on the head, but the wound was not such that he would have died from it, if he had not received more. On seeing this, the others, who were gathered around them, at once drew their swords to strike him. As the wounded count moved to seek refuge in the queen's chamber, Rui Pereira, who was the nearest, ran him through with his sword, and he at once fell to the ground dead.

The others sought to inflict more wounds upon him, but the Master told them to hold back, and none of them was bold enough to strike him again. The Master at once ordered Fernando Álvares and Lourenço Martins to go and close the gates, lest anyone get in, and to tell his page to rush through the city, crying out that they were killing the Master. This they did.

When he killed the count, the Master was 25 years old, going on 26. The count was slain on 6 December 1383.

Chapter 10

Concerning what the queen said on the count's death, and other matters that came to pass

L et us leave the page to go whither he was dispatched and meanwhile let us examine what took place in the queen's palace. The hubbub and commotion which they all made when the count was slain resounded noisily in the chamber where she was, for it was close by. Indeed, some thought that it was caused by people who had not attended the king's memorial, had just then arrived and were giving vent to their grief.

The queen was shocked on hearing the commotion and got to her feet without knowing what to think. She told those with her to find out what it was all about. The others hastily looked through the doorway and announced that the count had been slain. On hearing this, the queen, though in great fear, cried out: 'Holy Mary, help me! They have killed a good servant of mine! He dies a martyr's death, because they have killed him for no reason whatsoever! But I promise God that tomorrow I shall go to the Church of São Francisco and will have a big fire made there and will make such protestations of my innocence as ever a woman did in such circumstances!' This was something which she had very little inclination to do.

On seeing what had happened, the other people present, men as well as women, thought that the hour had come when they would all be killed and dared not leave through the doors but made off through the windows, some of them over the rooftops, while others rushed down the stairways, heedless of the number of steps, so that each one escaped as best he could.

João Gonçalves, the queen's secretary, was busy consulting the book of vassals but, when he realised what was happening, he began to run off, as also did all his assistants, each one through the best way out that he could find.

The Master now made his way from that spot to a nearby terrace. The queen then said, 'Go and ask the Master whether I'm going to die as well.' In great fear they went to ask him, but he replied very gently, 'Tell my lady the queen, whom God protect from evil, to be at ease in her chamber and not to be afraid, because I haven't come here to cause her any harm but only to do what I've done to this man, for that is what he truly deserved from me.'

When they took this answer to her, her reaction was to declare, 'If that is the case, then tell him to vacate my palace.' She gave that command because she was extremely anxious to see the Master leave, for she was uncertain whether or not her life was in jeopardy for as long as he remained there.

At this point, when Lourenço Martins came back from closing the doors, he observed a quantity of silver sitting on a table that led to the kitchen. He picked it up and slipped it into his tunic. Taking it to the Master, he said, 'Upon my word, my lord, there's enough here to cover your expenses for today.' The Master answered him harshly, telling him to put the silver back where he had found it, for he had not come for that purpose, but in order to do what he had done. Lourenço Martins did as he was told.

The noblemen who belonged to the retinue of Count Juan Fernández and those who lived with him, because they had no knowledge of what the Master had done, were now heading, fully armed, for the queen's palace. But, when they reached a point very near to the palace, a tumult was already beginning to break out among the people in the streets, and some of those who had fled from inside the palace told them not to go there, because the count was already dead and the doors were closed. They added that, as so many of the people were heading towards the palace, according to what was being said, then, if they were to go there, not one of them would escape but would meet with a disastrous fate.

They, therefore, went back to where they had come from, and each one set about finding a safe place in which to hide, for fear that at that dread hour all those who belonged to the party of the queen and the count would be killed.

Chapter 11

Concerning the tumult in the city when people thought that the Master was being killed, and how Álvaro Pais made his way there and many others with him

The Master's page was sitting astride his horse at the door when they told him to dash through the city as planned. He charged off at full gallop, shouting and bellowing through the streets, 'They're killing the Master! They're killing him in the queen's palace! Help the Master, they're killing him!' Finally, he reached the house of Álvaro Pais, which lay a long way off.

When they heard this, the people poured out into the streets to find out what was happening. Once they began to discuss the matter, their courage grew in their excitement, and each man started to take up arms as best and as fast as he could. Álvaro Pais, who was armed and at the ready, wearing a coif[17] on his head as was the custom at that time, hurriedly mounted on a horse, something he had not done for many years. All his supporters were with him

---

[17] Padded leather or mail head protection. It could be worn under a metal helmet or on its own, as the primary head protection, as seems to be the case in this passage.

as he yelled out to everybody he met, 'Come on, friends, let's go and help the Master, for he's King Pedro's son!' Both he and his page shouted this out as they galloped through the streets.

The sound of their voices echoed through the city, and everyone heard their cries that the Master was being killed. Just like a widow who had lost her king, and as though the Master stood in her husband's place, they all rose up with weapons in their hands, dashing in the direction of where it was reportedly happening, in order to save the Master's life and prevent his death. Not holding back from going there himself, Álvaro Pais shouted out to them all, 'Let's go and help the Master, my friends, let's go and help him, for they're killing him for no reason at all!'

The people began to join him, and there were so many of them that it was a strange sight to see. There was no room for all of them in the main thoroughfares, and so they also made their way along rarely used alleyways, with each man anxious to get there first. When they asked one another who was killing the Master, there was no shortage of those who answered that it was Count Juan Fernández acting on the orders of the queen.

God so willed it that they all experienced the same heartfelt urge to avenge the Master. The palace doors were already shut before their arrival, and, when they reached them, the words they began to utter were menacing, 'Where are they killing the Master? What's become of him? Who shut these doors?' All manner of different cries were to be heard. There were some people who said they were sure that the Master was already dead, because the doors were closed, and who urged that the doors should be broken down so that they could get inside and see what had happened to the Master or discover what was afoot.

Some of them shouted out for firewood, demanding that a fire be lit to burn down the palace and with it the traitor and the treacherous queen. Others were busy calling for ladders for them to climb up, so they could see what had become of the Master. The hubbub caused by all this was so loud that they could not come to any agreement among themselves nor decide upon anything at all. This was not just the situation at the palace door, but also all around the palace, wherever men and women were to be found. Some women were rushing up with bundles of firewood, while others were bringing quantities of dried gorse to kindle the fire, with the naïve intention of burning down the palace wall with it, and all were uttering insults against the queen.

From high up [in the palace], many people were shouting out that the Master was alive and that Count Juan Fernández was dead; but nobody was willing to believe this, retorting, 'If he's alive, show him to us, and then we'll see him.' When the Master's followers observed how this huge agitation was growing bigger and bigger, they urged him to reveal himself to the crowds, for otherwise they would break down the doors or set fire to them, and once the people had forced their way in, his followers would be unable to prevent them from doing whatever they wanted.

At that point, the Master appeared at a great window which overlooked the street where Álvaro Pais and the vast bulk of the people were gathered. Calling to them, he said, 'My friends, calm yourselves! I'm alive and well, thank God.' Such, however, was the people's confusion, for they already believed that the Master was dead, that some of them persisted in arguing that this man was not the Master. At last they all clearly recognised him and were overjoyed when they saw him, saying to one another, 'What a great mistake! He's killed that treacherous count but didn't kill that treacherous queen at the same time. Just as you believe in God, you can be sure that she will still cause some great harm to befall him. Just think of their evil scheme: they sent for him, when he had already set off on his journey, simply in order to bring him here so that they could treacherously kill him. What a treacherous woman she is! She's already killed one of our great lords,[18] and just now she was trying to kill another. Never mind, only evil results will come to her from these deeds of hers.' Undoubtedly, if they had made their way into the palace, the queen would not have escaped death. Indeed, it was already quite miraculous how many of her party and that of the count had actually been able to escape.

The Master was at the window, and everybody looked in his direction as they called out, 'My lord! My lord! Look at how they sought to cause you a treacherous death, God be praised that He saved you from that traitor! Please come down from there, and the Devil take that accursed palace! Don't remain there a moment longer!' As they uttered these words, many of them wept with joy at seeing him alive. When he realised that there could be no doubts about his safety, he came down and rode along on his horse, accompanied by his followers and by everyone else, so many people that it was a marvellous sight to behold. The people happily swarmed around him and called out, 'What do you command us to do, my lord? What do you want us to do?' Though he could scarcely be heard, he answered that he was very grateful that they were asking him but for the time being there was nothing more that he needed from them.

The Master then headed for the admiral's palace,[19] which was where Count João Afonso, the queen's brother, was lodging and where he was due to dine.

---

[18] They are referring to King Fernando. There was a popular belief that Leonor's adultery had caused the king to fall ill and eventually die, or at least had contributed to it.

[19] So called because it belonged to the descendants of the Genoese navigator Emanuele Pessagno (in Portuguese, Manuel Pessanha), whom King Dinis appointed hereditary admiral of Portugal in 1322.

As he made his way along the street, the well-to-do women of the city appeared at their windows, joyously calling out, 'God keep you, my lord. God be praised for protecting you from such terrible treachery as they were preparing for you.' That was because at that stage no one could imagine anything else.

In this way he proceeded until he entered the Rossio, just as the count was approaching with all his retinue, as well as other honourable men who were awaiting him, such as Afonso Eanes Nogueira, Martim Afonso Valente, Estêvão Vasques Filipe, Álvaro do Rego and other noblemen. When the count saw the Master arriving as he did, he joyfully embraced him, declaring, 'God keep you, my lord. I am aware of the great troubles from which you have rescued us. You deserved this honour more richly than we did. Come then, let's go and dine at once!' Thus they went to the palace where the count had his lodging.

As they were about to take their seats at the table, the Master was informed that the city dwellers wanted to kill the bishop and that he, the Master, should rush to help him. Indeed, he was anxious to do so, but the count then addressed him as follows: 'My lord, do not trouble yourself with this business, as to whether they kill him or not. Even if he dies, we shall not lack some other bishop, a Portuguese, who will serve you better than he did.' At the count's words, the Master set aside his good intentions, and the bishop was killed in the way that will be described in the next chapter.

Chapter 12

How the Bishop of Lisbon and others were killed and cast down from the cathedral tower

While the whole city was involved in this turmoil and people were accompanying the Master through the area close to the cathedral, a number of them remembered that when they had passed that way with Álvaro Pais, they had shouted to those aloft to ring the bells, yet, whereas the bells were ringing in the Church of São Martinho and in the other churches, those in the cathedral had refused to ring them. They discovered that the bishop was upstairs [above the cloisters] and that he had ordered the doors to be locked. As he was a Castilian, it was said at once that he belonged to the party of the queen and the count,[20] and that he had been aware of the treachery and death which they had sought to inflict on the Master. They said that that was why the

---

[20] Juan Fernández Andeiro.

cathedral bells had not rung out and they alleged this and many other reasons as to why he should be under suspicion. There were even plenty of people who would readily confirm that those were the true facts. At once a large portion of the people grew incensed with a wild fury, demanding immediate entry to the cathedral to take instant vengeance on the bishop.

The bishop was a native of Zamora, and his name was Don Martín. When he was the Bishop of the Algarve, he had succeeded to the bishopric of Lisbon through the influence of Gonçalo Vasques, a licenciate in canon law, who had won it for him from Pope Clement,[21] so that he, Gonçalo Vasques, might become Prior of Guimarães. This bishop was a great man of letters and a highly esteemed churchman, who ably administered his church. He lodged above the cloisters, so that he could constantly appear at the canonical hours and at divine service. It was his intention to order the construction of houses there for all his canons to live in, in order to enhance their chances of serving the church better.

That day, while he was at table with the Prior of Guimarães, whom until then he had not seen for over a year, they heard a great hubbub coming from the nearby queen's palace, with women wailing and the loud noise of people's voices in the streets round about and everybody yelling out that the Master was being killed. When the bishop heard this great hubbub growing ever louder, he concluded that this was no trivial matter and, to ensure their safety from anything that might happen, he left the table at which he was and went downstairs to the cloisters, along with the Prior of Guimarães and a notary from Silves, who had arrived that day to discuss some matters with the bishop.

Accompanied by these two guests and some members of his household, the bishop made his way to the highest tower of the cathedral, where the bells are, having first ordered that all the church doors be barred from the inside. As we have mentioned, when Álvaro Pais had passed that way, bound for the palace, people had shouted out to those aloft to ring the bells. The venerable man had no idea as to what the hubbub was about and, knowing that the sound of bells ringing in such a church would cause great turmoil throughout the city, he had great doubts about doing so.

When the people realised that the cathedral bells had not rung out and that the bishop was in the tower with the church doors powerfully barred and that they could not easily batter them down, they brought ladders, got in through a window and swiftly flung the doors open. There then entered as many as sought to do so, yet very few when compared with the number outside. With common accord they all cried out that they should mount the stairs to see who was in the tower, find out why the bells had not rung out as in the other

---

[21] The Avignon Antipope Clement VII (1378–1394).

churches and, if the cause was the bishop, then they should hurl him down from the tower.

Silvestre Esteves, who was an honourable man and the city's proctor, the city's deputy governor, and others, headed up a narrow spiral staircase, which could only be ascended in single file and by which nobody could enter the tower, as long as those above desired to defend it. Bearing in mind that he was a Castilian and of a nationality opposed to theirs, the bishop was very fearful about their coming together in this way, as any sensible person might well be, and so at first he refused them entry. Nevertheless, as he considered himself to be blameless, as well as being a person of standing and a churchman, and having first obtained from them his own safe conduct and that of those who were with him, those below gained entry to the tower. When they asked him why he had not given orders for the bells to be rung, when the people were crying out for them to ring, he made his excuses by gently advancing his own good reasons and did this in such a way that they were all satisfied with his answer.

However, blind rage, which amid such events pays heed to nothing, now started to flare up so much in the minds of the people who were at the main door of the church that they began to shout out to those who were aloft, demanding to know what they were doing and why they did not hurl the bishop down. These were their words: 'Watch out that we don't come up there, because, if we do, you'll all come hurtling down with him.'

Those up above, who had no desire to inflict harm of any kind on the bishop, shrank from carrying out the deed. On the one hand this was because he was a bishop and on the other because he was their prelate, not to mention the safeguards which they had granted to him. They were at a loss as to what to do.

Rage quickened the hearts of everybody below and in great fury they started to shout out as they all looked upwards, 'What kind of delay is this, that you don't throw that traitor down? What is happening? Have you become Castilians like him? Has he bribed you not to do it and have you reached some understanding with him?'

Then they all began to swear that if those up above did not cast the bishop down, they themselves would go aloft, and all those up above would come crashing down. As every fear is understandable when a person is in danger of death or something similar, those aloft were terror-stricken. At once the bishop was slain with many wounds and swiftly hurled down to the ground, where he was belaboured by many other blows, as if by so doing the people were earning forgiveness for their sins, for his flesh felt nothing any more. They stripped him of all his vestments, stoned him and threw many ugly insults at him, until eventually the men and the street urchins grew bored, having robbed him of all that he had.

Likewise, his guest, the Prior of Guimarães, was hurled down, because a squire who bore him a grudge and who went aloft with the members of the city council saw a suitable opportunity to kill him and, having looked for him all through the tower, found him in hiding and slew him. As nobody had any regrets at his death, because he was with the bishop, and as there was nobody to take his body away, they cast him down from the tower.

As for the wretched notary, who was as little to blame as the others, they began to bring him down, to insult him and to push him about, saying that, as he had been with the bishop, he was aware of the treachery. They punched him hard with their fists, then they started to stab him until they killed him. That was how all three died, while others escaped. The corpses of the prior and the notary lay there all day and night.

At once, that very day, a group of undesirables threw a rope around the bishop's legs as he lay there naked and summoned the street urchins to drag him off, while a country yokel led the way, bawling out, 'Behold the justice commanded by our master Pope Urban VI[22] to be inflicted upon this treacherous and schismatic Castilian for not clinging to Holy Mother Church.' Thus they dragged him through the city, with his private parts laid bare, till they reached the Rossio, where the dogs began to eat him, for no one dared bury him. When the corpse had been much gnawed away, it was buried the following day in the Rossio. The other two were then buried in order to remove the sight and the stench.

Though to some people such acts seemed wrong and disgraceful, not a soul dared to speak out against them.

---

[22] The Pope in Rome (1378–1389) at the beginning of the Great Schism in the Western Church (1378–1417). Shortly before he died, and against the opinion of some of his counsellors, King Fernando had taken the side of Antipope Clement VII as part of his peace agreement with the King of Castile (see *CKF*, Chapter 156). However, the people's hostility towards the Castilians made them indifferent to that change in Portugal's official position.

Chapter 13

How, after dinner, the Master went to seek the queen's pardon, and concerning the discussion that took place between them

After the Count of Barcelos and the Master had finished dinner, which we mentioned in the chapter before last, they were visited by Count Álvaro Pérez de Castro, Rui Pereira and other honourable noblemen. The Master conversed with the two counts and stated that he recognised that he had caused the queen huge displeasure by killing Count Juan Fernández in her palace and that it seemed to him to be appropriate, subject to their agreement, that he should go and seek her pardon. Once they had agreed that it was indeed appropriate, they all rode through the city and headed for the queen's palace.

The queen was in her chamber and dressed in mourning, as was her custom. They passed through the doorway and bowed before her. The queen rose to receive them. When the two counts entered, the Master's men also made their way in and stood there, fully armed. When she saw them enter in this way, the queen complained when she addressed them, 'Holy Mary, help me! Just what is the meaning of this discourtesy? Is this the way to enter my chamber? What do you want? Are we all to meet together in council?' They fell silent and quietly stood there without saying a word. On seeing this, she said, 'Proceed, then! Since this is God's wish, you're welcome.' She resumed her seat on the dais and bade the counts sit down. The Master then sat down, and the two counts each took their seats on opposite sides. Once they were seated, Count Álvaro Pérez addressed the Master as follows: 'My lord, tell the queen your purpose in coming here. Afterwards we shall discuss other matters.' Then the Master and the counts rose and knelt before the queen, and the Master began the following speech:

'My lady, he who does not err has no need to beg for pardon. But I have erred against you, and it is right that I should seek your pardon, even though God is aware that my intention was not to err against you, nor to cause you distress or offence. But events disposed themselves in such a way that what I did needed to be done in your palace. For that reason I seek your most gracious pardon, since I did not kill this man to cause you distress or to show you disrespect; rather, I so acted in order to protect my own life, for I believed that, for as long as he remained alive, my life would never be out of danger. It is for killing him in your palace that I seek your pardon and not for anything else. Indeed, God, who knows all things, is well aware that the death I inflicted on that man was a death which he had deserved from me for a very long time. Nevertheless, I ought not to have slain him in your palace. Accordingly, my lady, kindly extend unto me your most gracious forgiveness. Moreover, if you pardon me in this matter, God will still make for me a time when I shall serve you in those undertakings which you will command of me and which I shall regard as being to your service.'

While the Master spoke, the queen gave no sign that his reasoning was pleasing to her; on the contrary, she remained silent, and her countenance displayed her sadness. The other persons present looked at her and, as his reasons were sound, awaited the favour of a reply from her. Realising that she was not going to give an answer, Count Álvaro Pérez addressed the queen as follows: 'My lady, what is this, then? Won't you answer what the Master says to you? Won't you pardon him? In my opinion, he has spoken to you very well, for no man is obliged, even before God, to do more than seek forgiveness if he has done wrong. Since that is what he seeks from you, you ought to pardon him, especially as he is the son of a king. Besides, the mistake which he committed was not so great, nor made in so unseemly a way as to prevent him from performing greater services for you.'

As the queen made no answer to this, she was then addressed by her brother, the Count of Barcelos. 'What is this, my lady? Why don't you pardon the Master? The count has spoken well in saying that no man is obliged, even before God, to do more than plead for forgiveness when he has done wrong. Furthermore, since that is what he seeks from you, as he is the son of a king, he would always and at all times repay you for it with good and meritorious service. Forgive him, therefore, since he recognises his own shortcomings so willingly. This is the right time for you to pardon him.'

On hearing this, the queen was forced to reply and scornfully declared: 'What is the purpose now of all this talk of forgiveness? What is the point of all these arguments? He has already pardoned himself! Go on, then, you who are my brother, tell me instead what penalty I should exact! It seems to me to be quite pointless for someone to plead for something which he has already got. Since he is already pardoned, it serves no purpose for him to seek further pardon. Let's therefore give up this discussion and turn to other more important matters.'

The Master then answered her as follows: 'My lady, if this matter is irksome to you, let's talk no more about it. Let us henceforth discuss whatever you deem to be appropriate.'

'Let us, therefore', she said, 'now discuss the fact that people are saying that the King of Castile wishes to enter this country earlier than at the time laid down in the treaties.'

The Master said: 'That, my lady is indeed an appropriate subject for us to discuss, even though much discussion has taken place about it already. In fact, if matters are as people say they are, then in my opinion, as I have already said, you must send him a direct message, solemnly requiring him not to do so. He is a reasonable man, and it is my belief that he will not proceed, if you require that from him.'

'But let us suppose', she replied, 'that I send him a message with that requirement and he answers that he has no wish to consent to it?'

'Without a doubt', said the Master, 'if you were to send him a message with that requirement, and if he were unwilling to acquiesce, then you would be bound to assemble your forces and strive with all your might to prevent him from entering the country.'

The queen began to smile scornfully and declared, 'Oh, what fine words those are! When my lord the king was alive, with all of you around him, you couldn't do it. How are you going to do so, now that he's dead, and all your hopes are buried with him?'

On hearing these words, Count Álvaro Pérez sprang to his feet and said, 'Arise, my lord, and let us be gone, for it seems to me anything we say will find no favour here.'

At that, the Master and the Count of Barcelos got to their feet, and they all took their leave of the queen. As they were passing through the doorway of her chamber, she looked in their direction and caught sight of Count Juan Fernández, still lying in the very spot where he had fallen when the Master had slain him. She called after them, 'Holy Mary, help me! Just how cruel can you be? Have you no pity for that man, his dead body lying there, so dishonourably? Considering at least that he was a nobleman like you, take pity on him and arrange his burial, just don't let him lie there like that!' But they took no notice and went off to their homes.

Count Juan Fernández continued to lie there dead, covered with an old carpet, because nobody dared lay a hand on him to bury him. He was dressed in a close-fitting doublet of red satin under a tabard of fine black cloth, with trimmings and sleeves, a fine figure of a man of some forty years of age. After night fall, when it was quite dark, the queen gave orders for him to be buried as secretly as possible in the Church of São Martinho, which was nearby.[23] That same night she left the palace where she was and moved into the castle keep, where she had another residence.

---

[23] The queen was in the Palace of the Princes, Paço dos Infantes as it was known in Portuguese, next to the Church of São Martinho, outside the castle walls.

Chapter 14

How the citizens [of Lisbon] tried to rob the Jews, and how the Master forbade them to do so

After the great tumult with which the people of the city reached the queen's palace and in which the bishop was killed in the manner in which you have heard, there grew up among them a sense of union fostered by mortal hatred against anyone who did not share their opinions, with the result that nowhere was safe for anybody with a different view. Nobody went to work, and their sole occupation was to gather in groups to discuss the count's death and what had happened.

In addition, as it was being said that the King of Castile was making his way in the direction of the realm, they also discussed how it was to be defended. Some people mentioned the name of Prince João, saying that the kingdom was his by right. Others declared that that was impossible, because he was already held captive in Castile, would never be released and might well be put to death for that very reason. As he had indeed been taken prisoner, there was no need for another prince in the country than the Master of Avis, who was a son of King Pedro,[24] just like the other Prince João, and that they should adopt him as their king and liege lord.

Having spent the rest of the day in such discussions, the next morning the people began all over again. Each person expressed an opinion on these matters, and among them there emerged a new agreement, according to which they declared that it was quite all right to rob certain wealthy Jews who dwelt in the Jewish quarter, such as Dom Yehuda, who had been chief treasurer of King Fernando, and Dom David Negro, who had been a trusted counsellor of his, as well as others. From them the Master could acquire very great wealth with which to maintain an honourable estate. As these people conversed with one another as to how to put this plan into operation, a large and excited crowd began to gather round them.

As soon as they realised what was afoot, the Jews did not bother going to the queen. Instead, a number of them rushed to the houses belonging to João Gil, which were close to the cathedral and in one of which the Master had spent the night. They told the Master that the excited city folk were preparing to rob and kill them all and they pleaded with him to hasten to their aid, lest they should all be killed. The Master told them to take the matter to the queen,

24 By Teresa Lorenzo.

for it was not his place to get involved. Nevertheless, they persisted all the more, begging him to help them urgently.

Counts João Afonso and Álvaro Pérez, who were with the Master, realised that he was making excuses and, owing to their pity at the Jews' entreaties, addressed him with these words: 'My lord, please go there before they start and don't let them do any such thing. Once they start, it will be very difficult for you to dissuade them.'

The Master mounted up, accompanied by the two counts, and they rode straight to the Jewish quarter. On arriving there, he came upon large numbers of the city folk, who kept coming to join the others. They were all in a state of excitement and ready to burst in and steal. The Master then said to them, 'What, then, is this, my friends? What deed is this that you plan to carry out?'

'My lord', they answered, 'these Jewish traitors, Dom Yehuda and Dom David Negro, who belong to the queen's party, have vast treasure hidden away. Our wish is to confiscate it from them and give it to you, because we want you to be our liege lord.'

'Friends', he said, 'don't do any such thing. Leave this matter to me, for I'll resolve it.'

'My lord', they said, 'that is not the way. We'll go and get the traitors from their hiding-places and bring them to you. Then you shall have all that they possess.' Though the Master told them not to contemplate any such action, whereas they insisted that they would, he was in great difficulty as to how to deflect them from what they were intent on doing.

The two counts then addressed the Master, 'My lord, if you wish to find the best solution, leave this place at once, and all these people will depart with you and will give no further thought to what they want to do right now.'

The Master did exactly what they said, and everybody went with him along the Rua Nova. As few of them were left behind in the Jewish quarter, the riot broke up. In the Rua Nova the Master told Antão Vasques, who was a judge in Lisbon's criminal court, to arrange a proclamation on behalf of the queen that, at risk of certain penalties, no person should dare enter the Jewish quarter with intent to do any harm to the Jews. However, the judge declared that he would indeed arrange for the proclamation, but on behalf of the Master himself and not of the queen. The Master forbade him to do so, but Antão Vasques ignored the prohibition and had the proclamation made in the name of the Master.

When the people heard the proclamation, their hearts were filled with joy, and they said to one another, 'What are we waiting for? Let's take this man as our liege lord and make him our king.'

On hearing this said, the Master smiled to himself and praised God greatly in his heart for having caused the people to have such feelings on his behalf.

He and the two counts then rode back to the cathedral, where they dismounted and went in to hear Mass.

Chapter 15

How Queen Leonor behaved towards the Master and towards a number of others to whom she was not well disposed

If the ancients, who praised women of just renown, had lived at the time of Queen Leonor, they would have made a grave mistake in what they wrote, if they had not included her among the ranks of the most distinguished. That is because, if the gift of beauty, so highly prized by everyone, has given certain women never-ending fame, that gift had been bestowed on her abundantly, accompanied by a winsome graciousness, so much so that, however much beauty a woman might wish for, she would be immensely contented with what nature bequeathed to Queen Leonor. Along with this, she displayed skill and tact in her manners, not to mention great wisdom. Nor was she lacking in any aspect of what is appropriate in a prudent woman.

She was a resolute woman of great courage, and one who searched for ingenious ways to strengthen her position. From the very beginning of her reign women learned from her how to adopt new ways of dealing with their husbands, and how to disguise one thing as another, more perfectly than in bygone times it is found that any other Queen of Portugal had achieved.

She had certain ways of handling people towards whom she was not well disposed and in such a manner that they were never conscious of the fact. Indeed, whenever she planned to inflict great harm on someone, she caused deadly disasters to befall that person while outwardly displaying quite the opposite intent. Accordingly, though she entertained such a mortal hatred for the Master, owing to the death of Count Juan Fernández, that any ill that might befall him would be for her an insufficient revenge, nevertheless, her strength of character enabled her to achieve what few people would be capable of, namely that she displayed no outward sign of her dislike for the Master, as though he had never caused her any offence. Rather, on those few days on which she later spoke with him, when she was [still] in the city, her remarks and answers in addressing him were always courteous and never betrayed any ill will.

Two days after the death of Count Juan Fernández, at the request of the
Master, she released Fernão Lopes,[25] the Master's squire, of the payment of
100 *dobras* which were being demanded from him to settle a debt incurred
by his father-in-law, Lourenço Eanes, who had been the high steward of King
Afonso.[26] Not only did she give no hint of the rancour which she felt towards
the Master, but she also behaved in the same way towards others whom she
had the same reason to dislike. On the contrary, in her remarks and in the
matters which she dispatched, everything was carried out in an agreeable
manner and with a good grace, as she bided her time awaiting the chance to
take the revenge which she so deeply desired.

Chapter 16

How the queen left Lisbon for Alenquer, and
concerning the manner of her departure

Owing to the discord stirred up among the people, as we have mentioned,
and to the efforts of those who supported it to promote their point of
view, the queen was plunged into deep reflections mixed with an element of
fear. Not only was she unsure of how the Master wished to proceed in her
regard, but also she feared the city dwellers, both men and women, who, as
she knew, spoke against her very harshly. For these reasons she was uncertain
of the best way in which to preserve her life and honour. Having considered
many different possibilities she concluded that the best solution for the time
being was to leave the city for somewhere safer. She then decided to make
for a town of hers called Alenquer, some 8 leagues distant from Lisbon.

She left mid-morning, accompanied by all the ladies and damsels of her
household and by all her supporters, namely: Count João Afonso, her brother;
the Master of Santiago, Dom Fernando Afonso; the Admiral Master Lançarote;
Gonçalo Mendes de Vasconcelos, the queen's uncle; Martim Gonçalves de
Ataíde; Pedro Lourenço de Távora; João Afonso Pimentel; Vasco Peres de
Camões; Aires Vasques de Alvalade; João Gonçalves [Teixeira], commander-
in-chief of the crossbowmen; and Lourenço Eanes Fogaça. She was also
accompanied by all King Fernando's ministers, such as Álvaro Gonçalves, the
comptroller of finances, Gil Eanes, the chief justice, and many other *criados*
of the queen and of King Fernando.

---

25 This is not the chronicler.
26 Afonso IV of Portugal.

As for Dom Yehuda, the king's former chief treasurer and comptroller of finances, who was afraid of the people owing to the huge grievances which he had caused them when he had occupied those offices, he dared not venture out in public quite as other people would. He put an arming cap[27] on his head and took hold of a lance, as if he were a page, so as not to be recognised.

Basquin [de Sola] and Martin-Paul, two Gascons who had remained from King Fernando's day, brought up the rear, along with a number of lances, to protect the mules, for fear that the people of Lisbon would be on their heels.

The queen reached Alverca after a swift march and lunched there, before leaving for Alenquer to sleep. As she entered the town gates, she was addressed as follows by Gonçalo Mendes: 'Now, my niece, I believe you will be safe, rather than in Lisbon.' The queen did not respond to these words; indeed, she said nothing at all. But there was no shortage of people in her retinue who, on the way, had looked back at Lisbon and said, 'Let an evil fire burn it, and let me one day behold its destruction, ploughed under by oxen.'

The queen remained there for some days, her supporters lodging both in the town and outside it. No watch was kept, and there was no other protection than the town gates, which were left open by day and by night.[28]

Chapter 17

How the Master made his preparations to go to England, and how he sought forgiveness from Vasco Porcalho

As human deeds are judged on the basis of what was intended rather than the ensuing outcome, let no one have any inclination to censure the Master, when considering the events which then followed, by claiming that he took steps to kill Count Juan Fernández out of a wild urge to reign or hold some kind of sway over the kingdom, rather than for any other reason. That was never his intention, nor did any such urge well up in his heart. On the contrary, it was merely in order to carry out a noble deed and to avenge the dishonour inflicted on his brother, that he greatly risked his own life and

---

[27] Padded coif, usually made of linen, wool, even leather, used to protect the head from chafing against the helmet, bascinet, or mail coif, and to improve the fitting of the head protecting equipment. It could also be used on its own, as in this instance.

[28] Thus demonstrating that defence against the people of Lisbon was not really seen to be necessary.

honour by involving himself in this act, having decided to abandon both the kingdom and his mastership on that account, as in fact he had wanted to do.

Indeed, as soon as the queen left for Alenquer, while he remained in Lisbon, he decided, for his own life and safety, to leave for England, as he saw that it was unwise for him to remain in the country. He ordered all necessary steps to be taken to prepare for his departure in two *naos*[29] moored in the city harbour laden with merchandise.

Highly discreet and honourable man that he was, he awaited the due time to depart. As he was obliged to pass through certain places where danger normally lurks, against which human ingenuity and resistance are of no avail without the special help of that Lord Who governs all things, and as, too, he wished to clear his conscience, among the things which he did first, he called for Vasco Porcalho, who was the grand commander of his Order. He explained to him in detail, as the queen had explained to him after his arrest, that he, Vasco Porcalho, had indicated to King Fernando that he, the Master, wished to go to Castile to join Prince João to fight against his country and for that reason the king had ordered his arrest and on no other grounds.

The Master said: 'Consequently, I bore such a grudge against you that I intended to kill you. Later, I decided that it was not a very honourable thing to do, though you said those things, and I lost all my ill feelings towards you, in such a way that not until now, with you among my followers, have I explained this to you.'

The Master then went on to give his reasons for abandoning what he had intended, adding, 'For all that I am not bound to seek your forgiveness as I do, nevertheless, openly and freely, I now ask you to deign to forgive me for the grudge that I bore you at that time.'

---

[29] *Naos* were usually one- or two-masted ships with a capacity of up to 200 tons and features specifically Iberian in comparison to the north European 'cog' and the 'hulk' of the Hanseatic League. These are the ships that eventually evolved into and coexisted with the much larger 'carracks', and that were used both for commerce and warfare. At the end of the 14th century, shipbuilding technology was undergoing a process of evolution whereby different types of vessels were favoured by different regions in Europe, though all subject to cross-influences, including from the Mediterranean, in an effort to improve capacity, speed, and manoeuvrability. For this reason, it has proved impossible to find an English word that can accurately represent the Portuguese and Castilian *naos*, frequently mentioned by Fernão Lopes in his chronicles. As a solution, the translators decided to maintain the original *nao* and *naos* for these Portuguese ships and their counterparts from other Peninsular kingdoms. See: Filipe Castro, 'In Search of Unique Iberian Ship Design Concepts', *Historical Archaeology*, 42:2 (2008), 63–87.

The commander was amazed and astounded at this, saying, 'What a wicked and treacherous woman the queen is! She is evil in every way! As for me, my lord, I owe you a great boon in that you were so furious with me and yet rejected both killing me and inflicting any other harm upon me. I thank God and am deep in His debt for enabling you so well to perceive the truth as it was and not in some other form. For I swear to you, my lord, upon my soul, that I have never said such a thing, nor has it ever crossed my mind.' He then began to swear that he had never said such a thing nor even knew about it; he declared that the Master had been very wrong not to have told him this after abandoning his ill feelings towards him. 'You may be sure, my lord', he said, 'that, if I had known this when you killed Count Juan Fernández, then I could never have restrained myself from killing her.' The Master replied that he should not be concerned about it, for he believed that he was telling the truth. They then dropped the subject and talked of other matters.

Chapter 18

Concerning the reasons why the Master wished to leave the realm and set off for England

Authors have advanced a number of reasons why the Master decided not to remain in the country and leave for England, and it is desirable that you should be aware of some of them.

In the first place he was much afraid of the queen, owing to the death of Count Juan Fernández, though, while she was in Lisbon, she never gave a hint that she bore him any ill will on that account. But the Master knew her for a woman of great determination and one who was highly vengeful towards those who earned her displeasure, causing their downfall and bringing about their death by unthinkable and underhand methods. In particular, as she was likely to govern and rule over the kingdom for a number of years, he was quite certain in his own mind that his life would always be in peril. Furthermore, as it was common knowledge that she had written to the King of Castile, urging him to make haste and invade the country in order to fulfil her wishes, any sensible person could easily see that, having inflicted such distress on the queen, the Master was far from being safe.

Other factors also led the Master to want to leave the country, such as his clear recognition that many feared siding with him for fear of the queen and her relatives. Others abandoned him completely and went their way, as did Vasco Porcalho, Martim Eanes de Barbuda (also a commander of his Order) and García Pérez [del Campo], the cellarer of Alcántara, who had gone over to him.

Consequently, in view of these considerations and of others which we shall not bother to mention, the Master's firm intention was to leave the country.

Chapter 19

The reasons which the city folk gave to the Master as to why he should stay in the country, in which case they would adopt him as their liege lord

While the Master was getting ready to leave, provisions having been loaded onto his ships and mangers installed for the animals, all the city folk, both the people of standing and those of little account, were filled with apprehension.

Many factors were seen by them as clear signs of another war, but nobody could anticipate with any degree of certainty just what outcome recent events would have. The country's population and especially the people of Lisbon were greatly troubled when they realised the very unpredictable nature of these circumstances, which gave grounds for the expectation that the country would be laid waste.

Could there be anybody in the city who at that time felt safe and free from fear on recognising that the queen had left the city bearing them all such a deep grudge for the way in which they had rallied to the Master on the occasion of the death of Count Juan Fernández? This was all the more the case when, as people said, she had written to the King of Castile, urging him to head for the kingdom at once and with all due speed. Everyone understood that the sole purpose of his coming was to make them his subjects and to destroy both those who had been against the queen and those who had participated in the death of the bishop. The hearts and minds of everybody in the city were given up to profound thoughts, as they pondered on the conflicting results, both good and bad, which could ensue from these events.

One source of their concern was that, in consequence of the death of King Fernando, they found themselves to be bereft of any firm assurance that peace would continue, as the King of Castile had no desire to honour what was contained in the treaties and was heading for the realm with every intention of seizing it. A second cause for concern was that they expected to be subjected to the power of the Castilians and feared that they would be subjugated by them, as though by mortal enemies.

On the other hand they greatly feared the queen when they recalled the dreadful harm which earlier had been inflicted on those who had opposed her marriage to King Fernando. Furthermore, when Count Juan Fernández had been killed, they had not only helped the Master against her, but had also uttered vile words and insults which she had found quite intolerable. Consequently, suspecting that they would find themselves at the mercy of the queen, whose vengeful tendencies they knew well, they grimly awaited the execution of her vengeance against them.

In addition, they considered that, if the King of Castile were to invade the kingdom and enter Lisbon in his fury, both because they had not allowed a banner to be raised on behalf of Queen Beatriz his wife throughout the city and because they had united against his mother-in-law, then they were bound to undergo great harm to both their lives and their property, which they would be unable to oppose.

Moreover, even if they were to choose to suffer a siege and defend the city against the King of Castile, they would not be able to hold out for very long. In the end the city would be captured, and the whole country would be subjected to Castile, because everybody expected that whatever were to happen in Lisbon would also happen everywhere else. Another matter that greatly troubled the common folk was that in the city there were large numbers of Galicians and Castilians, as well as many supporters of the queen, either because they were her *criados* or because they had received favours and positions from her. They feared that such people, in circumstances where they wished to defend themselves from them, would take the queen's side and would present a total obstacle to them.

When they contemplated this situation, nobody knew what the outcome would be.

Chapter 20

Concerning the reasons which the city folk gave to the Master as to why he should not leave

The people were now riotous and busy discussing these issues, about which they had great doubts. As they recognised the Master to be a man whose great authority best befitted him to defend them, they were all anxious to have him as their lord. Talking the matter over among themselves, they declared, 'Why are we hanging back? Let's adopt this man as our defender. So great are his discretion and fortitude that he will be capable of overcoming any dangers that might confront us.'

Then they went to see him, pleading with him not to abandon both them and the entire kingdom to the mercy of the Castilians, for the realm had been won with such sacrifice by the kings from whom he was descended. Indeed, they were quite sure that the queen had hastily summoned the King of Castile, and, were he to invade the country with a powerful army, he was bound to seize control of it, if there were none to defend it. As for them, they would suffer a wretched and miserable subjugation, and for that reason they pleaded with the Master not to leave, but to stay in the city, for they were eager to adopt him as their liege lord, to govern and rule over them in every respect.

If by any chance Prince João were to come back, and the kingdom were to be his by right, then they would accept him as king, but not otherwise. But, as matters were as everybody believed them to be, they would adopt the Master as their king and liege lord. They urged him to take immediate possession of the treasury, the customs house and the arsenal, as well as of all the other royal rights and property. They would give him possession of the castle and fortress of the city. They would write letters to be sent all over the country to explain what was happening, for they were sure that a majority in every town would be of the same mind, lest they fell under domination by the Castilians. They added that, as they had sided with the Master over the death of Count Juan Fernández and considering the events that had ensued, they were at the mercy of the queen's hatred and, on that account, unless they had someone to protect them, their lives and property were bound to be in great jeopardy.

With these and similar arguments they all strove to persuade the Master not to leave the city and to remain in the kingdom as their defender, but he excused himself, with good and gentle arguments, and encouraged them as much as he could with comforting words that none of them would accept. But he conceded nothing whatever to any of their requests in this matter. Nevertheless, whenever the Master rode through the city, he was accompanied by common folk, as though treasures were dropping from his hands for all of them to grasp.

The people took great pleasure in following him about, some of them grabbing at the reins of his mount, others at the hanging folds of his clothing. All of them shouted to him, as loudly as they could, not to abandon them, but to stay in the country as their lord and ruler, each one promising him some share in his wealth and possessions, and each one offering his very life in the Master's service. The Master would gaze at them, smiling in his delight at what they said, and so they accompanied him like that all the way to his lodging, before wending their way home.

Chapter 21

How Queen Leonor gave orders for the Master to be murdered, once she knew that he was intending to leave for England

Just as a lover's thoughts are hasty in the urge to possess the loved one, similarly a person who is full of hatred is no less keen to take vengeance on the one who is hated. Thus, just as, when one experiences deep love, a variety of thoughts spring up as to how to achieve the object of one's desire, similarly, when one feels deep rancour against a person, one does not stop devising a variety of ways in which to quench the deadly thirst that arises from one's anger. Thus, with womanly intent, which is generally very keen to seek revenge, and with the immense courage with which nature had endowed her, Queen Leonor could not at that time turn her mind to anything other than to recurrent thoughts about every means by which she could wreak full vengeance upon the Master. She was well aware that he was in a hurry to leave for England on ships that he had already provisioned. Having realised that none of the requests or entreaties from the people could in any way hold him back, she was convinced that the King of Castile could not come swiftly enough to arrive before the Master's departure by sea.

Consequently, setting aside her decision to avenge herself through the King of Castile's invasion, she decided to make different plans, whereby, either through death or imprisonment, the Master could not possibly escape. Her plans were as follows.

When she was quite certain that the Master was on the point of leaving the kingdom, she concluded that that was the most opportune moment for her to kill or arrest him. It is said that she gave orders for conversations to be held in great secrecy with the masters of those ships, especially the master of the *nao* in which he was intending to sail, promising them outstanding rewards if they agreed to carry out her proposals. These were that, when the ships were sailing off the coast of Atouguia,[30] which is 14 leagues from Lisbon, the masters and their seamen were to take to their boats and head for land. Once the ships had been abandoned by their sailors, they were bound to be swept towards the shore, and the Master would inevitably be captured or killed. This scheme seemed to her to be the swiftest and most convenient way of achieving her objective.

---

[30] This is present-day Atouguia da Baleia, quite close to the coast near Peniche, roughly 54 miles (87 km) from Lisbon.

It may be assumed that this plan appealed to those to whom it was put, because, without delay, when once she learned that the Master was in a hurry to embark and no longer wished to linger in Lisbon, she discussed this matter with Vasco Peres de Camões.

The queen was so determined in her intent that, even before she had ascertained whether the Master had set sail or not, she twice sent Vasco Peres de Camões from Alenquer to Atouguia with a number of men under his command to wait there so that, as soon as the plan had been put into effect, they could either bring the Master back to her under arrest or bring news that he had been killed. When the queen learned for certain that the Master had not yet departed, and that the citizens of Lisbon were resorting to every means in order to have him as their liege lord, she stopped worrying about this plan until such time as she could be sure whether he was leaving or not.

Chapter 22

Concerning the discussions which Álvaro Vasques held with the Master about his departure for England

As you have heard, the people were remarkably worried about their safety and the defence of the country; therefore, even though the Master made excuses, arguing that he could not remain in the kingdom, nevertheless, the people persisted in following him about, pleading with him daily not to abandon them.

As it was widely rumoured that the Master was going to England, and when Rui Pereira saw the large number of people who gathered round him, all crying out that they wanted him to be their lord, he countered the Master's arguments with one of his own:

'Shall I tell you something, my lord? They're saying that you're going to England, yet it's my view that this place is as good as London.'

Then a gentleman squire, Álvaro Vasques de Góis by name, called the Master to one side and said, 'They say, my lord, that you're planning to leave here and go to another country. Is this true?' The Master answered that it was.

'What is your reason for leaving us in this way?' he asked.

The Master said: 'My reason is the coming of the King of Castile, for he's certainly heading this way. There is also the fact that all the nobles are on the queen's side and that she bears me a deadly grudge arising from the death of Count Juan Fernández. I'm convinced that she intends to inflict as much harm and disgrace upon me as she possibly can.'

'So, where are you heading for, once you leave?' asked the squire.

'I intend to go to England', said the Master.

'What sort of life do you plan to lead there?' asked Álvaro Vasques.

'I aim to serve the King of England in any war against his enemies', answered the Master, 'and to win the honour and fame that all honourable men love to pursue.'

Álvaro Vasques said: 'Truly, my lord, I'm not quite certain of your intentions in this matter, but I beg you to tell me this: even though you will spend as much time as you like there and though you will serve the king very well, as I'm sure you will, when do you think that there you'll win by force of arms a city as noble as Lisbon, the city in which you now stand and in which the citizens offer themselves and all that they possess, even their very lives in your service, in order to help you? If it is your intention to serve in another land in order to win honour by force of arms, then where better can you serve and earn greater fame than in the land which was won by the noble kings from whom you descend and in which you were born? Especially in the company of people who so courageously and sincerely desire to offer you their support and service?'

When the Master heard these arguments, he was very impressed, so that he began to ponder on how he might stay so as best to preserve his honour and advantage.

Chapter 23

How Friar João da Barroca came to Lisbon and his way of life there

Though this chapter could be narrated more briefly and more simply, nevertheless, in order to satisfy both our own wishes and those of others who may well take pleasure in such matters, we shall state, without bothering to cite specific authors, that there are four kinds of [divine] revelation, two of which are physical and two of which are spiritual. The physical ways are external, whereas the spiritual ways derive from the soul.[31]

---

[31] Fernão Lopes draws his classification of dreams from chapter 3 of the widely-known commentary by the 4th-century Latin writer, Macrobius, on the Dream of Scipio, chapters 9–26 of Cicero's *De Republica*. Such was the popularity of Macrobius's classification and description of dreams, that in the Middle Ages he was considered to be an authority on them.

The main physical kind occurs when our eyes are open so that we can see the sky, the earth and other things. Such revelation or demonstration is not perfect, because it does not enable us to perceive the true nature of the things that we see. The second kind occurs when we see from without an entity that has a hidden meaning within itself, as when Moses beheld the burning bush,[32] by which was revealed the incarnation of the Son of God.

As for the other two ways, which are spiritual, one occurs when, through the eyes of the soul and enlightened by the Holy Spirit, we get to know something. The other occurs when the human spirit, coupled with native insight and ability, enables us to examine some entity, which we truly succeed in getting to know later, just as philosophers came to know the courses of the stars, as well as other things.

Likewise, revelations in dreams occur in five ways: a plain dream, a vision, a visitation, a hallucination, an apparition. The last two sometimes occur through overeating; other times through lack of food; other times because of our great love for somebody; other times out of strong fear; other times through thinking deep and melancholy thoughts; and sometimes owing to Satan's deception, when he turns himself into an angel of light. Nobody is able to give a clear interpretation of these two forms of revelation.

A visitation is when a man of upright character receives a visit from God or some angel, telling him what he or someone else should or should not do. A vision is when what someone sees in dreams is what he later sees clearly with his own eyes, as in the dreams in which Pharaoh saw the kine and the ears of corn.[33] A plain dream is when someone sees something which, on his own, he is incapable of explaining or knowing, and for which he needs someone to interpret it for him, as in the dream of Pharaoh's cup-bearer.[34]

If, then, it was by one of the aforesaid ways, or, indeed, by some other means that we have not mentioned, that there came about the arrival of Friar João, who was later known as Friar João da Barroca, all that we know is what we have found written down in a number of histories which speak about him. These histories relate that, some considerable time before the Master killed Count Juan Fernández, there lived in Jerusalem a devout Castilian, who dwelt confined within four walls. He received by revelation an order to go to the port of Jaffa, where he would find a ship ready to sail for Portugal and to the city of Lisbon; he should board it, and it would take him to that port.

This righteous man left the cell in which he lived and, on reaching the port, he found the ship in readiness, just as he had been told. He immediately

[32] Exodus 3.
[33] Genesis 41.
[34] Genesis 40.

went aboard. God then directed his voyage in such a way that they reached Lisbon, a city in which he had never set foot. When night fell, he asked to be taken to a lofty hill close to the Monastery of São Francisco, where there was a small hovel. He asked them to lock the door and just leave open a narrow window, so that he could see out, adding that God would provide him with all that he needed.

Those that had taken responsibility for him did as he asked, and he remained there, shut in. So, with this righteous man living there, leading a harsh life in his confinement, people began to have so great a devotion for him, visiting him and bringing him alms, of which he accepted very little, that they all came to regard him as a saint and believed that God revealed to him much of what the future held. Some also went to seek his advice as to how to save both their souls and their possessions.

Chapter 24

How the Master came to speak to Friar João da Barroca, and concerning the answer which he gave him

As intelligent people commonly seek advice and avoid relying solely on their own judgement when they undertake great deeds, the Master decided that it was appropriate to consult religious people, and not just to count on what had been said to him by Álvaro Vasques, Rui Pereira and others. That was because, in order to undertake the task which they were asking of him, it was essential to have not only the support of the people, but also the prayers of the righteous and the help and grace of God.

Accordingly, the Master went to consult Friar João da Barroca, because of the great reputation accorded to him throughout the city on account of his righteous way of life and the sound advice that he gave to those who went to visit him.

Some say that this conversation took place at the request of the virtuous Friar João, with whom Álvaro Pais had spoken, telling him how perturbed he was that the Master was set on leaving the country. Moreover, Álvaro Pais told Friar João that he should by all means advise the Master not to leave, because God wanted him to be the ruler and lord of this land. Others relate that the Master simply went to talk to Friar João in order to receive useful advice as to what he should do.

Whichever is the case, the Master went to see him, explained to him his position and told him everything that had transpired between him and the people of Lisbon. He told him how they were all insisting on having him as their liege lord and were urging him not to leave the kingdom. He told him all the other reasons that had been advanced in his consultations with many of them as to why he should nevertheless remain in the country. He went on to say that, in spite of that, he could not see any way in which this could be done without endangering both himself and the people of the city. That was because the King of Castile was heading for the realm with a huge army and because most of the towns and castles had already declared for him. In order to mount any defence against such an invasion he would need a large force of his own, as well as a vast amount of money to pay the soldiers' wages. In addition, it was immediately essential to capture the city's castle, as it was hostile to the city, and such an action would be very difficult to carry out with the necessary dispatch.

The Master explained in detail to this righteous man all these and yet other arguments which, in his view, prevented him from going ahead. Friar João answered all of them in such a way that the Master was very pleased with his replies and took great courage from them. Friar João told him that on no account should he leave the kingdom, and that he should begin to fulfil what he had to do with the utmost daring and courage, because God wanted him to be Portugal's king and liege lord, as well as his descendants after his death. In order to seize the city's castle, he should build a wooden protective device, of the type known as a 'cat':[35] the castle would at once be captured without much delay and very few soldiers would be needed.

When the Master heard that answer he was amazed at the words of this righteous man: beginning to be filled with immense courage, he took his leave of him, pondering deeply on what he now had to do.

Chapter 25

How it was decided to send a message to Queen Leonor proposing her marriage to the Master and safeguarding the inhabitants of Lisbon

For all that few books mention it, one should not omit how the Master reacted after he had spoken to Friar João, both on that occasion and on several others, concerning whether he should leave the country or remain

[35] The word 'gata' in Portuguese and 'cat' in English mean the same, the animal and the siege war device. It consisted of a protective wooden and hide covering to shelter a group of soldiers attacking a castle, and which included a pole with a small ram and pick used to claw at the stones of the castle walls to open an access hole.

there. Since he was giving much thought to how to handle the very difficult problems which the situation demanded that he should resolve, he sent for Álvaro Pais and a number of the city's inhabitants who had spoken to him about it. He told them that he had pondered long and hard on what they had mentioned to him on a number of occasions in urging him to remain in the kingdom. He added that he could foresee so many difficulties which prevented that course of action from going ahead in accord with both his honour and their own wellbeing, that he had always had great doubts about doing so. He consequently entreated them to think very carefully about the matter, because it was not the sort of thing to undertake lightly; indeed, if they could find an effective way to proceed with what they wanted, then he was ready to set it in motion; otherwise it would be preferable not to go ahead and, rather, to look for a different solution.

After discussing the matter at some length, a number of citizens came to the conclusion that, in order to avoid the kind of harm which had befallen the realm in the wars in King Fernando's time, and in order to resolve the issue in a better and more advantageous way, it was a good thing for the Master of Avis to marry Queen Leonor. They said that she would rule the country as regent for a certain number of years, as stated in the treaties, and that meanwhile it could so happen that the King of Castile would have a son by Queen Beatriz. That son would be brought to Portugal and reared there, as had been set down in the agreements. During all that time the Master would share the regency with the queen. When once the time arrived in which that son were old enough to reign, the Master would act as the king's lord protector and would be the major figure both in the realm and in the Royal Council. In that way the country would enjoy peace and quiet, and they, the citizens of Lisbon, would be safeguarded from the queen in respect of their uprising against her. Moreover, the Pope, on seeing how much good flowed from this arrangement, would readily issue a dispensation for the marriage to take place.

The Master was informed of this in discussion with those who were entitled to consult with him. It was decided that there were advantages in the proposition, for the reasons which we have expressed and for many others which certain people indicated, and that it was appropriate to put it before the queen in order to discover what her answer would be. After debating who should go to do this, they decided that it was best to send Álvaro Gonçalves Camelo, who later became Prior of the Hospitallers, and the aforesaid Álvaro Pais, citizen of Lisbon.

On their arrival at Alenquer they received a great but false welcome from the queen, especially in the case of Álvaro Pais, against whom she bore a deeper grudge. Once they had spoken to her on the subject for which they had been sent, the queen would not come to any agreement with them with regard to a marriage.

As for safeguards for the city's inhabitants because they had united against her, some say that the outcome was as follows: since she was a wise and prudent woman, she realised that, if she did not give the people the safeguards which they wanted, then, as they were all still in revolt, the result could be even worse, and she would have no chance of taking her revenge on them as she wished; therefore she gave them the safeguards which their envoys requested. Indeed, in order for them to be all the more assured of these safeguards and lest there be any doubt about them, it is said that she pretended to receive Holy Communion by taking an unconsecrated host. Then she gave the envoys letters of safe conduct, which allowed them to leave.

It so happened that, after the queen took up residence in Alenquer (as we have mentioned), the aforesaid noblemen[36] and others who were present with her started to speak in her presence about those things which each one of them most regretted having left behind in Lisbon, making plain just how troubled they were at losing them. On hearing this conversation, the queen retorted, 'For my part, nothing troubles me more than leaving behind the bascinet and coat of mail belonging to Álvaro Pais.'

'Why do you say that, my lady?' they said. 'Are those arms so good that you could not buy equally good ones?'

'Not at any price', she replied, 'but if anybody were to hand them to me, I'd pay him whatever price he asked for.'

They were all puzzled as to what armour this could be but then they realised that she had said this because Álvaro Pais was bald and because of his scalp.[37] A number of those who heard this went and told Álvaro Pais, who took steps to leave all the more quickly, and the envoys headed back to Lisbon.

Before they left Alenquer, Count João Afonso had a word with an acquaintance of his, a squire, who had a wife in Lisbon and was accompanying the envoys, telling him that he could clearly see how Castile was against Portugal, and how Portugal was against itself. The squire ought to understand that there could be no future for a crazy scheme devised by two shoemakers and two tailors who wanted to have the Master as their liege lord. He ought, therefore, to leave Lisbon and come and join the queen's party, if only to protect his own possessions.

[36] See Chapter 16.
[37] The original Portuguese play on words is untranslatable. It seems probable that the Portuguese word 'cota', as used here, means not only 'coat' (as in 'coat of mail'), but is also applied here in the sense of 'scalp' or 'bald pate', the skin that 'coated' the head.

'This is unbelievable!' said the squire. 'When I'm here I get the impression that things are exactly as you say, yet, the moment I'm there, it seems to me that you're all worthless and that everything you tell me is just so much hot air.'

Chapter 26

How the Master agreed to stay [in Portugal] as ruler and defender of the realm, and concerning what was said in the city council chamber about his decision to stay

While Álvaro Gonçalves and Álvaro Pais were acting as envoys in Alenquer, the people of Lisbon became deeply concerned when they learnt that the King of Castile was heading towards Portugal and discussed the situation as follows: 'Why are we bothering to send messages to the queen and simply delaying matters even more? Let's approach the Master and firmly request him graciously to accept taking on the task, without any restrictions, of defending this city and this realm. We shall serve him with our very lives and possessions and we shall give him all that we have. Throughout the kingdom that is what all other true Portuguese will do as well. Let nobody trouble themselves any longer with sending messages to the queen or with any answer which she might send back.'

Then the common people, freely and without heeding the sentiments of those few who were opposed to the idea, requested the Master graciously to accept the title of ruler and defender of the realm. Realising just how strong was their intent and acknowledging too the advice of Friar João and of the other people who had discussed the matter with him, he decided to accept the undertaking, provided that they all assembled that very day in the Monastery of São Domingos, so that he could address them about what his intentions were in staying in Portugal, in response to their persistent entreaties. They replied that they were delighted.

When [later] that day many people gathered together in the monastery, the Master explained to them his reasons for having planned to leave the country, which we have mentioned. He went on to describe how they had repeatedly pleaded with him that he should nevertheless stay behind as their defender and how he had excused himself on grounds which he at once indicated to them. However, since their insistence was so powerful that, despite everything, he should not leave but remain in the city, then, to serve and honour his country, he had now firmly resolved to stay, provided that they found the means to serve and support him in a position of honour and dignity such as was required to defend the realm.

With one voice, without waiting for a single spokesman to speak on their behalf, all those present shouted out that they were only too pleased to serve him and to help him with their very lives and possessions, even unto death in his service. Then the Master replied that, since they said that they wished to serve him, he was pleased to assume the task of being their defender and to commit his person to whatsoever undertaking was needed for the greater honour of the realm and in defence of its people.

When the Master agreed in this way to assume the duty of ruling the kingdom, the people lost all their feelings of distress, and their hearts rejected all their former fears. They were all filled with joy and, with high hopes of a blessed outcome, they strove to press ahead with their task, deeply trusting that God would surely help them. They told the Master at once that, since there were many distinguished citizens who were not present, they should be summoned to the city council chamber, to have explained to them all the reasons for everything which was being proposed, so that they might all agree to what they said and wanted to do.

The Master said that this was a good idea, and the very next day everybody was summoned to the city council chamber and, once they were assembled, it was explained on behalf of the Master that all the humble folk accepted him as their ruler and defender and that now they too were being asked whether they were pleased to agree to what the common folk had accepted.

Not one of them answered; indeed, they all fell silent. Some of them whispered gently into the ears of those who were sitting next to them. Consequently, nobody gave any answer indicating that he or she agreed to anything which the others said. That was not because they were displeased at the idea of the city and the realm being defended from their enemies, but because they all doubted whether such an undertaking could go ahead and have a successful outcome, even though the opinions of the common people ran counter to that. Besides, they were greatly afraid of the queen, who might inflict terrible punishments upon them, as had been the case in the time of King Fernando, when they had opposed the queen's marriage to him.

While those who had been summoned were filled with doubts and gave no answer to what was said to them, large numbers of common folk were present, among them a cooper, Afonso Eanes Penedo by name, who had been present along with all the others when they had gathered in the Monastery of São Domingos and when they had accepted the Master as their lord. Noticing that not one of the distinguished figures in the city who were present had spoken, he began to pace up and down and, placing his hand on a sword that he wore at his waist, he proclaimed: 'What can you be thinking of? Why can't you accept what has been accepted by all these people here? Really! Are you still hesitating to adopt the Master as the ruler of this realm and as the man to take charge of defending this city and all of us in it? You don't appear to be true Portuguese. I tell you: that's the way you'll cause us all to end up in the hands of the Castilians.'

They were meanwhile discussing the matter among themselves, but they offered no answer, as they should have done, simply because these prominent people were gripped by fear, for the reasons which you have already heard about. Then, once more, placing his hand on his sword, the aforesaid cooper addressed those to whom that demand had been put: 'What *are* you doing? Do you wish to accept what is being proposed to you? Otherwise, say that you don't wish to, for in this matter I've risked nothing more than my neck, and anybody who doesn't wish to accept the proposal should pay at once with his neck before he can leave.'

All the common folk present said the same, and, when those who had been summoned [to the council chamber] recognised the strength of their emotions and saw that it was quite bootless to adopt a contrary approach, they accepted everything that the others had promised. Accordingly, everything was set down in writing and duly signed by their own hands. In that way the Master was adopted as ruler and defender of the realm, and, in the very process of ruling and defending, his virtue and daring were fully revealed, as you will see in due course.

Chapter 27

How the Master employed officials to manage his affairs, and what heading he instructed should be placed on his letters

When once the Master had received from all the people of Lisbon their acceptance of him as their lord, he set about preparing the defence both of the city and of the entire kingdom.

Two seals were immediately made, a pendant seal and a [wax] seal stamp, both of them showing the undifferenced arms of Portugal; between the castles the cross of the Order of Avis was added in exactly the way it is currently displayed. The Master installed Doctor João das Regras, who was a very learned man, as his chancellor of the great seal. This was the heading which he adopted for all his correspondence: *Dom João, by the grace of God, son*

of the most noble King Pedro, Master of the Chivalric Order of Avis, Ruler
and Defender of the kingdoms of Portugal and the Algarve.

The Master appointed to his council the aforementioned Doctor João
das Regras, plus Dom Lourenço, the Archbishop of Braga; João Afonso de
Azambuja, who later became Archbishop of Lisbon and then a cardinal;[38]
Doctor Martim Afonso, who later became Archbishop of Braga; João Gil,
licentiate at law; and Lourenço Esteves the Younger, the son of Lourenço
Esteves, a former counsellor of King Pedro. Both these last-named were
appointed high court justices and magistrates of the Master's council. As
comptrollers of his finances he appointed João Gil and Martim da Maia, and
as treasurer of the Mint he appointed a merchant named Master Persifal.
Another merchant, named Lopo Martins, was made chief justice of Lisbon.
João Domingues Torrado became treasurer and receiver general of revenues
from houses and shops. The Master also distributed other offices among such
people as he deemed fit to serve him and thought suitable for the good of
the country.

An immediate order went out throughout the city that twenty-four men,
two from every craft, should undertake to be part of the city council, in order
that everything that it was necessary to decide for the sound government of
the city and in due service of the Master should meet with their approval.

Many other offices were given to people whom it would take too long to
name, as in a kingdom which was beginning to be newly constituted. In the
midst of all these arrangements the emissaries who had been sent to Alenquer
arrived with a reply and letters from the queen. The Master refused to read
them and immediately tore them up, much to their satisfaction when they saw
his pure and wholesome desire to seize the task of ruling over and defending
those who wanted to help him.

It is important that you should be aware that, as soon as the Master took on
the title of ruler and defender of the realm, many of those who were the queen's
criados, protected by her or members of her family, at once left the city, either
to join her or to make off elsewhere. They headed out of Lisbon because they
were afraid of remaining there when they realised that the people's emotions
were running high and for fear of the King of Castile. Before they departed,
they collected together all their belongings in chests and bundles as best they
could and left them for safe keeping in friends' houses. On being informed
about this property by several people, many of those who came to join the
Master asked him to award it to them; without further delay, without knowing

---

[38]   Also known as João Esteves de Azambuja, he was made Bishop of Coimbra in
1398, Archbishop of Lisbon in 1402, and cardinal in 1411.

whether the quantity was large or small, he granted to them all that they were asking for. Many people greatly profited from this.

Álvaro Pais, who had been of great help to the Master in what he had achieved, as you have already heard,[39] realised how this request had started and was very aware that some people were telling the Master not to give away people's possessions in this way, because it would be better if he, the Master, were to have them himself. One day, he addressed him as follows:

'My lord, allow me to give you a piece of advice which will greatly help you to advance your cause.'

'What advice is that?' the Master replied. 'If it's sound advice, I'll be delighted.'

'My lord', said Álvaro Pais, 'This is what you should do. Give away what isn't yours, promise what you don't possess and pardon those who haven't acted wrongfully against you, and that will greatly assist you to achieve the objective at which you're aiming.'

The Master said that this seemed to be good advice and acted accordingly, that is to say, in every place which declared for him he distributed the belongings of those who were in the queen's party or who were on their way to join the King of Castile. In the warrants authorising these donations he proclaimed, 'This is because the said person has done us a great disservice by siding with Don Juan, who calls himself the King of Castile.' He promised offices and lands and other things which he hoped to gain later on. He also pardoned killings and other evil deeds committed by all those who requested this of him, provided that they were neither acts of treachery nor a breach of faith. A further provision was that those acts were to have been committed before the first day of December, the month on which he had killed Count Juan Fernández in the year 1383. This pardon was issued on condition that on certain days they should come to Lisbon in order to serve him at their own expense and for as long as the war lasted.

From the property which had been hidden the Master gained a huge quantity of treasure from the countess, the wife of Count João Afonso Telo, the queen's brother, which she had stored for safe keeping in the Monastery of São Domingos, when the queen left for Alenquer. The treasure consisted of silver, gold, gems, precious stones and other objects. Though it had been secretly hidden away above the main gate, tucked inside between the architrave and the roof, there were plenty of people who knew where it must be, and it was all taken to the Master.

[39] In Chapters 5, 6, and 11 above.

Chapter 28

How Prince João learned that the Master, his brother, called himself ruler and defender of the realm and how he reacted to this

Since we are not greatly concerned about certain written reports which we have come across here, we shall confine ourselves to the following account, which appears to make sense. It tells us that when the Master took on the task of ruler and defender of the realm, notwithstanding the arguments which, as you have heard, were put to him by Friar João da Barroca, his intention was not, however, to reign, but simply to enhance his good name. In addition, as he felt sorry for the land where he was born and as he had a deep sympathy for the common folk who were pressing him so very hard, he took on this task and for no other reason, because he hoped that Prince João, his brother, would somehow find a means of being freed from prison, then make his way to Portugal and could thus win back the kingdom and be its lord, according to the case defended by some. Such an outcome would bring the Master great honour, would be a praiseworthy achievement, and everybody would be greatly indebted to him.

After the Master had resolved to tell the prince of his plans in the best way possible, it happened that a certain squire, who was one of the *criados* of Prince João (for some of them were scattered throughout Castile and others throughout Portugal), learned that the Master, the prince's brother, had assumed the task of ruler and defender of the realm, and yet that, according to others, he was nevertheless planning to leave the country. The squire decided to inform the prince, so that he should be fully apprised of all this and be able to give him, the squire, appropriate instructions. Knowing that the King of Castile had ordered that any person who served the prince, if found in the place where he was held captive, would be arrested and held at His Grace's pleasure, the squire made his way there as stealthily as he could and made his confession to a friar. Through this friar he succeeded in informing the prince of his reason for coming, telling him that it was being said that his brother intended to go ahead with his plan to rule and defend the realm, and was prepared to be under siege in Lisbon from the King of Castile or to confront anything else that might arise; accordingly, the squire sought to be graciously told what the prince wanted him to do.

The prince was delighted to receive this news, because of the circumstances of his imprisonment. He sent a message to the squire, urging with all his might that both he and all his *criados* should go and join the Master and enter his service; he added that this was the best way in which at that time they could serve him, the prince, and which would bring him greatest pleasure. Furthermore, the squire should tell the Master that it was the prince's earnest request and entreaty that, as his brother, the Master should declare himself King of Portugal, if he wished to see him once more a free man, because otherwise he believed he would never be released. Some accounts relate that the prince forwarded to the squire his personally signed letter of credence. Leaving Toledo, the squire went to meet João Lourenço da Cunha, who had been the husband of Queen Leonor, as well as others of the prince's *criados*, and told them everything which had been transacted between him and the prince. All those who heard about this then left for Lisbon and went to join the Master, who welcomed them and greatly rejoiced at their coming. When he saw his brother's message, he wrote no further to him concerning his plans for the governance of the realm.

Chapter 29

Concerning the message which the queen sent to Gonçalo Vasques de Azevedo before she left for Santarém, and the words he addressed to the town's inhabitants

It is true that historical accounts are much more easily understood and remembered if they are neatly and perfectly organised than if they are presented in any other manner. Though it is our intention, in respect of the account which we wish to set down, that it should be written in a good, clear style, nevertheless we are confronted by such a huge number of separate stories, especially at this point, that they disrupt our best intentions. There are several reasons for this: the King of Castile is on his way to invade Portugal; Nuno Álvares is likewise heading for Lisbon; the Master and the common people are striving to capture the city's castle; throughout the kingdom townships are rising up against the governors of their castles; some groups are rising up to challenge others; so many other events are simultaneously taking place that it becomes impossible to narrate them with reference to the exact dates when they came about.

It is our opinion that it is better to relate first some events and then others (despite the fact that such an approach does not please certain people), than it is to bundle events together in a confusing muddle which is far harder to understand. That being so, let us begin by taking the queen to Santarém, and then we shall speak about the highly praiseworthy Nuno Álvares and how he came to Lisbon to serve the Master; then we can go on to relate how the castle of Lisbon was taken and, after that, recount other events as best we can.

Consequently, we want you to grasp that, when the queen learned that the city folk had adopted the Master as their ruler and defender, and that he in his decrees was already using that very title, further feelings of belligerence were stirred deep within her being, along with the deadliest thoughts as to how to thwart his efforts. For that reason, after pondering on all manner of schemes and having turned them over in her mind, she decided to leave Alenquer for Santarém. Prior to that, the townsfolk of Santarém had risen up against their governor, when, at his command, the banner [of Queen Beatriz] was borne through the town, as you have already heard.[40] On that account she was uncertain whether the townsfolk were well disposed towards her; indeed, she remained in grave doubt because of their actions, especially at that time owing to the uprising in Lisbon, and concluded that, ahead of her arrival there, it was best to discover by some means what their intentions were.

She wrote to Gonçalo Vasques de Azevedo, who was the Governor of Santarém, requesting him to address, as best he could, the leading citizens of Santarém and to discover what their feelings were towards her. Whatever he found out from them, he was to communicate it to her afterwards in the way he deemed best to be of service to her. On a given day Gonçalo Vasques sent out a call to the respectable townsfolk to gather together in the church of São João de Alporão, in order to discuss certain matters with them. After they had all assembled there, he summoned them to a great courtyard outside the church and addressed them as follows: 'Good townsfolk of Santarém, you know full well that I am your neighbour and a native of this country. You know that this town is where I have my possessions and my houses and that I have more here than anywhere else. For that reason I have always loved this town and its people. Believe me when I say that I would most willingly do anything to bring about your greater honour and benefit.

'Now, my friends, it so happens that, when last night I lay thinking about a number of matters concerning my affairs, I started to consider a particular matter, for the good of both your honour and mine and in the interests of all the inhabitants of this town. If you approve of what I have to say, then God be praised; if, however, you deem a different approach to be better, then whatever you all agree upon I shall join you in agreeing to it. That is because my wish is to share in every good fortune that comes to this township and, if need be, even to share in adverse circumstances. For that reason I have decided to

[40] See *CKF*, Chapter 176.

speak to you about the following matter. You know well what happened to the queen recently in Lisbon and how the Master killed Count Juan Fernández in the very palace where she resided. You must have heard about everything that followed on from that and how the queen left the palace and made her way to Alenquer.

'As you well know, it is no surprise that the inhabitants of Lisbon do this kind of thing, not to mention other uprisings in the past; that is because they are people of very mixed origins and, between them, give vent to a variety of opinions and cause many uprisings. As the queen is in Alenquer, which is a place where she cannot be accorded the same dignity as she would receive if she were here, I believe that it would be better if you were to send her a message requesting her graciously to come here to this town, pointing out that, in your view, it brings her neither honour nor advantage to remain so close to Lisbon in a township like that, and that, at all events, she will be far safer here than where she is at present. Whether such a message will please her or not, she will appreciate your sense of duty towards her, and you will earn praise for it. As I considered that this would be the honourable stand for both you and me to take, I decided to tell you so. Do as you think best.'

At that, they all answered that he had spoken very well, that they welcomed what he had to say and that they would send the queen a letter to that effect. He answered that, since that was the case, he would act as messenger to her, would tell her of the goodwill which he had felt that they showed towards her and would explain that they were ready to carry out anything in order to promote her honour and be of service to her.

Gonçalo Vasques then left, declaring that accordingly he would make his way to Alenquer earlier than he had envisaged. When he arrived there and told the queen of the reply which he had received from them, she was very pleased. She wrote a letter to the townspeople expressing her immense gratitude for everything which they had written to her and for the goodwill and readiness to serve her which they had shown; she told them that she held them to be good and loyal subjects and that they should be assured that in view of this she would grant them many favours in response to whatsoever they requested of her.

Chapter 30

How the queen left Alenquer for Santarém, and concerning the arguments which she advanced to the townsfolk before she departed

When the queen learned from Gonçalo Vasques, who was Governor of Santarém at that time, that its townsfolk were ready to serve her and that they were pleased that she was going to make for that town, she made arrangements to leave Alenquer after celebrating Christmas. She left Vasco Peres de Camões as governor of the castle and Martim Gonçalves de Ataíde as guardian of the town. Before she left, she gave orders for the honourable men of the town to assemble and addressed them as follows: 'My friends, you know full well that this town belongs to me and that you all owe me obedience. Besides, you have seen the turmoil in Lisbon when the people rose up with the Master. Indeed, I know not whether he is master gunner or master of bombards. I am puzzled about what kind of rage or stupidity drove them to do such things. Nevertheless, you should pay no heed to their stupidity and avoid any uprising such as theirs: rather, you should be peaceful and loyal, as you always have been. By so doing, you will enhance your standing and good name, as well as performing a great service to me, for which I shall always reward you with favours whensoever you request them.'

At that, they all replied that the town and all its inhabitants were hers and ready to serve her, adding that they would not side with anyone but her, nor obey any command unless it were hers, as she was their queen.

She declared that she was very grateful to them for that pledge and then she left for Santarém. She was accompanied by the counts her brothers, as well as by the Admiral Master Lançarote, João Afonso Pimentel, João Gonçalves [Teixeira] de Óbidos, all those who belonged to Lisbon's court of justice, along with several knights and squires. However, they amounted to only a small number of people. When she reached Santarém, the most honourable townsfolk went out to greet her, including the Jews, carrying their Torahs.

She rode a packsaddle mule wearing a great black cloak which hid her face, and in that way she made her way to the castle. Gonçalo Vasques, who was its governor, asked to be released from his duties and received his release in writing. The queen was lodged in the castle, and Gonçalo Vasques went off to his own dwellings.

Count João Afonso lodged in the main fortress of the castle, which at that time was well garrisoned and entirely fortified in itself. Nobody was permitted to leave or enter, except when bearing written authorisation, and every night a watch was kept over the town for fear of the people of Lisbon, who were opposed to the queen. A few days later, Count Gonçalo left for Coimbra, as he knew that the King of Castile was approaching, and he, Count Gonçalo, was uncertain about the future course of events.

But it now behoves us to leave aside this theme and go back to speaking of Nuno Álvares, and not just about his lineage and upbringing, but also about his journey to Lisbon to join the Master.

Chapter 31

Comments from the author of this work before speaking of the deeds of Nuno Álvares

When writing this particular section, without wishing to compel anyone to listen, we intend, in respect of this man's achievements, to adopt the approach taken by certain preachers, who within their homily insert the life history of the person about whom they are preaching and then, having completed it, bring the subject of their sermon to an end. As for us, though we have already made certain references to Nuno Álvares, it would be appropriate if his glorious deeds, which are described below, were to lead some people to inquire about the origins of his lineage and to ask about their very beginning. That said, by discontinuing for a while our chronological order and before approaching that topic, as we shall do briefly, we shall first of all make the following comments by way of a prologue, which he certainly deserves.

Experience teaches us that no person is born without certain contradictory characteristics and that nobody is by nature so calm as never to be upset; furthermore, it is very demanding to behave temperately when enticed by idle pleasures. For those reasons a man is deemed to be honourable, if in a continual struggle he overcomes his natural desires and if he is never found to be at fault, such as would result from blameworthy behaviour. If such determination brings great honour, then the man of whom we wish to speak truly earns it. In an unceasing fight and with huge strength and forbearance he so successfully repressed the sins of the flesh that none could censure him for any obvious shortcoming.

If we could relate at length his prudent deeds, that would be for us a most satisfactory commemoration, yet a task which is more pleasurable than easy. Yet who could give a worthy account of the laudable accomplishments of this noble and virtuous man, whose prowess and circumspect actions, were they all to be set down here, would occupy a large portion of this book?

It would certainly give us immense pleasure, if in recounting them we could organise our presentation of them in the same way as those who write down the events during the lives of those to whom they happen, praising each noble deed in turn, for each and every virtue is well worth proclaiming; but now, after his passing, and in view of the death of most of those who were his companions, we are no longer in a position to spend time on his noble actions, except on those of which there are a few lingering details.

We would, therefore, much prefer to spend a long time reading and hearing about the benefits brought by his achievements, rather than to occupy ourselves for a brief spell in recounting them and putting them in the right order, especially as we cannot escape those people who take delight in finding fault and who habitually devote their censure to serving whatsoever purpose or faction they choose; indeed, we cannot say anything which they would not judge to be blameworthy. That is because certain malicious people may declare that we praise him more than is merited by his deeds, even claiming, as we have said, that nobody in this world is wholly without defects, and exaggerating certain trivial characteristics of his, in order to make them seem greatly reprehensible.

Others will perhaps declare that the praise [from us] is less than he actually deserves and will consider his achievements to be of greater value than they receive in our narrative; such people will censure us for our audacity and presumption in wanting to set down in writing what we can no longer do in any detail. Others will want to give an account of just as many noble deeds, wrought by someone less worthy of high honour and of lesser standing, and will supply reasons why such a person should be equal in stature to this much greater man.

However, although certain people did indeed accomplish great and reputable deeds, the nobility of which we have no intention of overlooking, we cannot find anyone among them who, ascending in tireless determination from one virtue to the next, could compete with him in so many blessed achievements. Having mentioned the part played by such men, whose duties are always acknowledged, nevertheless, owing to the fact that nothing was written down during his lifetime (though there clearly existed a strong wish to do so, along with painstaking reflection on the matter), and despite our account being relatively brief and our style so impoverished, we intend to record his truly remarkable accomplishments. These, though they displease some people, yet, by awakening in others a beneficial envy, may well spur them into performing similar actions.

Chapter 32

Concerning the lineage from which Nuno Álvares descended, and who were his father and mother

With regard to the order in which events occur in this world, we should reflect that the first thing which needs to be known about this man is the source of his lineage. For that reason, before we commend his noble deeds as praiseworthy, let us see who his father and mother were and from whom they were descended.

It so happened that in Portugal there was once a great and honourable nobleman, distinguished in both rank and lineage: his name was Gonçalo Pereira. His was a great and eminent household, and he enjoyed the fellowship of many honourable relatives and *criados*. He was very generous and liberal both to his own people and to strangers; indeed, it is written that his generosity was such that, on one occasion when he was in Pereira, he gave away sixty horses to noblemen who were close followers of his.

Anyone wanting to read an extensive account of the ancient origin of his lineage should consult the *Livros das Linhagens dos Fidalgos*,[41] Title 21, paragraph 11, where he can find out about it in detail. Gonçalo Pereira fathered several children whom we shall not bother to mention, other than the one who, like his father, bore the name of Gonçalo Pereira: he became Archbishop of Braga and was one of the major prelates that there has been in Portugal.

This Archbishop Gonçalo Pereira fathered a son, Brother Álvaro Gonçalves Pereira by name, who became Prior of the Order of the Hospitallers. This man received great honours, became immensely rich and was of noble character. He left the country, and, travelling in great state, accompanied by a goodly retinue of squires and other men-at-arms, made his way to the [Order's] monastery on the island of Rhodes. He journeyed there with twenty-five horsemen, and, as a reward for his honourable deeds, the Grand Master invested him with the rank of prior.

After he became Prior of the Order, he performed many noble actions to increase the Order's holdings, among which were the castle of Amieira, which is both very strong and very beautiful, the palace and dwellings of Bom Jardim,

---

[41] The Portuguese *Livros de Linhagens* (Books of Noble Lineages), were repertories of the noble families (including their Galician and Castilian ramifications), from just before the foundation of the realm to the time when they were written. There were three of them, of which the third, from *c.* 1343, compiled by Pedro, Count of Barcelos, is the most comprehensive and best known and is the one mentioned in the text.

near Sertã, which is a fine construction and very pleasing to look upon, and the fortified mansion of Flor da Rosa, which is close to Crato, both defendable and well constructed, and where he built a great church, devoutly dedicated to the honour of the Blessed Virgin Mary. To add to that honour, he ordered that a new commandery be installed there, amply endowed in order to enable its commander to live in an appropriate style.

This prior became a counsellor of three kings of Portugal, namely King Afonso [IV], King Pedro and King Fernando, by all of whom he was loved for his beneficence, especially by King Fernando. Prior Álvaro Gonçalves lived to a great age and fathered thirty-two sons and daughters, among whom was one Pedro Álvares, who succeeded his father as Prior of the Order of Hospitallers and later became Master of the Order of Calatrava in Castile. Pedro Álvares was the son of one mother, but Nuno Álvares [another of Prior Álvaro's sons] was the son of another mother, whose name was Iria Gonçalves, a native of Elvas. He was born in the month of June, 1360.

His mother was a very noble lady, both before God and to the world, living in great chastity and abstinence, performing many acts of charity and much given to fasting, neither eating meat nor drinking wine for a period of forty years.

Chapter 33

How Nuno Álvares was brought to the Court of King Fernando and how he received his first arms from the hand of Queen Leonor

According to what certain writers have set down in their books, Prior Álvaro Gonçalves Pereira, being both sensible and intelligent, was reportedly an astrologer and a man of great wisdom. Whenever any of his children were born, he dedicated himself to the astrological interpretation of the birth. Thanks to his astrological knowledge he was convinced that one of his sons would always be victorious in every battle in which he took part and would never be defeated. They say that throughout his life Álvaro Gonçalves believed that this talent would be the lot of his son Pedro Álvares, who after his death became Prior of his Order, and with that in mind he always singled him out among his brothers.

Other writers give a contrary account, and this version we find more satisfactory, because they say that in the household of Prior Álvaro Gonçalves there was a widely read and very knowledgeable astrologer by the name of Master Tomás. They record that it was from this man that the prior learned that one of his sons was due to be victorious in his battles and this was Nuno Álvares Pereira.

This is clearly demonstrated to be the case, because, when Prior Álvaro Gonçalves arrived at the palace of King Fernando to deal with certain matters, he begged a boon of the king, namely that he should receive Nuno Álvares as a resident in his household. As this was pleasing to the king, he granted his request. The prior then departed to his estates and made ready to send his son to the Court. Before sending him, he called for Martim Gonçalves do Carvalhal, who was the uncle of Nuno Álvares and his mother's brother. He made him swear an oath that he should never mention to Nuno Álvares a certain matter which he wished to disclose to him. Once he had promised to keep the matter secret, the prior then told him that he was intending to send his son to the Royal Court and Martim Gonçalves along with him as his tutor. For that reason he begged him to assume the responsibility of carefully rearing him, and he assured him that his son would be gifted with great prowess and would always emerge victorious from every battle he joined, provided that he held close to God in all his undertakings and did nothing that was a disservice to Him.

Having made these arrangements, the prior left for the Royal Court just at the time when King Fernando was at war with King Enrique. The prior passed through Santarém and took some of his forces with him, as well as some of his sons, among whom was Nuno Álvares, a boy of thirteen years of age, who had never yet taken up arms. While the forces of the King of Castile were heading for Lisbon, where his liege lord was present at that time, the prior commanded Nuno Álvares, though he was still a boy, to ride forth alongside his brother Diogo Álvares, an honourable knight of the Order, and go with several members of his household, whom he ordered to accompany them, in order to find out what the Castilian troops were doing. Yet, since they made for the very area through which it was reported that the Castilians were travelling, but did not see any of them, they headed back to town.

They arrived at the castle where the king and queen were lodging at the time and, while they were dining, the king and queen sent for them and asked them where they had been and what they had discovered there. They fully answered all the questions that were put to them. While discussing the matter, Queen Leonor, being a lady well versed in the manners of the Royal Court and habitually gracious in her speech, declared to the king, in a playful way, how much it would please her if she were to adopt Nuno Álvares as her squire. The king replied that it was a commendable thing to do and that he would adopt his brother Diogo Álvares as his personal knight.

Then the queen told Nuno Álvares that by her own hand she wished to adopt him as her squire and that she did not wish him to receive his arms from the hands of anyone else but hers. On hearing this, though Nuno Álvares was still a boy, he expressed his acknowledgement that she was doing him a very great favour and that it would be pleasing to God if he were to serve her with noble and meritorious deeds; with that, he kissed her hands. Since the queen wished to put her words into good effect, she sent for an appropriate suit of armour for Nuno Álvares, but, as he was of a tender age, they were unable to find any armour that was small enough for him. At that point the queen was informed that the Master of Avis possessed a suit of armour which he had used when a boy and which would be suitable for Nuno Álvares, and so she ordered it to be brought for him.

When they brought it she immediately bestowed it on Nuno Álvares, and thus he received his very first arms from the hand of Queen Leonor, and from that time forth she always regarded him as her squire.

Chapter 34

How the prior proposed to his son that he should seek to get married, and how his son agreed and married Dona Leonor de Alvim

While Nuno Álvares was a resident in the king's household, when he was little more than sixteen years of age, it so happened that a lady from the province of the Minho became a widow; her name was Leonor de Alvim, and she had been the wife of a noble knight named Vasco Gonçalves de Barroso. This lady was of noble birth, honourable in every way, and very wealthy in her earthly possessions, both chattels and landed property.

Knowing of her wealth and good repute, the prior sent her a message proposing that she should marry his son Nuno Álvares, and, when João Fernandes, the Commander of Flor da Rosa, went on the prior's behalf to present this proposal of marriage to her, the lady replied that they should inform the king and find out what His Grace commanded should be done, for she would not go against what he commanded. João Fernandes returned with this message, and the prior reported it to the king, requesting him to attend to the matter favourably. The king was pleased at the proposal and summoned her to him with a letter.

While the prior was dealing with this matter, Nuno Álvares was at home and had no knowledge of it. One day the prior sent for his son when nobody else was present and addressed to him the following words: 'Nuno, although you are just a boy and of a tender age, it seems to me that it would be very suitable, in God's service and a worthy thing for you to do, if you were to marry. In the Minho there lives a most noble lady, who is young and very virtuous, and therefore it is my wish, please God, that you should marry her. For that reason I would like to know what you think about it.' He said nothing more than that.

Quite apart from being naturally courteous to everyone, Nuno Álvares was much more so towards his father, as well as being very obedient and compliant to his wishes. Yet when he heard what his father had to say he was somewhat perturbed. One reason was the bashfulness which he habitually felt in his father's presence, the other was his raising the subject of marriage, a thing that was extremely remote from his own wishes. That was because at that time he was still of tender age, and all he cared about was his good comportment and that of those who accompanied him. He also enjoyed riding in the hunt for all sorts of game, without any thoughts of love for any woman, not even in his imagination. Rather, he often read story books, especially the story about Galahad and the Round Table. As he found that in such stories, Galahad, owing to his virgin state, had accomplished great and noteworthy deeds, which others were unable to achieve, he was very keen to emulate him in some way. Often he pondered on whether, with God's help, he should remain virginal. For that reason he found himself to be far removed from what his father had said to him about his marriage. Nevertheless, in order to obey him and to give a reply to his query, he answered him as follows:

'My lord, you speak to me about marriage, which was something about which I had no warning. I beg you, therefore, to favour me by giving me some time to think about it, and then I'll be able to give you an answer.' His father told him that his request was very acceptable, though he was quite amazed at his answer, given that he was such a young man, and told his mother, Iria Gonçalves, all that had passed between, them urging her to persuade him to agree to this marriage. Nuno Álvares's mother talked to him but was unable to alter his view, or shift him away from his original intention. Nuno Álvares was then approached by his cousin Álvaro Pereira and by Álvaro Gil de Carvalho, who was a great friend of his, and after listening to their insistent arguments he consented to do as his father wished.

Meanwhile, Leonor de Alvim arrived at Vila Nova da Rainha, where the king and queen were lodging. They warmly welcomed her, and the king immediately informed the prior, who joined them over there with his son Nuno Álvares. As soon as they arrived, the wedding took place, and Nuno Álvares and his lady were married without further celebrations, because she was a widow. The next day the prior departed with his son and daughter-in-law, heading for the estates belonging to the Order, and to a place named Bom Jardim. There Nuno Álvares lay with his wife Leonor, who from that time onward could truly be described as 'Lady', for though she had been described in such a way beforehand, she was in fact a maiden, because her first husband had never lain with her, which was a secret she had always kept honourably to herself.

Chapter 35

How Nuno Álvares left for his own house, and the way in which he lived

Nuno Álvares enjoyed himself with his wife in his father's house for several days, but then he left, and they travelled to the province of the Minho, where her own dwelling was located and where she had her own estates. There he was made very welcome and received visits from the nobles of the area, who offered him their friendship, as is the custom.

Nuno Álvares was a man of few and gentle words; indeed, his noble and friendly demeanour and his resort to sweet reason were a source of great pleasure to everyone. He was more given to hunting large than small game, though he practised both, as circumstances required. In his household he had daily twelve to fifteen squires and twenty to thirty men on foot, according to what was required for his estates. All of them were brave and capable men: indeed, he never relied on any other men so completely as he relied on these for as long as he lived.

He never did anything out of rancour or hatred, but in the matter of exorbitant expense and because such was the custom in the land, he sometimes went beyond the bounds of reason. Nevertheless, never so much that he lost his fear of God, for he always attended Holy Mass and lived a decent and honourable life alongside his wife, by whom he fathered three children: two who died at birth, and one daughter who was named Beatriz and later became a countess and a very noble lady, as we shall relate further on.

After three years had passed, his father the prior passed away at a very great age in Amieira. Nine sons, including Nuno Álvares, and nine daughters attended his funeral. Once the funeral rites had been duly completed, he was taken to the Church of Flor da Rosa, which he had built. Then his son Pedro Álvares, Nuno's brother, was made prior, though Brother Álvaro Gonçalves Camelo, who was Commander of Poiares at that time, held the right to succeed to the office of prior, but King Fernando ordered that Pedro Álvares be made prior.

After this, King Enrique having died, his son King Juan reigned in Castile. As King Juan was at war with King Fernando, you have heard how Nuno Álvares, along with his brother Pedro Álvares,[42] was summoned to guard the frontier, how he tried to challenge Juan de Osórez, who was the son of the Master of the Castilian Order of Santiago, how, with his brother who at the time was lord of the marches in Lisbon, he took part in a skirmish there, and what he did in order to be with the king in the battle that had been expected to take place at Elvas.[43] [You have also heard] how, after the death of King Fernando, he had wanted to join with the Master in killing Count Juan Fernández, and, as at the time this did not come about, how he took his leave of the Master and went after his brother, whom he caught up with in Ponteval.[44]

As you have already heard all this, it is important to go back to writing about what happened to him during the time of the Master's ascendancy, after he, Nuno Álvares, left the city of Lisbon, which was the point at which we ceased recounting his [previous] deeds.

Chapter 36

How Nuno Álvares discovered that Count Juan Fernández had been killed, and concerning the discussions which he held with his brother on this matter

When Nuno Álvares left Lisbon, since the plan to kill Count Juan Fernández had not yet been brought about, as we have duly explained,[45] and when he had talked about it with the Master, he headed off to join his brother Pedro Álvares, catching up with him in a place called Ponteval, which lies some 12 leagues away from the city. While they were there together, Gonçalo Tenreiro arrived bearing a message from the queen to the prior, urging him to continue in her service and indicating that she would reward him with many favours and that she would obtain a pledge from her son[-in-law] the King of Castile that he would do the same. Nuno Álvares and many of the others who were with the prior were far from happy at this, especially Nuno Álvares, who was

---

[42] See *CKF*, Chapters 120–21. According to Chapter 33 above, Nuno Álvares had been accompanied by his brother Diogo Álvares.

[43] See *CKF*, Chapters 137–38 and 151.

[44] See Chapter 4 above.

[45] See the close of Chapter 4 above.

greatly displeased, so much so that he could not resist speaking to the prior, saying that it was inadvisable to lay himself open to such an approach. The prior did not care for his argument but said nothing and left, making his way to Santarém.

While the prior and his retinue were there, Nuno Álvares took up lodging in Santa Maria de Palhais. One evening, after dinner, he went out and made his way down to the riverside to relax, in a spot close to the Church of Santa Iria. Passing a sword-smith's door, he noticed that he was holding a fine well-tempered sword. Taking hold of it, he asked the sword-smith whether he would temper one of his swords in the same way for him. The sword-smith answered that he would indeed do so and that it would even be a far better sword. Nuno Álvares sent for his sword at once and gave orders that it be given to the sword-smith to temper.

Next day Nuno Álvares went back there in the evening and found that the sword had been tempered just as he wanted it. He was delighted with it when he took hold of it and commanded one of his men to pay the sword-smith well for his trouble. The latter answered him, 'My lord, I want no payment from you at this time but wish you every good fortune. Indeed, you will return here as the Count of Ourém. Then you will pay me what I deserve.'

'Do not call me "lord"', said Nuno Álvares, 'for that I am not, but it is nevertheless my wish that you be well paid.'

'My lord', he replied, 'what I say is the truth: this will soon come about and be greatly pleasing to Almighty God.'

Indeed, events occurred just as he had predicted: a short while afterwards he returned there as the Count of Ourém and paid the sword-smith well for tempering his sword. Just what happened you will hear in due course.

At this point news reached Santarém that the Master had killed Count Juan Fernández, and that likewise the Bishop of Lisbon and others had been slain. When Nuno Álvares heard this, he went straight to his brother the prior and told him of the news that he had received. He added that this was God's work, for God's wish was to remember Portugal, especially as the city folk wanted to adopt the Master as their ruler and defender; in particular they wanted him to defend the realm against the King of Castile, who was reportedly preparing to invade the country. He went on to say that, as these things were already in train, he was now begging him, most earnestly, to come over to the Master and help him to defend the kingdom.

The prior showed little enthusiasm for anything that Nuno Álvares had to say to him on the matter, declaring that it was dangerous, a very bad beginning for the people, and the consequence would be that great harm would befall the realm. Anyone thinking that matters would proceed in the manner indicated by Nuno Álvares was insane. Nuno Álvares replied that it was not a bad beginning: the Master had acted well and done what he ought to do in avenging the dishonour brought upon the king his brother and in showing himself ready to defend the realm which his forefathers had won by dint of their extreme efforts. He asserted that Portugal had always been a free nation, was not subject to Castile, and that there was no reason for that to happen now.

The prior repeated that the subject was not worthy of discussion and that Portugal was in no position to defend itself against the King of Castile, who was extremely powerful; besides, most of Portugal would side with him because of the promises made to him in accordance with what was contained in the treaties. Nuno Álvares replied that those promises were not fit to be kept, for the simple reason that the king was himself breaking the treaties. Moreover, every member of the nobility could go to the aid of the Master and without incurring any blame. The Master would be able to assemble 1,000 men-at-arms and many foot soldiers with whom he could confront the King of Castile in battle. Besides, it was far better for the Master to venture forth with them at his side to fight against the King of Castile than for them to be subject to Castilians and to let them lord it over them as they saw fit.

The prior declared that matters had not reached a point where it was possible for such an undertaking to begin and end safely and well. For that reason they should not discuss the subject any further. Realising that the prior was far from accepting his intent, Nuno Álvares spoke to his brother Diogo Álvares, urging him, despite everything, to join him in going to assist the Master. Diogo Álvares expressed his approval, and they both resolved to go ahead.

Chapter 37

How Nuno Álvares revealed to his followers that he intended to go to Lisbon in order to serve the Master

The prior left for his own estates, making his way via Golegã. His brothers Nuno Álvares and Diogo Álvares did not go with him but travelled to Lisbon, where the Master was, and as they had previously agreed. However, when they were still some 3 leagues away from the city, Diogo Álvares regretted his decision and announced that he wanted to rejoin his brother the prior. Unable to dissuade him from his intent, Nuno Álvares found himself obliged to take his leave of him and arrived that day at a village named Ereira, where he spent the night. Once there, he called his squires aside and said: 'Friends, I want to tell you a secret. It concerns a great challenge which I keep deep in my heart and that secret is this: I imagine that I can see a very deep pit, full of darkness. I am inclined to believe that any man who jumps down into that pit can never escape from it, except through some great miracle born of God's willingness to favour and rescue him. Yet I cannot resist what my heart tells me, which is to jump down into the pit. For many days you have been my companions, and I have come to recognise your noble intentions towards me and my deeds. For that very reason, I am informing you of this, because, despite everything, my great desire is to jump down into the pit. As for those of you who are content to jump down with me, I shall regard that action as being of the highest service to me. The others, who are loath to do so, can go their own ways and do with their lives whatever they regard as more profitable.'

On hearing this, the squires were filled with consternation and did not know what to say. However, they did answer him, saying: 'Nuno Álvares, you know very well that we are your followers and are ready to serve you. But this matter about which you have spoken to us is indeed very obscure and difficult for us to grasp. Not one of us knows what answer to give you. For that reason, kindly tell us what it is, so that we can know about it, and then we shall give you our answer as we see fit.'

Nuno Álvares then went on with his explanation and declared to them: 'Friends, the pit which I behold and which is very deep and dark is the great quest which, as is reported, the Master is keen to undertake in defence of this realm against the King of Castile. It is my understanding that whosoever joins him in that quest will face a very grave and dangerous challenge. Nor can such a man even think of escaping from it, except by the grace of God. As it is my intention to go and join the Master and serve him in his quest, I have therefore asked you whether it is your wish to come with me as my companions.'

They then answered him, saying: 'Nuno Álvares, we are your followers and are at your service. We are ready to go with you in this quest which you want to pursue and in any other pursuit which you feel will bring you both honour and profit, however great the danger may be, even to the point of giving up our bodies and our lives in your service.'

Nuno Álvares thanked them in the most generous terms, declaring that he was ready to reward them for anything which they might do to enhance his honour and profit, as the honourable *criados* and good friends that they were.

Chapter 38

How Nuno Álvares reached Lisbon, and what he said to the Master

Next day Nuno Álvares went on his way, while the queen was still in Alenquer in the company of the counts her brothers and of many others, as we have indicated. When he reached Alverca, he decided to spend the night there. The queen learned that he was heading for Lisbon to join the Master and was inclined to send out some soldiers to arrest him, declaring to those present, 'Have you noticed the stupidity of Nuno, whom I raised since he was a mere boy? Are you aware that he has abandoned the prior his brother and is now heading for Lisbon to join the Master?'

Some of those present who had a liking for Nuno Álvares answered: 'My lady, you have no grounds to order his arrest. Though he's making for Lisbon, you don't know what his reasons are for going there. He's perhaps going with such determination and intent as will enable him to serve you even better from there than if he came directly to you here.'

Nuno Álvares found out about this situation while spending the night at Alverca. As he was greatly apprehensive that the queen would have him arrested while he was on his way, he spoke to his squires, warning them that, if that were to happen, it would nevertheless be preferable for them to let themselves be killed than to be taken prisoner. All that night they never laid down their arms nor unsaddled their mounts. Next day, Nuno Álvares reached Lisbon and went at once to speak to the Master. The latter gave him a warm welcome, adding that he was delighted at his arrival and that for some time he had looked forward to seeing him. The city folk were likewise very pleased to see him and all confirmed the Master's welcome.

Two days after Nuno Álvares arrived in Lisbon, he made his way to the Master's palace, addressing him as follows: 'My lord, for a very long time it has been and still remains my great wish to serve you. Yet before now it has not been my good fortune to be able to do so. As you have now attained such standing as leads me to believe that I shall be able to achieve something which I have sought for so long, I now most willingly offer you my own person and my humble service. I beseech you henceforth to regard me as freely and entirely devoted to you and to make such use of me as befits a man who is very ready and willing to be of use to you.'

The Master thanked him warmly for his noble intentions, because he had recognised his honourable qualities for a long time. He now welcomed him as his follower, just as he had said. Indeed, he made him a member of his council, joining the others who already belonged to it. Thereafter the Master never did anything about which Nuno Álvares did not know.

Chapter 39

How the mother of Nuno Álvares came to divert her son from serving the Master, and what happened as a result

Iria Gonçalves, the mother of Nuno Álvares, was at this time in Portalegre, a town that lies 4 leagues[46] away from Crato,[47] which was where the prior had arrived with his brothers. When she heard that her son Nuno Álvares had not come back with them, she at once hastened to Crato to ask what had become of him, her son. The prior announced that he had remained behind in Santarém and that he was expecting him daily. She answered that it looked as though he was little concerned about his brother and had never really liked him; this he had now made plain, since, despite his being in the prior's company, he had not bothered to bring Nuno Álvares with him.

Iria Gonçalves left at once for Lisbon, where she discovered that Nuno Álvares was now to be found. She told him just how serious and dangerous she felt the action was that he was keen to undertake, in going to serve the Master and help him to defend the realm against the whole of Castile and most of Portugal. She deployed many lively arguments as to why the course of action which he was taking could not succeed and why he could not thereby add either to his profit or honour. Determined to go ahead, Nuno Álvares plied her with opposing arguments which dismantled everything that his mother said. So much were they locked in argument that, though she had come to press her son to serve the King of Castile, Nuno Álvares induced her instead to promote the Master's cause.

When they both finally came to agree that what Nuno Álvares said was right, Dona Iria spoke again to him as follows: 'My son, just as I now give you my blessing, since you have chosen to serve the Master and remain at his side, I beg you always to serve him faithfully and well and never to desert him in any way, whatever may happen. As for me, I shall immediately arrange for Fernão Pereira your brother to come and join you in serving the Master.' Nuno Álvares answered that he would do as she asked.

---

[46] About 14 miles (just over 24 km).
[47] Crato is located 12 miles (c. 20 km) due west of Portalegre.

Knowing that Dona Iria was in the city and that she had come to dissuade her son from his wish to serve him, the Master went to visit her in the house in which she was lodging. He told her how it was his intention to make himself available to defend the realm and that he understood that her only reason for coming was to dissuade her son from his wish to serve him. He therefore urged her not to get involved in the matter and not to impede her son in any way, for the causes to which he wished to devote himself were the service of God and the honour of the realm. It was his hope that God would direct his actions so well that her son would emerge with his honour greatly enhanced. As their discussion continued, she answered him by saying how very pleased she was that her son would remain with the Master to serve him and that accordingly she had given him her blessing.

Dona Iria then went back to where she had come from and spoke to her son Fernão Pereira, offering him such guidance that he at once departed with his followers and made his way to Lisbon to join the Master.

Chapter 40

How the Master addressed the members of his council as to whether he should stay in the kingdom or leave it

We now go back to narrating the Master's actions, which we left off in order to take the queen to Santarém and to bring Nuno Álvares to serve him. In that very period when Nuno Álvares joined him, the Master was greatly troubled and torn by conflicting thoughts. That was because a number of members of his council asserted that he should not wait in Portugal for the advance of the King of Castile with his powerful army but should travel to England. They brought to bear many reasons why he ought to do so and predicted sundry profitable and assured outcomes that would ensue, declaring, among other matters, that as a result of departing in that way he could thereby count on such military support as would enable him to return to the country later and recover the realm with very great honour and without losses to the people nor harm to the land.

Others were completely opposed to this opinion, dismissing the reasoning of such counsellors with contrary arguments. Such were Nuno Álvares, Rui Pereira, Álvaro Vasques de Góis, Doctor João das Regras, Álvaro Pais and Doctor Martim Afonso, who all said that for the Master to leave would neither be honourable, nor in the service of Almighty God, nor in his own best interests because, if he were to leave the country, it would be forsaken and have nobody to defend it. Besides, the King of Castile would seize the city and the other townships which were opposed to the Master, and would give them to such individuals to defend them and would fortify them in such a way that they could not be recovered afterwards except by dint of great toil and the spilling of much blood. For those reasons they entreated him to remain in the kingdom and not to abandon it, for God had summoned and chosen him for this purpose and would direct his actions, adding greatly to his honour and to his renown.

The Master listened to these arguments from both sides. For all that those who were advising him to leave the country were advancing positive and reasonable arguments as to why he should do so, the Master's immense courage and great desire to perform acts of chivalry made him lean towards remaining in the country after all and towards undertaking any venture to defend the realm.

Nevertheless, those who were advising him to take the opposite course of action greatly impeded those thoughts to the point where he began to have doubts. One day, after dinner, the Master summoned his council, including Nuno Álvares. When they were all assembled, the Master addressed them as follows: 'My friends, you are aware of the great danger in which this kingdom finds itself, and how, in accord with what some of you say, if I were to leave the kingdom, it would be utterly lost and fall into the hands of the King of Castile; you are aware too that such men argue that it would be preferable to die honourably in defence of this land than to be subjected to the servitude which its enemies would inflict on us. As for me, let me tell you that it is my firm intention, by which I shall abide, never to leave this country, if that is something on which you are able to agree.'

The members of his council who were of this persuasion declared that the Master had spoken very well and they were delighted with his reasoning. They begged him to go ahead and not to heed any other advice. They added that they and all the others would serve him honourably and faithfully and that they placed their hopes in Almighty God, trusting that He would bring the Master's actions to such noble fulfilment as would bring great honour both to him and to the realm.

After the lengthy debate which they devoted to this matter, they all agreed that the Master should remain in the kingdom and not leave. They then began to discuss other matters, including how to capture the castle.

Chapter 41

How the Master had wanted to attack Lisbon's castle, and how he took it without a fight

After the conclusion of the matters about which you have been hearing, the Master announced that one of the obstacles which he had to confront was the city's castle, for it stood against him and was loyal to the queen. It was essential to capture it, in order to prevent the city from harmful attack from any of the forces in the castle, should they wish to mount such an assault on the city. Nuno Álvares and the other members of his council said that he should not feel hampered by such an obstacle and should not be troubled about it, because God, Who had given him the city, would likewise give him the castle.

Now it happened that, when the queen pondered on past events, her heart was often filled with sombre thoughts; while still in Alenquer at that time and fearful about what was later to ensue, she spoke to Count João Afonso, her brother, who was the Governor of Lisbon and who had many honourable vassals in the city, requesting him to send them a message urging them to take refuge in the castle, along with their squires, in order to be safe from anything that might happen.

The count agreed that this was a good step to take and spoke to Afonso Eanes Nogueira, who was there present and was one of his vassals, telling him to make his way to the city and to urge those who were his followers to take refuge in the castle. Afonso Eanes went to Lisbon, but all those to whom he was due to speak were secret disciples of the Master and held opinions greatly contrary to what they had formerly believed, as they now supported him against the queen. When Afonso Eanes spoke to Estêvão Vasques Filipe, as well as to Afonso Furtado, Antão Vasques and other honourable knights in the city, he found that they had shifted away from what he expected to hear from them. Deciding not to broach the matter with others, he headed for his lodgings, got himself ready as best he could and took refuge in the castle through the postern gate,[48] accompanied by ten to twelve squires.

When Afonso Eanes took refuge in this way, shouts went up throughout the city as people called out, 'Treachery! Treachery! Come and help the Master! They want to kill the Master!' On hearing this, the city folk became greatly

---

[48] The postern gate was a secondary gate in a city or castle walls, usually in an inconspicuous location, allowing people to come in and out quietly and without attracting attention. It could be quite useful in a siege, allowing supplies to be brought in, or messages to be sent out, but it could also be used to let the enemy in. For this reason it is known as a 'porta da traição' (traitor's gate) in Portuguese.

excited, took up arms and rushed to attack the castle, simply because the Master, when he decided to seize the castle, had taken up lodging in the bishop's palace, which is close to the castle. When those who had made their way to the castle realised that what they had been told was untrue, they came back very angry and uttered all manner of threats against anyone who dared to get involved in such an act.

Martim Afonso Valente was one of the honourable figures in the city and was the governor of the castle on behalf of Count João Afonso, the queen's brother. He received a request to hand the castle over to the Master and not to allow himself to be a source of harm either to the city or to the realm, since he was a true Portuguese. All sorts of reasons were given as to why he should do so. Martim Afonso pleaded the excuse that he was in no way able to do this, since he had made a solemn promise and would be disgraced and greatly dishonoured, just as all his descendants would be.

The Master then commanded an attack on those in the castle. He ordered the construction of a wooden device known as a cat,[49] so that if the shallow moat that the castle then had was filled in, this cat could go over it and come up to the castle. Then, from under its protection, it would be possible to claw at the ramparts and get through into the castle. Those on the outside called out to those inside the castle to surrender it to the Master their lord; otherwise, they swore to God that they would put Constança Afonso on top of the cat. Constança Afonso was the mother of Afonso Eanes Nogueira and sister[50] of the wife of Martim Afonso, the governor of the castle. They also said that the same would happen to the wives and children of everyone in the castle, and then they could hurl down from above fire and stones on whomsoever they chose. In fear of this, a number of the defenders told the governor that they would rather go outside and not help to defend the castle than risk killing their wives and children in the manner in which they were being threatened.

At this point, even before the cat had been built and the moat had been filled in for the cat to go over it, Nuno Álvares told the Master that he wanted to go and speak to Martim Afonso Valente and Afonso Eanes Nogueira about the castle, for he believed that they would hand it over to him. The Master said that he was pleased at the idea, and so Nuno Álvares went to the castle and plied Martim Afonso with many reasons as to why he should hand over the castle to the Master. He told him that it was undesirable that, because of him,

---

[49] See Chapter 24, note 35, above.

[50] According to Jorge Almeida, Afonso Eanes Nogueira's mother was the mother or stepmother of Martim Afonso Valente's wife, not her sister. See Jorge Almeida (ed.), *Crónica da Regência e do Reinado de D. João I* (Porto: Húmus, 2015), p. 104, note 2.

the city should be lost and the kingdom put at risk. That was something which, as the true Portuguese that he was, Martim Afonso could in his heart never agree to. If he were to act in any other way, everyone would bitterly resent it, and he would deserve to be stoned [to death] by all the people in the city.

Martim Afonso listened to these and many other arguments which Nuno Álvares put to him, observed how the entire city showed great hostility towards him and noted the attack that they were mounting on the castle. Moreover, as those who were with him were saying that, if the siege were to be conducted in the way described, they would not be prepared to sacrifice their wives and children in order to help him to defend the castle, he consequently realised that he had not the means to hold out for very long. Martim Afonso, therefore, told Nuno Álvares that he was content to hand over the castle to the Master but that he would first inform the queen and Count João Afonso, owing to the promise which he had made.

Nuno Álvares declared that the date until when they would refrain from attacking [the castle] should at once be determined and that Martim Afonso should hand over hostages as a warranty, lest help should arrive in the meantime. Then Martim Afonso gave assurances that, if no help reached him within forty hours, the castle would be surrendered to the Master without further contention. Afonso Eanes Nogueira was then placed as a hostage in the power of Nuno Álvares, who took him back with him to his own lodgings.

When the city folk discovered that the castle was subject to a temporary truce, they all rushed up there with their weapons at the ready. All that night a heavy guard was posted on it, as they slept around the hill with many candles burning and kept very careful watch to forestall any help which might come to the governor of the castle. Martim Afonso was quick to send a squire to Alenquer to inform the count of where he stood with the city folk and how they were keen to attack him and in what way. When the squire told the count that the city folk were threatening to place the wives and children of all the defenders on the cat, and that they could kill whomsoever they wished, the count smiled saying: 'They've really hoodwinked you with that ploy, making you think that you have to surrender the castle! You'd better tell me that you wanted to give them the castle, so you've given it to them! It looks to me as though they've filled you with fear to scare you off, just like the fox at the foot of a tree, threatening the crow with its tail, while the crow up the tree had the cheese in its beak, just to make the crow drop it.[51] You're all just like

---

[51] Fernão Lopes seems to have crossed Aesop's fable of the fox and the crow with another traditional fable where the fox threatens a bird high up in an oak into giving him one of her young lest he would cut down the tree with his tail and eat them all up.

that, you've been stricken by an irrational fear of what you couldn't hold and, in order to surrender the castle earlier, you've agreed to a deadline which leaves no chance for help to reach you. I haven't got enough men here to go and help you, and, even if I had, the deadline is so short, that there wouldn't be even enough time to get the horses shod.'

The squire answered that Martim Afonso had been unable to gain more time and that even the deadline which they had set him was given very begrudgingly.

The count then spoke to the queen and told her about the means by which the city folk sought to attack the castle. Her answer was that, since that was how things were, he should give the order for the castle to be surrendered, because, later, whoever held the city would also hold the castle. The squire went back with this message, and, when the deadline came, the castle was surrendered to the Master on 30 December. He took up lodging in it and had it searched and the gates removed on the city side as advised by the entire population.

Having surrendered the castle to the Master, Martim Afonso came forward with the other inmates to serve the Master. Along with Afonso Eanes and all the others, he always served him faithfully and well.

Chapter 42

How the castle of Beja was captured, and how Admiral Master Lançarote was killed

Before these events, in view of how Count Juan Fernández had been slain and the uprising in Lisbon had taken place, the queen had dispatched letters throughout the kingdom, both to the governors of the castles and to the leading citizens in towns large and small, complaining about what had happened and instructing them how to proceed in declaring their loyalty to her daughter Beatriz. She also wrote to the King of Castile, urging him to make every effort to head swiftly into Portugal. He was in fact already in Guarda, as in due course you will be able to see. Consequently, both because of his advance and the fact that all the most prominent people in the kingdom were on the queen's side, loyalties were declared and banners were flown on behalf of her daughter, just as she had instructed in her letters. But these declarations of allegiance and this flying of pennants and banners, under the title[52] which

---

[52] Namely, that of Queen of Portugal.

was being proclaimed on her daughter's behalf, were very hard for the ordinary folk in the villages and townships to swallow. Since they were in no position to contradict such prominent figures, their hearts were filled with anguish as they consented, with fear and dread, to what they could not gainsay.

That is what occurred in Estremoz: there, João Mendes de Vasconcelos, who was Queen Leonor's cousin and governor of the castle, gave orders for allegiance to be declared to Queen Beatriz, and for her banner to be flown. Lopo Afonso and Lourenço Dias, along with other citizens, paraded it through the town, but when they noticed that the rest of the populace were troubled and discontented with what was happening, they immediately declared it essential to install an executioner's block and axe in the main square for beheading those who opposed what they were doing.

While this wrangle took hold of people's hearts and minds, setting some against others, it became common knowledge throughout the land that the Master had consented to take on the role of ruler and defender of the realm, that he had captured the castle in Lisbon and now held it in his power. This was very pleasing to some of those in the kingdom, especially ordinary humble folk. By contrast, those who were on the queen's side were much troubled by it, although they thought it all so much vainglory.

It so happened that in Beja the governor was one Gonçalo Vasques de Melo, who was in charge of the castle and had declared his allegiance to the queen. At this point the queen again wrote letters to the council in Beja, instructing them to always maintain their allegiance to her, adding that, if the King of Castile should chance to pass that way, they should welcome him into the town without any fear whatsoever, because he would defend them from anyone wishing to cause them any harm and would confer many favours upon them in return.

When the letters were received by the leaders of the community, they proclaimed throughout the town that on the next day everyone should go and listen to the message contained in the letters sent by Her Grace Queen Leonor. On the following day Estêvão Mafaldo, João Afonso Neto, Master João, Rui Pais Sacoto, Mendo Afonso [de Beja] and other prominent figures from the town all gathered together and held a separate meeting by the small entrance door of the Church of Santa Maria da Feira; there they began to examine what the queen had written.

As for the common people, many of them had assembled long before in the church square, waiting to be told what the news was that the queen had commanded to be announced. They were all impatient to find out, and one of them, Gonçalo Ovelheiro by name, called out to the rest of them, 'Is nobody here going to find out what's in these letters? Or what message is this that the queen has sent?' There then spoke up a worthy squire, named Gonçalo

Nunes de Alvelos, who was neither one of the leaders of the town nor one of the ordinary folk. Turning to Vasco Rodrigues Carvalhal, he asked, 'Do you want to help me? Why don't we go and find out what these letters have to say?' Vasco Rodrigues said he was happy to do so. Some thirty others joined them and they went to where the leaders of the community were to be found. Gonçalo Nunes addressed them as follows:

'What are these letters which you are reading and about which we know nothing? Is this town, by any chance, going to be maintained and defended just by the four or five of you gathered in this spot? Of course not! It'll be by us, who live here.'

Estêvão Mafaldo then asked, 'What faction is that, bringing you here like this?'

Gonçalo Nunes answered him, saying, 'This is no faction! But we want to know what is in those letters.'

Then Mendo Afonso spoke, saying that it was right that he should ask and right for them to see the letters. Then they all went into the council chamber, with some of the common folk among them. When the letters had been read out, they gave them to a notary for him to announce them to those outside. The latter then went outside and addressed them as follows:

'My friends, this is the situation: there is no reason for me to linger on what is written here. In the end, the issue is this: do you wish to stand with the queen or with the Master?'

As though with one voice, they all answered, 'With the Master! With the Master!' As for the leading citizens, when they heard this, they immediately left, each one heading off home, without daring to appear again.

At this point, and without further delay, the people noticed that men-at-arms were appearing at the castle. Then they all started to shout out, 'The castle is in arms against us! The castle is in arms against us!' Gonçalo Nunes swiftly mounted his horse, and the rest of them all armed themselves and started to attack the castle at once. On seeing this, the governor set fire to two towers in which many supplies were stored, lest the townspeople should make use of them, if the castle were to be captured. When those inside the castle defended themselves fiercely and wounded some of those attacking from outside, the townspeople set fire to the castle gates. Once the gates had burned down, they made their way in on a Wednesday at the hour of the midday meal. The governor was captured but taken to safety by certain people who had a liking for him.

Gonçalo Nunes and Vasco Rodrigues at once took charge of the castle and declared their allegiance to the Master, patrolling and keeping watch over the town in his name and with all the gates closed. While they were keeping watch over the town in this way, as they had done for a few days, there arrived late one evening, riding a mare, a man from Campo de Ourique. He told those on watch to inform whosoever was in charge of governing the town that on that very afternoon Master Lançarote had arrived at a village known as Os Colos, which is 9 leagues away;[53] and that the admiral was bound for Odemira, which is in the kingdom of the Algarve, intending to lead an uprising in the Algarve and declare allegiance to the King of Castile.

On learning this, Gonçalo Nunes took 50 horsemen with him, as well as 100 crossbowmen and foot soldiers. They rode through the night, with the result that they reached Os Colos at daybreak. The admiral and his men had already saddled up, ready to ride off. Armed as they were, they were all taken prisoner, along with their Moors, both men and women, and their pack-mules, with all the possessions which they were carrying. Having seized their weapons and their animals, they let the admiral's men go free, but the admiral was brought into the town on a mule. Once he had arrived, they put him in the castle's main keep, whereupon he vehemently addressed them as follows:

'My friends, send me as a captive, under guard, to my lord the Master. Please don't kill me without a reason.'

They told him not to be afraid. But, while Gonçalo Nunes went off to deliver to the Master everything which they had captured from him, the townspeople became fearful that the admiral would cause an uprising in the castle. One day they all headed there and told Vasco Rodrigues to throw him out. Afraid of what they might do, he went off home and left the admiral in the keep. On realising this, the admiral began to prepare his defence as best he could. When they shouted up to him to come down and not to be afraid, he had no choice but to do so, hoping that they would show him pity and compassion, yet they inflicted on him a grim and dishonourable death, and so he ended his last days.

Chapter 43

How the castles of Portalegre and Estremoz were captured

In the very way you have heard about, the people rose up in other towns, and there was a great rift between people of rank and ordinary folk. This conglomeration of ordinary people, who were gathering in this way at the

---

[53] About 31 miles (c. 50 km).

time, was referred to in those days as 'the common herd'.[54] At the outset the grandees ridiculed ordinary folk and called them 'the Lisbon Messiah's people' for believing that the Master was bound to save them from subjection to the King of Castile.

Once they had summoned up enough courage and had become united, the ordinary folk called grandees 'schismatic traitors'[55] for siding with the Castilians in order to hand over the kingdom to someone to whom it did not belong. Not one of them, regardless of rank, dared to contradict this or to speak out on his own account, because he knew that, if he did so, a grim death would swiftly follow, without anyone coming to his aid.

It was wonderful to see how much courage God instilled in the common people and how much cowardice in the others: the very castles, which former kings by force of arms and after a long siege were unable to capture, were forcibly seized, before midday, by the common people, poorly armed, leaderless and scantily armoured[56] though they were.

One such was the castle of Portalegre, governed by Dom Pedro Álvares, the Prior of the Order of the Hospitallers. On his authority it had declared allegiance to the queen, just like the other castles. Yet the ordinary folk of the town came together one Thursday morning, began to attack it and, before midday, with God's help, it was captured.

Similarly, the people of the town of Estremoz became mightily aroused and proposed to the governor that he and his men should abandon the castle and make their way into the town, because otherwise they did not feel safe from him. João Mendes [de Vasconcelos] announced that he would not do that at any price, because it would bring him great dishonour and cause him to be blamed. On receiving his answer, the townspeople decided to attack the castle. They brought a cart into the main square and set about placing in it the wives and children of those who were inside the castle with the governor, who were all natives of the town.

On seeing this, those in the castle told João Mendes to surrender it to the townspeople, because otherwise they were disinclined to help him. Realising the predicament that he was in, he sent word to those outside asking them

54 'Arraia miúda' in Portuguese. The common people as a group also belong to Fernão Lopes's gallery of heroes.

55 This is a reference to the Great Schism in the Church (1378–1417). The Castilians sided with the Avignon Antipope and the Portuguese with the Pope in Rome.

56 Fernão Lopes uses the phrase 'ventres ao sol', literally 'bellies in the sun', a powerful image stressing the commitment of these simple men, unable to afford adequate armour and yet fighting with their bellies unprotected, thus leaving them vulnerable to a fatal wound.

to send a trustworthy person to whom he might speak, adding that he would come to an agreement with them.

Accordingly, they sent to the castle Friar Lourenço, the warden of São Francisco, along with others. João Mendes advanced many arguments to prove that he did not side with Castile, asserting that he was a true Portuguese, just like them. But, as his arguments availed him nothing, it was decided that he should nevertheless leave the castle and that it should be handed over to one of the townspeople, who would keep watch over it.

The governor conceded that he was content to do this, simply because he was in no position to do anything else. The castle was handed over to a squire named Martim Peres. The governor then made his way at once out of the castle and departed for Moura, which Álvaro Gonçalves held in the name of the King of Castile. Those on the town council gave orders for the removal of the gates of the tower and those of the castle which faced the town; they also ordered the demolition of that section of the parapet and of the battlements. From then on the castle was watched over and patrolled in the name of the Master and placed in the power of the common people.

Not only the menfolk, as has been stated, but also the womenfolk had formed a group taking the Master's side and did so against anyone who did not declare their allegiance to him. The outcome was that one day Mor Lourenço, the ragpicker Margarida Anes and other women rose up and were involved in a heated argument with Maria Esteves, the mother of Nuno Rodrigues de Vasconcelos, declaring that her son had slandered the Master and that he was a supporter of the Castilians. Indeed, they took it upon themselves to kill him and hurled him down from the ramparts.

Chapter 44

How the Governor of Évora sought to declare his allegiance to the queen, and how the castle was captured by the townspeople

Álvaro Mendes de Oliveira, the Chief Provincial Governor of the town of Évora, who at that time held the castle in the queen's name, heard what was happening in a number of townships and realised that events similar to what was happening to others could also happen to him. Recognising this, and recognising too that he had no forces available with whom he could defend the castle, other than a handful of *criados* of his, such as Gonçalo Eanes Melão, Martim Bravo, Rui Gil and up to seven or eight others all told, he sent for Martim Afonso Arnalho, who was a merchant and at that time a judge and married to a lady-in-waiting of Queen Leonor. He also sent for Gonçalo Lourenço, who was the deputy governor, as well as Vasco Martins Porrado, who was the town council clerk, Rui Gonçalves, who was a land surveyor, along with Martim Velho, the merchant Álvaro Vasques and other worthy men of the town. When they all assembled in answer to his summons, he put to them many arguments on behalf of the queen, whom he wished to support, with the result that they all agreed to join with him and help to defend the castle on her behalf.

That very day, once they had all hurried inside the castle and this had become known throughout the town, Diogo Lopes Lobo, Fernão Gonçalves da Arca and João Fernandes his son, who were among the men of rank who lived there, together with all the townspeople, immediately rose up against them and attacked the castle. This they did by climbing on top of both the cathedral and the slaughterhouse, which are lofty buildings from which they were able to attack them with crossbows and from which they shot many bolts at those inside the castle, a building which was very strong owing to its towers, ramparts and surrounding moat and which was very difficult to capture without immense effort.

In order to bring about their surrender more quickly, they seized the wives and children of those who were inside defending the castle, and placed them on carts, all tied together, which was a ploy, in such circumstances, which the common folk customarily resorted to in those days. They went up to the castle gates and shouted out to those up above to come out and abandon the castle at once, or else they would set fire to all the wives and children and do so in their very presence and where they could see it happen. Once they had said this, they began to set fire to the gates amid the tumultuous hubbub of a huge crowd. On seeing this, the governor addressed those who were with him inside the castle. Lest they should fall victim to the uncontrolled rage of the mob, they agreed to surrender the castle to the people without further ado. The agreed arrangement was that they be allowed to leave the castle and depart from the town in safety and with their honour intact and that they would leave the castle to the people unconditionally. Subject to these terms and once they were safely held, they were turned out through the postern gate, but only after all the town's gates had been locked, lest the common people should rob them once they got outside.

The castle was strong and it is certain that it would not have been captured as swiftly as it was, were it not for the way in which the wives and children of those inside the castle had been placed on the carts. When the castle was captured, it was at once looted of everything in it and many parts of it were demolished. They set fire to it inside in such a way that, with the burning of its interior and all its contents, the castle was utterly laid waste and dilapidated, so that no part of it was defensible. The postern gate was immediately battered down, so that nobody could use it either to enter or to leave the castle.

The governor made his way to join Fernão Gonçalves de Sousa, who was in Portel and had declared for Castile; a number of the others joined Pero Rodrigues da Fonseca, who was the Governor of Olivença; yet others went to Payo Rodríguez [Mariño], the Governor of Campo Maior, for both of them had declared for the King of Castile. The castle was captured on 2 January 1384.

After this had happened, the people of Évora wrote at once to the Master to tell him what they had done. He swiftly sent letters to the main participants in the event and to Martim Gil Pestana, who was the town's lieutenant, declaring that he had seen the letter from the town council concerning the highly praiseworthy actions which they had all undertaken in the service of God, for the greater honour of the realm and in his own honour. For that very reason he was bound to reward them with many favours as the honourable and loyal servants that they were, adding that he trusted that God, Who had been the beginning of their great deeds, would also be their righteous middle and end. Accordingly, he entreated them, as true natives of the realm, to strive and so conduct themselves that no harm should befall either him or themselves.

Chapter 45

How the townspeople rose against the abbess, and how they set about killing her

Once the castle had been captured as we have described, the townspeople became passionately aroused, far beyond what good practice normally allows. They began to be driven by a wild rage, inventing all manner of new grudges against people who had done them no wrong. Unrestrained in their power, they showed contempt for those whom they had at the outset regarded as leaders, for example, men like Diogo Lopes Lobo, Fernão Gonçalves and other prominent figures in the town. Treating such men with suspicion, they declared that, if they took pleasure in serving the Master and owed him allegiance, then they should go to Lisbon to serve him and assist in the defence of the realm. Realising that there was nothing to be gained by disputing the matter, they did exactly that and went to join the Master.

The major figures in this disturbance were Gonçalo Eanes, a goatherd, and Vicente Eanes, a tailor, who carried on doing just as they pleased, calling out their rallying cry, '*Abite! Abite! Aqui dos dabite!*'[57] What is more, when some people in the mob shouted, 'Let's go and kill so-and-so, let's go and rob him!', then that is exactly what happened, without any of the leading citizens being able to help the man, even if they wanted to intervene on his behalf.

At this time the nuns and the Abbess of São Bento, a convent not far from Évora, happened to be staying in some of its houses in the town which were situated in the town's ruined wall. They had come there out of fear and dread of the war which was then openly breaking out. With the common people so aroused and with nothing else with which to occupy themselves, a sudden voice cried out (so certain accounts tell us), shouting that Gonçalo Eanes, the goatherd, one of the leaders of the mob, had spoken to the people and said, 'Let's kill that treacherous abbess: she's a relative of the queen and a former member of her household.'

Others supply a different account, which appears more reasonable and goes as follows: they say that, on hearing how they were behaving and what they were doing, the abbess uttered the following words in such a way that the mob found out: 'Just look at those drunks! Just see how drunk they are! Never mind, they're bound to come to grief if they carry on like that!'

Now, whichever way it came about, the instigation against her was not unavailing. They at once went to look for her in the houses in which she was lodging but they did not find her there, because she had gone with her nuns to attend Mass in the cathedral, as was her normal practice. On seeing that they were looking for her, one of the women who kept house for her where she was staying rushed to the cathedral to warn her about them.

Owing to her great fear of them and realising that there was no way in which she could defend herself against them, the abbess left the Mass and took refuge in the sacristy. She took hold of the Communion cup, where they say that the consecrated Body of Christ was at that moment reserved, and grasped it tightly. Those who did not find her in the house rushed to the cathedral to seek her out there, making their way in and yelling out their rallying cry of '*Abite! Abite!*' When they had all arrived they asked where she was, revealing just how keen they were to find her.

There came out to meet them Gonçalo Gonçalves the dean, Mem Peres the precentor and other clergy, seeking to deflect them from their intent. Yet they did not succeed in dissuading them from what they wanted, however much

[57] 'Abite' is an enigmatic expression for which there is no known translation. According to Fernão Lopes's own words, above, it is an 'apelido', a rallying cry to fight against an enemy.

they preached at them in the name of God and the Blessed Virgin, telling them to leave her alone for the time being and not to take her out of the church, for they, the clergy, would keep her prisoner and well guarded, in order to submit her to the law, were it the case that she had done or said anything wrong. For that matter, not even the abbess's anguished prayers and entreaties succeeded in quelling the savagery of the people's rage. Rather, without any reverence for Our Lord, Whom she held in her hands (that very Lord whose reasoning was unbeknown to us and Who at that time permitted the people to use their power without restraint), they wrested the cup from her hands and dragged her out of the sacristy.

As they were hauling her through the cathedral, and before they reached the stairway door, one of them lunged at her fiercely and tore away her mantle and her headdress, leaving her hair uncovered. As they pressed ahead, and before they reached the main door, another man lunged at her and cut away the folds of all her vestments, so that her legs were laid completely bare, as well as part of her pudenda. In this dishonourable fashion they dragged her out of the cathedral and hauled her along the Rua da Selaria[58] to the main square. There one of them struck her a blow on the head with his cleaver, from which she fell to the ground dead, whereupon the others began to slash at her, each one as he saw fit.

Then they left her [body] lying in the square and went off to eat and look for other amusements. Once night fell, those who had killed her came back and, tying a rope around her legs, they dragged her off to the Rossio, close to where the cattle are corralled. After abandoning her dishonoured body there, a number of them were moved by this sight, took it away by night and buried it secretly in the cathedral, because they did not dare to do so openly.

Chapter 46

How the city of Oporto declared allegiance to the Master and raised banners in his name, and concerning the part played by the people

You should know that, once the Master had assumed the role of ruler and defender of the realm and learned that the King of Castile was approaching with his forces and intending to invade, he dispatched letters

---

[58] Saddlers' Street.

at once to a number of towns, both large and small, as well as to certain individuals, notifying them that they well knew that these realms were on the point of being lost. He also told them that the King of Castile was on his way to seize them and subjugate the people, contrary to what had been laid down in the treaties which he had promised to uphold. This they should regard as a really grave and extraordinary fact, to the extent that it was preferable they should all venture forth and die confronting it than that they should fall into such hateful servitude. As for him, for the sake of the honour and defence of the realm and of all those whose native country it was, he had set his hand to the task of ruling and defending them, which was a cause that, with the grace of God and their noble assistance, he intended to pursue to the end. He therefore requested all men with a noble heart, as true Portuguese, to declare their allegiance to Portugal and to pay no heed to any letters to the contrary which the queen or the King of Castile might send them.

Among the places reached by his message was the city of Oporto, where his letters were not listened to in vain. Indeed, when the letters had been examined, the people all gathered together at once, with great determination and at the ready, especially the humbler folk, for a number of others among the common people hesitated and were afraid to set about such a task.

Then those who were called 'the common folk' told a certain man, one Álvaro da Veiga, to carry the flag through the city in the name of the Master of Avis, but he refused to take it, arguing that he ought not to do so. They immediately called him a traitor, saying that he was on the queen's side, readily stabbing him so many times that it was an extraordinary sight to behold. After this man was killed they did nothing else that day, but they all assembled the following day with their flag unfurled in the main square, having decided that it should be carried by Afonso Eanes Pateiro, an honourable man of the town. If he refused to carry it, they would kill him on the spot, just like the other man, but Afonso Eanes had learned of this from some of his friends. Very early in the morning, knowing that they would invite him to carry out this task, he made his way to the main square, where everybody had gathered to carry the banner through the city and, before anybody could tell him to carry it, he took hold of the flag, crying out in a loud voice which everyone could hear, 'For Portugal! Portugal! For the Master of Avis!'

Then Afonso Eanes mounted a fine great horse which was standing there ready for that very purpose and bore the flag with immense dignity through the entire city, followed by a huge crowd, clergy as well as laymen, and with everybody shouting out with one voice, 'Long live the Master of Avis, ruler and defender of our Portuguese realms!'

They made their way through the city and reached the cathedral, which for a very long time had been a place where no one was permitted to be buried. They started to ring the bells and have Masses said; they dug up the dead from where they had been buried and brought them into the church, and nobody dared to speak out against this.[59] A certain friar then preached a homily well-suited to the purpose they had in mind, concluding that they should all be of one heart and mind and that there should be no discord among them; rather, they should serve the Master faithfully and with all their will, as true Portuguese, since he was standing ready to defend the realm and to rid it of subjection to the King of Castile.

They were all very pleased with what the friar had to say in his sermon. Thenceforth there was no disagreement among them; rather, their common aim was to uphold and further the Master's intentions. Just as you have already heard, the common folk in many towns seized the castles from their governors, which places, to avoid prolonging matters, we shall not mention, declaring their allegiance and carrying banners through town, crying out, 'For Portugal! Portugal! For the Master of Avis!' Family ties and friendship were of no avail to anybody who failed to share their intent; instead, all those who sided with the queen were put to the sword.

Just imagine the rifts between parents and their offspring, between siblings, between spouses. Arguments and excuses which anybody sought to make on behalf of his or her cause just fell on deaf ears. But when someone said, 'So-and-so is one of them', nothing could preserve that person's life, nor was there any form of justice which would free such a person from their hands. This applied especially to the more honourable and high-ranking people in the towns and villages, many of whom found themselves facing death and were robbed of all that they possessed.

Some of them fled in terror to those towns which had declared for the King of Castile. Others left the kingdom, abandoning their property and all their possessions, which the Master at once gave to anyone who so requested them. The common people went in pursuit of them, and so willingly hunted and captured them that it was as though they were fighting for the Holy Faith itself.

[59] Only the aristocracy, the clergy and, from the 13th century onwards, rich burghers could be buried inside the church. Common people were buried in the space outside the church.

Chapter 47

Why the Master sent ambassadors to England, and concerning the reply which came back to him from that country

R eason dictates that, when they wish to tackle a major undertaking, a large number of people can bring it to a conclusion better than can a small number, no matter how daring the latter may be. That is why the Master, along with his council, decided that it was best to have [other] forces to help him. They agreed to send a request to the King of England, asking him to see fit to give leave for soldiers of his kingdom to come as mercenaries, paid according to their wishes, to aid the Master against his enemies.

It was decided that Lourenço Martins, one of the Master's *criados*, who later became Governor of Leiria, and Thomas Daniel, an Englishman, should travel to England as envoys. They left the city aboard two *naos* in December [1383]. Afterwards, it was agreed to send Dom Fernando Afonso de Albuquerque, who was the Master of the Order of Santiago, and Lourenço Eanes Fogaça, who had been King Fernando's chancellor of the great seal and whom the Master dubbed knight in Lisbon cathedral before he left.

You should know that this Dom Fernando Afonso de Albuquerque, who had been in the town of Palmela, came with all his supporters to join the Master in Lisbon, greeting him as his lord and becoming a vassal in his service. However, despite this, as he had been made Master of Santiago by Queen Leonor and for fear that he might side with the King of Castile and hand over to him the fortresses which he held as Master of Santiago, it was declared wiser for him to go as an ambassador, to keep him at some distance from such an opportunity. Besides, since there was greater honour for the Master of Avis to be represented by such emissaries than by men of lower rank, they all agreed that he should go.

They embarked in two vessels, the Master of Santiago in a *nao* and Lourenço Eanes aboard a barge,[60] completing their voyage a week later, on a Friday, when they landed at Plymouth, which is an English town. Having obtained horses there, they rode to London, where the king[61] was to be found at that time. They were well received by him, as by all the great lords and

---

[60] *Barca* in the original Portuguese, a smaller version of a galley with a sail and normally thirty oars; it could be used for many purposes such as cargo, scouting, patrolling, raiding and conveying important passengers.

[61] Richard II.

nobles of his court. After they had been to speak to the Duke of Lancaster, the king decided to hold his Privy Council in the city of Salisbury, when once the duke had arrived. The envoys explained their mission, the conclusion of which can be summed up as follows: once their country, by the king's intervention, had been duly liberated from its enemies, then any help which the Portuguese could provide, both in galleys and in the physical presence of their soldiers, they were very ready to place at his disposal, wherever he might choose to employ them in his service. Furthermore, if the Duke of Lancaster were inclined to come in person to claim the kingdom of Castile, which rightfully belonged to him by reason of his wife, then the time was ripe, and all Portugal was ready to help in this. The Master of Santiago and Lourenço Eanes had plenipotentiary authority from the Master of Avis and the cities of Lisbon and Oporto to sign this agreement and any others.

Once the king had agreed to this, along with all the members of his Privy Council, he was pleased to announce that any men-at-arms who wished to go as mercenaries to help Portugal were free to do so. Indeed, the king swore a promise that he would do no less to provide all the help he could in this enterprise than he would do in defending his own kingdom.

While the Duke of Lancaster was away in Calais, negotiating a truce with the King of France, and was expected back early so that the king could entrust him with choosing the best way to proceed with this undertaking, the Master of Santiago and Lourenço Eanes were consequently busy in the meantime dispatching men-at-arms and archers, owing to the urgent need of them in Portugal. Nevertheless, there were very few of them, among whom the leaders were Elias Blyth, Cressyngham and Guilhem de Montferrand, a Gascon knight. Once they were ready to depart in two *naos*, the Master of Santiago sent Lourenço Martins to the aforesaid town of Plymouth to assemble and dispatch them by ship from there. On arrival he too embarked with them and sailed back to Portugal, as we shall indicate in due course,[62] though the Master of Santiago and Lourenço Eanes Fogaça were very angry that he came back in this way.

The English were so pleased to provide this aid which the Portuguese had sent ambassadors to request from them that there were many who lent them money in order to pay the wages of the troops, whom they were poised to send out at once. Among those who lent money were Sir Nicholas, who was the Mayor of London, and Henry Bivembra, a knight, who loaned them 3,500 nobles, plus others who lent greater or lesser amounts as best they could. With these monies and from merchandise which they requisitioned from its

---

[62] In fact, the return of Lourenço Martins from Plymouth is not recorded elsewhere in this chronicle.

Portuguese owners whom they found there, against a written warranty that they would be repaid later, the soldiers were kept happy and only too willing to travel out.

You can see from the following letter the reply which the King of England sent to the Master of Avis concerning the aid which at that time was being requested of him:

> Richard, by the grace of God King of England and Lord of Ireland, to the great and most noble lord João, by that same grace Master of the Order of Chivalry of Avis, ruler and defender of the kingdoms of Portugal and the Algarve, our highly valued friend, wishes of health and firm friendship.
>
> Very recently we were pleased to welcome the noble and excellent knights Fernando, Master of the Order of Santiago, and Lourenço Fogaça, Chancellor of the Great Seal of Portugal, your ambassadors, whom you had sent to us. We understand clearly all that they have told us on your behalf. Certainly, most valued friend, we thank you wholeheartedly for the goodwill which you show for us and which the gentlemen of your land express on your behalf, as we can see both in your deeds and from what we know about you.
>
> With regard to what they have declared to us concerning your offers, both of galleys and of other aid from your kingdoms that might prove advantageous to us, we heartily thank you. An agreement has been reached between your ambassadors and the members of our Privy Council, about which the aforesaid Lourenço will supply you with fuller details. As for the aid which would be advantageous to you and to your allies in your kingdoms, we have authorised your aforesaid emissaries to recruit from our land, under promise of payment, as many men-at-arms and archers as they wished. Indeed, that authorisation, in view of the rebellious wars in which we are currently involved, is a concession which we would not grant quite so readily to anyone else.
>
> We are keen that you and your allies should participate in a treaty which we are at present negotiating in Calais with our adversaries from France and Castile. We would have liked your ambassadors to give their consent to this, but they excused themselves, saying that they had no such mandate from you. As they brought no mandate, our own envoys in Calais have urged us to write to you, and the French have likewise and on their own behalf written to the occupier of Castile, indicating that the truce (which we made with the aforesaid adversaries and which was to last until the first day of next May) should be kept by both sides. If our common adversary refuses to consent to this, we reserve to you full freedom to be protected and defended by our troops.
>
> We believe it to be appropriate to write to Your Grace to enable you to arrange that this request be put to your adversary as soon as you possibly can. Our intention would be that, having noted his answer and after giving

careful consideration to the matter, we would be in a position to devote our attention to our common defence.

In the meantime, stand firm, trusting in God, in the sure belief that the King of Kings, Who is just and never abandons those who fight for justice, will not forsake your endeavours but, rather, will cause you to become a glorious conqueror and win a great and honourable victory. Noble and excellent sir, may the Lord God guide you in all your enterprises, and may you live a long and happy life. So written.

Chapter 48

How the city of Lisbon made a contribution to the Master in helping him to raise money

You have already noted from the reign of King Pedro how much the Kings of Portugal did in order to amass treasure and have wealth available, in order to have ample sums to disburse, whensoever they needed to defend their realms, or otherwise go to war, if they deemed it necessary.[63] You also noted how hard they strove to ensure that the said treasure should never be so depleted that it became necessary to impose taxes on the people. Yet King Fernando strove just as hard to waste his treasure on unnecessary and bootless wars!

He not only spent all the treasure which had been handed down to him by earlier monarchs but he also imposed new taxes on property sales and changed the coinage much to the harm and detriment of all his people. The consequence was that, when the Master took on the task of ruler and defender of the realms, he had no financial resources with which to wage war, nor even to grant favours to those who came forward to help him to mount any kind of defence. When, therefore, everyone realised that, in order to be free from subjection, it was incumbent on them to tackle this huge deficit, they decided to help and serve the Master by providing him with sums of money, and by the city [of Lisbon] promising him a contribution of 100,000 *libras*, which included 1,000 *dobras* paid by the Moors and Jews who resided there. These sums were paid to him in small coins and in 'white' money, as well as in silver. 'White' money was the name given at that time to *graves*, *barbudas* and *pilartes*.[64] These coins were collected by certain people in the parishes. The order went out that any person taking money out of the city would lose

---

[63] See *CKP*, Chapters 11 and 12.
[64] See *CKF*, Chapter 55.

it all, and that anyone seizing it from that person would receive one-fifth of it. It was seized from several people who were taking it out clandestinely, and the proceeds were given to the Master.

Apart from this, the Master requested several people from the city and from its district to lend him sums of money, as he believed that they were in a position to do so. They all willingly offered him anything with which they could help him. The Jewish quarter lent him 60 silver marks, apart from what they paid as a contribution. The clergy also, in crosses, chalices and other ornate objects, lent him any silver which they could manage without, so that the cathedral, along with twenty other churches in the city, provided him with 287 marks, of which the cathedral gave 87, and each of the other churches gave according to what it had freely available.

The Master ordained that the Treasurer of his Monies should be a merchant named Persifal. To him were handed over all the sums of money and silver which we have mentioned, as well as 900 silver marks which the Master had in his chamber, along with many other coins and 'white' money, not to mention other coins from Castile, all of which were handed to him by Afonso Martins, the Master's private secretary.

Chapter 49

How the Master decided to mint money, what was the alloy used and what was the design from which it was minted

When once the Master had set about minting money, he immediately decided to mint silver *reais*. But first you should be made aware that, at the time, when the Master declared himself ruler and defender of the realm, its currency was what we have already mentioned, namely: *dinheiros* from the reign of King Afonso IV, nine of which were worth one *soldo*, with 20 *soldos* being worth one *libra*; *barbudas*, which were valued at two *soldos* and four *dinheiros*; *graves*, each of which was worth 14 *dinheiros*; and *pilartes*, which were worth seven *dinheiros*, as was duly written down when we spoke of the debasement of the currency brought about by King Fernando.[65] The currency also included *reais* of standard silver worth 10 *dinheiros* each, 56

---

[65] See *CKF*, Chapter 55. Interestingly, despite Fernão Lopes's implicit criticism of King Fernando's practice of funding warfare through currency debasement (however unusual it might have been to earlier Portuguese custom), it was not actually reversed

of which constituted one mark. We shall now explain why such names were given to these coins.

When King Fernando went to war against King Enrique, as you have heard, there accompanied him in the invasion of Castile a large French force known as the White Company. They were armed in the following fashion: they wore bascinets with visor, arming cap and camail, and these [items together] were known as a *barbuda*. The coin of that name was stamped on one side with a saltire, in the middle of which was a shield displaying the five *quinas*,[66] while on the other side there was a *barbuda* with its visor. These men-at-arms carried *graves* with small banners on their tips: these weapons are nowadays called 'lances'. The youths who wore their *barbudas* over their pourpoints were known as *pilartes* and later they came to be known as '*grave* bearers'. Nowadays we call the *barbudas* 'bascinets with camail' and the youths, 'pages'.

From the names given to that armour and those weapons the names of the coins were derived. The *grave* was stamped with a lance bearing a small banner on its tip, while on the other side was a saltire and the *quinas*. With these coins circulating together, the crossed *dobra* was worth 5 *libras*, the Moorish *dobra* 4½, and the gold franc from France 4. The mark made from standard silver was valued at 11 *dinheiros*, or 22 *libras*.

The Master decided to mint a new coinage consisting of silver *reais*, which were standardised at a value of 9 *dinheiros*, with 72 of them to the mark. Then he changed the standard so that other *reais* of the same weight were worth 6 *dinheiros*. Next he had others minted of 5 *dinheiros*. By the minting which he ordered to be carried out under the law of fiscal enablement, he earned enough to cover his expenses. Some people write in their accounts that these first *reais* which the Master ordered to be minted were very useful for treating some ailments, with the result that many people set them in silver and wore them [on a chain] round their necks.

When once the Master began to reign as king, he ordered the minting of standard *reais* of 1 *dinheiro*, each one of which was worth 10 *soldos*. Later, he ordered the minting of other *reais* of 3½ *libras*, standardised at 3 *dinheiros*. When he decided to capture Ceuta, as you will hear in due course,[67] he ordered

---

by King João I, former Master of Avís. Rather, though Fernão Lopes never says as much explicitly, it was practised by him with considerable variation and subtlety.

[66] The five shields which are displayed on the arms of Portugal.

[67] In fact, the account of King João's reign written by Fernão Lopes goes up to around 1411. It does not, therefore, cover the seizing of Ceuta in 1415. The *Crónica da Tomada de Ceuta* (Chronicle of the Conquest of Ceuta) was written by Gomes Eanes de Zurara, who succeeded Fernão Lopes as royal chronicler.

the minting of coins known as 'white' *reais*, each of which was worth 3½ *libras* and was standardised at 3 *dinheiros*, and of which there were 72 in a mark.

For as long as these coins lasted, so many changes were made in both their alloy and design that it would be tedious to describe them. The outcome was that a crown came to be worth 150 'white' *reais* of 35 *libras* each, then 1,500 of 3½ *libras* each, that is to say 5,250 *libras* all told. Consequently, what in King Fernando's time was found to be 1,173 *dobras* was later found to be worth no more than 1 *dobra*. He was obliged to make these changes by the demands of the wars which he so frequently waged against the King of Castile. These wars caused him huge expenditure which he was unable to avoid, and on that account it is appropriate to take note at this point of a very profitable saying, which every king and prince ought to bear in mind whenever confronted by such demands, and for which there is no other remedy possible: 'It is better for a land to suffer than for land to be lost.'

By such changes and the minting of coins and with the help of Almighty God the Master defended the kingdom of Portugal and achieved peace with its enemies, though his people felt the harmful effect of certain shortages.

Chapter 50

How the Master licensed certain people to mint coins and provided upkeep for many people

L eaving aside the reasons amply advanced by certain writers who argue how advantageous it is to the realm for all who are able to do so to mint coins, let us simply record how the Master went about it and make no further comment.

For that reason it is important for you to know that at the time when the Master had his coinage minted, because he believed it was to his advantage and profit, he licensed Lisbon's city council to mint a quantity of silver to assist them in their expenses. This was not just for the soldiers whom the city had to pay, but also for a growing number of items necessary at that time for its defence.

Similarly, he licensed Doctor João das Regras and others, without taking any profit from what they minted, but all the coins they produced were handed over to him. Having minted this coinage, the Master at once provided upkeep for the nobles and officials belonging to his household.

In this way 100 *libras* were paid to both Doctor João das Regras and Doctor Martim Afonso, along with others as appropriate. 100 *libras* were also paid to Dom Afonso, who was the son of Count Álvaro Pérez [de Castro], and to Dona Leonor Teles, who was the wife of Dom Pedro de Castro,[68] and to Dona Beatriz his sister. As for the rest, there is no need to provide any specific account.

But what shall we say about the noble qualities of this virtuous lord? Despite the fact that his mind was at this time divided between so many separate worries, which this undertaking so obviously required, he did not neglect spiritual matters. Sparing no expense, he immediately ordered a highly honourable memorial ceremony for the soul of his brother King Fernando, giving the responsibility for it to Antão Rodrigues, who was the Prior of São Nicolau.

He also provided upkeep for certain devout persons, urging them to pray to God on behalf of himself and the realm. Accordingly, Friar João da Barroca, as well as anchoresses Margarida Eanes and Maria Esteves, received 4 *soldos* a day. He also enacted a most remarkable deed which earned great praise from everybody, as they all deemed it to be a case of outstanding magnanimity: this was because some men had already been taken captive by the Castilians, as the war was already being vigorously waged, yet they could not afford to pay their ransom. The Master arranged for them to be freed from captivity, paying on their behalf all that they had to give for that purpose, while for others he paid out large sums to help bring about their immediate release from the hands of their enemies.

In this and similar actions, he began to be greatly loved by his people, who recognised his great generosity and the good-natured grace with which he dispensed such gifts. They also recognised the depth of his faith, how well-informed he was and his immense wisdom in taking on the governance and rule of his country, so much so that they all considered themselves to be truly fortunate to have him as their lord.

Chapter 51

How the townspeople of Almada declared for the Master, and how he went to attack Alenquer

As old habits teach us, and as acquaintance with them convinces us even more, nowhere does envy have a cosier place in which to dwell than in the courts of kings and great lords. As the Master often took counsel with

---

[68]   Queen Leonor's niece, the daughter of her brother João Afonso Telo. Pedro and Beatriz were also the children of Count Álvaro.

his followers as to how to proceed with his great enterprise, he sometimes talked to Nuno Álvares, but separately, telling him things about which the others had no knowledge. Thus it came about that this common evil, namely envy, took a powerful hold on the hearts of members of the Master's council, men like Rui Pereira, Álvaro Vasques, Doctor João das Regras and all his other close advisers, when they realised that the Master was holding special conversations with Nuno Álvares and actually following his advice. Their resentment was so deep that they all secretly agreed that they would always oppose any advice that Nuno Álvares gave to the Master, however noble and well-reasoned it might be, and that they would never abide by it – and, indeed, that is what they did.

Nuno Álvares found out about this secret compact and said nothing about it to any of them. One day, when the Master was speaking in his council about a matter of considerable importance, Nuno Álvares answered with his own opinion, a reply that pleased the Master, so that he took a decision in accordance with what he said. As the Master was so receptive to the arguments of Nuno Álvares, the other members of his council were far from pleased with this and argued vigorously against it, deploying all manner of reasons as to why it was bad advice.

On realising this, Nuno Álvares began to laugh, as he knew only too well why they were reacting in this way. When the Master noticed this and asked him why he was laughing, he explained to him the situation and why it was that they disagreed with what he had to say. The Master was greatly taken aback at their envy and addressed them in such a way that they abandoned their approach, and from then on everyone always reached a common consensus.

Among the matters which were discussed in that council meeting was how essential it was that the township of Almada should declare in favour of the Master, as it occupied a key position on the river [Tagus] in the event of the King of Castile wishing to dispatch a fleet against the city of Lisbon. Indeed, as the town did not possess a castle and a governor charged by his very allegiance with its defence, it would be easy for him to take the town. The Master regarded this as good advice and made his way to Almada, where the townsfolk welcomed him and declared themselves to be his supporters, ready to serve him. It was the first day of January, 1384.

On returning to Lisbon from Almada, he at once decided to lay siege to Alenquer, a township with its own castle, which lies at a distance of 8 leagues from the city [of Lisbon], where the queen had lodged after the death of Count Juan Fernández before leaving for Santarém, as you have already heard.[69] The governor of this town was Vasco Peres de Camões, who held

---

[69] In Chapters 16 and 29 above.

it on behalf of Queen Leonor. Having gathered together up to 200 lances, though not many crossbowmen and foot soldiers, the Master went and spent that night at Castanheira, which is a league away from Alenquer, and very early next morning he arrived near the town. He lodged in the Monastery of São Francisco, while Nuno Álvares was lodged at the house of Vasco Martins de Alteiro, who was married to his sister.

Early that afternoon, the Master's soldiers skirmished with those from Alenquer at a spot known as the Gate of Soure. The Master arrived and ordered a retreat, because his men were receiving injuries from the crossbows firing from the ramparts. However many times they attempted skirmishes, it availed them nothing, both because the town was very strong, and as they had no siege engines with which to attack.

This, however, is the point at which to break off this part of the narrative and leave the Master in Alenquer, and the queen in Santarém; rather, let us go and see what the King of Castile did in his own country, when he received news that King Fernando had died.

Chapter 52

How the King of Castile ordered the arrest of his brother Count Alfonso

It came to pass that while the King of Castile was in Puebla de Montalbán, which was where he stayed after we left off narrating his activities,[70] he received the news that King Fernando was dead. As soon as he heard this, the very next day he immediately summoned to his chamber his brother Don Alfonso, who was the Count of Gijón. He told him that he had received news that his father[-in-law] King Fernando had passed away. For that reason, in order to be safe from Don Alfonso, since he was married to King Fernando's daughter [Isabel], and since he feared that he would rush into Portugal and stir up strong feelings in that kingdom, he had decided to arrest him.

The count was astounded to hear this and entreated him to continue keeping the promise which he had made to him when they had received the Body of

---

[70] To be exact, when Fernão Lopes last spoke of the King of Castile, he left him in Torrijos (*CKF*, Chapter 171); and according to Pero López de Ayala (*Crónica del Rey Don Juan*, 1383, Year 5, Chapter 7), it was there that he heard about King Fernando's death. But immediately afterwards he went to Puebla de Montalbán, where he arrested his brother.

Christ together. The king answered that he was not interested in his arguments, because he was quite certain that, after the count had left Gijón and had come in answer to his summons, he had committed a grave error in sending letters to Portugal in disservice to him, the king.

The count swore that he had never done any such thing and [again] entreated him to keep his promise, but the king, who paid no heed to what he said, handed him over as a prisoner to Don Pedro Tenorio, the Archbishop of Toledo, who brought him out of the palace, where some fifty horsemen awaited him. He entrusted him to one of the most honourable members of his own entourage and, then, he made his way to where the count was staying and arrested the countess his wife, sending her straightaway to Toledo, which lay 5 leagues away. The count was also taken there and, as he remained a prisoner there for a long time, the king gave the territory of Noreña to the Church in Oviedo and confiscated to the Crown all other property which the count possessed in Asturias.

Chapter 53

How the King of Castile ordered the arrest of Prince João of Portugal

You have already heard us talk[71] about how Prince João had gone over to Castile and how he had been brought to join the king's court owing to his sister Princess Beatriz, who was the wife of Count Sancho. Thus it was that the king gave him Alba de Tormes, Manzanares el Real and other townships. Yet he did not enjoy quite the well-to-do standard of living that befitted his status, for his daily entourage never exceeded ten to twelve retainers who were always with him. Other noblemen, however, who had a strong liking for the prince because of who he was, greatly honoured him, showed him hospitality and kept him company both in his own house and on the way to the palace. Such men included Don Juan, who was the son of Don Tello, King Enrique's brother, who possessed ten times as many houses as the prince, the Marquess of Villena and Pedro Fernández de Velasco, who never failed going anywhere with a team of 150 mules. He also enjoyed the company of Juan Duque and his brother Ruy Duque, as well as of other worthy noblemen of the king's household.

---

[71] In *CKF*, Chapter 106.

When the King of Castile married Princess Beatriz, knowing that King Fernando was very frequently ill, they immediately began to fear that the prince would reign after King Fernando's death; they also began to be unsure of him and to arrange ways of preventing him from doing anything on his own account that the king did not know about.

Some of his supporters understood this situation and repeatedly drew it to the prince's attention, but, as a man who could never harbour malicious thoughts, he attached no importance to what they had to say. No sooner had the king ordered the arrest of his brother Count Alfonso than he also ordered García González de Grijalba to arrest Prince João in the prince's apartments. He ordered that the prince be told that he was not arresting him for anything which he knew to be against his, the king's, service, but that he was afraid, now that King Fernando had passed away, that certain Portuguese would acclaim him king and would cause a disturbance in the country contrary to what was laid down in the treaties. Moreover, he should be held prisoner at the king's pleasure until such time as the latter was reassured about this.

Other writers assert that the prince's captivity came about differently. They claim that, as soon as King Fernando passed away, certain people in Portugal immediately and hastily wrote to him to tell him that his brother the king was dead, urging him to consider what it was that honour demanded of him in this situation; on receiving this news, he went to the king and showed him the letters. They say that the king greatly thanked him and then ordered his arrest. At all events, whichever way it happened, the king commanded that a strong guard be placed on the prince and that he be held at the king's pleasure; he also prohibited any of his followers from setting foot in the city to which he had ordered the prince to be taken.

Chapter 54

How King Juan arranged exequies for King Fernando in Toledo and how he went about it

Once Count Alfonso and Prince João had been made captive, as you have heard, the king decided to arrange a memorial ceremony for King Fernando in the city of Toledo. He commanded that everything there should be duly and properly prepared and waited in Puebla de Montalbán until this had been done. When they brought him the message that everything was ready, the king made his way there, as did the queen also. The king wore a black tunic, and the queen, dressed in black woollen sackcloth, made her way in a litter, which was covered in black drapes, so that no one could see her.

The Portuguese who accompanied her were dressed in white woollen sackcloth, and the women likewise. When they arrived, it was already time for vespers.[72] They left their horses at a church which is very close to town, and all the noblewomen of the city went to join and accompany the queen. They took the queen to the cathedral, where there was already a raised platform bearing a coffin, everything most appropriately arranged.[73]

When they entered the cathedral door, all the Portuguese gave vent to their grief, including the queen and the women from Portugal. After vespers were over, it was already late, and so they retired to their respective palaces in the city. In the queen's palace, both her sitting-room and bedroom were hung with dyed black cloth. Next morning the king and queen set out for the cathedral, where a high platform had been prepared for them. When they passed through the doorway, the mourning began again as at vespers. Then the king and queen withdrew, and the king removed his black garments and put on a long mantle of cloth of gold lined with ermine and worn open on the right side. At that time such robes were known as Lombard mantles.

The queen was likewise dressed in the same rich cloth, and their baldachin and seating area were draped right down to the ground in the selfsame cloth of gold. Once the king and queen had duly taken their seats on the platform, they were approached by a procession led by the Archbishop of Toledo, dressed in a rich cope and with his mitre on his head, along with all the canons and clergy of the city, who were reciting their prayers. A banner bearing the arms of Castile, and the signs of Portugal sewn on below, was carried in procession and then placed between the king and the queen.

The king then sent for Vasco Martins de Melo, who had journeyed from Portugal with the queen, and he came at once into the king's presence. The king declared that the most honourable title in his kingdom was the position of lord lieutenant and that, in order to reward him for coming from Portugal with Queen Beatriz his wife and also to acknowledge him for being the honourable man that he was, he was making him his lord lieutenant in both Castile and Portugal. He urged him to take hold of the banner and to raise it up high on his, the king's, behalf, as was the custom whenever a new king is acclaimed. Vasco Martins replied that this was a very great favour to bestow on him, but that he could not assume such a duty, because he was a vassal of King Fernando and was his chief of the royal guard, and because there was

---

[72] That is 6 pm.
[73] The coffin was, of course, empty.

a possibility that a war might break out against the country of which he was a native and he would then be accused of treason.

Chapter 55

Concerning what happened when the banner was raised on behalf of the King of Castile

When the king realised that Vasco Martins was unwilling to take on the duty of being his lord lieutenant, he sent for Juan Hurtado de Mendoza, gave him that office and handed him the banner. Juan Hurtado received it from him as a very great favour and immediately raised it on high. The trumpets began to blare as they all shouted out, 'Long live the king! Long live the king! Long live King Juan of Castile and Portugal!' With that, they carried the banner out of the cathedral.

Ready at the door was one of the king's horses, saddled up to carry the banner throughout the city. There too, on horseback, were Juan Núñez de Toledo and others, all holding white spear-poles with pennants, waiting to accompany the banner. The lord lieutenant mounted up, and they inserted the banner into the sling on his saddle. Juan Núñez then cried out in a loud voice, urging everyone to declare, 'Long live the king! Long live the king! Long live King Juan of Castile and Portugal!' Then they all began to charge along after the banner as it headed on its way.

While they were joyously rushing along, the wind tore apart the stitches which held the Portuguese signs sewn on beneath, leaving them dangling down. In addition, the horse carrying the lord lieutenant stumbled against an outer quoin of the cathedral and broke one of its rider's shoulders, bringing him down with it as it fell. Some of those who saw this happen took it to be a very bad omen and said among themselves that the King of Castile would never become King of Portugal.

Some said to the king that it was not right for the Portuguese signs to be in an inferior position like that, so that he issued immediate orders that both sets of signs be displayed equally on his escutcheon. As for those Portuguese who were mourning the death of King Fernando, when they saw what had happened, both when the banner became unstitched and when the horse that was carrying the lord lieutenant fell, they were very pleased and said to one another that God would never make King Juan the King of Portugal.

At this point, the king and queen stepped down from where they had been seated and dressed themselves in the mourning garb which they had been wearing earlier. The archbishop also put on the appropriate vestments again and said Mass on behalf of King Fernando. Once the mourning was over and the exequies completed, they went off to eat and then left at once for Puebla de Montalbán, where they had been lodging, remaining there for up to ten days.

Chapter 56

How King Juan held a Royal Council to consider whether it was right to invade Portugal, and how he decided to do so

While the king was in Puebla de Montalbán, he summoned a Royal Council to consider whether it was right to invade Portugal at once with all his might, in order to make himself master of that kingdom, or what his approach should be. That is because, once he learned that King Fernando had passed away, he immediately summoned companies and men-at-arms with which to invade Portugal. On this issue he held a major council meeting which lasted for days, because there were two opposing viewpoints.

Most members of the council, those who tendered the best and most sensible advice, spoke as follows: 'Sire, Your Grace must not and cannot rightfully invade Portugal in this way with your armies, for that is laid down in the treaties which were signed between you and King Fernando. Rather, it is most important and in your interests, in accordance with the way in which they were sworn, that you should keep and fulfil them in every respect and adopt such an approach to the people of Portugal as not to invade their country by force of arms. By so doing, you will be true to your promises and to those which we made along with you; otherwise, by invading Portugal with all your might, you will be unable to avoid harming that country, at the very least as regards its food supply, and thus there would grow up immense hatred between Portuguese and Castilians, which would not be in your interests.

'By contrast, were Your Grace to invade with a small force, that could prove to be very perilous for you. For that reason it does seem appropriate that you should make your way to Salamanca, which is close to Portugal, and for the present you should not send for any troops. From there you should send your envoys into Portugal, notifying that country's grandees and men of power that you have learned of King Fernando's passing and [reminding them] that, as they well know, his daughter Queen Beatriz, your wife, has inherited the kingdom, as is laid down in the treaties and agreements which were drawn up and sworn on oath. Accordingly, it is your wish to keep and fulfil everything contained in those treaties, in line with what Your Grace has sworn and signed. Moreover, if they consider that there is anything to add to or remove from those treaties which may be to the greater benefit or honour of their kingdom, you are ready to put that into effect, provided that Your Grace's honour and interests are protected. You should urge them to send their envoys to Salamanca, so that you may learn of their response and come to an agreement with them about everything which you feel to be to your advantage.

'Furthermore, it seems to us to be appropriate that, when their envoys come to see Your Grace, you should honour them profusely, sharing with them your riches and jewellery, and that you should tell them that it is your wish and would be your great pleasure to adopt such measures in their regard as would be both to your advantage and of benefit to their country, and would bring great honour to its citizens.

'Likewise, Your Grace can remind them that they should be well aware that in the treaties sworn and signed between you and King Fernando it is laid down that the governance of the realm should pass to Queen Leonor, your mother-in-law, until such time that you have a son who reaches the age of fourteen, and that that son should be reared in Portugal from three months after the day of his birth and under the supervision of his grandmother. Tell them that you are pleased to keep and uphold that condition, and that, if they consider that there exists some better means of ruling Portugal, by some ruler or rulers drawn from their kingdom, in some way which they may deem to be more beneficial, and which preserves your honour and best interests, then you would be pleased with that measure and would wish to adopt it. Let the messengers whom you send to Portugal announce that to the noblemen and great lords to whom they speak. They will be pleased at such an approach from Your Grace, their hearts will be at peace and thus they will be ready to serve you.'

Other members of the Royal Council, who were not counsellors in the true sense of the term, realised that the king was very keen to invade Portugal and, having neither regard for the treaties nor for the oaths which both he and his followers had sworn to keep, and no regard either for the penalties which they would incur, were they to go against all or some of the treaties, instead, simply in order to be obsequious to the king, praised all his arguments, declaring that it would be perfectly appropriate for him to invade Portugal with all his might, without any regard for agreements. Indeed, they declared to him that he was not bound to honour such treaties, because they were reached contrary to his honour and even contrary to the law, and that therefore the treaties should not be kept.

Rather, it was to be preferred that, before the Portuguese had any warning about this, he should invade the country with his forces, in order to regain the rights which he had there and that, if there existed any other agreement to be considered in this regard, then it would be to his greater advantage to establish his position within Portugal than to linger in Castile. The king, who was extremely keen to conquer the country, by hook or by crook, went along with this reasoning and praised what they had to say.

Those who had spoken earlier demolished these arguments, deemed them to be reckless and lacking in sound reasoning, and addressed the king as follows: 'Sire, the greater the standing of Your Grace, all the more must you avoid censure in any way. Just as delay in tackling just causes is undesirable, by the same token unseemly haste in undue undertakings is considered to be a bad way to behave.

'We cannot believe that any invasion of this sort can bring about such benefits as will not be all the more harmful. At the least you will find yourself doubly lacking, both in being untrue to what you have promised and in betraying the oaths which you swore in that respect. How can it be said on your behalf that you were led astray in the treaties and that they ran counter to your honour and benefit, as these men say, when so many law authorities, and wise and sensible members of your council were summoned, before you decided to give them your consent?

'In addition, sire, in the oath which you took at Badajoz, approving everything drawn up by your proctor, in respect both of your marriage and of the succession in that kingdom after the death of King Fernando, Your Grace testified and guaranteed that these matters had previously been seen and examined by you and that you had been advised about each and every clause maturely and at length. That is what is written and laid down in the treaties. In such circumstances how can it now be claimed that these treaties were drawn up to your disadvantage? These men make that claim in order to follow your whim but not to produce any reasons about what by right you are in a position to do. Rather, Your Grace is breaking his own word, and we are perjurers and guilty of falsehood.'

Anxious as he was to invade Portugal and in the belief that with his vast army he would be obeyed and that he would seize the realm, the king entertained no doubts about doing so and attached no importance to any advice to the contrary.

Chapter 57

How the Bishop of Guarda told King Juan that he would hand the city over to him, and how the king made a final decision to invade the country

While the king was nursing his great urge to invade Portugal, though he still hesitated a little because of the large number of advisers who opposed him on this, there was present at the time a certain Bishop of Guarda, the chancellor of Queen Beatriz, who had journeyed with her from Portugal for her marriage, as you have heard.[74] The bishop informed the King of Castile that the town of Guarda, of which he was the bishop, was very strong, stood on the Portuguese frontier and that all the other people who lived there were his own *criados* and would do as he told them, so that if he were to be favoured by the king's advance on the town, he would be there to give him an immediate welcome.

The king was very pleased at what the bishop told him, which greatly increased his desire to invade Portugal by any means. He at once left Puebla de Montalbán, where he had been staying, and sent for companies and men-at-arms to hasten to join him from wherever they happened to be.

The king and queen arrived at the bridge of Alcolea, which the archbishop[75] was at that time building across the Tagus. The archbishop gave orders that they and their party should be given all that they needed. They remained there for two days and then left for Talavera, from where they went on to Plasencia. There the king informed his Royal Council that the Bishop of Guarda had told him that he would hand Guarda over to him and asked the counsellors what their opinion was in that respect.

Some of them repeated that it was his sovereign duty to uphold the treaties which he and the Portuguese had signed and mentioned again the oaths taken and the penalty clauses to which he and his proctors would be subject if they broke them; for that reason they should in no way set them aside. They added that, if he were to enter the town in that manner, the Portuguese would be afraid of him and would say that he wanted to take over the land against their will and to their great sorrow; also, that the governance of the kingdom, in accordance with the treaties, belonged to Queen Leonor his mother-in-law, and that he had no right at all to do so. Those who gave him this advice went

---

[74] In *CKF*, Chapter 160.

[75] Don Pedro Tenorio, Archbishop of Toledo. The bridge is close to Talavera and is still known as El Puente del Arzobispo, 'The Archbishop's Bridge'.

on to say, in order to dissuade him, that they knew that in the town of Guarda there stood a very fine castle, held by Álvaro Gil de Cabral, who was not of the bishop's party, and that it was inadvisable to enter the town without at once seizing the castle. On those grounds they urged him not to rush matters until things offered him a better and more advantageous opportunity.

Other counsellors, whose sole interest was to tell the king what he wanted to hear, declared that it was preferable for the king to leave at once and seize the town, which was the main one in the province of Beira. This was a vast area where there were very wealthy and honourable knights and squires who would at once join with him, because they would much rather be under his governance and subject to his power than be ruled by his mother-in-law Queen Leonor. Keen to seize the kingdom by any means and setting aside all the oaths and promises of which you have heard, the king declared that this was excellent advice and commanded the bishop to journey ahead of him, so as to have everything in readiness to ensure his welcome into the town.

Chapter 58

How the King of Castile invaded Portugal, and concerning a number of noblemen who went over to his side

The Bishop of Guarda set off and made his way to that town. The king left Plasencia and reached Perosín, which is close to Fuenteguinaldo. There he received a message from the bishop, informing him that he held the town in readiness for him and that he should make haste to arrive there early next morning, because the townspeople and those who lived in the surrounding area were already aware that he was approaching. Were he not to arrive by that time, it would then be doubtful whether he could have the town, because they would all be prepared for him, and he, the king, would then find it difficult to cope with their opposition.

On receiving this message, the king left Perosín that afternoon and journeyed through the night, along with the queen, arriving at Guarda early next morning. He was accompanied only by some thirty men-at-arms, who were among the officers who accompanied him daily. With his clergy in procession, the bishop went out to receive him as honourably as possible, and thus the king and queen and their retinue entered the town, with the king taking up lodging in the bishop's palace.

Álvaro Gil did not go out to meet him but remained quietly in his castle, without revealing which side he was on. There did arrive, however, Vasco Martins de Melo, who had accompanied the queen [from Portugal] and who was lodging in Fuenteguinaldo; on leaving Perosín, the king had sent him the order to follow him to Guarda, but his brother Martim Afonso, who was a great lord and held Celorico and Linhares, was the first to come and join the King of Castile, becoming his liegeman in Guarda. It greatly displeased his brother Vasco Martins that he had set out to become the king's vassal ahead of anybody else.

The next day the king was joined by a number of men-at-arms for whom he had sent, namely some 200 lances.[76] After three days there arrived the Count of Mayorga, as well as Pedro Fernández de Velasco, Pedro [Ruiz] Sarmiento and other captains with some 500 lances. Noticing that Álvaro Gil had not come to speak to him nor even emerged from the castle, the king told Martim Afonso de Melo to make him come and talk to him.

Martim Afonso did so and brought him under safe conduct; he spoke to the king, then went back to his castle and did not speak to him again afterwards. The next day Vasco Martins [de Melo] sent a message to Álvaro Gil through his son Martim Afonso, telling him that he had acted very nobly in not joining the King of Castile, nor should he surrender to him, for he assured him that the king would not lay siege to him: he was simply passing that way and would be continuing his journey. He added that, were it so to happen that the king should seek to besiege his castle, he, Vasco Martins, promised that along with his sons and his men, he would join Álvaro Gil and his men and would help him to defend the castle.

The king was angry that Álvaro Gil did not speak to him further and had not joined him. He was, however, joined by several knights and squires from that area while he was in Guarda, namely Martim Afonso de Melo, who was the first; Vasco Martins da Cunha, his son Martim Vasques and other sons of his; Fernando Afonso de Melo, Álvaro Gil de Carvalho and others. The king received them very well and told them to pay him all due homage through the fortresses which they held. They paid him this homage by welcoming and recognising his wife, Queen Beatriz, as their queen and liege lady and him as her husband. Nevertheless, they did this on the understanding that the treaties, as drawn up between himself and King Fernando, would be honoured. The king was greatly perturbed that they were imposing such a condition on their

---

[76] Lance, in this context, refers to the Castilian military unit of a knight with two horses and perhaps one squire or page. The number of troops joining the King of Castile may, therefore, have been much higher than the 200 mentioned in the text by Fernão Lopes.

fealty, yet he accepted it, because he could do nothing more about it for the time being.

For all that these knights and squires came to join the king, nevertheless certain authors write that they were not happy with the king's welcome nor with the way in which, in their view, he received them; and, just as quickly as they had come to join him, they soon began to plan among themselves to leave at once. It is claimed that there were two reasons for this. The first was that the king was a man of few words and of a far from cheerful disposition, whereas they were accustomed to King Fernando who customarily gave people a warm and lavish welcome. The other reason was that the king did not distribute money to them immediately: indeed, he was not in a position to do so, having invaded the kingdom in a hurry in order to gain possession of it, without bothering to wait for money first.

Chapter 59

Concerning the reasons which Beatriz Gonçalves gave to her son for not handing over his castles to the king

An honourable nobleman from that area, Gonçalo Vasques Coutinho by name, was the Governor of Trancoso, Lamego and other townships. As he was in Trancoso when the king came to Guarda, the king believed he would come and join him as a number of others had. According to some writers he was inclined to do so, but others indicate in their books a number of reasons why he failed. Some relate that at that juncture he sent a squire with letters of credence, one to Vasco Martins de Melo, and the other to Vasco Martins the Younger, his son, who would die following the battle [of Aljubarrota], as you will hear in due course,[77] requesting them to advise him as to what approach to adopt in relation to the king's invasion of the kingdom, as he had noticed that many noblemen of that area were going to join the King of Castile, and informing them that he would do nothing in this regard without their advice.

Such writers report that they sent back messages to say that Gonçalo Vasques should not join the King of Castile, because he was merely travelling on his way without any intention of besieging either him or others, even though they had not gone to join him. Other writers tell us that it was not for that reason at all but because his mother Beatriz Gonçalves was there with him and, when he asked her what approach he should adopt, seeing that the King

---

[77] In *CKJ2*, Chapter 43.

of Castile was invading the country in the way he did, his mother answered him as follows: 'My son, men gain at the expense of the stupid and the hasty, and, when it comes to matters that need pondering, haste is always harmful. Kings and powerful men often think they can bring to a speedy conclusion what they greatly desire, and sometimes things don't turn out as they expect. The King of Castile is invading this realm, thus breaking the treaties, as we can clearly see. Yet, even though certain nobles have gone to join him and have become his vassals, many others are displeased at his invasion; rather, the people at large are aggrieved and consider that the king is doing what he ought not to do, which is true, because he is breaking the agreements which were signed between him and King Fernando. Lisbon has adopted the Master as its ruler and defender, when its people learned that the King of Castile was keen to invade. Throughout the kingdom there are other towns, great and small, which share that attitude with the Lisboners. As a result, these events have started something which cannot now be easily abandoned, for all that some people say that the declaration which Lisbon and the other places have made against the king is just so much hot air. Therefore, it seems to me that your best approach is to hold back until you can see what end God is bringing to these affairs, for in that way you can then take whatever action you feel appropriate to enhance your honour and benefit.'

Gonçalo Vasques took this to be good advice and believed what his mother was saying. This was the reason why he did not go to speak to the king; it was not the [aforesaid] first reason which certain writers have put forward.

Chapter 60

Concerning the message which Queen Leonor sent to certain town councils after the death of Count Juan Fernández

In the month[78] immediately prior to that in which there began in Castile the new dating from the birth of Our Lord Jesus Christ, namely 1384, which is the year 1422 in the Era of Caesar, the queen was to be found in Alenquer, after the death of Count Juan Fernández. She had sent letters to certain town councils, in which she made it widely known how distressed she was at the

---

[78] December 1383.

death of her husband the king, and how, with his passing, the kingdom now belonged to his daughter Queen Beatriz.

Moreover, she added, lest these realms should be joined to those of Castile and in order to keep the two crowns permanently separate, just as till then they had been, as it had been laid down in the treaties and as King Fernando had ordained in his will and testament, she had taken charge of ruling over them, for as long as it was necessary, even though she found this to be both physically arduous and grievous to her soul. Nevertheless, she was doing this in order to keep them in safety to reward them for the very great service and honour which she had received from them.

She told them that, when she was in her palace in Lisbon, busy deciding what was necessary both in God's service and for the benefit of the realm, the Master of Avis had turned back from the mission on which she had sent him, namely to impose due respect on the townships of his Order and on others in that area. She told them that he had killed Count Juan Fernández and, for that reason and because of the tumult which had broken out in the city, she had made her way to Alenquer.

She also declared that she was sending them a message of complaint about those events, so that they might share in her indignation, and that it was not her intention to pursue them with wilful vengeance but only to uphold the law and see that justice be done. Furthermore, she intended to send a message to the King of Castile, urging him to hold back from invading the kingdom, in order to avert any harm which might befall them and to guarantee the separation of the two kingdoms, which would remain in great doubt if her daughter the queen and the king her husband started to rule over them at once. This message was, therefore, to notify them of this, as they were people worthy of her trust, and so they might understand that her intent was to further the benefit and honour of each and every one of them.

Chapter 61

How Queen Leonor wrote to King Juan, urging him to invade Portugal, and her purpose in doing so

When the queen sent these letters out all over the kingdom, the substance of which we have briefly described, they caused everybody to feel ill at ease, to be greatly disheartened and to feel a deep uncertainty about the outcome of such events. It was a very grievous matter for them to learn that the King of Castile might head for Portugal on seeing the country hanging in the balance and with a view to incorporating it wholly into Castile. That was the reaction of the great majority of ordinary people, who were not on the queen's side.

Moreover, some considered that the king would hold back from such an invasion, given what his mother-in-law had written to him and the way in which she had expressed it, especially on account of the treaties, which were the subject of solemn oaths and pledges. Others totally abandoned any hope when they took stock of all manner of different events which were taking place throughout the kingdom and when people were already saying that King Juan was moving in great haste to take immediate possession of the realm.

Meanwhile, the king invaded, as you have already heard. While he was in Guarda in that month of January which we have mentioned, there arrived anxious letters from Queen Leonor, letters which ran very much counter to what she had previously written to the councils. That was because in those first letters she assured them that it was her intention to send a message to the king, urging him to hold back from invading the kingdom, to preserve them all from any harmful consequences. However, in these letters she informed the king of everything which had taken place in Lisbon, including the death of Count Juan Fernández, whom the Master had slain in her very presence in the royal palace, as well as of the death of the bishop and the others who that day were slain in the cathedral. She also reported how, fearful and greatly upset, she had left Lisbon and made her way to Santarém, where she now remained for the time being. For that reason she was now requesting him to hasten at once to Santarém, because she felt herself to have been greatly dishonoured by the Master of Avis and by the inhabitants of Lisbon. Indeed, it was her opinion that they had no wish either to show him any obedience, or to have Queen Beatriz his wife as their liege lady.

The queen referred to the discord in Lisbon, the uprising of its inhabitants, how the Master was their captain and leader and how he had put himself forward to defend them, calling himself in his edicts ruler and defender of the realm, all of which would be an opportunity for his aggrandisement. Nevertheless, she added that she had brothers and great and powerful noblemen who were her kinsmen and who possessed plenty of fortresses with which they could provide King Juan with great assistance of various kinds. Besides that, there was the town of Santarém, where she now was and which was one of the finest towns in the realm, and for that very reason it was most important that he should head for Santarém with all due haste.

The King of Castile was very pleased when he saw Queen Leonor's message. For one whose great wish was to invade Portugal, her letters, when they arrived, in no sense caused him to hold back but spurred him on in pursuit of his goal, so that the very next day he decided to set forth.

Accordingly, it is important that you should know that the reason why the queen wrote these letters, as some authors assert in their books, was the deep resentment which she felt towards the Master of Avis and others in the kingdom of whom she was suspicious. She felt the same both about the people of Lisbon and about those of a number of places which sided with them. It was her belief that, after the King of Castile arrived, he would use the immense power of his army to force them to obey him and that he would inflict her vengeance on all of them, especially on the men and women of Lisbon; she declared that she would never be avenged upon the latter until she had filled a cask with their tongues.

Undoubtedly, if matters had ensued in the way which she contemplated, then the most ruthless justice would have been meted out at her behest to the inhabitants of Lisbon in response to what she knew that they were saying about her, especially at the time of the count's death. After she had been thus avenged and the kingdom fully pacified, King Juan would then return to his own country, and she would remain to rule in Portugal with her honour restored; thereafter, nobody, however important he might be, and still less the common folk, would dare to gainsay her, for fear of similar revenge. Once she had been avenged, and once the country was tranquil again, the king would journey back to his own country and she would remain in Portugal exactly as she intended.

Chapter 62

How the King of Castile continued on his way and reached Santarém

The king left Guarda at once, made a pilgrimage to Santa Maria de Açores, had a midday meal there and went on to spend the night in Celorico, a township which Martim Afonso de Melo had already ceded to him. There he remained for four days before setting off again and making his way to Coimbra, which was held by Count Gonçalo, who was the brother of Queen Leonor. Her uncle, Gonçalo Mendes de Vasconcelos, was also there.

However, these men did not go out to [meet] the king, nor did they welcome him into the city, thus revealing their displeasure towards him. Consequently, he made his way to Miranda [do Corvo], which was where the Count of Viana lived.[79] The count went forth to welcome him, became one of his supporters,

---

[79] João Afonso Telo, Count of Viana do Alentejo, second son of João Afonso Telo de Meneses, First Count of Ourém, Queen Leonor's uncle.

and there the king stayed for one day. Next day he left early in the morning and went to spend the night at Chão de Couce. The following day he ate at Ceras and spent the night in Tomar. There the king assumed that he would be joined by the Master of the Order of Christ, who was the nephew of Queen Leonor, being her sister's son. When the king reached Tomar and discovered that he had left, he was furious, because it was his belief that he would become one of his supporters, just like the others. Nevertheless, the king installed himself in the Master's residence in the main square.

According to the account of a certain author, what actually happened was that the Master was on his way to join the king, in order to offer his allegiance and serve him. However, a knight of his Order, seeing him set out and knowing what he intended to do, addressed him as follows: 'My lord, I believe that you are going out to welcome the King of Castile, to join with him and to offer him your allegiance. Yet, my lord, if you consider this matter carefully, it is plainly something which you should avoid doing until you can see what outcome all this is likely to have. Once you see the direction things are taking, you will then be in a position to do what you feel is right in order to preserve your honour and best interests and remain free of recrimination.'

As a result of these and other arguments which were put to him, the Master was persuaded not to go any further. He went back to Pombal and stayed there. As the king was spending the night in Tomar, a guard was mounted in the vicinity, resulting in a skirmish in which a certain Henrique Alemão was killed, along with five or six of his companions.

The king departed at midnight and reached Golegã by morning. There he ate a meal before continuing his journey to Santarém, accompanied by his wife Queen Beatriz. 2 leagues before they reached Santarém, those who were with Queen Leonor assembled, though not in a single party, but one at a time, as each man saw fit to do so. They went forth to greet the king, kissing both his hand and that of his queen, and offered them their allegiance. Among these men were Gonçalo Vasques de Azevedo and João Gonçalves Teixeira; on behalf of Queen Leonor they told the king that his mother[-in-law] warmly commended herself to him and that he was most welcome, as she had wanted to see him in Portugal for a long time.

As for Queen Beatriz, before she reached the vineyards of Santarém, she halted a while, in order to adorn herself appropriately, because she was dressed in travelling attire. The king sent ahead Pedro Fernández de Velasco and Pedro Sarmiento, instructing them to await him at Chão da Feira, the market-place, which is in front of the castle gateway. They did as they were commanded, and Gonçalo Vasques and João Gonçalves returned to Queen Leonor.

Chapter 63

How the Master [of Avis] went back
from Alenquer to Lisbon

A s for the Master [of Avis], whom we left in Alenquer, he sent men out
to spy on the King of Castile, after they told him that he was in Guarda.
This was in order to find out the strength of the army that was accompanying
him and what route he was intending to take. Some days before King Juan
arrived at Santarém, a message reached the Master, informing him that he
was heading straight there, that his forces were somewhat scattered and that
there were not many with him.

The Master told Nuno Álvares that the King of Castile was heading down
through the country and would very soon be in Santarém, adding that he
thought it best for them to return to Lisbon, in order to ensure all due protection
for the city. Nuno Álvares answered that, even if they went back to Lisbon,
the King of Castile would know the route to take to attack the city just as
well as they, whose duty it was to defend it. Rather, his advice was that, while
the King of Castile was advancing with a relatively small force, and before
heavy reinforcements could join him, a watch be kept on his movements, so
that, when he reached the Santarém area, they could block his approach and
engage him in battle; that way they could easily defeat him and such a victory
would greatly advance the Master's cause.

The Master declared that this was excellent advice but that it could not be
achieved without danger to himself, as their own numbers were very small.
At this point he received another message, telling him that the King of Castile
was due to reach Santarém that very day. Consequently, the Master set off
with his forces and made his way back to Lisbon.

Chapter 64

How King Juan spoke with Queen
Leonor and conducted her with him to the
monastery where he took up lodging

A few days before the King of Castile arrived at Santarém, he sent ahead
Pero Carrillo, his chief herberger,[80] to ask Queen Leonor to make

---

[80] Official responsible for the allocation of lodgings to members of the royal
household.

arrangements for accommodation and quarters to be provided for his troops. She consulted the nobles and lords who were with her, and they agreed that neither the king nor those who accompanied him should be accommodated in the town, rather that the king should be lodged in one of the monasteries, whichever he saw fit, and that his forces should find lodging outside the town as best they could. Realising this, the herberger did not return to the king, but stayed there to await his arrival. Those within Santarém began to keep better watch over the town than before, as though it were on a war footing.

Some relate that, although Queen Leonor had summoned the King of Castile and was very pleased that he had come, yet, as a wise and very perceptive woman, she was uncertain in her heart whether the king would demonstrate by his actions the approach which she so keenly desired. They add that, as she was afraid of many things and unsure of anything, she hesitated to emerge from the castle and place herself in the king's power, for fear of what, indeed, was to happen afterwards. Therefore she did not want to come out to speak to him. Instead, she wanted the king to take up lodging in one of the monasteries, and they would later agree on how they should meet to discuss matters. Indeed, Martim Gonçalves de Ataíde, Gonçalo Rodrigues de Sousa and other noblemen told her that in no way should she place herself in his power, because it could happen that the king would detain her until she yielded the town to him, along with the other places which had expressed their allegiance to her.

Gonçalo Vasques and João Gonçalves both told the queen that in no way should she do so but, given that it was her daughter and son-in-law, whom she had summoned from their kingdom by her very own letters, it would be highly discourteous and would cause the king to be deeply suspicious and irritated, were she not to emerge at once to greet and speak to them. They said this, particularly as they had formed the view, when they went to meet him, that the king was well disposed towards her and wished to please her in any way he could.

These authors relate that, at this point, the king, along with his wife Queen Beatriz, reached Santarém after vespers on Tuesday, 12 January. Queen Beatriz was seated on a saddle-mule, shrouded in mourning, and was accompanied by Dona Beatriz de Castro and other ladies and damsels. The king's following comprised 180 armed horsemen with their lances raised and trumpets blaring, but many more arrived later that evening.

They go on to say that the king and his queen dismounted in a great open space before the castle gates, as did all the nobles, ladies and damsels who accompanied them. Once they had all dismounted, Queen Leonor was informed. She came out in a troubled mood and covered by a great black cape which hid her face, and on the arm of Vasco Peres de Camões, and a few others with her. The moment he saw her, the king came forward to greet her, and she was embraced both by him and by her daughter. In tears, Queen Leonor addressed the king at once:

'Sire, my son, I have a complaint to make about the Master of Avis. That man slew Count Juan Fernández in my very own palace, right by the train of my gown, and threw me out of Lisbon, yes, me and all my supporters and followers.'

The king answered that it was for that reason that he had come, namely to please her, to restore her honour and to avenge her for all that had been inflicted on her. Thereupon Queen Leonor took her leave of the king and her daughter, wanting to go back into the castle, and the king would have let her do so, had it not been for Pedro Fernández de Velasco, who said that it seemed to him to be reasonable that the king should take her with him, on the grounds that neither he nor her daughter had seen her for a long time, and this he urged him to do.

Despite this, the queen sought to re-enter the castle, requesting the king, since he was not yet installed in his lodging, to let her go for the present, as the next morning she would go and visit him and her daughter. However, the king insisted that she should go with him. The king and Queen Beatriz led her by the arm, one on each side, and conducted her to the Monastery of São Domingos, where the king was due to take up lodging.

However, since from the very beginning of this work we have continued to present differing opinions, so that each reader may adhere to what seems to him the most satisfactory viewpoint, we shall mention another version of the story, which is greatly at odds with the above. One author gives an eye-witness account, claiming that Queen Leonor was already on the castle drawbridge when it was announced that King Juan was approaching; he claims that the king and Queen Beatriz arrived together, that they embraced her and that her daughter kissed her hand. What words passed between them nobody heard; the king then motioned Queen Leonor a short distance away from her daughter and spoke briefly to her, without anybody hearing what they were saying, and then he took her to the monastery of São Domingos. That was how she left and not otherwise. That very night 200 lances stood guard to protect the king, as they continued to do thereafter.

Chapter 65

How the king decided to enter Santarém and how it took place

As to the discussions which that night the king held with his mother-in-law Queen Leonor, nobody has clearly set them down in writing, except for what they say the king said to her, namely that he could not, on her behalf, inflict vengeance on the Master of Avis nor on the others involved in the way she wished, nor could he subjugate any town, large or small, which had declared against her, unless she first yielded to him and to her daughter the governance of the realm, governance which she was due to hold in accordance with the treaties. Changing her mind and her plan, the queen resolved to do so.

According to certain authors, the advice given to the queen by several of those who found out about this was of no avail, when they said that she could not hand over the governance which had passed to her on the death of King Fernando. They argued that this would run counter to his last wishes, which were held to be legally binding; furthermore, such a renunciation was against the treaties, to which she could neither add anything, nor from which she could subtract anything, without the consent of the prelates and people of the realm, just as the treaties laid down. However, she replied that they had no grounds for raising doubts on this issue, for they knew only too well that King Juan, with her daughter Queen Beatriz, was supreme lord of the kingdom of Portugal and that nothing could any longer be done about this situation. Early next day, the Wednesday, a notary was summoned at once, and a document was drawn up in which she renounced all rights to the governance of the realm, governance which was due to pass to her, and bestowed it on King Juan and her daughter.

Very early on the Thursday morning Queen Leonor came back to the castle and dismissed Gonçalo Vasques de Azevedo, who was its chief governor. She sent for the knight João Gomes de Abreu, who was one of the high-ranking residents of the town, and told him that, at midday, he should order the opening of the Leiria gates, which were locked and guarded by local men; then the King of Castile would enter with his wife and troops to take up lodgings in the town. In his answer João Gomes begged the queen graciously not to require him to allow the King of Castile and his men into the town; it was preferable, he urged, that they should be accommodated in the monasteries where they were and out in the surrounding area, where they would be provided with supplies in return for payment, rather than that the town be subjected to their might and that everybody be plunged into turmoil.

The queen grew angry at this and raged at João Gomes in the following words: 'What? So you don't want my son-in-law and daughter to come into the town? Let me tell you that, if you refuse, I shall let them in through this castle gate and out through the gate which leads into town. Besides, although I've given orders for them to be lodged in the house belonging to Gonçalo Vasques de Azevedo, they'll be installed in yours instead!'

João Gomes then answered and said, 'My lady, what I said was in good faith, believing it to be in your best interests. However, as it displeases you, I shall do everything you ask.'

That very day, after the midday meal, the gates were immediately opened up. Having eaten, the king headed towards town mounted on a horse, preceded by a group of his men, all mounted and armed, with raised lances. First, all the streets were requisitioned from the castle as far along as the Church of Santo Estêvão (close to where the king was due to lodge) and from there as far as the fortress, and many men-at-arms were installed on foot in these streets. Queen Leonor commanded the Jews, bearing their Torahs, to greet her son-in-law and daughter outside the town, and this they did.

When the king reached the castle gate which was close to the Chão da Feira, Queen Leonor was already there on horseback. The king led her mount by the reins, with Queen Beatriz her daughter behind her, led by the Prince of Navarre. The king was wearing a coat of plates and holding a citron branch. They entered by the Leiria gate and proceeded along the street until they reached the house of Gonçalo Vasques de Azevedo, where they were to be accommodated and which was close to the Church of Santo Estêvão. Queen Leonor also lodged in the same quarters as the king.

Also on that very day the castle and the fortress were handed over to the king. The man who held the castle on behalf of Gonçalo Vasques was removed, and his place was taken by Lope Fernández de Padilla. In the fortress they installed the brothers Garci and Sancho de Villodre, along with eighty lances. As for the king, he was protected in his royal quarters day and night by a guard of fifty men-at-arms.

Chapter 66

How King Juan handled the justices of the realm, and how he impaled his arms with those of Portugal[81]

While the king was in Santarém, which is one of the best and most noble towns in the kingdom of Portugal and one of the richest in all provisions, he received every day prominent captains bringing many soldiers from his kingdoms. Queen Leonor's herberger together with the herberger of the King of Castile distributed sectors of the town to each one, according to rank, both within the town itself and in the surrounding area. Nobody was exempt from providing lodging, except in the Jewish quarter, where they did not lodge owing to Dom David Negro and two high-ranking Jews who were allied to Queen Leonor. From the very outset the Castilians adopted an honourable attitude both towards those with whom they were billeted and in the purchase of food.

When the King of Castile arrived, all the justices and officials of King Fernando's time were present with the queen in Santarém, having accompanied her when she left Lisbon. Among these were King Fernando's chancellor of the great seal, Lourenço Eanes Fogaça; the latter's clerk [of the crown in chancery], Gonçalo Peres; Doctor Gil do Sém; João Gonçalves, Fernão Gonçalves and Lopo Esteves de Leiria, all three of whom were licenciates at law; Rodrigo Esteves de Lisboa; Gonçalo Peres, who was the Prior of Ourém, and Gonçalo Eanes, both of whom were bachelors in canon law; these men and others dispatched all of Portugal's affairs with great deliberation and according to law [in King Fernando's time]. On the King of Castile's arrival, he chose not to meddle with their duties but ordained that each one should continue in office; this also applied to the secretaries and all other officials.

He made Gonçalo Martins, who was a bachelor in canon law, his proctor. All of them received from him two months' payment and in his name they dispatched the kingdom's affairs as though they understood that it was already his. The chief justice of the Court, Gil Eanes, together with one of the King of Castile's magistrates, presided over the town's legal affairs and heard cases which had arisen between the Castilians and the Portuguese.

---

[81] The heraldic term 'impaled' means the arrangement of two coats of arms side by side in one shield along a vertical centre line. The husband's arms are in the dexter half, in the position of greatest honour, and the wife's in the sinister half. As the terms 'dexter' and 'sinister' refer to the right and left of the shield's wearer, to the onlooker they appear to the left and right respectively.

Though the King of Castile had formerly already described himself as 'the King of Castile, León, Portugal and the Algarve', in Santarém he began to present his titles with much greater clarity, because of legal verdicts and other legal decisions affecting the realm, and did so by raising banners displaying his arms with the *quinas* on the fly end, as you have already heard.[82] When the king arrived, he instructed Lourenço Eanes Fogaça, who had been King Fernando's chancellor of the great seal, to bring him the seals which he held, both the stamp and the pendant seals, so as to have them broken up and destroyed and to have others made displaying the arms and signs of Castile, impaled with those of Portugal. He told him that, as soon as they were made, he would at once hand them over to him, as it was his wish to have no other chancellor in the country but him.

Lourenço Eanes carried out the king's command and handed him the seals but with little desire ever to have any seals back again or to be the king's chancellor. Indeed, one day, in order to get away safely together with his clerk Gonçalo Peres, he spoke as follows to the King of Castile: 'Sire, both I and Gonçalo Peres, your clerk of the crown in chancery, are away from our wives: mine is in Lisbon and his is in Évora, wherefore we request Your Grace's gracious permission to allow us to go and fetch them, both for their greater safety and so that we might serve you better.'

The king consented to their request, thinking that it was all just as Lourenço Eanes said, but they went [directly] to the Master and offered him their services. The Master dispatched Lourenço Eanes to England, as you have heard,[83] and later he sent Gonçalo Peres to Oporto, as we shall relate in due course.

As for the conjoining of arms [of both realms], the king effected it as follows: he divided the round seal down the middle, so that in the dexter half appeared the undifferenced arms of Castile, and the sinister half displayed the undifferenced arms of Portugal, that is to say, the bordure running along the border and the line of partition was surrounded by castles, and inside there were the five escutcheons of the *quinas*;[84] the letters which bordered the whole seal proclaimed: *Johannis Dei gratia, Regis Castelle et Legionis, et Portugallie.*[85]

---

[82] See Chapters 54 and 55 above, in which Fernão Lopes refers to the arrangement whereby the Portuguese arms were first of all sewn on beneath the Castilian ones; by this time they are impaled.

[83] In Chapter 47 above.

[84] More precisely, the *quinas* are the five escutcheons scattered with a semé of bezants argent.

[85] '[The seal of] Juan by the grace of God, King of Castile and León, and of Portugal.'

His title on letters and any other documents read as follows: 'Don Juan by the grace of God King of Castile and León, and of Portugal, Toledo and Galicia', and of the other places which were customarily mentioned. Such were his seals and the title he took at that time and for some time afterwards.

The town community of Santarém took the decision to provide an immediate contribution to the King of Castile: 30,000 *libras* were voted to him by the high-ranking men of the town, a sum which later became the Master's, once he was king, since he acquired it from those who had been in receipt of such monies. King Juan decided to mint money in Santarém, ordering the minting of a quantity of silver *reais* of seven *dinheiros* and bearing a crown, as well as of other coins of lesser value.

It is also said that Queen Leonor gave the King of Castile many jewels that had been left by King Fernando; he thanked her for them most warmly, and from the very outset they were in full and very friendly agreement with one another.

Chapter 67

Concerning the noblemen and knights who were with King Juan in Santarém, and what happened to Gonçalo Vasques in respect of the wages which he ordered to be paid to his soldiers

While King Juan was in Santarém, from among the noblemen of the realm, the following great lords and captains were present there with him: Don Enrique Manuel de Villena, the son of Don Juan Manuel, who was the Count of Seia and held Sintra; Dom Pedro Álvares Pereira, who was Prior of the Order of the Hospitallers; Count João Afonso, Queen Leonor's brother; the Count of Viana;[86] Gonçalo Vasques de Azevedo, who held Torres Novas; Vasco Peres de Camões, who held Alenquer; João Gonçalves Teixeira, who held Óbidos; Diogo Álvares and Fernão Pereira, brothers of the said Prior of Crato [Pedro Álvares Pereira]; Vasco Martins da Cunha, along with Martim Vasques, Gil Vasques and Vasco Martins his sons; Vasco Martins de Melo; João Afonso Pimentel; João Rodrigues Portocarreiro; Martim Gonçalves de Ataíde; Afonso Gomes da Silva; Fernão Gomes da Silva; Martim Afonso de Melo and his brother Vasco Martins, along with their sons; Fernão Gonçalves

---

[86] Queen Leonor's cousin; see Chapter 62 above, note 79.

de Sousa; Gonçalo Rodrigues de Sousa; and, throughout the kingdom, many other noble knights who held mighty fortresses in obedience to the king's command.

Of these great lords and nobles who came to Santarém the king ordered a number to return to their towns and villages, whereas others remained in his company. It is important that you should know that all the great lords and noblemen who remained there with him, as well as those who went back to the castles which they had already offered him, were in receipt of wages authorised by the king with which to pay for a certain number of lances who would serve him. Among those nobles was Gonçalo Vasques de Azevedo, to whom he authorised payment of wages for 100 lances.

Gonçalo Vasques possessed a great household and came accompanied by many honourable squires who resided with him, for example Rodrigo Eanes de Buarcos, Vasco Rodrigues Leitão, João Rodrigues da Mota and other similarly reliable men. One day he went to the palace, having left instructions to his bursar to pay wages to all his men as he had previously ordained. The bursar placed three heaps of money on a table, one consisting of florins, another of silver *reais* and the other of general coinage. When he asked the squires to take the money, not one of them wanted to. They would just pick up the florins, laugh at them and then put them back in their place. At supper time Gonçalo Vasques returned to his lodgings and did not know what to think when he saw the money was still there; so he asked his bursar why he had not distributed the money as instructed.

'Well, sir', he said, 'I invited them all to collect their money, but not one of them chose to accept it.' Gonçalo Vasques fell silent for a little while, as he suspected why they were doing this; he then ordered the money to be put away and the table to be laid. He then called them all to one side and said: 'You are all men whose honour I very much wish to enhance and in whose interests I very much want to procure the favour of my liege lord the king, and by whatever means. It therefore surprises me that you do not choose to accept his wages, which are paid to enable you to serve him as soldiers in my company. The fact is that I held such an opinion about you (and I don't just say this with regard to the King of Castile, who is a great lord whom we are all expected to serve) that, even if I became a Moor and went off to Granada, to live there for ever, I believed you would become Moors along with me and would serve me in whatever pertained to my honour. Yet now it seems that I was mistaken about you, because what I see is quite the opposite, and, that being so, I beg you to tell me why you are behaving like this.'

They all stood silent until Vasco Rodrigues replied: 'Let me explain: seeing that they're all tongue-tied, and that not one of them chooses to speak, I shall speak both on their account and mine. Under no circumstances will they or

I accept wages from the King of Castile, or even from you, with a view to serving him. We will all choose to take our leave of you rather than accept his wages and be his soldiers. However, were you to adopt the stand taken by the Master and by Lisbon, then let me tell you that you would have no need of gold or silver or any other money to give us. We would all willingly devote our bodies, our lives and our possessions to serving and dying alongside you, wherever you went. That is our final decision, from which we shall not turn, and, if anyone tells you otherwise, then he's a liar; you should neither believe nor trust him, no, not even me, were I to say such a thing to you.'

On hearing this, Gonçalo Vasques was amazed and said that, since that was the situation, he had no intention of harming them nor of forcing them to stay; rather, he would take steps to see that none of this became public. He then obtained the king's agreement to his moving to Torres Novas and to staying there to mount guard over the town, which he duly did. As for his men, when they realised that it was his wish to serve the king and support his objectives, they gradually left him and went to Buarcos to join his son, Álvaro Gonçalves, who had declared for the Master. They sailed with the Oporto fleet, when it later went to Lisbon, as we shall relate in due course.[87]

Chapter 68

Concerning the townships throughout all areas of the realm which declared for Castile

As we have spoken of those nobles and great lords who joined the King of Castile, it is right that we should mention the townships which declared their allegiance to him and promised to obey him, so that you can see how he had a large portion of the kingdom under his command and throughout every region. That is not to say that the people resident in such townships willingly yielded them to him or declared their obedience; rather, it was the governors and high-ranking figures in each township who offered allegiance to him, and forced humble folk to declare their allegiance along with them.

Such was the case with Lope Gómez de Lira in Braga, who gave himself the title of bailiff on behalf of the King of Castile.[88] By imprisoning certain

---

[87] In Chapter 131.

[88] In fact, Lope Gómez had taken over as bailiff of Braga by command of King Fernando, following the suspension of its archbishop, Dom Lourenço Vicente, in October 1377. Lope Gómez belonged to the group of *emperogilados*, i.e. Galicians

residents of the town and the clergy from the cathedral chapter, he forced them to declare allegiance to the King of Castile and to obey him as their liege lord by paying homage to the Archbishop of Santiago. That situation arose because the said Lope Gómez entered the town against the wishes of both the town council and the cathedral chapter and ushered in the Archbishop of Santiago, along with further forces from Galicia who came with him. He then issued a proclamation throughout the town requiring all its people, both clerical and lay, to go at once to the cathedral cloisters to pay homage to the King of Castile and his wife, to accept them as their liege lord and lady and to serve them both in peace and in war. As for those who refused to do so, he would banish them from the kingdom of Portugal and would confiscate their property and possessions.

In addition, the people were at the mercy of the castle, which dominated the town. Its governor was Vasco Lorenzo, the brother of Lope Gómez, and he threatened the people that, if they did not do as Lope Gómez demanded, they would be annihilated. Terrified, they all did as he wanted. In this and other similar ways the people of Portugal handed themselves over to the King of Castile, though against their will.

Here, you should believe that a fearful outcry went up throughout the realm when, as we have described, the news came that the king had left Castile for Portugal, when the people were assured of his intention to invade the country and when they realised that such an invasion could only be a source of great tumult and discord. This invasion had such an effect on human understanding as to produce many differing opinions. Consequently, although love for their country and their natural affections drove many noblemen and governors of castles to declare for Portugal, rather than for Castile, there were nevertheless others who, filled with greed mixed with evil intent, along with some who were afraid of losing their honoured positions, while keen to gain even greater standing, opted for the opposite course. As a result, the kingdom was rent asunder and split into two.

Indeed, very few places and very few noblemen actually sided with the Master to offer him their help; all the others went over to the King of Castile and obeyed his command, so that throughout the various areas of the realm the following fortresses favoured Castile:

In Estremadura: Santarém, Torres Novas, Ourém, Leiria, Montemor-o-Velho, the castle of Feira, Penela, Óbidos, Torres Vedras, Alenquer and Sintra.

---

loyal to the faction of Pedro I of Castile, who, after his death, settled in Portugal during King Fernando's reign. See *CKF*, Chapter 25.

In the Alentejo: Arronches, Alegrete, Castelo de Vide, Crato, Amieira, Monforte, Campo Maior, Olivença, Vila Viçosa, Portel, Moura, Noudar, Mértola and Almada.

In Minho: Lanhoso, Braga, Guimarães, Valença, Melgaço, Ponte de Lima, Vila Nova de Cerveira, Caminha, Viana and the castle of Neiva.

In Trás-os-Montes: Bragança, Vinhais, Chaves, Monforte de Rio Livre, Montalegre, Mogadouro, Mirandela, Alfândega, Lamas de Orelhão and Vila Real de Panoias.

In Beira: Castelo Rodrigo, Almeida, Sabugal, Monsanto, Penamacor, Guarda, Covilhã, Celorico and Linhares.

When he set out, and even before invading the country, the King of Castile had under his power these fifty-four townships, as well as others which we do not care to mention. Yet, though the rich and the powerful, such as castle governors and other noblemen, declared their allegiance to the King of Castile, all the people in their heart of hearts were opposed to him and to Queen Leonor. As a result, as we have said, there took place sundry uprisings in a number of places, with castles being seized from their governors. In these places the people declared their allegiance to the Master of Avis and wrote to him, indicating that they wanted to be his supporters and to help him both materially and on the field of battle. This was the case in Évora, which they seized from Álvaro Mendes de Oliveira, in Estremoz, which was captured from João Mendes de Vasconcelos, as well as in Beja and other townships, as you have heard.

As for those townships which sided with Castile, the king sent them as many soldiers as he deemed necessary to enable the governor, by resorting both to those soldiers and to his own *criados* and friends, duly to defend the town; that was because the governors were far from confident about the residents of such places, in the light of what they realised was happening around them.

From the fortresses which had declared their allegiance to Castile, their Portuguese governors set out on sorties, robbing and raiding those districts which had sided with the Master, where they plundered and looted and killed, as though those districts deserved this for some fault which they had committed. As a result, those who ought to have been the defenders of the people, and to have rescued them from the hands of their enemies, those were the very men who killed and persecuted them and inflicted on them every cruelty possible.

Oh, what a grievous and deadly war was this to behold: Portuguese seeking to slay other Portuguese! Men born from the selfsame womb and reared in the selfsame land willingly and wantonly killing one another and spilling the blood of members of their own families!

Chapter 69

How the ships bearing fish from Galicia were captured

Just when this new war broke out among the Portuguese, not to mention the one they waged against the Castilians, and while the Master was in Lisbon, as we said, on a certain Monday morning, the first day of February 1384, there appeared at the mouth of the Tagus a galley from Castile, five balingers[89] and a large *nao*. As the weather was inclement, the merchant vessels anchored downstream from Restelo, at more than a league away from the city. The *nao* and the galley remained further downstream, between Oeiras and Santa Catarina,[90] a good distance away from the balingers.

The Master was informed that some of these ships were from Galicia, laden with flour and other provisions, and had come to meet the Castilian fleet, as they believed it was already besieging the city. Other ships were laden with dried fish for Aragon. Having made certain that all these vessels belonged to his enemies, the Master immediately ordered two galleys, two *naos* and three barges to be prepared. After two days they were at the ready and equipped with weaponry and ship's company.

Having come to anchor, these ships did not think they would undergo any harm from the people in the city, believing that they would be so preoccupied with preparing for the expected siege that this would give them plenty to think about and leave them no opportunity to take note of anything else. What happened was that before dawn the Portuguese *naos* and barges launched an attack on these ships. The Castilian galley, on seeing the Portuguese galleys and other sailing ships approaching, abandoned its anchors, took to flight and got away; the smaller vessels were all captured and brought to port in the city, without putting up any further resistance, which would have been pointless.

The new and mighty *nao* of 200 *tonéis*[91] had been well fitted out by a Jew named Don David from La Coruña. Realising what was happening, she hastily unfurled her sails, though the weather was unfavourable. She tried to find a way out taking advantage of the current opposite the fortress[92] and sailed against the headwind as best she could. The [Portuguese] galleys skilfully hugged the shoreline, while one *nao* and two barges pursued the [Galician]

---

[89] Small, fast one-masted ships of about 50 tons lading, with a shallow bottom, and usually employed in coastal trading. They could operate equally well with sails or a set of rowers.

[90] Santa Catarina is nowadays the suburb known as Dafundo.

[91] About 38,433 gallons (174,720 litres).

[92] This fortress is the Palácio da Alcáçova, in front of which the river is narrower.

nao into a very choppy sea, whipped up by a strong wind. As there was considerable distance between them, they were already losing any hope of catching up with her.

The Master was in his palace watching, as also were many city folk. When he saw the immense advantage held by the Galician *nao*, as compared with his own ships, he cried out to those present, 'She's getting away!' Just as he uttered these words, the ship's cross-jack yard, some 18 feet long, broke off, so that she was forced to heave to and was captured by the Portuguese, without putting up any further resistance and even without anyone being injured. The Master and everyone in the city were overjoyed at this fortunate occurrence, especially at a time when there were so many shortages, for on board these ships they found lots of dried fish: hake, conger eel, octopus and sardines, both smoked and salted, as well as large quantities of flour and other provisions.

It is important that you should know that, though it was everybody's duty both to provide and to make available anything that each person felt to be of common use and of general profit to the city, there were nevertheless some people who were so possessed by greed, which so easily gripped their hearts, that it drove them to apply to the Master, requesting him to sell them that fish, so that they could take it out of the country, lured as they were by the vast profit which they felt it would make. With a semblance of fine words, each one of which was inimical to the common weal, they argued how greatly it would profit him and be in his very best interests. But the Master, who was far from lacking in good sense and sound judgement, retorted that nobody should speak to him about any such thing, as it was his view that God had brought him all this, so that he could provide everyone with a good Lent, which was just approaching. He added that those merchants who were making this application were driven by their greed for profit and were revealing only too well how little they sympathised with the common folk and with how they were to be defended, and all that at a time when there was such a shortage of food and other necessities.

So it was, then, that the city was amply supplied with an abundance of fish, and that thereby it proved possible to pay the noblemen and other soldiers their wages in fish, news of which greatly displeased the King of Castile when it reached him in Santarém.

Chapter 70

How the Count of Mayorga sent a challenge to the Master, and how Nuno Álvares answered it

A mong the great lords who accompanied the King of Castile was a certain Count of Mayorga, Don Pedro Álvarez de Lara,[93] the bastard son of Don Juan Núñez de Lara. He was a great man-at-arms and a valiant knight of vast renown.

In this regard some writers say, when praising the feats of Nuno Álvares, that, when he was with the Master in Lisbon and heard about the count's repute and prowess, it occurred to him to challenge him to mortal combat, with thirty men against thirty. They say that he sought the Master's permission and that he explained why he was inclined to do this, adding that the Master consented. They further relate that Nuno Álvares sent a challenge to the count, which the count duly received, that the day and place were arranged, and that Nuno Álvares was in readiness. However, the Master later realising how their toils and troubles were ever increasing forbade Nuno Álvares to go ahead; for that reason he did not proceed with his challenge.

Nevertheless, another historian, whose account is in our view more reliable, narrates the story quite differently, and we think this version is more satisfactory. He tells us that a minstrel, Anequim by name, who had been a member of King Fernando's household and had stayed on in that of Queen Leonor, often visited the King of Castile's lodgings. This man was in the habit of addressing everybody he knew as 'my dear friend' and was addressed by them in the same way. As he customarily visited the houses of great lords, he announced one day that he wanted to go to Lisbon to see the Master of Avis and to entertain him. When the Count of Mayorga heard about this, he summoned him into his presence and said:

'My dear friend, is it true, as they say, that you're going to Lisbon?'

'Yes', he said, 'I want to go there to see the Master.'

The count, said: 'In that case, I want to ask you to do me a favour: I want you to tell the Master that, if he contradicts me and says that he is not committing treason and an evil act in stirring up the country and wanting to be its supreme lord, a position which by right belongs to my liege lord the king and to his wife, then I shall challenge him to combat in that regard and shall make him acknowledge my claim. So I ask you to tell him so plainly.'

---

[93] Usually known as Don Pedro Núñez de Lara.

Anequim answered that he promised to tell him and would bring back the Master's reply. Hence he went to Lisbon and, while in conversation with the Master, he passed on the count's message. As soon as he had finished and before the Master could say a word, Nuno Álvares, who was [also] present, answered Anequim in the following words: 'There is no reason why my lord, the Master, should resort to combat against him, but in regard to his expressed intent I shall willingly take up his challenge. Moreover: if he denies to me that my lord the Master, and the rest of us Portuguese, are at his side fighting a just war to defend our very lives and possessions; also, if he refuses to accept that the King of Castile has with evil intent done what he should not have done and invaded this country before he was entitled to, breaking those very treaties which he was committed to keep, losing thereby any rights in this realm which he did have; and if he refuses to accept that, therefore, this realm belongs to my lord the Master, here present, as the son of King Pedro, as he indeed is, then I shall meet him in mortal combat, and shall make him acknowledge my claim, fighting one against one, or two against two, or any number he cares to choose. Please tell him so.'

They then talked about other matters, and a few days later Anequim went back to Santarém. The count asked him whether he had delivered his message to the Master, and he answered that he had, giving him the reply which Nuno Álvares had made.

'Who is this Nuno Álvares?' asked the count.

'My lord', he answered, 'he is a brother of Dom Pedro Álvares, the Prior of Crato.'

The count replied: 'I don't know what sort of a man he is, nor do I know him. I'm not interested in any man other than the Master in person, nor will I enter into combat with anyone but him. As for parentage, we both descend from the lineage of our kings and, with regard to our mothers, we are both bastard sons. If, therefore, he refuses my challenge, I likewise have no intention of meeting in the battlefield or of entering into combat with anybody else.'

At this juncture, with the Master taking steps to counter what he expected would soon come about, now that the King of Castile was in Santarém and he himself had left Alenquer for Lisbon, he at once ordered all the inhabitants of the Lisbon area to make their way into the city and bring with them as many provisions as they could carry. For fear of the Castilians, who, they were told, were already roaming the country, these inhabitants set off with their wives, children, cattle and pack-animals, and with as much as they could bring with them and made their way into Lisbon. Others crossed the River Tagus into the Ribatejo, seeking to save their lives, each one as he saw best.

Oh, what a grievous sight it was to behold, all those men and women heading for the city in droves, both by night and by day, with their children in their arms or leading them by the hand, the fathers with other babes on their shoulders, and their mules loaded down with household goods and anything they could carry! That was how all the inhabitants from the surrounding area made their way into the city, before the King of Castile could arrive.

Chapter 71

How Nuno Álvares went into the Sintra area in search of provisions, and how certain captains from Castile arrived at Lumiar

Since the Master realised that one of the things which were most essential to him, as he was about to be besieged, was a plentiful supply of provisions, he decided, before the King of Castile's arrival, to send men out to forage for food in areas which had not declared for him, in order to provide the city with as much food as possible.

He sent Nuno Álvares to Sintra, to bring provisions from that area, sending with him some 300 lances, both squires and citizens, and a few foot soldiers. Sintra had declared for the King of Castile and was governed at that time by the Count [of Seia] Don Enrique [Manuel de Villena] and by soldiers with whom he was well capable of defending it. Nuno Álvares roamed all around the surrounding area without encountering anybody to hinder him. He amassed plenty of provisions, both livestock and wheat, as well as other foodstuffs, and they loaded all this onto mules, with which they had come well prepared for this purpose. Nobody emerged from the town in an attempt to prevent him doing so.

The King of Castile, who was in Santarém, had just a short while beforehand sent forth Don Pedro Fernández Cabeza de Vaca, who was the Master of Santiago, Pedro Fernández de Velasco, who was his lord chamberlain, Pedro Ruiz Sarmiento, who was the Chief Provincial Governor of Galicia, and with them 1,000 lances consisting of valiant men-at-arms. Their mission was to reach the outskirts of Lisbon in order to begin to lay siege to the city, and they were to prevent those inside the city from making any sorties into the surrounding area and causing any damage whatsoever. On the night after Nuno Álvares left Sintra with his booty, he received a message informing him that these forces were in Alenquer and were preparing to attack him. Consequently, a number of his company immediately left and made for the city [of Lisbon].

Next day those who had remained behind urged him to hurry away and not wait for these forces to arrive, but Nuno Álvares refused to do so, gave no heed to anything they said and proceeded slowly and steadily with the train of booty he was driving. On the way and much against everybody's wishes he waited till midday to see whether the Castilians would arrive to confront him.

In Lisbon the Master, on learning about this, sent out Rui Pereira, Nuno Álvares's uncle, along with 150 lances, to help him. As the day wore on, realising that the Castilians were not going to attack them they made their way into Lisbon with all their spoil and were warmly greeted by the Master. The Castilian captains whom we mentioned were approaching with their forces with a view to catching up with Nuno Álvares and taking from him the plunder which he had seized. However, as Nuno Álvares had already been back in the city for a whole day, they took up lodging in Lumiar and in the villages round about, without advancing any further. This took place on 8 February 1384.

Chapter 72

How the Master took the decision to go to Santarém to do battle with the King of Castile and the reasons why it was not done

We have already described how, when the King of Castile reached Santarém, all his men were billeted throughout the town, lodging with people of high rank, those of medium standing and those of humble status, with the result that there was nobody in the town with whom they were not billeted.

At the very outset of their accommodation they began by behaving well towards their hosts but after a few days they started to lord it over them, submitting them to so many instances of unreasonable and outrageous behaviour that all the local people considered themselves to be deeply offended. That is because they wrested their very possessions from their owners; moreover, they would eject two or three inhabitants from their houses and make them lodge somewhere else, closeting them all together in one house, without allowing them to take anything out of their houses, not even bedclothes, but simply the clothes they were wearing at the time.

They flung other men out of their houses but kept back their wives and slept with them; in other cases, they did this before their very eyes, much to their anguish, announcing that everything that these men had was now theirs and that they possessed nothing; they insulted them with vile and foul taunts and a torrent of disreputable abuse. If any man tried to speak or answer back, they at once threatened him with death. Other men they bound hand and foot and left them like that all night. Yet others dared not leave their houses to go anywhere else without a pass, for otherwise they were arrested and ill-treated; to such an extent that many abandoned all they possessed and fled to Lisbon and other towns. This went so far that certain men from Santarém, as well as other Portuguese who were with the King of Castile, sent messages from time to time to Lisbon, urging the Master to sail there in barges to do battle with the King of Castile, adding that they would help him to do so.

The Master first discussed this matter with Nuno Álvares and then with other members of his council: they all agreed that it was a good idea to go ahead. Afterwards, however, when once the Master set about studying how to put it into effect, he decided not to proceed, nor to make for Santarém in barges, which are boats that can only transport small numbers of men, when what was needed was to convey large numbers. In addition, the barges would reach no further than Muge, which lies 2 leagues away from the town, because there the waters of the Tagus were very shallow, preventing them from heading further upstream. But the main reason for having doubts about this undertaking was uncertainty as to whether the messages received were genuine or a contrivance of the King of Castile whereby to kill or capture the Master and all those accompanying him. For that reason the project was abandoned.

Chapter 73

How Queen Leonor wrote to Count Gonçalo, her brother, telling him to hand Coimbra over to the King of Castile

As at the very beginning the queen was in agreement with the King of Castile, she gave him to understand that he could easily seize and possess every town in the country because the leading figures in the kingdom were relatives of hers or of his wife; furthermore, everybody else who held towns and castles was under an obligation to her on the grounds of having belonged to her household or having received her favours. She added that, though there were a number of miscreants who had declared against him by indicating that they wished to oppose him, he should not trouble himself about the craziness of such men, for they were fools in pursuit of foolish notions based on vain hopes.

Moreover, she would write to her brother, Count Gonçalo, and to her uncle, Gonçalo Mendes de Vasconcelos, both of whom were in Coimbra, which was one of the main cities in the land; they would declare their allegiance to him and would hand the city over to him, even though they had not gone out to greet him when he had passed that way. If necessary, she would accompany him there as she would to the other townships, whensoever they were hesitating about handing themselves over to him.

Prior to this, according to what we have found in a document, Count Gonçalo had gone to Oporto to attend a memorial ceremony for King Fernando; the queen had written to him, requesting him to go to Coimbra, and had written to its honourable citizens, urging them to welcome and treat him with all due honour. He then went to Coimbra, accompanied by 100 lances. Occupying the castle and pleased at his arrival was its governor Gonçalo Mendes, uncle to the count and to the queen. It is said that, once the count had taken up lodging in the city, his uncle made him a promise that he would not hand over the castle, nor should the count hand over the city to anybody, without their mutual agreement. That, therefore, was the situation in Coimbra.

After the count's arrival he was joined there by João Rodrigues Pereira, João Gomes da Silva, Álvaro Gonçalves Camelo (who later became Prior of the Hospitallers), Nuno Viegas, Nuno Fernandes de Mariz, Nuno Fernandes de Penacova, Pero Gomes de Seabra, Martim Correia and others. Consequently, he had there with him 350 lances and was very secure and at ease.

When the queen spoke to the king, as we mentioned earlier, he asked her to write to her brother and to Gonçalo Mendes, urging them to hand the city over and to declare their allegiance to the king, for which he would reward them with many favours. We found that the letter which she wrote went as follows:

> Brother and friend, whom I love most fondly, I believe that you are well aware that I have renounced the governance of this realm and placed it in the hands of my son[-in-law], the King of Castile. It is my belief that thereby I did my duty, because, as you can see, my daughter would otherwise have been unable to regain this land and have authority over it, judging by how things have begun to turn out. As I know that your uncle, Gonçalo Mendes, though he has done me homage on behalf of Coimbra, cannot hand it over against your will, therefore I beseech you, as my brother and friend, in whom I have every confidence, kindly to declare your allegiance to the King of Castile, your nephew by marriage, accepting him as your liege lord. Thereby you will do your duty in fulfilment both of my honour and yours, and the king will reward you for it with many favours and will enhance your status. That is because it would be quite unacceptable both to me and to you, were the Master to gain control of Coimbra, thereby bringing dishonour on our lineage.

The queen likewise wrote to Gonçalo Mendes, pointing out that he was well aware of the honour and privileges which she had bestowed upon him, including the governorship of the castle, for which he had paid her homage. Accordingly, she besought him, without further ado, to declare his allegiance to her son[-in-law], the King of Castile, and to hand the castle over to him. By so doing, he would fulfil his duty towards her, bring her great pleasure and do her a great service. She assured him that the king would reward him with many favours, even more generously than he could imagine.

Chapter 74

Concerning what happened to certain men who emerged from Lisbon to fight the Castilians

While these letters are on their way to Coimbra, and some reply is to come back, let us see what was done by the Master of Santiago, by Pedro Fernández de Velasco and by Pedro Ruiz Sarmiento, whom we left in Lumiar, as you have heard.[94] One day, after they had taken up lodging in the villages a league away from the city, there was a foray of horsemen from the city ordered by the Master, led by João Fernandes Moreira, accompanied by a number of foot soldiers and crossbowmen. They headed for a large field known as Alvalade Grande, intending to provoke the Castilians into setting out against them and to lure them close to the city.

When the Castilians discovered that they had gone to that field, they sounded their trumpets, and their captains rode forth, accompanied by large numbers of their men, and the Portuguese turned back. As the Castilians drew closer, the Portuguese could not move forward fast enough not to be overtaken by them. Many were killed or captured, and João Fernandes himself was slain. Were it not for the vineyards where they took refuge, because the Castilian horsemen could not break through there, their enemies would have inflicted on them even greater slaughter.

The Master himself had gone forth that day, along with Nuno Álvares and some 300 lances from the city, as well as foot soldiers and crossbowmen. They took up battle formation on a ridge above the Church of São Lázaro, which is roughly two crossbow shots away from the city. There the Master awaited the arrival of the Castilians, who were following hard on the heels of those who had gone out as far as Alvalade, so that they would find him ready to confront

---

[94] In Chapter 71 above.

them. When the Castilians arrived and saw them drawn up on foot and in battle formation, they baulked at dismounting, decided among themselves not to give battle on that occasion and returned to the villages where they were billeted. As for the Master, he went back with his men into the city.

Chapter 75

Concerning the arguments which Nuno Álvares expressed to Count Álvaro Pérez de Castro and his son, and how the Master decided to do battle with the Castilian captains who were in Lumiar

Setting aside all bias, if you just stop to consider the Master's remarkable achievements, then it is certainly true, when we comment on this passage in our text, that he deserves huge praise. That is because, despite his great courage and daring, equal to that of the strongest and most virtuous heroes, there were nevertheless many adverse circumstances which were there to confront him, since he could see the vast bulk of Portugal ready to assail a tiny Portugal that still held out. Likewise, he knew that several of those who were heading to join him were feeble and faint-hearted when giving advice; moreover, he was led to regard others as suspect and of doubtful loyalty.

However, these and all the matters that you can well imagine, which were greatly disadvantageous to him, failed to move him from his firm intent; his immense and lofty courage remained undefeated by such storms. A typical case occurred after Count Álvaro Pérez de Castro came to join him: one day the Master related to him and his son all the events which had befallen him up to that point and told them what his intentions were.

As for the count, who was more inclined to favour the success and honour of the King of Castile than to support the Master's honourable cause, he held his achievements in low esteem, telling him that he had begun a difficult undertaking and that he, the count, was very doubtful as to whether the Master could bring it about with honour. In this way, a man who ought to have given him strength, having come to serve him, uttered these and similar words, which were enough to discourage him from everything which he had undertaken and was so keen to bring about.

Nuno Álvares, who was also present, simply could not tolerate his line of argument, nor could he hold back from addressing him. Here is his reply: 'Sir count, just let me tell you, since you have taken up with my lord the Master and honourably intend to serve him, that such arguments and advice as you have given him are neither honourable nor helpful to the common good. What is more, he should not believe a word of it but should go ahead with his plans and in no way turn back. I don't say this just in opposition to the King of Castile, who is a great and powerful king, but even if it were in opposition to every king in the world, the Master must continue to defend himself and defend all those who are subject to him. That is because he has the courage and good right to do so and because, except for him, there is nobody else in Portugal who is equipped to do this. Besides, all honourable Portuguese have good reason to serve and help him to follow through with what he has begun, offering their lives and possessions even unto death. Almighty God, who has summoned him to this task, will ensure that his deeds go from strength to strength, protecting and leading him to the goal that he desires. Anyone who is willing to serve him well and loyally will have ample time in which to demonstrate it.'

The count was angered by the way in which Nuno Álvares spoke to him, retorting at once, 'What's that, Nuno Álvares? How dare you speak to me like that? Aren't you ashamed to speak so freely?'

'Not at all', said Nuno Álvares, 'I don't regret a single word, only that I uttered so few.'

Dom Pedro, the count's son, then addressed Nuno Álvares: 'Have you no shame, Nuno Álvares, in speaking to my father like that?'

'None whatsoever', he replied. 'I'm not ashamed of what I said to your father nor of what I say to you. I said what I was bound to say in the service of my lord the Master and not for any other reason.' At this point, before they could exchange any more words, the Master ordered them to be silent, and they promptly obeyed.

When the Master realised that the Castilian captains had been at their ease in Lumiar for a good two weeks and had not left the place but merely skirmished from time to time near the city, he spoke to the Master of Santiago [in Portugal], to Nuno Álvares and to all the members of his council, announcing that it seemed to him to be a good idea to go and do battle with them. Rui Pereira, João Lourenço da Cunha and all the others present agreed that this should be done.

While they were discussing who the captains were who had come with the Castilian forces and were mentioning each one by name, whenever they said, for example, 'One of them is so-and-so, the Master of Santiago', the face of Count Álvaro Pérez would become contorted, and he would say, 'Ah, what a child!' Whenever they said, 'Oh, and such-a-body is one of them as well', he would reply with 'Now there's a simpleton!' Then, referring to another captain, he said, 'Ah, what a young puppy!' In this way he gave each one of them a special label, leading people, by his grimaces, to believe that it was a bad idea to do battle with them, and declaring that, in his view, they were honourable and excellent captains leading a vast army; moreover, since they received little trouble from them, the Portuguese should not be concerned about their presence there.

The Master declared that it was intolerable that, much to their vexation, the Castilians were so close to the city, without their reacting to it as they should. Then all his followers assembled their forces and made ready for the next day. The Castilians swiftly heard about this and hastily left, some of them heading for Alenquer, while others made their way to Torres Vedras, refusing to await their attack. On hearing of this, many of the Portuguese rushed to Lumiar and found the villages nearby abandoned, with pans still on the fire and meat still on skewers, which, in their hurry to depart, they had not had time to eat. Indeed, if other writers give a different account, from a viewpoint contrary to the truth, then it should be rejected.

Chapter 76

Why discord broke out between Queen Leonor and the King of Castile

People say that malice drinks most of its own poison, and this can certainly be said about Queen Leonor. That is because, lodging as she was in the same residence as her son-in-law the king, not many days passed before she began to dislike the king's company, and before he began to feel the same about her. They say that the displeasure which in the main the queen felt towards him began in the following way.

In Castile the Jewish chief rabbinate fell vacant at the very time when the queen sent the message to Coimbra about which you have already heard.[95] The post was sought from the king in Santarém, where he was, and, learning of this, Queen Leonor approached him on behalf of Dom Yehuda, King Fernando's former treasurer, and a trusted counsellor of hers. The king avoided granting this to her and acceded to the choice of his wife Queen Beatriz on behalf of Dom David Negro, who had likewise been a counsellor of King Fernando and was a wealthy and very honourable Jew who had begun to serve Queen Beatriz as soon as she had arrived in Santarém. Since Queen Leonor was a stout-hearted woman who was always used to getting her own way and who bore in

[95] In Chapter 73 above.

mind the approach she had adopted in bestowing on the king the governance of the realm, not to mention other matters, and since he had refused to accede to her choice for the rabbinate, which was in itself a trivial matter and the very first thing she had sought from him, she drew the conclusion that from then on she could expect little from him, especially as they were so different from one another both in character and in the way they discussed matters.

It is said that she was so furious with the king that she declared to a number of those who had accompanied her from Lisbon: 'Just see what sort of great lord this man is! Just what favours can we expect from him when he refuses to grant me such a trivial request? What favour is he ever likely to grant to me or to you? In fact, I swear to you that, if you want to take my advice, you'd all do well to go over to the Master, for he's your fellow-countryman and a great lord who will offer you better things. As for me, who would like to do so, I no longer have the means. Indeed, I expect things to get steadily worse for me, in view of the approach I now realise that the king adopts. Let me assure you that, if I could leave this place like you and with my honour intact, I wouldn't stay here a day longer.' In fact, that is what most of them went on to do, namely to go over to the Master.

It is also related that the reasons why the king began to dislike the queen's behaviour derived from the fact that he found that she talked very freely, with a way of speaking which was inappropriate for a widow, especially when so little time had passed since King Fernando's death and while she was still dressed in mourning. When he drew this to her attention in a private conversation, and her character proved resistant to such advice, this meant that after any argument they never parted in agreement.

Chapter 77

How King Juan left Santarém, bound for Coimbra, with the intention of taking it

As a result of these events the queen began very much to blame herself for what she had set in motion, not only for inducing the king to invade the kingdom, but also for renouncing the governance of the realm and bestowing it upon him. So, leaving to one side her original thoughts about this, it is said that she secretly sent letters to several places which the King of Castile planned to win over to his cause. In these letters she urged them, even if the king went there in person and she went along in his company, that they should not be handed over to him, however many arguments she might advance, or which she might get others to put forward. Among these places was the city of Coimbra.

At this point there came back a reply to the first message which she had sent to Count Gonçalo and Gonçalo Mendes, which you have already heard about. In his reply the count stated that he was very pleased at what she had written, but that her proposal could not be put into effect in any way, unless the king were to go there with his army, threatening to lay siege to the city with a view to its capture. That was because, otherwise, he doubted whether those who were there with him would agree to it; moreover, she should in any case accompany the king and not do anything else. Having noted this message, the king was very pleased with it and decided to leave with his army at once, taking both queens along with him. That day he reached Torres Novas, where he spent the night. The king and his wife lodged in the outskirts, whereas Queen Leonor took up separate lodgings and was guarded throughout the night by Castilian men-at-arms. The next day, when she realised this, she exclaimed to those who accompanied her, 'What's this? Am I to be guarded by Castilian troops? I can see that from now on I'm a prisoner.' On hearing of this, the king declared that he was doing it for the best and in order to ensure her safety, along with other disingenuous arguments.

He left Torres Novas and along his route he passed by Tomar and other townships. From these he met with a poor reception and he found the gates of the townships locked. The king told his followers privately that, before leaving Santarém, he had strongly suspected that he would be received in just such a way in these places.

Chapter 78

How King Juan reached Coimbra, and concerning certain things which happened there

The king arrived at Coimbra with a great army and took up lodging in the Palace of Santa Clara, close to the city bridge. The Count of Mayorga lodged in the Monastery [of Santa Clara], Count Pedro [of Trastámara] lodged in the Monastery of Santa Ana, accompanied by his brothers Alfonso Enríquez and Alfonso Enríquez the Younger. Count João Afonso de Barcelos, João Rodrigues Portocarreiro and Juan Alfonso Cabeza de Vaca[96] took up lodgings

---

[96] The *Diccionario Biográfico Español* online gives his full name as 'Juan Fernández Cabeza de Vaca'. The change in the Portuguese text to 'Affomsso' may

in the Monastery of São Francisco, whereas Dom João, the Count of Viana, camped nearby in a tent. Fernão Gomes da Silva and several knights lodged in the houses near the Church of São Martinho, in the bishop's enclosure, while others were billeted in the Monastery of São Jorge in walled gardens and in other places in that area.

After they had all been comfortably accommodated, they committed no offence nor showed any desire for combat. Rather, the Count of Mayorga and others made their way into the city every day to converse with Count Gonçalo and Gonçalo Mendes de Vasconcelos, and there they ate and drank with them. Through these emissaries the king requested them to hand the city over to him and to declare their allegiance to him, assuring them that he would pay the wages of all the soldiers who were with them, as well as promising immense favours to one and all. In addition, he indicated many reasons why they should do so. But Count Gonçalo replied that they would only hand over the city to the one to whom it belonged by right.

The king took note of the count's reasoning and sent back a message to say that the count should consider it right to hand the city over to him and that he would make him lord over the whole of Estremadura as far as Oporto; alternatively, he would give him towns and villages in the kingdom of Castile, wherever he chose and whatever contented him most. He should not pay any heed to his rank as count, for he would enhance his status and give him a much greater title than that. Those who delivered this message strongly urged him to accept, but he always gave the same answer as he had previously given. Consequently, the king sent him a further message to request that, as he did not wish to hand the city over to him and as he, the king, had the governance of the realm, he should remain where he was, without going to war with him about it.

The count answered that, if his sister without his advice and that of those with whom she ought to discuss the matter, had done what she had done, then she should deal with the matter herself, because he had nothing to do with it, and that the answer he had given was the one he would continue to give, no matter how many times they brought it to his attention.

One day the Count of Viana happened to cross the River [Mondego], in the direction of Vila Franca, and they arrived at a place called Arregaça, whereupon Martim Correia emerged from the city with a group of his men, plus a handful of foot soldiers and four crossbowmen. There followed a brief skirmish, in which six of the city's foot soldiers were killed and three were taken prisoner. While Martim Correia and the others with him were heading

---

have arisen out of a confusion with a later Bishop of Coimbra, João Afonso (or João Esteves) de Azambuja, or from a scribal error.

back, a certain squire from the king's household gave chase so carelessly that his horse hurtled with him into a vineyard, where foot soldiers from the city came out and slew him. The king witnessed him being killed and stripped of his armour. On seeing this, those in the king's encampment killed two of their prisoners.

After this, there sallied forth the Count of Mayorga and Pero Díaz de Cuaderma; on the other side there also sallied forth Count Gonçalo, Gonçalo Mendes and others. These latter captured a Castilian squire by the name of Garci de Villodre. Early the next day they sent him back to King Juan, along with all his armour. From then on there was no further conflict, except that from time to time one or the other side shot arrows at their opponents. Nuno Fernandes [de Penacova] discharged a shot from a windlass crossbow and struck an honourable knight called Juan Alfonso de Bolaño, killing him.

Chapter 79

Concerning the arguments which Dona Beatriz de Castro put to Alfonso Enríquez and what his answer was

If we are to relate this story in full, so that you become better informed as to why the King of Castile sent Queen Leonor out of the country and as to whether or not he had a just reason for doing so, let us see what a certain author tells us in his chronicle, for it presents us with a lengthier account than any other with regard to what happened.

It is important for you to know that the king hung on for a few more days, waiting to see whether Count Gonçalo or Gonçalo Mendes would change their minds. You should also be aware that Queen Leonor, who had given up her earlier hopes and was now suffering sad and bitter regrets, plainly revealed a troubled countenance, which enabled anybody to read her grim thoughts. Noticing this, Dona Beatriz, who was the daughter of Count Álvaro Pérez de Castro and a lady-in-waiting of the Queen of Castile, was one day discussing matters of the heart with Alfonso Enríquez, who was the brother of the king's cousin Count Pedro and who was greatly in love with her. This is what she said to him: 'You're well aware that Queen Leonor, who reared me in her household and raised my status by making me lady-in-waiting to her daughter, is now in great trouble, as we can all see. In my opinion, she expects the situation to get even worse, because matters aren't proceeding either according to the king's wishes or to hers. For that reason they are more at loggerheads than anybody can imagine. So, since you tell me that you love me so much as to want to marry me, I'm going to reveal to you something which I've been thinking about. If you were man enough to be able to get your brother the count to agree to what I've been planning, then I'd be only too happy to do all that you wish and require of me. In that way our marriage would be even better, and our honour would be greatly enhanced.'

'There's nothing', he replied, 'which you ask of me and which I can do for you, and which my brother can do in my honour, that we shall not most willingly accomplish. Just tell me what will please you.'

When once they had sworn and solemnly promised that these matters must be kept a close secret, Dona Beatriz began to present her plan as follows: 'You can see only too well how the affairs of this queen who reared me in her household have taken such a turn for the worse and very much run counter to what we all thought. If she doesn't escape from the king's control, then nothing but great dishonour will befall her. Consequently, if your brother the count, who is a man of great stature (and in my view he has a good relationship with her), were to devise a way by which she could be out of reach of the king's power and installed in the city with her brother the count and with us too alongside her, then her honour would be fully restored, and we would be even more honourably married. Let me add this: if your brother were able to do this and she were to be given back her total freedom, it would be no great surprise if she were later to marry him and thus share with him the governance of the country. After all, she has so many brothers, kinsfolk, and *criados* that she would be bound to gain control of the realm, and she would regain the governance that she formerly held.'

When Alfonso Enríquez heard these arguments, along with many others which they discussed in this regard, they struck him as being so well thought out that at once he willingly agreed to make every effort to bring her plan about, declaring that he would immediately discuss matters with his brother. For her part, she would discuss the plan with Queen Leonor.

Chapter 80

Concerning the discussions which Queen Leonor held with her brother Count Gonçalo

Dona Beatriz discussed her plan with Queen Leonor, and Alfonso Enríquez did so with his brother [Count Pedro]. The queen was very pleased with the advice, and Count Pedro no less so. Having talked the matter over at some length, they agreed to send Alfonso Enríquez to discuss it with Count Gonçalo. On learning about it, he was very pleased that such a plan was being considered.

That evening Count Pedro and his brother went into the city, both unaccompanied, to discuss the matter with Count Gonçalo, and Count Pedro told him everything that he wanted to do in this regard. Count Gonçalo said that he was very grateful to him and that, if he were to proceed with the proposal, then in himself he would gain a very good friend, who would do anything which would bring him honour, adding that he would await them with his men on the night when they would be ready. In order to do these things more secretly and to allay all suspicion, several of Count Gonçalo's men went under safe conduct to speak to Queen Leonor, as well as to Count Pedro, creating the impression and leading the king to believe that everything was being done to serve his best interests and to bring about his early take-over of the city.

Moreover, Queen Leonor expressed to King Juan the view that she should discuss the matter openly with her brother, to see whether she could change his mind in the course of their conversation, so that the king could take possession of the city, since in discussions with others it had proved impossible to get the count to agree. The king declared this to be an excellent suggestion but, though he did not know what was being transacted between them, he did not feel sure that there would not be any trickery. He therefore ordered the construction of a raised platform on the bridge in such a fashion that her brother could not seize her even when they were conversing together.

When the day for the discussion arrived, Count Pedro took Queen Leonor by the arm and she was accompanied by some twenty others. Count Gonçalo was already on the bridge with three or four of his men. When the queen arrived, he bowed low, took her hand and kissed it, whereupon she declared, 'A man kisses the hand that he'd like to see cut off!'

'My lady', said the count, 'That's true, but not in the case of yours!'

She replied: 'Well, if it's not true of my hand, why don't you give this city to my son[-in-law] the king, as I command you to? You amaze me! You know only too well the honour which I've given you, the enhancement of your status which I've bestowed upon you, and how you would not have set foot in this city were it not for me, yet you will not do me the honour of handing it over to the one to whom I command and beg you to give it.'

'What you say is true', he answered, 'and I'll happily hand it over to you at once, if you agree to come and join me here.'

'I'm a prisoner', she replied, 'and I can't go and join you there.'

He said: 'It's my opinion, precisely because I can see that you're a prisoner and in somebody else's power, that I would commit a great wrong if I were to hand the city over to the one who has taken you prisoner. But since you've acted as you pleased without my advice or the advice of those with whom you should discuss matters, then you'd better come to terms with him.'

'I can see', she said, 'that I've been abandoned by you and all my kinsmen, people to whom I've granted great favours and done much good.'

Likewise, those who were with the queen began to tell Count Gonçalo that they thought he was doing wrong in refusing to hand the city over to the king, when he could see that his sister was grievously at odds with the king because of that place. Were he to hand it over, the king would extend to him many favours, and they would be guarantors thereof.

'What I *will* do', said the count, 'is this: if the king, accompanied by 100 lances and bringing Queen Leonor with him, wishes to come and dine with me in this city, I shall give him a very fine meal.'

'The king would do no such thing', replied the queen. 'Those are just empty words.'

'Well, if you don't want to do that', he answered, 'then I don't know what else I can do.'

Then they all withdrew, but the two of them exchanged words that nobody could either hear or understand.

Chapter 81

Concerning the conversations between Queen Leonor's brother Count Gonçalo and Count Pedro

After her discussion with Count Gonçalo, Queen Leonor gave King Juan to understand that she was hoping that he, the king, would very soon take control of the city, despite the discussion which she had held with her brother, as a result of other matters which she had discussed with him afterwards. It is said that this was done in order to arrange sufficient time to put into effect what she and Count Pedro had plotted against the king. Here follows the way in which the aforesaid author describes the plan.

King Juan was to be killed one night by Count Pedro and a number of his followers; the count and all his men were then to install themselves in the city, as well as Queen Leonor along with him. Once married, Count Pedro would then immediately declare himself King of Portugal and she would continue as its queen. In that way she would remain liege lady of the realm as set down in the treaties, having renounced it [before] as she should not have done, because she could not do so according to law. She would then enter negotiations with the Master and go ahead with what she had to do.

However, Count Gonçalo knew nothing about the [planned] death of the king, nor about his sister's [intended] marriage to Count Pedro, nor, indeed, that the latter was going to declare himself king. That was because, when he discussed the matter with him, Count Pedro revealed none of his plans, except that he would install himself in the city along with Queen Leonor in order to wrest her from the King of Castile's control, thus making it plain to him that he was displeased with the king, owing to the eminence and favouritism which the king gave to Pedro Fernández de Velasco. In fact, with the many kinsmen he had, and the remaining troops of the King of Castile, who he believed would go over to him, Count Pedro believed that he could fulfil his plans. In particular, that was because the queen greatly encouraged him, telling him that they were in a position to achieve all that they wanted, owing to the kinsfolk and *criados* on whom she could count, not to mention those of King Fernando, who held many fortresses up and down the country, which they would at once hand over to him rather than to the King of Castile, so as to ensure that the realm remained fully independent.

It is important for you to know that a Franciscan friar was the main emissary who conveyed the messages relating to these matters from Count Gonçalo to the queen and Count Pedro, and he it was who brought back their replies. However, he knew nothing about the [planned] death of the king, nor of the other matters, since these had not been disclosed to Count Gonçalo. Whenever the friar went to speak to Count Pedro about the secret which the latter shared with the queen, the count immediately went to tell the king that the friar had come to see him and had spoken to him about the handover of the city. He explained why he was holding back and was doing everything for the best, and the king was very pleased at this explanation, since he expected every day to take control of the city.

Now it so happened that the friar who was handling this mission was personally acquainted and very friendly with the aforesaid Dom David Negro, on whom the king had conferred the rabbinate which we mentioned previously. For fear that, in the turmoil that was bound to ensue, when once Count Pedro and Queen Leonor had installed themselves in the city, some harm might befall this Jew and the small children that he had with him, the friar thought fit to advise him to leave the encampment and make his way into the city, while he, the friar, would find a means by which he could safely install him there with his honour intact. In the utmost secrecy, he informed him of this in writing, telling him that he should make his way there before a certain day which he then indicated.

On reading this message, the Jew could not have been more alarmed when he realised that it ran counter to the hopes entertained by the king and everyone in the encampment. Deeply uneasy, he urgently contrived for the friar to go and see him very privately, as the special friend that he was. The Jew asked him just what was implied by the written note which he had sent him. The friar answered that it might well happen that, on the day when it was said that the city would be handed over, such a tumult could break out as to endanger those in the encampment, and that he, the Jew, might suffer some mishap. For that reason, he had informed him of this. That was as much as the friar told him, so as to avoid revealing anything further.

The Jew was a wise man and understood only too well how much secrecy was involved in these matters. He pressed the friar so hard in the name of their friendship, with promises that he would in turn reveal to him other important matters affecting the encampment, that the friar disclosed to him in very great secrecy the following plan. On a given evening, once Count Pedro had sent a message indicating that he was in readiness, a bell would be rung in the city to announce that Count Gonçalo was emerging accompanied by a body of men; Count Pedro would be ready for this and would order a trumpet blast to show that he was about to ride against Count Gonçalo and counter his attack; while riding forth in this way, Count Pedro would take Queen Leonor with him. As Count Gonçalo showed that he was taking flight, Count Pedro would chase after him, showing in his turn that he was defeating him, would force an entry into the city and would install himself there with his brothers, all of his men and the queen; this and no other would be the true handover of the city. However, the friar was not able to reveal to Dom David how Count Gonçalo and Count Pedro, as soon as this had been accomplished, would return with all their men, attack the encampment, seize Queen Leonor (if Count Pedro had not already managed to take her with him) and slay the king and certain others whom they had decided should meet the same fate.

After they had discussed these matters at some length, the friar swore the Jew to the utmost secrecy, and the latter promised him that he would keep the secret and would make every effort to leave the encampment before the appointed day. With their friendship enhanced, they then took their leave of one another.

Chapter 82

How what Count Pedro was intending to do was discovered, and how he fled to Oporto

Too anxious to delay informing King Juan about all this, the Jew immediately hurried off to tell him everything which he had discussed with the friar. On hearing this, the king was greatly alarmed and could not believe what the Jew was telling him, despite his assertions that what he said was true. It was not surprising that the king did not believe it, since Count Pedro was his first cousin, being the son of Don Fadrique, the Master of Santiago and brother of King Enrique, who was the father of King Juan.

At this point the king sent for Queen Beatriz and told her all that the Jew had said. The queen had at once no difficulty in believing it, declaring, 'Let me tell you, sire, that I've always been suspicious of this man, because of the great affection which I saw him show for my mother, though I've never mentioned this to you before now.'

When the day dawned on which the plan was due to be put into action, the king summoned the Count of Mayorga, revealed to him everything that the Jew had said and added: 'Secretly warn all your men to be armed and in readiness this evening, and you along with them, for when Count Pedro pretends to ride out against those from the city. You and your men are to yell out, 'Treachery! Treachery! Count Pedro's treachery!' Then you should arrest him and as many of his men as you can, or kill them if they're unwilling to surrender.' He also told one of his knights to arrange guards to be posted that evening on Queen Leonor, so that she could neither be seized nor installed in the city.

Guarding the king that evening was Count Pedro's responsibility, and he strove as best he could to prepare what was necessary in order to complete what he had undertaken. And since the task was now very difficult and dangerous to carry out, he took so long in going to the palace that the guards on duty were due to stand down, and thus the king would be left with no guard at all.

For this reason, the Count of Mayorga told the king that he thought it best if fifty of his own lances were to come to the palace, lest it be without a guard at such a time. The king was happy to agree to this, and at once they swiftly came and stood in readiness. At this point, a squire, who was one of those whom Count Pedro had let into the secret, was walking through the palace to take note of what they were doing. Suspecting that Count Pedro's secret had been discovered when he saw those men arriving, arrayed as they were, he hurried to his side and said, 'My lord, what are you doing?' 'What do you mean?' came the reply. 'I assure you', said the squire, 'that troops loyal to the Count of Mayorga are already in the palace and are armed in readiness for guard duty.'

On hearing this, Count Pedro felt that he had been found out and was so disturbed that he did not know what else to do, other than that he, his brothers and as many as possible of his men should swiftly gather up their best possessions and head for the bridge. When Count Gonçalo learned that he was making off in this way and was not taking his sister [Queen Leonor] with him, he was very surprised and asked him why he was leaving in such a fashion. Count Pedro replied that he had been found out and was fleeing in fear of his life, because the king was bound to order his death.

Count Gonçalo was far from being convinced by this, believing that it was all talk and not the truth. Accordingly, he refused to let Count Pedro into the city, adding that, with things as they were, he should go and lodge in the outskirts, whereupon he went to the Monastery of Santa Cruz and stayed there. Meanwhile, the king had not gone to sleep and was fully armed in his chamber waiting for the signal that was due to be given by the city. However, when he realised that time was passing and found out that Count Pedro had already fled, he grasped that Count Pedro had learned what had been revealed to him. That very night the king ordered the arrest of Dom Yehuda, Queen Leonor's trusted adviser, as well as Maria Peres, her lady-in-waiting, because he believed that they knew about the plan.

The king did not succeed in finding out immediately whether Count Pedro was now inside the city or outside but, when he learned that he was in the outskirts, he ordered 1,000 lances to ford the river to arrest him. Finding out about this, Count Gonçalo sent him a message telling him to get himself to safety. Consequently, Count Pedro rushed away to Oporto as fast as he could go. On his arrival there, and when he had related what had befallen him, he was allowed into the city, even though they did not wholly trust him, wondering whether he was planning some deception. The reason for this was that, without knowledge of the secret plan, nobody could imagine anything other than that, on behalf of King Juan and with his consent, he had left his presence in order to seize some town.

Some said that they should kill him, others that they should let him be. Finally, they decided to keep him under close observation, but without holding him prisoner, until such time as they had informed the Master [of Avis] of his arrival in Oporto and received his orders as to what to do with him.

Chapter 83

Concerning the words exchanged between King Juan and Queen Leonor in respect of these events

The king's feeling was that morning took a long time coming before he could know the truth and be certain as to what had happened. At last dawn broke and, having attended a very early Mass, he ordered Dom Yehuda to be brought to his chamber, along with the lady-in-waiting [Maria Peres]. Nobody else was present other than the king, his wife the queen, the Prince of Navarre,

Dom David (who had revealed the secret) and a clerk to write everything down. On the arrival of Dom Yehuda and Maria Peres, the king ordered that they should be stripped and submitted to torture. The Jew declared that there were no grounds for dishonouring him in this way, indeed he would state the truth of the matter. He then began to explain how Queen Leonor had written to all the governors of the castles which they had passed, urging them not to hand them over to the king. He also reported on all the conversations with Count Gonçalo which had taken place up to that point and how they were about to install Count Pedro and Queen Leonor in the city. He described how Count Pedro planned to declare himself king, having first killed King Juan, and mentioned all the other matters which we have told you about. Maria Peres then made the same confession, and everything was written down and confirmed by them.

The king then asked them whether they would say the same thing in the presence of Queen Leonor, and they said that they would. Next the king sent for Queen Leonor, who was led by the arm by the same knight whom the king had commanded to keep a watchful eye on her. Despite being brought to the king as though a prisoner, she entered fearlessly, without revealing any change in her demeanour, since she was a woman of great courage. She entered the chamber alone and without any other company. On seeing the Jew who had revealed the secret, she forcefully challenged him, 'So here you are, Dom David! You who are the cause of my presence here!' To this the king retorted, 'The one who saved my life has far more right to be present than the one who had plotted my death.'

The king then asked the clerk to read out to Queen Leonor everything that the Jew had said against her. On hearing what he had confessed, she complained at him, 'You treacherous dog! You said that about *me*?' 'Yes, I did', he answered, 'That is what I said and what I now say is the truth and what really happened.'

'You're a liar and a treacherous cur!' she retorted. 'And, if that *is* what really happened, then it was on *your* advice to me.' Just as she was about to dispute the matter, Queen Beatriz broke in, 'Oh, mother! Oh, my lady! In the space of a year would you really like to see me widowed, orphaned and disinherited?'

The king said: 'Now look, there is no point in arguing further. I have no wish to kill you, out of respect for your daughter's honour, even though that is what you deserve from me, and it would be quite wrong for you to continue in my company and for me to remain in yours. But what I *shall* do is send you to a highly respected convent in Castile, where queen dowagers and kings' daughters have resided in the past, and I shall arrange for you to receive such upkeep as will enable you to live well and honourably there.'

Queen Leonor answered the king quite fearlessly, saying: 'Do that to a sister of yours, if you have one, and dispatch her to that convent to be a nun. But you'll never get me to be a nun, and nobody will ever witness such a thing. This really is a fine reward for you to bestow on me! I gave up the governance of the realm and handed to you the greater portion of Portugal and now, at the words of some wretched dog, who is so terrified that he'll say that God isn't God, you accuse me of raving, in order not to keep the promises which you made to me and on which we received together the Body of Christ in Santarém. Let me tell you just what people will say about this: they'll say that if you want to kill your dog, first give out that it is mad.'

Disregarding what Queen Leonor had to say, the king gave orders for the lady-in-waiting to be made a prisoner but forgave the Jew at the behest of Dom David. Nothing more was done at that time.

Chapter 84

How Queen Leonor was taken to Castile

King Juan consulted on this matter with those with whom he needed to discuss it, declaring that it seemed to him to be perfectly reasonable to order the arrest of his mother-in-law, to dispatch her to some convent in Castile and to ban her from remaining any longer in Portugal as a result of what had happened.

Some members of his Royal Council stated that the king was quite right in what he said and that he should give orders for it to be carried out, adding that, if the queen remained any longer in the kingdom, she would send messages to the noblemen who held the fortresses, urging them not to hand them over to the king, nor to go over to his side. Such a thing would be very much against his best interests and would constitute a major setback to all that they had set in train.

Others declared that it was wrong for the king to arrest his mother-in-law the queen, and for him to do what he intended, given that she had renounced the governance of the realm, which she was duty-bound to hold as set down in the treaties, and had conferred that governance on him. Furthermore, she had handed over to him the town of Santarém and other castles, as everyone was well aware; in particular, since she was the mother of his wife Queen Beatriz and was a lady held in the greatest honour, they considered it unreasonable and undesirable for the king to send her away in this manner. However, the king adhered to the first of these opposing viewpoints, namely that it was right to arrest her and take her away to Castile; so, she was at once handed over to Diego López de Estúñiga.

The king then left Coimbra and made his way back to Santarém, from where they set out with the queen, to take her to Castile and install her in the convent at Tordesillas. While on the journey she very furtively wrote letters to Martim Eanes de Barbuda and Gonçalo Eanes [de Abreu], of Castelo de Vide, urgently pleading with them, with many reasons why they should do so, to make ready to snatch her away, while still on her journey, from those who were conveying her to Castile. Unfortunately, the letters were delivered so late that they had no opportunity to carry out her request, and so she was taken to Castile and to the aforementioned convent.[97]

As for Maria Peres, she was tortured into confessing where Queen Leonor had put a quantity of gold, silver and other gems; indeed, it is said that in Santarém she confessed that many things were to be found in the house of a worthy man of that town whom the queen greatly trusted, and that the king took possession of most of them.

Chapter 85

Concerning the message which the people of Alenquer sent to the Master [of Avis], and how he answered them

On learning that Queen Leonor was a captive in Coimbra and how the King of Castile was treating her, the inhabitants of Alenquer all agreed that it was right to go over to the Master, though cautiously and subject to certain conditions. They sent Vasco Martins de Alteiro and Álvaro Fernandes do Rego to convey their message to Lisbon. On entering the Master's presence and after presenting their credentials, they made the following proposal: 'Great lord, the honourable men of Alenquer and we along with them, bearing in mind that we are all Portuguese and all born in this realm, consider it right that we are bound to love its honour and interests, especially [standing] against those who wrongly and illegally seek to harm and wage war on it, just as

---

[97] Recent scholarship indicates that she died in the Convent of Nuestra Señora de la Merced in Valladolid, Castile, at a date between 1403 and 1410. See Isabel de Pina Baleiras, 'Portugal, 1385- A people's choice or coup d'état?', in Ana Maria S.A. Rodrigues, Manuela Santos Silva, Jonathan W. Spangler (eds), *Dynastic Changes Legitimacy and Gender in Medieval and Early Modern Monarchy*, 1st Ed. (Abingdon: Routledge, 2020), pp. 43-68, note 44.

the King of Castile is doing at this time, along with those who are helping his party, in his wrong and illegal endeavour to force it to undergo grim and severe subjection. Accordingly, we agree that it is better for us to declare our allegiance to you and to hold this town on your behalf and in your name. We do this on the following condition, namely that, if Queen Leonor is released, though she is currently a prisoner in the King of Castile's power, and if she is freely restored to power, in such a way that neither King Juan nor anybody else can restrict or otherwise wrong her against her will, then you should vigorously confirm the donation to her of Alenquer in line with what was laid down by your brother King Fernando. Moreover, as for the revenue and entitlements which in the meantime you will receive from the town, you should arrange for them to be handed over to her, wherever you wish, and should confirm the town's inhabitants in their ancestral rights and traditions.'

The Master answered them and said that, since he was mindful of their noble intent in respect of the honour and defence of the realm and since he honoured the queen as though she were his own mother, he would do everything he could to preserve her honour. He went on: 'Were she to seek to maintain the honour and defence of this realm, which is what we believe she will do henceforth, considering the approach to her adopted by the King of Castile and his ill-treatment of her, we are pleased to grant to her what you and your inhabitants are asking for. This we say, provided that they [the town's inhabitants] declare their allegiance to us forthwith, make ready to preserve the honour and defence of this realm and remit to us the revenue of the town. We grant and confirm that, once the queen is able to exert her power freely, she shall have the town of Alenquer just as she formerly did, on the condition that, when once the town is handed back to her at our behest, she should swear and promise that she does so to promote the honour, noble heritage and defence of this kingdom, not only against the King of Castile, but also against all who venture against it. Furthermore, if she fails to do so and gives advice to do the opposite, either in word or deed, then the grant that we make shall become null and void. The honourable men of Alenquer shall be expected to rise up against her and to wage war (as well as to seek peace) on our behalf. In addition to confirming to them their rights and traditions, it is our intention to acknowledge this with many graces and favours.'

Then the Master issued documents to them in respect of all these matters, and on receipt of this reply they went back to report to the inhabitants of Alenquer, who became the Master's supporters.

Chapter 86

How King Juan came to leave Santarém, and concerning the Royal Council he held on whether to lay siege to Lisbon

The King of Castile, having realised that he needed more companies of soldiers than were present with him, and with matters developing in ways he did not anticipate, had already commanded the Marquess of Villena, the Archbishop of Toledo and Pero González de Mendoza, whom, for that purpose, he had left behind in Torrijos, near Toledo, to send him up to 1,000 well-equipped lances. These were made ready and dispatched to the king just as he had commanded.

On 10 March the king left Santarém with all the forces which he had mustered there, taking with him his wife Queen Beatriz. He left a knight named Lope Fernández de Padilla in charge of the castle and, in the other fortress, known as the Alcáçova, he left another knight by the name of Fernán Carrillo. They were both provided with sufficient troops to guard everything.

The king went to Alenquer, where Vasco Peres de Camões came out to greet him, handing the town over to him and making all due homage. The same was done by Fernão Gonçalves de Meira in respect of Torres Vedras and by João Gonçalves Teixeira, who had been captain of the crossbowmen in King Fernando's day, in respect of Óbidos; this was against the wishes of the inhabitants of these townships. The king took up lodging in Bombarral, a village in the Óbidos area, and stayed there for some four days, before leaving again for the township of Arruda, where, out of fear, a number of the inhabitants took refuge in a cave, thinking it would provide a means of defence or escape. On finding out about this, the Castilians thrust fire into the cave, and some forty inhabitants were burnt to death.

Grooms of the bedchamber went ahead to prepare the chamber where the king was due to take up lodging and, on entering it, came upon two men hiding there, armed with swords and with daggers in their belts. They seized them and held them prisoner until the King of Castile arrived; when they appeared before him, and he learned about how they had been discovered, he addressed those present as follows:

'Even though these men assert that they had hidden out of fear, this surely can't be true; rather, they came here on the Master's orders, so that they could kill me while I slept.' He duly gave the order for them to be hanged.

At this point the king summoned his Royal Council on whether to lay siege to the city of Lisbon, or whether to advance through the entire country waging war, since a state of war now so openly existed between the Portuguese and the Castilians.

Some of his counsellors told him that it was inopportune to lay siege to the city, on the grounds that numbers of his troops were already beginning to die from the plague, and that this would cause them much greater harm if they were all together in one spot than if they were dispersed throughout the country; moreover, it would be preferable, since a large portion of the realm was rebelling against him, to go forth and subject it to his power, punishing those who refused to obey him, rather than to lay siege to the city at that time. This was especially so, since, even if he were to pitch his encampment around Lisbon, the city would not thereby be totally surrounded, because access by sea was not impeded, and his fleet had not arrived to impose a blockade on its use. Furthermore, he had no siege engines or other devices with which to create havoc in the city, and, even if he had, they would be of very little avail, owing to the large number of people who were inside the city walls; for those reasons it was better not to lay siege to Lisbon.

Other counsellors were totally opposed to this view and declared that, the moment his fleet arrived, he should immediately lay siege to the city, because Lisbon was the pre-eminent city and the capital of the kingdom; all other towns and cities were watching to see what would happen in Lisbon, so that, once it was seized, the whole of Portugal would be conquered. Besides, the Master was in the company of many of those who, along with their forces, had declared against King Juan; with the Master were also the city's inhabitants, as well as others who had flocked to it from the surrounding area. This being so, their food supply could not last for long, and for that reason they would not be able to defend the city against the king for very long either; he was bound to seize it in due course, despite their resistance.

The king thought that the latter argument was the right one. Trusting in this advice, which later proved to be detrimental to him, he decided that, as soon as his fleet arrived, he would at once lay siege to the city, and that, meanwhile, he and his men would find the surrounding villages and area much more amenable to what he wanted.

Let us now leave the king at his ease, waiting, along with all his forces, for his fleet to arrive, since for the time being there is nothing more to relate in his regard. Let us see what the Master did over this period, along with Lisbon's inhabitants, to prepare the city's defences, for they had a good fifty days freely available to them for that purpose.

Chapter 87

How the Master decided to appoint Nuno Álvares Pereira as Officer of the Marches for the Alentejo

In the midst of these events which we have described and which you have heard about, many messages reached the Master in Lisbon, in which he was told that many townships and castles in the Alentejo were declaring their allegiance to him, and that the inhabitants of these places were forcibly seizing them from those who were holding them on behalf of the King of Castile; these messages were received with the greatest pleasure by the Master and by all those who were with him.

While this good news was arriving, he received a new message which caused considerable concern, because a number of town councils in that province told him that, owing to their declarations of allegiance to him, which greatly irked the King of Castile, the king had commanded his High Admiral Fernán Sánchez de Tovar, after getting the fleet ready for its attack on Lisbon, to assemble his men and head through the Alcántara area, to where the Master [of the Order of Alcántara] was to be found. These forces, along with Juan Alfonso de Guzmán, who was the Count of Niebla, and Dom Pedro Álvares, who was Prior of the Order of the Hospitallers, as well as other great lords and their companies, were to attack the townships which had declared for the Master and lay waste that entire area; after that, they were to join the king in laying siege to Lisbon. They had laid siege to Portalegre for five days, cut down vineyards and olive groves and created immense havoc. This was what they were doing wherever they went, and for that reason the people of this area were pleading with the Master to send them some captain under whom they could all assemble, in order to drive the enemy out of their province.

The Master discussed this occurrence with a number of those whom he trusted. When they came to discuss Count Álvaro Pérez de Castro and whether it was advisable to send him there, great doubts were raised about him, because he was a kinsman of Queen Leonor, not to mention other reasons which we shall touch on in due course. Likewise, when discussing others, they had certain doubts about them also, so that the Master eventually said that he could see no one more suited to such a task, nor more desirous of carrying it out, than Nuno Álvares Pereira, provided that it pleased him to take up the charge. Doctor João das Regras was very much against this, declaring that for so important an undertaking it was essential to send someone of mature authority, and considerable wisdom, who had knowledge of warfare; besides, Nuno Álvares had brothers among the enemy, not to mention other reasons which he advanced as to why he should not be the man to go.

The Master did not heed those who opposed his view and spoke to Nuno Álvares, entrusting him with the enterprise and advancing every noble reason to bolster his courage and to explain why he placed his trust in him, reasons of the kind that were expedient in such circumstances. Without any greed for honours or gain, but solely to serve his liege lord and to defend his native land, Nuno Álvares accepted his task and commission, as one who most willingly nurtured a deep desire to serve the Master in anything that might come his way. Everybody then learned that Nuno Álvares would be going as officer of the marches for the province of the Alentejo. He arranged to take with him some forty honourable squires from within the city. This was not for the Master's security,[98] as some write, but because it was always his wish to have in his company men who by their deeds were worthy of being called men.

We shall list here, for you to see and always to remember, the names of a number of those who went with him: João Vasques de Almada,[99] Pedro Eanes Lobato, Rui Cravo, Afonso Peres da Charneca, Antão Vasques, Vasco Leitão, João Álvares, Master Manuel [Pessanha], Álvaro do Rego, João Lobato, Estêvão Eanes Borboleta, Lopo Afonso da Água, his brother Lourenço Afonso, Lourenço Martins Pratas, Diogo Durães, and Diogo Domingues, the son of Domingos de Santarém. These men and other honourable squires, both from Évora and from Beja, who at that time were in Lisbon and had come to join the Master, because, uncertain as to their allegiance, the ordinary folk had cast them out of their towns and villages, now set out in the company of Nuno Álvares when he departed.

Chapter 88

Concerning the banner which Nuno Álvares ordered to be made, and about the powers which the Master gave him

When Nuno Álvares took on this undertaking, as we have said, and thinking that, not only in major matters, but also in very minor ones, we should always seek help from that Lord, without Whom nothing can have

[98] This apparently strange possibility, as the final sentence of this chapter reveals, is due to uncertainty about their allegiance and to the alleged desirability, 'as some write', of removing them from proximity to the Master of Avis.

[99] Brother of Antão Vasques de Almada and son of Vasco Lourenço de Almada, a family of staunch supporters of the Master of Avis.

a worthy beginning or end, he decided, deep in his soul, to cling to God as his principal guide in all that he did. He also resolved to direct his worldly actions to the very best of his ability and in every instance within the limits of his human frailty.

Thus, since it is important, wherever the greatest dangers lie, devoutly to recall that Lord on Whose help man so much relies, Nuno Álvares ordered a banner to be made, on which there was a white field with a great red cross in the middle. In the first quarter, on the flagpole side, was depicted the image of Our Saviour Jesus Christ crucified, with His Mother and Saint John close by. In the second quarter, on the fly side of the banner, was the image of the Blessed Virgin, with her Blessed Son in her arms. In the first of the two base quarters, the dexter, on the flagpole side, had Saint George, in armour and kneeling, with his hands joined in prayer and looking upwards, while the sinister displayed Saint James in the same posture, each one of them with his bascinet in front of him. By this means, when the banner was unfurled, in such places where it was appropriate, and he beheld the images of Our Saviour and His Blessed Mother, his heart would be more devoutly uplifted into calling on Their aid. In the corners of the banner were placed four small shields bearing his family coat of arms, a cross argent voided on a gules field.

The Master gave Nuno Álvares letters to present to every town or village which had declared for him, announcing that he was sending him to that region as its officer of the marches and defender, and ordering them to be ready to carry out his commands and to supply him with whatever things he required from them in the Master's service and in defence of the realm, as though he, the Master, were there in person. And to bolster the courage of those who accompanied him, as well as of those others who would come to join him, so that they would more eagerly carry out whatever tasks were entrusted to them, and since the hope for swift reward makes great travail seem but slight, Nuno Álvares begged a favour from the Master: he wished to be granted the power to distribute the property of any persons who did not declare for him, and requested that, if such property had been distributed by him in the first instance, rather than by the Master, his distribution should be regarded as valid. He also requested the power freely to give out monies and to grant other favours and honours to whosoever deserved them.

Not simply in this regard, but also in respect of the allegiance from the castles and the administration of justice, not to mention all other matters, the Master conferred on him plenipotentiary powers. Nuno Álvares was immediately paid a month's salary and then made ready to set out.

Chapter 89

Concerning the instructions which the Master gave to Nuno Álvares, and how he took his leave

Great affection and goodwill had grown up between Nuno Álvares and the Master ever since he first arrived and began to serve the Master. This was, according to what a number of authors have written, because both of them were men of great courage and led virtuous lives. Furthermore, since there is nothing which produces a greater bond between men than sharing the same noble objectives, the Master was reluctant to let Nuno Álvares take his leave of him in Lisbon when setting out from the city. Rather, when Nuno Álvares made his way via Almada and then on to Coina, which lies 3 leagues further on, the Master arrived aboard a galley and ate that day with him.

After they had eaten, the Master made for a spacious area nearby, taking with him Nuno Álvares and all his company. When they were all assembled, the Master addressed Nuno Álvares in such a way that many of those present heard what he had to say, as follows: 'Nuno Álvares, you know well the messages which have reached me from the Alentejo concerning those great lords and forces from Castile which are invading that region to wreak havoc there; you also know that the towns and villages which have declared for me have written pleading with me to send them a captain with whom they could join, in order to prevent the Castilians from wreaking any more havoc than what they have begun to do. Since I love and trust you, and because you are valiant and suited for this task, I have chosen you from among all the others, in order to send you to that region. As your companions I have given you these brave troops which are here present, for they are true Portuguese, and some of them are from my own household. It is my firm belief that, in whatever you happen to set your hand to, they will loyally follow you and will help to fulfil everything which is in my interests and to your greater honour. That is what I beg and order them to do, urging them to obey you and carry out your commands in everything you say, just as they would for me. I shall deem it a great service to me and, for acting in that way, I shall confer on them great favours.'

They all joyously answered him, declaring that it gave them immense pleasure to do so, and that they would most willingly carry out what he said. The Master then turned to Nuno Álvares to say that he entrusted to him the brave troops which he was taking with him, asking him to treat them well and to provide for them generously, as he was sure that he would; indeed, doing so would bring him much pleasure and would be of great service to him.

Nuno Álvares replied that he was very happy and willing to do this. He then kissed the Master's hands, as did all the others with him. The Master then left for Lisbon, and Nuno Álvares set out with his men for Setúbal.

Chapter 90

Concerning a ruse employed by Nuno Álvares to test his men's mettle

That day Nuno Álvares reached Setúbal, planning to lodge there and spend the night in the town. However, since they were still undecided as to which side they were on, the inhabitants refused to greet him and would not even let him into the town. In the light of the intentions they showed and of this shabby welcome, he turned about and went off to spend the night in the outskirts of the town, taking up lodging there along with his troops.

Now consider how praiseworthy Nuno Álvares is for his great skill and foresight in his approach to the war that was about to begin. Surely, he deserves to be portrayed as an example to great and courageous men; indeed, there is no hero of note whom we might seek to praise, whose talents he does not in some measure share. Since he realised that he was leading certain young men who, as yet, had no experience of danger, while there were others whose intentions he knew nothing about, he decided to test what their mettle would be when confronted by their enemies. On the grounds that there were large numbers of the King of Castile's forces at that time in Santarém, and lest some of them should advance down the bank of the Tagus without his knowledge, wreaking havoc, Nuno Álvares declared that he thought it right to post his guards and scouts a league away, in the direction of the castle of Palmela. He gave the task of directing and posting these guards and scouts to a knight named Lourenço Fernandes de Beja. Nuno Álvares had a private word with him, urging him to come back at night and in a great hurry, announcing that Castilian troops were attacking him.

Lourenço Fernandes went off to position his guards and scouts. Then, when Nuno Álvares was asleep that night in his lodging, Lourenço Fernandes suddenly arrived, urging Nuno Álvares to get ready at once because Pedro [Ruiz] Sarmiento was about to attack him with 300 lances, and asserting that he had seen fires in the places where the Castilians were lodging. Nuno Álvares showed that he was very pleased at this news and ordered trumpets to be blown. All armed and at the ready, his men at once gathered around him, just as dawn was beginning to break. Nuno Álvares set out with his troops and, as soon as he left the outskirts of Setúbal, he drew them all up in due battle formation; thus they advanced, ranged on foot over a good league, facing in the direction where Lourenço Fernandes said that he had seen the fires.

When once it was broad day, he announced that the fires he had seen were those of muleteers who had corralled their animals in a great valley, and so they turned back. Nuno Álvares looked over his troops and saw that they were all present, with no one missing, and that they had shown the daring and willingness necessary to tackle anything that might befall them. He was delighted with them when he saw just how eager they were.

Chapter 91

Concerning the way in which Nuno Álvares chose from his men those who were to serve on his council

The following day Nuno Álvares summoned most of those accompanying him, announcing that he wished to discuss with them a number of matters that would both benefit them and be of service to their liege lord the Master of Avis. He began as follows:

'My friends, I'm about to tell you what thoughts I've been having concerning our enterprise. It is important, nay sensible, that from time to time we should receive messages from the Master and also that he should receive messages from us. Similarly, we should receive frequent information about our enemies, so as to enable us to avoid any harm they might inflict on us and to hinder their attempts to do so with as little risk as possible. With regard to such matters it is important for us to have our own council, in order to reach a decision on every issue and on what we consider might best be of service to our liege lord the Master, as well as bringing honour to you all. However, if we were to constitute a council from everyone now here present, that would be quite preposterous, and its deliberations would swiftly become known to those outside the council, which does not befit good warriors. As I see it, therefore, the best way to proceed will be that, when such issues as these crop up and require your advice, I should discuss the matter with a group of you, so that, with your agreement, we can decide on what you think is the best way ahead. However, were I to choose a number of you myself, in the belief that they were the best men to advise me, then those who are their equals would at once take umbrage and would be forever disgruntled, maintaining that out of disregard for them I had not chosen them for the council and had not considered them good enough. Therefore, I think it best if those from Lisbon elect from their number those they deem suitable to discuss confidential matters with me. The same applies to those from Évora, Beja and other towns, if there are any; in such a way I shall be able to hold council meetings with them as is appropriate. Afterwards, they can explain to you whatever needs to be revealed and can require of you whatever things pertain to each and every one of you.

'Likewise, since we fight in a just quarrel and a righteous cause in defence of our country and since we believe that God is a just judge, let us cleave unto Him to seek His help. If we do that and trust firmly in God, then, few as we are, we will vanquish many enemies. In addition to that, I recommend to you that our help and assistance to our fellow-countrymen should be delivered in such a way that, as we make our way throughout the land in its defence, they should not experience the kind of harm which they suffer from their enemies. Otherwise, I shall be obliged to react by doing something which you will find disagreeable and which I would not want ever to happen.'

They answered him by saying that they were happy to do things in such a way, and that he had thought things out so well that they could not be bettered; moreover, in this regard as in all other respects it was their intention to carry out his wishes to the best of their ability.

Those from Lisbon then elected the following to serve on the council: João Vasques de Almada, Afonso Peres da Charneca, Vasco Leitão and Pedro Eanes Lobato; those from Évora elected Diogo Lopes Lobo, João Fernandes da Arca and Lopo Rodrigues Façanha; others were similarly elected. It was then that they began to address Nuno Álvares as 'My lord'.

Chapter 92

How Nuno Álvares summoned certain troops, and concerning the arguments he expressed to the entire force

Before leaving that area,[100] Nuno Álvares at once appointed his officers. One squire, Diogo Gil by name, he installed as his standard bearer; he also appointed a bailiff, a magistrate, a jailer and a treasurer to receive monies from the Master's treasurer. He made arrangements for his chapel and appointed a preacher. He attended Mass twice a day, something which no king or great lord was previously in the habit of doing.

---

[100] The area between Setúbal and Palmela.

Nuno Álvares then left with his troops and made his way to Montemor-o-Novo, where he halted for one day, because the honourable citizens of the town were not yet wholly committed to the Master's service. He spoke to them, advancing many arguments on the Master's behalf, with the result that they were happy in their resolve to declare their allegiance to him.

Next day, Nuno Álvares left Montemor and made for Évora, where he was well received and highly honoured. He discussed with the townsfolk what was needed for the town's protection and for the defence of the realm, at which they were very pleased, owing to his gracious words and warm approach to them; they were all happy to obey him, as though he had been their liege lord for a long time. From Évora he at once sent out letters to all the towns and villages in that area, summoning their people, with weapons at the ready, as behoved them, but without declaring to them what he wanted to do.

Despite the fact that he wrote to them that they should come to him with all due haste in the service of his lord the Master, there appeared only 30 lances, which with his own 200 lances, made a total of 230. As for foot soldiers and crossbowmen, his total force came to 1,000. With these forces he immediately left Évora and made his way to Estremoz. There he received definite news that those great lords from Castile,[101] along with their forces, were all assembled in the town of Crato, which had declared for Castile, and were heading to lay siege to Fronteira.[102] There were great numbers of them, and they were well equipped.

On receiving this message, Nuno Álvares, since he was lodging on the outskirts of Estremoz and had few forces at his disposal, gave immediate orders for everything to be enclosed in a defensive stockade and in such a way that they could hear if any forces attempted to attack him by night. Thus he waited at Estremoz for the troops which he had summoned but which had not come yet, not even those from Elvas and Beja, to whom he had written more times than to anyone else.

Nevertheless, because of his persistent letters, they felt compelled to go and join him. When they were all assembled, he mustered them in an open space. There were few men-at-arms, and they were not well equipped: on horseback there were only some 300 and, of those, just 180 wore bascinets; there were scarcely more than 1,000 foot soldiers and up to 100 crossbowmen. He addressed them together as follows: 'My friends, I believe that you already know that the Master, my liege lord and your own, has sent me to this area, so that with God's help and yours we might defend it from any harm or damage which the Castilians might inflict upon it, and in such a way as to give him

---

[101] See Chapter 87 above.

[102] This village lies some 18 miles (29 km) to the north of Estremoz.

a good account of ourselves. I have definite news that my brother, who is the Prior of the Order of the Hospitallers, along with the Master of Alcántara and Juan Rodríguez de Castañeda, as well as other lords, plus a vast army, are present in Crato, which is very near here. They are ready to march into this land, which belongs to my liege lord the Master, to do as much damage as they can. For that reason, it is my intention, with the help of God and accompanied by all of you, to go and find them before they can advance and to do battle with them. It is my hope that God will favour us by inflicting on them such a great defeat as will forever bring you fame and honour. Furthermore, you will perform an important and outstanding service to my liege lord the Master and will earn much happiness for yourselves in defending your country and your property, which is no less than what is expected of you.'

When Nuno Álvares had finished proclaiming these and other exhortations designed to bolster their determination and courage, they all answered him as with one voice, declaring that this was a weighty undertaking and not conducive to an immediate reply. They asked him to grant them time to think about it and discuss it among themselves; then they would reply and tell him what their feelings were. Nuno Álvares was far from pleased with this, realising the intent behind their words. Yet, though he had wanted an immediate response, it behoved him to be patient, since there was nothing else he could do.

Chapter 93

Concerning the reply that was given to Nuno Álvares, and how all his forces decided to accompany him into battle

The leading men from the various townships discussed the question with those who had accompanied them, as well as with one another, and great and divergent arguments emerged from their debates. Next day, when they had all reached agreement, they issued the following reply:

'Lord Nuno Álvares, we now well understand all that you proposed to us yesterday, yet consider it a very dubious undertaking for us to accompany you into battle against such an army, and for two principal reasons. The first is that it has as captains great lords and with them come vast and powerful forces. For they say that the following are coming: Don Juan Alfonso de

Guzmán, the Count of Niebla; Don Diego Martínez, the Master of Alcántara;[103] Pero González de Sevilla, the Governor of Andalusia; Juan Rodríguez de Castañeda; García González de Grijalba; Álvaro Pérez de Guzmán; Pedro Ponce de Marchena; Juan González de Carenzo; the cellarer [of the Order of Alcántara]; García Fernández de Villagarcía and Martim Eanes de Barbuda. They also say that Fernán Sánchez de Tovar, the High Admiral of Castile, is coming, as well as other great lords whose names we do not know, and that they are bringing with them 1,000 lances and more, all well equipped, along with many light horsemen, crossbowmen and a large force of foot soldiers. In view of our small numbers, such a conflict as the one proposed would be a very unequal fight.'

There then spoke up one Álvaro do Rego, a noble squire who accompanied Nuno Álvares: 'My lord, it's true that, as to vast and powerful forces, that is certainly the case, because I'm acquainted with most of the captains who are heading this way. Let me add that, leaving aside the other troops, there are more men of honourable rank among them than we have here of ordinary stock.'

This remark was answered by Pedro Eanes Lobato, another squire in the service of Nuno Álvares: 'As for me, my lord, let me say that I'd rather fight against all such great lords, so delicate as they are, than against hardy squires and men of toil who'd keep me busy all day, for these gentlemen who come here perfumed with rose-water and orange blossom are incapable of resisting long, and you'll swiftly overcome them.'

The men from the townships said: 'The second reason why many are hesitating, is that your brother Dom Pedro Álvares, who is the Prior of Crato, is coming, along with two other brothers of yours. They are very hesitant and scoff at the idea that you will fight your own brothers. It's more likely, they say, that they could all quickly meet with disaster and be betrayed, defeated and killed, and that the townships where they live could be seized by the Castilians, which would be of scant service either to God or to the Master. Therefore, in conclusion, the answer from us all is that we do not intend to accompany you in this undertaking.'

On hearing this reply, Nuno Álvares was greatly irritated in his heart but showed no anger and gave them a gracious answer as follows: 'My friends, I don't know what to say to you beyond what I've already said. Nevertheless, I still want to reply to what you've said to me. As regards your statement that the Castilians are approaching in huge numbers and are led by great captains and lords, so much greater then will be your honour and glory in defeating

---

[103] In fact, the Master at this date was Diego Gómez Barroso. He was elected in the final months of 1383, after the death of Diego Martínez.

them, for it has already often happened that small forces have defeated large ones, because every victory lies with God and not with men. As for the other matter which apparently gives you cause to doubt, namely that my brothers are in that army, you should in no way be afraid, may God forfend, that any one of you will be betrayed by me. That is because, in this matter, I do not consider them to be my brothers, for they come to lay waste the very land that gave them birth. I don't just say this against my brothers but truly I swear to you that, even if my own father were approaching, I would stand against him in the service of my liege lord the Master.

'For you to recognise this, if you are willing for us all to be companions in this enterprise, I swear and promise to you that I shall lead from the front, ahead of my banner, and shall be the first to start fighting. That way, you will be able to see how determined I am to oppose my brothers in this matter. Nevertheless, if it is your intention to proceed as you have told me, then let those who wish to return to their towns and homes leave with God's protection. As for me, along with these few noble Portuguese who accompany me, I intend to meet my brothers in a pitched battle.'

On hearing him pronounce these words, those who doubted now gained the courage to follow and accompany him, all declaring with one voice that they wanted to go with him.

'Now, my friends', he said, 'I request of you that those who wish to go with me in this quest should cross over this brook; those who don't wish to do so should remain on this side.' They told him that they would all cross over. Yet, despite saying this, there were some who inwardly regretted doing so and revealed that they had spoken more out of shame than out of any desire to go ahead. This was especially the case with Estêvão Eanes the Younger and Mendo Afonso de Beja, who could not help declaring openly that they were going there at a very inauspicious time and would never come back from the conflict.

Nuno Álvares pretended that he had not heard them or heeded their words, so delighted was he at the reply which they had all given, namely that they wished to go with him. Delighted as he was, and confident that they would all accompany him, he at once decided that very early the next day they would set forth to do battle.

At midnight or a little later, while Nuno Álvares was asleep in his lodging, Álvaro Coitado came to him in great haste, announcing that Gil Fernandes and Martim Rodrigues from Elvas already had their horses saddled and their armour on and were intending to leave for Elvas, as they did not wish to go with him into battle. On hearing this, Nuno Álvares got up at once and went to where they were already giving orders to load up their pack-animals. 'My friends and brothers!' he said, 'Is this worthy of you? Abandoning such honourable deeds, when God has prepared you for them? And going back on your word, just to head back home?'

He addressed Gil Fernandes in particular: 'Even you, Gil Fernandes, whom I thought and still think to be one of the most honourable servants in this country on whom my liege lord the Master relies, how can you show yourself to fall short in an undertaking of this importance?' He added that he valued him alone more highly than all the men who came with him. They made their excuses with good arguments, but he answered them with even better ones, so that they changed their minds and agreed unconditionally that they would accompany him into battle.

Chapter 94

Concerning the discussions which Nuno Álvares held with Ruy González

As morning came without further problems, Nuno Álvares at once gave orders for the trumpets to be sounded and left with all his men for Fronteira, which lay 4 leagues away and was where the Castilians would be heading. On the way he sent a number of his light horsemen ahead to seek news as to where the enemy lay.

At this point, little time passed before a Castilian squire, Ruy González by name, who had formerly lived alongside Nuno Álvares in his father's household and was at this time living in the household of Pedro Álvares his brother, arrived at speed on horseback, heading for Fronteira. He went up to Nuno Álvares, who received him very well and inquired of him the whereabouts of his brother and the other great lords from Castile. His answer was that they were already at Fronteira, which lay about a league and a half away from where he had encountered Nuno Álvares. The latter asked him what they were doing and received the answer that they were planning to attack the town. Urging him to tell the truth, Nuno Álvares then asked him what his purpose was in coming, whether he was a spy or whether he bore a message and, if so, from whom. Ruy González answered him as follows: 'Lord Nuno Álvares, you are well aware that in this matter, just as in any other, I will never tell you anything but the truth. You can be sure that your brother and the great lords and forces of Castile have been informed that you were equipped and ready to seek them out and do battle with them. They are so surprised at this that they find it very difficult to believe, when you have so few troops as they know you have and yet are engaged in bringing it about.

They have asked your brother for his opinion, but his answer was that he did not know, though he could assure them of one thing: if you had begun to do something in this regard, he knew you well enough to say that you would go ahead with it even unto death. The other great lords then requested him to send me to you to find out what your plans were, and that is why I am here.

'He also sent me to say that you should consider very carefully what you are undertaking, as it is highly unsafe, with the few forces that you have, for you to go into battle against so many great lords as there are at Fronteira. Indeed, he assures you that they have there such great and well-equipped captains that, even if King Fernando were alive, he would have a lot of work to do to enter a pitched battle against them; his opinion is that you are not acting sensibly, for, if you go into battle, there is no way you can defend yourself. Nor will he be able to help you in this matter, even if he wished to do so. Therefore, he would be very pleased, and sends you this advice as a brother, if you were to abandon your quest and choose one of two courses of action: either you go over to his liege lord the King of Castile, for which he guarantees you safe conduct, and who will grant you many favours and will add to your rank in a way that will please you; or you stay where you were in Estremoz and let his forces sweep across the country, as they have every intention of doing, and avoid your own downfall and that of the forces which you have there with you.'

On hearing these arguments, Nuno Álvares answered the squire as follows: 'Ruy González, I understand very well what you say. Briefly, my answer is this: tell my brother the prior that I don't want his advice on this matter, nor will God want me to believe any part of the message he has sent. Let him tell that to the other great lords too. That is because I shall in no way change the aim which I have set myself; indeed, with God's help I shall fulfil it. Instead, let them prepare themselves for a fight, because, with these few Portuguese whom I have with me, I intend to go into pitched battle against them. At this moment, I know of nothing I want more than to be in the thick of it. Before long, if it pleases God, I shall be there with them; let them have no doubt about that. So, Ruy González, my friend, I beseech you, out of your friendship for me, to deliver this message as fast as you can, even if you ride your horse into the ground. That's because I believe that you won't be able to go so fast that, with God's help, I'll not be very close to where the Castilians are to be found.'

Chapter 95

How Nuno Álvares went into battle against the Castilians and how he defeated and routed them

R uy González left, just as Nuno Álvares had recommended him to do, riding as fast as his horse could carry him at the trot and the gallop. Very soon he reached Fronteira, where the Castilian captains and their forces were encamped. On arrival he told the prior and the other great lords all that Nuno Álvares had said and what had been his reply [to their message]. When they heard this, they immediately halted the preparations which they had begun for attacking the town and diligently set about preparing to go into battle.

While they were beginning to leave the outskirts [of Fronteira], where they had been lodging, and were heading for Estremoz, from where Nuno Álvares had been approaching, Nuno Álvares had installed himself with his troops in a spot which was highly suitable for a pitched battle, namely Os Atoleiros ['The Quagmire'],[104] which lies roughly half a league before Fronteira. Once Nuno Álvares was settled in that position and was confident that the Castilians were on their way to do battle, he immediately commanded all his men-at-arms to dismount. With the few men that he had, he drew up his formations for the vanguard, rearguard, and the right and left flanks; then he drew up his foot soldiers and crossbowmen along the flanks, where he believed they would be in the best position to fight.

Fearing for the foot soldiers, lest they should fail him, owing to the vast numbers of the Castilians, he posted a number of men-at-arms among them with orders that, if they saw them turning tail, they should kill them. Having completed his battle formation, he began to make his way along the lines of men mounted on a mule, exhorting his troops with noble words, cheerful countenance and an agreeable attitude, telling them all to remember carefully four things and to store them in their hearts.

The first of these was that they should commend themselves to God and to His Mother, the Virgin Mary, urging Them to provide help against their enemies, since their dispute with them was just, and they should firmly believe they would receive that help. The second was that they were there to defend themselves, their homes and possessions and to extricate themselves from the subjugation which the King of Castile was seeking to impose upon them, contrary to all right and reason. The third was that they were there to serve their liege lord and achieve great honour which God would be pleased to grant

[104] The battle site lies some 12 miles (*c.* 20 km) to the north of Estremoz.

them very soon. The fourth was that they should firmly resolve to endure every tribulation and keep on fighting, not just for one hour but for a whole day, if need be.

Such were his encouraging words before he went into battle. No sooner had he uttered them than the Castilians were already very close at hand. Nuno Álvares immediately got down from the mule he was riding and took up his position alongside those who led the vanguard in front of his banner, as he had promised. It was the Wednesday of Holy Week in the month of April, and he had not yet eaten.

He knelt down on the ground and prayed before the image of the Crucified Christ and His Blessed Mother as depicted on his banner. Likewise, all his men knelt down with their hands raised in prayer, and many of them were in tears. He kissed the ground and rose to his feet; then he donned his bascinet (which he wore without a visor). Taking in his hands the lance borne by his page, he addressed his men as follows:

'My friends, let none of you doubt me, and let all of you who help me in your turn be assisted by God. If I die here through any faults and shortcomings of yours, let God hold you responsible for my death.'

The Castilians had been planning to fight the battle on foot, and that was what Nuno Álvares had foreseen. However, when they saw the Portuguese drawn up as they were, ready to die or to conquer, they changed their plans and decided to enter battle on horseback. They were full of daring, owing to their considerable numbers and their fine horses, believing that they would swiftly rout the Portuguese the moment they attacked them, which seemed to be what any reasonable man might think. They drew up their battle lines on horseback, and the light horsemen took up a separate position, along with the baggage train, on a slope covered with green wheat and very close to where the battle was due to take place.

Then the Castilians launched a mighty charge against the Portuguese, with their lances under their arms and solidly ready for the impact, yelling out loud, 'For Castile and Saint James'. Nuno Álvares and his men yelled back, 'For Portugal and Saint George', and each man lowered his lance, taking aim at his foe. The moment the horses collided with them, some fell to the ground with their riders, while others, even before reaching the Portuguese battle line, were wounded by bolts and spears launched at them by foot soldiers over the heads of the men-at-arms. With the horses rearing up, they threw their riders to the ground. Some of the wounded tried to retreat but, as they turned back, they collided with others and fell to the ground.

Likewise, reinforcements, which had been waiting behind in readiness, came up, but the same thing befell them as happened to the earlier ones. Nuno Álvares and his men attacked and killed them, so that it pleased God for the Castilians to be routed. Even though they joined battle with a will, they were defeated in a short space of time. At the first onset, forty Castilian men-at-arms were slain, and in the later onslaught a further seventy-seven. As for the Portuguese, not a single man was killed or wounded.

Among the dead were the Master of Alcántara, Pero González de Sevilla, Ruy González and the cellarer [of the Order of Alcántara], as well as other worthy but less prominent noblemen; among the wounded were the [High] Admiral, the Prior [of Crato] and García González de Grijalba. However, at this juncture, a number of authors advance two arguments which run counter to the truth. One of them is that the Castilians were routed owing to their poor battle formation; the other is that those who remained alive retreated and formed a single force, which the Portuguese did not dare to attack any further. That is something which ought not to be described in that way, whether to favour or to cover up some shortcoming, for the historian should not be an enemy of the truth but its recorder. The truth was as follows: the Count of Niebla, the Prior of Crato, the [High] Admiral of Castile and Martim Eanes de Barbuda (who called himself the Master of Avis), as well as other captains, along with many of their men, when once they realised that they were away from the field of battle, refused to go back to it and began to seek refuge, some in Crato and others in Monforte and the other places which had declared for Castile. While they were in retreat, some of the admiral's men urged him to turn about and return to the fight, as there were plenty of troops with which to confront the Portuguese, but he answered them, saying, 'A dead man gets no wages. Bring home our banner, for, when once a man has been defeated, there is no point in his going back into battle.' As for the assertion that the Castilians presented a poor battle formation, nothing could be further from the truth. That is because there were present in that conflict great lords and captains, both Portuguese and Castilians, schooled in battle, along with so many and such noble forces that, not just for Nuno Álvares with those few men he had with him, but also for a very lofty prince, there were ample numbers to draw up an effective battle formation and do battle with him; indeed, with precisely that dauntlessness and sound formation they had attacked them. However, Almighty God, in Whose hands lie every victory and the power to deliver many into the hands of the few, was pleased on that occasion to confer victory on the Portuguese. When they saw the Castilians in flight, Nuno Álvares immediately mounted his horse and with a very small number of his men (small, because in such haste few managed to find a mount) gave chase for a good league, before nightfall forced him to turn back. Indeed, several of his men told him that it was tempting God not to be content with the favour God had conferred upon him, and thus to give chase for so great a distance.

Then Nuno Álvares went back to the site of the battle and afterwards to spend a very short night at Fronteira.

As he was approaching the town, there arrived on horseback, fully armed and in haste, a squire who dived in among the Portuguese, in particular João Vasques de Almada, Pedro Eanes Lobato and others. After speaking to them, saying 'God keep you, my lords', he asked whether he would be safe among them. 'Yes, you will be', they said, 'but you ask the question very late!' Then they asked who he was and what he had come for. He replied that he was the son of Pero González de Sevilla and had come to find out whether his father was dead or a prisoner or what the circumstances were. They took him to Nuno Álvares who, once he had spoken to him and had discovered why he had come, certified to him his father's death and who it was who had killed him. Nuno Álvares then gave orders that he be well looked after and accorded every honour. Next day he commanded him to be given safe conduct.

Wherefore, let it be noted that Nuno Álvares was the first, in the memory of man up to this time, to fight a battle on foot in Portugal and win it.

Chapter 96

How Nuno Álvares captured Arronches and Alegrete

Owing to this first blessing which God had conferred on Nuno Álvares and the Portuguese, all those in that region who had declared for Portugal were immensely pleased. Thereafter, many willingly volunteered to serve him and obeyed his every command. Similarly, when the Master learned of this in Lisbon, where he was in readiness to withstand a siege, he was delighted at the news. It was quite the opposite with the King of Castile, then in the Óbidos area, who was far from pleased.

On the day after the battle, very early in the morning and without resting from his endeavours, Nuno Álvares got ready and left for Monforte,[105] where Martim Eanes de Barbuda, whom we have mentioned, was to be found. He was a Portuguese knight, renowned for being a good man-at-arms, and was accompanied by large numbers of troops with whom he had fled the battle. Nuno Álvares had it in mind that he would attack the town, if those in Monforte were unwilling to emerge to confront him.

After he reached Monforte, the troops who were inside the town refused to emerge, though they consisted of some 300 lances. Since the town was well fortified and had many troops inside its walls, and since Nuno Álvares had

---

[105] This township lies 18 miles (29 km) to the south of Portalegre.

no siege engines, he decided not to attack it. However, he stayed there for one day, during which time there took place several skirmishes between the Portuguese and those in the town in front of its fortifications, without anything significant coming about. On the morning of the next day, which was Holy Thursday,[106] Nuno Álvares walked barefoot on a pilgrimage to Santa Maria do Assumar, which lies a league distant and is a church held in great veneration. All his men accompanied him on foot.

When he arrived at the church, he found it to be filthy because of the Castilians' horses which they stabled there whenever they were passing that way. Before taking any rest, he ordered it to be cleaned and was the very first to begin to remove the dung.

At this point there arrived a message from certain Portuguese men, informing Nuno Álvares that he could seize Arronches,[107] a township which had declared for Castile, and that they would hand it over to him. Nuno Álvares was very pleased at this, leaving for Arronches and spending the night at Assumar. He sent a message to those who were to hand over the township to him, asking how this was to be achieved, and received a reply that very evening.

Well into the morning of the next day he rode off with his troops and reached the town, where he was duly received. Entering the town, his men began to attack the castle from all sides. In the castle were some honourable Castilian knights, namely Alfonso Sánchez, Gonzalo Sánchez de Guntes and Sancho Sánchez; with them were up to thirty lances, as well as other Portuguese.

There followed a major onslaught, in which the castle gates were set alight and battered down. All the inhabitants were captured, and Gil Fernandes seized Alfonso Sánchez and Sancho Sánchez, taking them with him as prisoners when he returned to Elvas with the troops native to this town. In Arronches the Portuguese took possession of horses and weapons, not to mention other things of profit to them.

Likewise, Alegrete,[108] which had also declared for Castile, sent Nuno Álvares a message, urging him to give orders for that town to be received on the Master's behalf. To receive the township, he at once sent there, along with a number of others, an honourable squire, Martim Afonso da Aramenha by name, who was a native of the town yet who lived in Portalegre. It was duly handed over, and in that way Arronches and Alegrete came over to the Master's side.

---

[106] Fernão Lopes has confused the days, having told us in Chapter 95 that the Battle of Atoleiros took place on a Wednesday, yet Nuno Álvares had now spent an intervening day, since Os Atoleiros, in skirmishes at Monforte.

[107] This township lies 15 miles (24 km) to the south-east of Portalegre.

[108] Alegrete is located some 10 miles (16 km) to the north of Arronches.

Nuno Álvares left his uncle, Martim Gonçalves, as Governor of Arronches. There he celebrated Easter. He dispatched many of his men back to their homes, telling them to be ready for when they received his summons. He then left for Estremoz, thence to Évora and finally to Montemor[-o-Novo].

Chapter 97

Concerning a raid into Castile carried out by the Portuguese, and concerning the booty which they brought back

If you remember well what you have been reading about, [you will know that] the King of Castile is in the Óbidos area, awaiting the arrival of his fleet, so that he can lay siege to Lisbon. While Nuno Álvares is resting, and the Master is waiting for the mighty siege, in the meantime let us, in order not to waste this interval, consider a number of matters, however trivial they may be, until the fleet arrives, at which point we will return to that part of our story.

It so happened, therefore, that since, as you have heard, many castle governors had declared for Queen Leonor, the Master dispatched Vasco Porcalho, who was the grand commander of his Order, to be Governor of Vila Viçosa and with orders that his men should eject García Pérez del Campo, who was the cellarer of the Order, because he was a *criado* of Queen Leonor and thus liable to suspicion.

With Vasco Porcalho thus declaring for him, the Master gave orders that Álvaro Gonçalves Coitado should be posted to Vila Viçosa, along with thirty squires who were natives of the town, because he too came from that same place. This Álvaro Coitado was a very great friend of Pero Rodrigues, who was the Governor of Alandroal. They both agreed to make an incursion into Castile, because none of those who had declared for Portugal had dared to make such a move. That was because Pero Rodrigues da Fonseca[109] was in Olivença with considerable forces, having 500 horsemen at his disposal, both men-at-arms and light horsemen. Consequently, the entire region was very afraid of him, and cattle were well guarded all along the Castilian border area.

Once matters had been agreed and the day named, Álvaro Gonçalves assembled his 30 squires, along with 150 foot soldiers from Vila Viçosa. Pero Rodrigues had 15 horsemen, as well as 50 foot soldiers from Alandroal,

---

[109] This nobleman had declared for the King of Castile; see Chapter 44 above.

so that in all they had 45 horsemen and 200 foot soldiers. Having gathered together, ready to invade Castile, they forded the Guadiana at night at Serva and reached the village common of Cheles just before dawn. They rounded up two herds of cows belonging to García González de Grijalba, captured 14 cowherds, uprooted their tents and loaded the beasts with their equipment. They made off with cows, bullocks and mares, along with their herdsmen, of whom just one escaped to give the news to Villanueva del Fresno and Alconchel, both villages which come under the jurisdiction of Castile.

Pero Rodrigues and Álvaro Coitado ordered the foot soldiers to drive these cattle and gave them ten horsemen to accompany them. The rest, along with the crossbowmen, followed as a rearguard, lest any forces should gather together to attack them. They drove the cattle through Ferreira and on to the cork-oak groves belonging to the Order [of Avis], situated between the townships of Alandroal and Juromenha, finally reaching the field near Pardais, where stands a church dedicated to Saint Mark. There they shared out the herd, with the captains receiving their just amount and each of the others the portion due to him. As for the one-fifth which pertained to Álvaro Coitado, he was unwilling at that time to accept it for himself but ordered it to be shared out among his men, at which they were all very pleased and duly thanked him for it.

In their booty they counted 700 bullocks, separated out into one of the herds; there were 1,400 cows, 26 mares and nine three-year-old colts, as well as a number of foals. The mares were given to Álvaro Coitado, who sent them to an estate of his near Benavente. This was the first cattle raid into Castile carried out by the Portuguese at the beginning of this campaign.[110]

Chapter 98

How Vasco Porcalho came to be ejected from Vila Viçosa because of suspicions which were entertained about him

After this cattle raid and seizure of booty was over, Pero Rodrigues discovered for certain that Vasco Porcalho, the grand commander, was receiving letters from Pero Rodrigues da Fonseca contrary to the Master's service. He arranged for this information to be passed on by one of his squires

---

[110] The Castilian and Portuguese villages mentioned in the raid carried out by Coitado and Rodrigues are all situated in the area to the south of Elvas and Badajoz respectively.

to Álvaro Coitado in Vila Viçosa.[111] When the squire arrived with this message, Vasco Porcalho happened to be in the town square. Álvaro Gonçalves made ready to arrest him, and he began by talking to a number of townspeople. Having secured the postern gate, where he posted crossbowmen and foot soldiers, with orders not to let anybody in or out, he ordered ten squires to be posted at the castle gate and commanded all the town's gates to be barred. Then, in great haste, he summoned Pero Rodrigues from Alandroal, which is a league away. On reading his message, Pero Rodrigues rode off with ten squires and sixty foot soldiers and very quickly reached Vila Viçosa.

Álvaro Gonçalves had already taken control of a huge tower which stands over one of the gateways and gave the order for the gate to be opened for Pero Rodrigues. The moment they saw each other, they entered into a discussion that nobody heard. Then they set off at once, with their forces and all the townsfolk, to the palace of the Order [of Avis], where the commander was already to be found, with fifteen squires, thirty foot soldiers and ten crossbowmen; in addition, the street leading to the palace was well defended by barricades.

The huge throng immediately battered down the barricade, with everybody yelling out, 'Death to the traitor and all his men! Death for selling us out to the King of Castile!' Though everyone was calling for the palace to be set alight, they were made to quieten down, and a message was sent to the commander telling him to come out, so that they could talk to him, or they would go in, whichever he preferred.

When once Vasco Porcalho and his men had been given assurance of their own safety, he emerged from the palace to speak to Pero Rodrigues and Álvaro Gonçalves. After they moved away from the crowd, the commander asked why they had taken steps to dishonour and kill him without due reason, surrounding his castle, where his liege lord the Master had installed him and where he, the commander, had pledged him his loyalty. He said: 'In that regard, it seems to me that you've neither acted wisely nor received sound advice. Indeed, the Master, whose *criado* I am, and of whose Order I am a brother, will neither be pleased at this, nor will he consider that you have been of service to him. Let me tell you that I intend to write to him, telling him of the evil and dishonour that you have brought upon me.'

After he had uttered these and other arguments, which he set out at some length, Álvaro Gonçalves answered his complaints as follows: 'Sir knight, do not be aggrieved, nor regard as evil any of the actions which we have taken or which we shall take, for not one of them has been done with a view to dishonouring or killing you. Rather, it is because we believe that what we are doing is in the service of our liege lord the Master. We have been told (and of

---

[111] This township is situated some 10 miles (16 km) to the south-east of Estremoz.

this we are sure) that you have been exchanging letters with Pero Rodrigues
da Fonseca, the Governor of Olivença, and that for three months you have
been a vassal of the King of Castile, have received favours from him and
promised to hand this town over to him. In addition, we have been told that
there are 300 lances in Olivença, who this very day were due to come and take
possession of this town. Since this would be a very great evil and extremely
harmful, inflicting a disservice on the Master, our liege lord, we wish to be
sure of you and require you to hand this castle over to us. Then you can go
to the Master, demonstrating to him that you are blameless in this matter and
serve him as he commands you. There is no further point in your resorting to
arguments and fancy excuses about this, for nobody will acknowledge them.
To be sure, today the castle will be levelled with the town, its drawbridge will
be smashed and everything else will be done that we believe necessary for the
town's security and in the service of our liege lord the Master.'

To this Vasco Porcalho gave a reply by which he sought to show that
the foregoing was not the case, but they told him not to devise any further
arguments, because he knew very well that what they said was true. They
pressed him to hand over the castle, because for the time being they believed
that they could not trust him. Not being in a position to do anything else,
Vasco Porcalho summoned Lopo Gil, a squire on whom he greatly relied,
and ordered him to go with them, hand the castle over to them and obtain
documents indicating how he was being forced to do this, for he protested his
innocence regarding any breach of the terms by which he had sworn homage
as the holder of that castle.

They then took possession of the castle and gave orders for the drawbridge
of the postern gate to be smashed and for the gateway to be walled up against
external entry. They arranged for the castle and the town to be defended as a
single unit. The commander made his way outside, along with all his effects
and followers.

Chapter 99

How the Master ordered the castle to
be restored to Vasco Porcalho

The commander departed for Lisbon, along with those who served him. The
Master received him well, despite the fact that Pero Rodrigues and Álvaro
Gonçalves had already written to tell him everything that had happened. Vasco
Porcalho lodged a serious complaint with the Master, asserting that he had

been greatly dishonoured and that this was out of envy and not because there was any truth in what they alleged.

The Master dismissed the whole incident with conciliatory words, personally made sure that he was well treated and continued in that fashion for several days. On one occasion when the Master was at table, the commander was waiting on him and at the end of the meal he duly poured water over his hands. After the tablecloths had been removed, the Master called the commander to him, saying: 'Commander, don't distress yourself about what has happened, because those who brought it about believed that they were doing it to serve my best interests. Nevertheless, it is my wish to place even greater trust in you than before. It is also my wish that your honour be restored and that they should hand back to you the castle of Vila Viçosa, which you previously held. If you are disloyal to me, you will be the vilest traitor in all the world, what with your being a brother in my Order and one of my knights and devising treachery against me! That is something I could never believe, nor do I believe that God so created you that you would strive to bring such disgrace on your name. I shall send you with letters to hand to Álvaro Gonçalves and Pero Rodrigues, as well as to the honourable citizens of the town, commanding them to hand back to you your castle, just as you previously held it. That is because I deem you to be both honourable and loyal. Indeed, I believe you to be a man who will carry out his duty and I shall confer favours on you for doing so. I command you to establish a firm friendship with those knights. They shall honour you on my account, and you shall treat them and the town community in the same way.'

On hearing this, the commander kissed the Master's hand, declaring that he esteemed it a very great favour for his honour to be restored, for he had already imagined himself, though blameless, to be counted among the dead. The truth was [he said], in his heart he had not contemplated any means by which he could have been of disservice to him; indeed, God forbid that he should ever fall victim to such a defect. These and other assertions were advanced by this traitor, as a result of which the Master was increasingly inclined to deem him blameless.

The Master then gave orders for his letters of credence to be written out, directing them at Álvaro Gonçalves, Pero Rodrigues and the town community and instructing them as to the approach they should adopt towards him. The commander took his leave of the Master and made his way to Vila Viçosa, where he and his followers lodged at the [nearby] monastery. He then forwarded the letters to Álvaro Gonçalves and to Pero Rodrigues, and the latter was greatly concerned when he read the message.

Leaving the town [of Alandroal] heavily guarded, Pero Rodrigues set off to discuss the matter with Álvaro Coitado. On reaching Vila Viçosa, he discovered that Álvaro Coitado had walled up all the town gateways with stones, and that the only one open was a postern gate which stands beneath a huge tower. Ten men-at-arms were stationed at that postern, as well as twenty foot soldiers and six crossbowmen, and that was the way through which Pero Rodrigues entered the town.

After he had spoken to Mécia Peres do Campo, Álvaro Coitado's wife, he went off to the tower where he was to be found. They showed their letters to each other and saw that it was the Master's wish that possession of the castle should be restored to Vasco Porcalho, just as formerly. Even though both they and the townsfolk were greatly disturbed at this, they agreed to carry out the Master's commands and summoned him back to his castle, since the Master wished him to hold it.

Chapter 100

How Vasco Porcalho used guile to arrest Álvaro Gonçalves

After Vasco Porcalho entered the town, he spoke to Álvaro Gonçalves and Pero Rodrigues, resorting to composed and unassuming assertions of the sort that tricksters habitually deploy, begging them to forgive him, if he had in any way offended them, and declaring that he was ready to serve the Master in anything that they might command or consider appropriate. Moreover, he promised to maintain a true and honourable friendship, in order to be united with them in affection and intention. Such was the nature of the affability which he showed to everyone that, when he restored the castle to how it was beforehand, they all deemed it to have been well done. He repaired the ramparts with stone and placed huge beams on top of the battlements. For himself he stored up firewood, meat and other things needed for defence, telling them that this was what the Master had ordered him to do.

As he did all this, he feigned great friendship with Álvaro Coitado, acting as godfather at the baptism of one of the latter's sons. Pero Rodrigues, the Governor of Alandroal, was also present at the baptism, but after they had all eaten a meal with Álvaro Gonçalves, Pero Rodrigues went back to where he had come from. Álvaro Gonçalves did not go to spend that night in the town's great tower, of which he was still in charge, and, as it was evening, Vasco Porcalho came to see him, explaining that, as godfather to his son, he had come to have a drink with him and to spend some pleasant time in his company. He stayed with him far into the night, until fifty squires burst in, as well as 200 foot soldiers whom he had hidden in the castle. Vasco Porcalho then arrested Álvaro Coitado, his wife and children, and anyone else who was with him. They were at once taken away to the keep of the castle, and Vasco Porcalho stole from his houses everything he possessed.

That night, 200 Castilian lances entered the castle and, once dawn broke, they gave a blast on their trumpets and hoisted their flag on the main tower of the castle, yelling at the top of their voices, 'For Castile! Castile!'

When the townsfolk saw the Castilians in their midst, they were greatly dismayed and deeply disturbed, not only at the capture of the town, but also at the arrest of Álvaro Gonçalves. They opened the postern gate, and people started to flee to Borba, both on foot and on horseback. The commander was delighted that the town was rid of them and that they had left in the way they did. The result was that he at once gave away the property of those who had left to his *criados*.

Then Vasco Porcalho began to behave as a bad neighbour towards Pero Rodrigues, the Governor of Alandroal, and Pero Rodrigues did the same to him in return. The people of Alandroal ran very short of food and were eating bread made from acorns and other coarse kinds of food. The commander, having arrested Álvaro Gonçalves, informed the King of Castile of the fact, urging him to send back a message as to what he wished he should do with him. Likewise, Pero Rodrigues wrote to the Master telling him that the treacherous commander, in whom he had placed his trust, had handed over Vila Viçosa to the King of Castile and taken Álvaro Coitado prisoner. This news greatly troubled the Master, who ordered Pero Rodrigues to place a heavy guard on the town of which he was governor.

Then the commander received a message from the King of Castile, ordering him to dispatch his prisoner Álvaro Coitado to the tower of Olivença, where he would be more securely guarded. Pero Rodrigues da Fonseca also received a letter, telling him to keep a close guard on him until receiving further orders.

Nuno Álvares learned that Álvaro Gonçalves had been taken prisoner, was greatly perturbed at this and wrote to Pero Rodrigues at Alandroal, urging him to make every effort to find out whether it was intended to transfer Álvaro Coitado away from Vila Viçosa. He wrote back to say that it was, but that he did not know how or when.

Nuno Álvares then sent him a number of squires, so that he could have them with him and work out with them, if possible, how Álvaro Coitado could be recaptured from the Castilians when they took him to Olivença. Among those squires were Afonso Peres 'the Black', who later became Governor of Vila Viçosa; Lourenço Martins do Tojal; Gonçalo Cão; Gonçalo Colaço; Lourenço Peres Cinza; Gomes Lourenço de Sampaio and other honourable squires, numbering sixteen in all. He ordered them to do all that Pero Rodrigues required of them. They repeated that instruction to him when they arrived, for which he thanked them most graciously and greatly enjoyed their company.

Chapter 101

How the Portuguese fought with certain Castilians, defeated them, and put them to flight

Not long after these squires arrived, the Commander of Zalamea and the Commander of Calatrava rode out one night from Vila Viçosa with a number of horsemen and foot soldiers. They carried out raids around Évora and throughout that district. While they were stealthily advancing in the middle of the night, a Portuguese youth, native to Borba, Rodrigo Valejo by name, was journeying as page to a Castilian called Diego González Maldonado. He ran away from his master on the road at nearly dawn and went to Alandroal to carry the news to Pero Rodrigues, the governor of the town, that those men had made an incursion and raided the area around Évora. He said that there were 200 foot soldiers, including *almogávares*[112] and others, and 100 on horseback, including some on jennets riding with them. He told the governor the road they were taking and the place they had said they were going to plunder.

When Pero Rodrigues heard this, he was very glad of the news, and much more so were the squires whom Nuno Álvares had sent there, because Vasco Porcalho had given away the property of some of those who were from Vila Viçosa. Pero Rodrigues immediately conferred with them regarding how they thought it best to proceed with such a matter. They all agreed that, although there were many of the enemy, they should go and await them on the road and attack them nonetheless.

Pero Rodrigues at once ordered those he would be taking with him to make themselves ready. With the squires of Nuno Álvares, there were twenty-six horsemen and sixty foot soldiers. They headed for Estremoz, riding as fast as they could as far as the road that runs from Vila Viçosa towards Évora. They took with them the youth who had brought the news, and he led them to the track along which the Castilians had passed, on the foothills of the mountain range.[113] There they agreed to wait for the enemy at the pass where a few men would be as effective as many. Having agreed that they would wait

---

[112] Soldiers trained for service on a border region. Formerly, the mission of the *almogávares* was to make incursions into Muslim territory.

[113] That is, the Serra de Ossa, a 2,000 ft (650 m) high mountain range.

there for whatever fortune God might choose to grant them, the horsemen and foot soldiers took cover in a hollow. Pero Rodrigues set two lookout posts, commanding views across a wide sweep of the plains below; he was at one of them. There they remained from the hour of prime[114] until midday, when they saw the foot soldiers approaching and driving along their plunder, as well as ten light horsemen with them as guards.

The train of plunder was astonishingly long, for they were driving 5,000 sheep and 1,500 goats; there were as many as 60 men and youths as well, roped together in three groups. All the foot soldiers accompanied the plunder, and with them the ten light horsemen; the men-at-arms protected the rearguard. They went on their way driving their plunder, feeling as secure as if they were in Castile. At this point the men-at-arms appeared, and as they rode along they gave the impression of being greater in number than they were. They pulled away from the road they were following, to go and raid Redondo, which was very close by, and skirmished around the town with some of those who were there.

When Pero Rodrigues and the squires saw this they said to each other, 'Now is the time to attack those foot soldiers who are marching toward us with their plunder, and also those light horsemen before they can get help from the men-at-arms.'

Then they divided into two groups, with foot soldiers and horsemen in each, and went to attack the Castilian foot soldiers and light horsemen as they approached. With the first blows they felled five light horsemen and fifty-three foot soldiers, with such wounds that they had no need of a surgeon to tend to them. Against their will they abandoned all their plunder and began to flee towards the mountains, those who were able to do so. The Portuguese, both foot soldiers and horsemen, and also those that had been held captive by the Castilians and who were then freed, pursued them in a deadly fashion, killing and capturing them as best they could, so that, in a short while, 123 of them were taken prisoner or slain, while the others escaped into the mountains. Pero Rodrigues at once took possession of the arms and mounts of the five horsemen who had fallen and with them made squires of five foot soldiers who had well deserved it, so that then there were thirty-one horsemen fit to fight.

The other five light horsemen who escaped went to give the news to the men-at-arms, telling them how their loot was now in the hands of the Portuguese and that many of their men had been taken or slain. In great distress they regrouped and, at the fastest pace they could sustain off the road, they reached the place where the fighting had occurred; they gathered on a very lofty hilltop from which they could easily see how many Portuguese there

[114] 6 am.

were. When Pero Rodrigues saw them up there, he agreed with the squires that, though the battle would be very uneven, they should attack the Castilians first, before they summoned up the determination to come out at them.

Then he stationed all the foot soldiers on one side, and ordered them to stay there and not to change their positions, no matter what they might see; that was because he and the squires intended to launch an attack on the horsemen, before they could organise an assault on them. If they could not defeat them, then they would retreat to where the foot soldiers were stationed, and the foot soldiers should not hesitate to splinter their spears and lances on the horses of the Castilians. Then Pero Rodrigues and the squires braced their lances under their arms and, all crying out, 'For Portugal and Saint George!' they launched an attack on the enemy. The commanders, with their men, rode towards them valiantly, calling back, 'For Castile and Saint James!' When the lances clashed together, ten Castilians fell to the ground, and two of the Portuguese.

After the lances had been lost they did battle with swords, and attacked each other with spirit. The Castilians fought in such a way, because there were so many of them, that, if it had not been shameful to do so, the Portuguese would have fled the field. The foot soldiers realised this and, seeing the battle was so unequal, in spite of the instructions they had received, they strove to bring their help at a time when it was much needed.

When they arrived, they began to jab with their spears at the horses of the Castilians, which caused their riders to fall to the ground. So much did the Portuguese horsemen and foot soldiers do to get the better of their enemies that they forced them to flee the battlefield. Lourenço Martins do Tojal and Gomes Lourenço de Sampaio, when they saw that the Castilians were being defeated and starting to flee, said to each other, 'Let's go after these commanders, since we know them; let's not allow them to escape us like this.' Then they pursued them, each riding after his own man. The commanders, with their immediate following, held back in order to rally their men together. Lourenço Martins and Gomes Lourenço rode in among them all, and each clashed with his own man, so that both their adversaries were knocked from their saddles. With both of them on the ground, their loyal *criados* rallied to them, and killed the horses of Lourenço Martins and Gomes Lourenço; both were left on foot and wounded. Then the commanders managed to remount. Pero Rodrigues rode up to aid the squires, who were in danger of being slain or taken captive. At that point the fighting broke off. Pero Rodrigues went back from there and told the squires to take the sheep to Alandroal, for their owners would come there to get them.

Having gathered his men together, he found that not one of them was missing, but twenty-five foot soldiers had been wounded, and eleven of the squires were also wounded, though in no danger of death. Of the Castilians, there where they had clashed with them, four horsemen died and nine were captured; six horses had been killed and nine were taken alive. On the Portuguese side five horses had been killed, but there was no lack of other horses and better horses to replace them.

Then the owners of the sheep came, each to retrieve his own, and they wanted to give Pero Rodrigues half of the livestock. But he would not take more than 300 goats and 100 lambs for the wounded to eat.

Chapter 102

How Álvaro Coitado was freed from captivity, and how the Castilians who were carrying him away were defeated

It was not long afterwards that one morning there arrived a spy whom Pero Rodrigues maintained in Vila Viçosa. He said that that coming night they were going to take Álvaro [Gonçalves] Coitado from Vila Viçosa to Olivença, and that he should consider what it was best to do. Pero Rodrigues at once called the squires into the spy's presence, and they began to speak of how they should proceed in the matter. They agreed that on this night they should set up an ambush near Vila Viçosa, in a pine grove well suited to the purpose, and that the spy should strive to find out the time when the prisoner would be moved, and how. They ordered him to go, and to bring them word at the pine grove.

After sundown Pero Rodrigues, with the sixteen of Nuno Álvares and fifteen of his own squires and fifty foot soldiers, departed from Alandroal, pretending that he was taking the road to Estremoz. After night had fallen, they turned back by another road, as secretly as they could, and went to the pine grove they had chosen. While they were there waiting for word from the man who had been sent to get news, it grew very late. They had received no news from any reliable informer from Vila Viçosa, and had no information except what that man they were waiting for had told them.

Seeing how long he delayed, they began to wonder if what he had said was true. Some said that this could be a trick on his part, a man whom Pero Rodrigues had trusted, and who had betrayed them. The one who feared this the most was Pero Rodrigues himself, so much so that he as well as the others would have been very happy to be far away from there, and not to have begun such an expedition. At this point, the two squires Lourenço Martins and Gomes Lourenço began to speak as follows: 'Pero Rodrigues, you have come here in the service of God and of the Master. When Nuno Álvares sent us to you, this was the principal mission he commanded to be entrusted to you, namely that Álvaro Gonçalves should be freed from captivity when they tried to take him away from here, if you could do so. Now, if this is a trap, it is already set, and we cannot escape it in any way; rather, we must try to free him by force of arms, ready for whatever may happen, whether here or on the road. Therefore, if it pleases you, we wish to go ahead with two foot soldiers, and we'll catch an informer if we can. You wait here, for we will return to you very soon.' Pero Rodrigues said that he was content with this, and that he would not leave there for any reason until they came back.

The squires left with two *almogávar* foot soldiers. As they drew near the town, they sent the foot soldiers to the outlying area, and they remained nearby, across from the postern gate. As they waited there, they saw many men on foot and on horseback. Two Castilian foot soldiers arrived, intending, by order of the commander, to accompany those at the postern gate. The squires took them captive at once and made them keep quiet. At this point, the two men who had gone with the squires came back to them and said: 'They are taking Álvaro Gonçalves from the castle now, and they have a mule ready for him to ride; it seems to us that there must be about 200 horsemen, by our reckoning, and many men on foot. They are calling to Alfonso García, their infantry captain,[115] saying that it is high time to leave if he is going to leave at all.'

'Now', the squires said, 'you remain here, and as soon as they start riding, let one of you come to tell the news and the other one follow them closely, and see for certain how many men there are, and what road they take.'

Then the two squires departed with those men they had captured and went to the pine grove. When they arrived, they told Pero Rodrigues and the others everything that had happened to them. While they were questioning the prisoners about the men who were in Vila Viçosa, the man Pero Rodrigues had been waiting for arrived, as well as one of those who had remained in the town to find out the road they intended to take. They both gave the following news: 'The commanders are coming with Álvaro Gonçalves, and they have with them about ninety horsemen and sixty foot soldiers, all picked men, and twenty-five crossbowmen. Alfonso Álvarez,[116] their infantry captain, is acting as their guide, and they are taking the road to Corte de Elvira;[117] any moment you will hear them passing by.' Then they began to mount their horses and, while they were getting ready, they heard the sound of the Castilians' horses.

---

[115] 'Almoçadém' in Portuguese. Many ranks in Peninsular armies used designations of Moorish origin.

[116] Named above as Alfonso García.

[117] This location has proved impossible to identify.

'What do you think will be best?' asked Pero Rodrigues. 'Where should we attack them?'

'It seems to us sound thinking', said the others, 'to let them get some distance from the town, and attack them at the edge of that grove of holm-oaks yonder.'

As they were speaking of this, the other foot soldier arrived with information, saying: 'The commanders are passing by: they're wrapped up in the biggest conversation anyone ever heard and they're riding along without any precautions whatsoever; they've no advance guard, nor any rearguard.'

Then Pero Rodrigues said: 'It seems right to me that we should confront them in that field beyond these thickets of rock-roses, and there is no reason why we should let them go any farther. They may hear us, and we'd find them better prepared for us. It's a clear night and not very dark; let's take them by surprise. Please God, they'll surrender Álvaro Gonçalves to us, as well as some of their horses and weapons.'

Then they rode at the greatest pace they could, and entered the road where the commanders were riding, and came up so close to them, that they heard the noise of the loud conversation they were carrying on among themselves. As they were beginning to emerge onto the plain, the Portuguese prepared to attack them; they fixed their lances under their arms, at the fastest gallop that their horses could manage.

The Castilians, when they heard them, made a great surge forward, and the commanders shouted in loud voices, 'It's nothing, gentlemen, it's nothing. Turn back, gentlemen.' As they were hastily reining back, a knight struck Álvaro Gonçalves a blow with his lance on the jerkin he was wearing, crying out, 'You traitor! You've betrayed us!' Álvaro Gonçalves threw himself off the mule to the ground, with a large shackle round his legs, and used the mule as protection.

Pero Rodrigues and the men who were with him rode to attack the Castilians; in the charge they made on them, a total of twenty Castilian squires fell from their horses, and their foot soldiers retreated to the hill, without doing anything worthy of mention. The Portuguese foot soldiers had no work to do other than to capture those squires who fell, to gather together the lances and adargues[118] that lay all over the field, and to round up mules, horses, sumpters and other pack-animals belonging to the commanders and other worthy squires who were in their company. There was no one to hinder them, because the enemies were defeated quickly and scattered through the thickets.

Since it was night and they were without a leader, they got down from their horses and ran off up the hill to escape. For this reason there were many

---

[118] Oval or heart-shaped leather shield.

horses left without owners, in addition to those which had fallen in the first charge. The commanders came out on a very rocky cliff, and abandoned their horses there, as did the others who were with them, and the horses made their way back to the plain.

The Portuguese did not know where Álvaro Gonçalves was and shouted for him, calling him by his name; he was lying in a large bed of rushes, and did not dare to answer, believing that it was Martim Eanes de Barbuda who was coming to seize him for the Castilians and take him captive on account of the ill will he bore towards him. By chance, Gomes Lourenço de Sampaio passed near the bed of rushes and, as he went around shouting for him, Álvaro Gonçalves recognised his voice and then responded. Joyfully, Gomes Lourenço dismounted from his horse, and helped Álvaro Gonçalves into the saddle, for he could not do it himself because of the shackle he was wearing. He fastened a spur on his foot and handed him a lance. Gomes Lourenço seized the horse of the Commander of Calatrava, who was the most renowned Castilian present, and they rode off to join the others. Pero Rodrigues was overjoyed to see him, as were all those there, telling him that they had come solely on his account. He thanked them as well as he could for their deeds.

The commotion was great in the town, and they rang all the bells they could, believing that it was Nuno Álvares attacking them, and the townspeople held this opinion according to what those who took refuge there told them.

In this defeat nine squires were taken captive, and sixteen horses were won, along with six mules, six sumpters, and twenty-five pack-animals with the provisions of a number of squires.

Ending the talk they had together, Álvaro Gonçalves took leave of Pero Rodrigues; out of all that they gave him he refused to take anything except eight horses. The sixteen squires that Nuno Álvares had sent, and also certain foot soldiers, went with him to Estremoz. Pero Rodrigues returned to Alandroal where, the next day, he gave six horses to six men whom he made squires, and he divided up all the other things and the ransom of the prisoners equally among them. Those who happened to remain in the town always received as good a share as those who went out with him.

Chapter 103

How Pero Rodrigues went to the aid of Álvaro Coitado so that he would not be taken captive by the Castilians

When Vasco Porcalho learned of the rescue of Álvaro Gonçalves, and how the commanders had been defeated, he was deeply vexed. In great annoyance he said in a mocking tone to those who were present: 'In truth, I consider it strange that none of you have ever asked me for your share of one-fifth from these raids that you make; 100 of you fight against 30, and always two dozen of you end up dead, and the others fleeing like sheep come back to this enclosure. With such honour as this, our good reputation will reach the king.'

That night he sent two spies to find out what Pero Rodrigues was doing, and what sort of troops had gone with him to the rescue of Álvaro Gonçalves, or whether he was still in Alandroal, for he was keen to hurry over there and accomplish some noteworthy deed, if he could. Certain men that Pero Rodrigues had sent out that night as spies seized an informer from the spies of Vasco Porcalho. The latter, learning that Álvaro Gonçalves was already in Estremoz and was due to leave that day for Borba, sent forty horsemen and thirty foot soldiers to go and wait on the road along which Álvaro Gonçalves was to travel, ordering that he should not escape them, whatever it took, but be taken dead or alive. Álvaro Gonçalves knew nothing of this.

Pero Rodrigues got news of this, and more, through a man from Vila Viçosa who came to tell him. As soon as he was assured about it all, he sent for those from the town [of Alandroal] and asked them what they thought he should do in such a situation. They said that he should do what he thought suited his honour, and that they were ready to help. He said: 'It seems to me that it is not right for us to allow a man to be lost, who cost us so much effort to set free. If we do not go to his aid, he may be captured or killed, a thing that I would not want to happen by any means.'

'Make yourself ready', they said, 'for we are ready.'

Then he rode with the men of the town community of Alandroal, and came to the town of Montalvão where he had been told that the commander had ordered the ambush of Álvaro Gonçalves. The Castilians had two lookout posts and, when they saw the Portuguese coming, they fell back, not willing to confront them, and Pero Rodrigues did not manage to catch any of them. Then he rode on to Estremoz, and found Álvaro Gonçalves, who had not yet left. He told him why he had come there, and Álvaro Gonçalves thanked him profusely. Pero Rodrigues told him to surround himself with good protection and precautions in order to escape harm.

Álvaro Gonçalves and Pero Rodrigues departed together then for the town of Borba. The following day, at mid-morning, Álvaro Gonçalves sent two squires to scout the area, and they spotted ten horsemen who were heading to raid the town of Borba. These got as far as the town, attempting to catch the two scouts, and seized twenty oxen that were grazing near the town. When they saw this, Álvaro Gonçalves and Pero Rodrigues rode against them to seize the oxen from them and did so before they could arrive at a spot where the Castilians had set up an ambush at a place called Orelhal. The ambush was discovered, and the Portuguese chased them at a gallop as far as the horticultural areas of the royal demesne near the town [Vila Viçosa], where they captured seven pack-animals belonging to Commander Vasco Porcalho. The Castilians did not dare to try and take them back, believing that they were faced with a greatly superior force.

Then Álvaro Gonçalves returned to Borba, and Pero Rodrigues to Alandroal.

Chapter 104

How Vasco Porcalho made a raid on Alandroal, and the booty he took from the Portuguese

Commander Vasco Porcalho, seeing the boldness that Pero Rodrigues and his followers were showing against him, wrote to Pero Rodrigues [da Fonseca],[119] the Governor of Olivença, telling him to order an attack against the town of Alandroal, from which he, Vasco Porcalho, was receiving very unneighbourly treatment. He said Pero Rodrigues da Fonseca could be sure that as soon as his raiders reached there, both the foot soldiers and the horsemen of the town would immediately come out and go after them, and not leave them until they reached the River Guadiana. That was because the foot soldiers of Alandroal could run as fast as the horsemen, and thus Pero Rodrigues da Fonseca's men could catch them and put them to the sword at their will, laying an ambush for them some distance east of the town.

As soon as he sent that message, he ordered twenty horsemen to make a raid on Alandroal, where they captured a few asses, which were taken back from them by men of the town community. These, returning to the town, told

[119] In Chapters 104 and 105, it is important to bear in mind the distinction between Pero Rodrigues, the Governor of Alandroal, who was loyal to the Master of Avis, and Pero Rodrigues da Fonseca, the Governor of Olivença, who was loyal to the King of Castile.

Vasco Porcalho that they did not intend ever to go there again, for they had been pursued so vigorously that if the road had not been long, they would have remained behind as their prisoners.

In great annoyance the commander took horse early in the morning, accompanied by 150 horsemen and 250 foot soldiers, and set up an ambush near Alandroal at a place called Pinheiro. Once it was fully daylight, he sent 20 horsemen to raid as far as the gates of the town; anything they might find, they should seize without fear. The light horsemen did as he commanded them, and rode as far as the gates of the town, capturing 700 goats. The men of the town came out against them: Pero Rodrigues with 10 horsemen and 75 foot soldiers. The horsemen took a different direction, so as to get in front; the foot soldiers had already taken the goats from the raiders, and the horsemen came across the ambush where most of the troops were. When they discovered it, they all headed directly back to the town, which was very close by.

To protect the foot soldiers, Pero Rodrigues advanced with them all close together until they neared the houses of the settlement of Mata, outside the walls. There they waited for their enemies and began to fight, with Pero Rodrigues on foot alongside his men. The battle being very unequal, the Portuguese were defeated by superior force. They fled to the town, taking refuge in the houses of Mata Street, which were all connected by internal passageways, and thus they escaped. Otherwise, most of them would have been killed or taken captive. But no more than five men were killed, who were very young and valiant and killed near the wall, but many were wounded. Pero Rodrigues received a wound. Two of the Castilians and fifteen horses died.

Vasco Porcalho then returned to Olivença[120] with great satisfaction, and took along those 700 goats, without there being anyone to hinder him. Pero Rodrigues, with his men, was greatly distressed by such misfortune; nevertheless, he delivered a speech to comfort them: 'My friends, this is how war goes in such matters. Eighty-five, against 350, can abandon the field without shame. As to those who died in defence of the kingdom, God will have mercy on their souls.'

[120] This seems to be a mistake. Vasco Porcalho must have returned to Vila Viçosa, from where he had launched the raid.

Chapter 105

How Pero Rodrigues da Fonseca set an ambush for the men of Alandroal, and what happened to him

Pero Rodrigues da Fonseca did not forget what Vasco Porcalho had told him in his letter. He rode out from Olivença with 200 horsemen and 300 foot soldiers, advancing one night to set an ambush near São Brás do Mosteiro, a full league from Alandroal. When it was morning he spoke to his men as follows: 'My friends, I would like to capture this town, and kill or capture those who dwell in it. If we can do it, as is my wish, we will do good service and give pleasure to the King of Castile, and we will succeed in all our raids. Since Vasco Porcalho killed some of the Portuguese the other day in an ambush that he set up, let us proceed in the following way. If those who go forward in the raid take some prisoners or anything else, they should pretend that they are attacking Terena. Some of the others should remain in front of the town, engaging our enemies as cautiously as they can. If they cannot find anything to capture, they should draw them as far away from the town as they can and inform us as secretly as possible. Once they are drawn away from the town, I and these squires will position ourselves between them and the town. Whoever recognises Pero Rodrigues of Alandroal should make every effort to capture him, and kill as many of the others as he can. For if he is captured, he will surrender the town at once, or else I will cut off his head at the town gate.'

The others, hearing these words, said that the plan was very good, but that it seemed to them wise to let Vasco Porcalho know, as he was well supplied with men and thus it would be much better and safer for him, Pero Rodrigues da Fonseca.

Pero Rodrigues da Fonseca said that he did not like the idea, because he wanted the honour for himself and for them. 'For today we will burn the gate of the town', he said, 'and after it is in our power, he will learn of it, and I do not wish it any other way.' Resolving on this decision, he selected forty of the best-mounted and most trusted light horsemen he could find and instructed them as we have said, commanding them to carry out his orders according to their own good judgement.

They raided around the town as they had been commanded. Pero Rodrigues, the Governor of Alandroal, had sent two squires out that morning in the direction of Vila Viçosa to scout. When the lookout saw the horsemen, he rang the bell and lowered the basket.[121] The men of the town, when they saw that, went forth on foot with lances and spears; those who did not have one of these carried instead six or seven sharpened staves as weapons. Pero Rodrigues had not wanted them to go out but, when he saw them ready to skirmish, he rode out with ten horsemen. They followed the enemies so closely that they could not go by the road that they had intended to follow; rather, armed with spears and darts, they began to flee towards where Pero Rodrigues da Fonseca was lying in ambush, quite unaware of any such situation.

When the Portuguese attackers and the Castilians ambushers found themselves mingled into one, there was such a great confusion among the latter that some could not mount their horses. Without noticing whether there were many or few enemies, they fled through the undergrowth as well as they could, both on horseback and on foot. Thus, fortune aiding the few and spreading fear and panic among the many, Pero Rodrigues da Fonseca fled with those who managed to join him; others did not reach Olivença for two days. In the encounter seven of the Castilian foot soldiers were killed, and two horsemen, and five of the light horsemen; thirteen horses were killed, and nine left alive. Of the men of the town, three horsemen and ten foot soldiers were wounded, and one was killed. They found many lances and spears that had been left on the field and returned with much rejoicing to the town.

Chapter 106

How Payo Rodríguez captured Gil Fernandes of Elvas

While these events were happening, the Master wrote from Lisbon, where he was at the time, to Gil Fernandes of Elvas, telling him to go and speak with Payo Rodríguez Mariño, the Governor of Campo Maior, to persuade him to declare loyalty to the Master, who would grant him many favours.

Gil Fernandes rode off at once, taking fifty men-at-arms with him, and went to Campo Maior. When outside the town next to a church that stands there, he sent a message, asking Payo Rodríguez to come forth from the castle and speak with him concerning things that were for his honour and advantage. Payo Rodríguez said that he would not come forth, but that Gil Fernandes should come to a place between the castle wall and the outer fortifications of the castle, and bring ten men-at-arms with him.

---

[121] The lowering of a basket, which was usually on top of a high mast, warned the inhabitants that there were enemies in sight.

Gil Fernandes said that he was content at that, but on condition that on both sides there should be granted a guarantee of safe passage, so that each would be safe from the other. Payo Rodríguez said that he too was content, and thus it was confirmed and agreed between them. Then Gil Fernandes selected ten men-at-arms, and went to the outer wall of the castle where they were to speak, and found Payo Rodríguez already there. When they came to embrace each other, Payo Rodríguez threw his arm around the shoulder of Gil Fernandes, so as to hold him, and with the other hand he removed his sword, saying, 'You're under arrest.'

Gil Fernandes was shocked when he heard this and had no way to defend himself, for Payo Rodríguez had so many men, who were so stationed that his ten squires could not help him. Rather, making an effort to flee when they saw what was happening, five of them were taken captive: Gonçalo Casco, Martim Vasques and Gil Lourenço, who were Gil Fernandes's cousins, and two others. While these were being captured, the other five jumped over the outer wall and went to join those who had remained outside. All of them, shocked by such treachery, returned to Elvas.

Gil Fernandes, having thus been made prisoner, had to pay a ransom of 2,000 *dobras*; he gave sureties and left his prison. When he arrived in Elvas, everyone was very pleased to see him, because, while he had been a prisoner, they had been very often raided by their enemies. As sureties for his ransom, the priests gave the crosses from the churches, and the laity goblets, swords, bejewelled belts and coins, and other things, all pledged to Payo Rodríguez, until the ransom could be paid. After it had all been handed over, Gil Fernandes took Sancho Sánchez and Alfonso Sánchez, whom he had brought as prisoners from Arronches, as you have heard,[122] and received for them a ransom of 2,000 *dobras*, of which 1,000 were given over to him at once, and the rest on a set day, according to his obligation, to Payo Rodríguez. Thus he paid everything and redeemed his pledge and his squires.

Chapter 107

How Gil Fernandes made a raid into Castile, and what happened to him

When this had been done, Gil Fernandes called for his friends, and gathered between them and other men of Elvas around 100 horsemen and 400 foot soldiers. He entered Castile openly, skirting Olivença and Alconchel, and

---

[122] In Chapter 96 above.

went to raid the lands of Jerez [de los Caballeros].[123] He brought away a large booty of cattle, sheep and prisoners.

As he was heading back towards Portugal with all this, the men of Jerez and other towns round about gathered together, around 300 horsemen and many men on foot, and followed him to a place called the Sierra de las Puercas. While they were there, the two groups not far from each other, some men said to Gil Fernandes: 'You know well that in front of you in Olivença you have Pero Rodrigues da Fonseca and Payo Rodríguez Mariño who is with him now, and that the two of them have some 300 lances and 700 foot soldiers to fight against you on your way back. If you wait for those who are coming up behind us to join with those who are in front, you will have a much fiercer encounter. It seems to us, therefore, that it would be wise for you to fight these men now; once they are defeated, the others will not want to encounter you.'

Gil Fernandes said that it seemed like good advice to him. But before he arrayed his men to go and fight, some of them hurried off to engage the enemy without him. When they attacked the enemy, they were repulsed, and some of them wounded. Gil Fernandes, when he saw them in that plight, came up speedily to their aid and said:

'Holy Mary protect us! What's this? Come back, come back, young men, for they are good for nothing.' Then he threw himself among them, encouraging his men. They attacked the Castilians with such valour that they were defeated and scattered, and fled from them, some across the field and others into the Sierra de las Puercas, for they did not dare to turn back and face Gil Fernandes.

As Gil Fernandes was coming back with his men and their booty, expecting to have another such encounter with those noblemen we have mentioned, the latter found out how Gil Fernandes had defeated the men of Jerez, and both of them agreed not to do battle with him. Without any hindrance Gil Fernandes returned with all the [captured] livestock to the town of Elvas. There was so much of it that anyone who wished to take some to eat was free to do so.

---

[123] Not to be confused with Jerez de la Frontera, the home of sherry, this village lies some 15 miles (24 km) to the south-east of Alconchel.

Chapter 108

How Gil Fernandes did battle with
Payo Rodríguez Mariño, and how Payo
Rodríguez was defeated and killed

For you to see in what manner Gil Fernandes was avenged for his captivity, although it did not happen very soon afterwards, we wish to relate it here, as we do not know whether we will have any further occasion to speak about his exploits.

It so happened that Payo Rodríguez Mariño sent twenty horsemen from Campo Maior to raid Elvas. Gil Fernandes went out after them with fifty horsemen, followed them for a very long way and captured four squires from among them. He paused on the approach to a hill called Segóvia, believing that Payo Rodríguez would make for there, since he had been sent for by his men. While they were waiting, some of Payo Rodríguez's men came on ahead, and Gil Fernandes captured two of them. Payo Rodríguez had eighty horsemen with him, very well arrayed. When he arrived, he established himself on a small rise at the edge of the road on the side of the hill, whereas Gil Fernandes was at the bottom.

On both sides there were no foot soldiers except for two that Payo Rodríguez had brought with him; one was a crossbowman, and the other threw stones by hand and caused considerable damage. At this point a good squire called Pero Fernández Viscaino said to Payo Rodríguez, 'I tell you, Payo Rodríguez, my advice is that you should not fight with Gil Fernandes.'

Nuno Fernandes Cogominho said: 'In truth, do you call that good advice? There are eighty of us horsemen here, well armed, and Gil Fernandes has no more than fifty over there, and all of them thieves and rascals, such as João Ruivano and Afonso das Vacas, and others of the sort, and you advise us not to fight with them! I tell you that if he misses this chance, it will be a long time before he gets another one as good.'

To this Pero Fernández retorted, 'Really, Nuno Fernandes, do you not see those good squires riding there alongside Gil Fernandes? Let Payo Rodríguez do as he likes, for I shall not abandon him and flee the field.' Nuno Fernandes was a powerful man and had seven squires of his own with him there, and moreover was a good fighter. Payo Rodríguez did not reply to either of them, and they continued disputing with each other for what must have been a quarter of an hour.

Then Gil Fernandes, observing this, spoke as follows to his men: 'Let's move away from them a little, and then they will muster the courage to come down to us.' When they began to move away, at once Payo Rodríguez rode hard to take higher ground than Gil Fernandes. Gil Fernandes, at a gallop, climbed another slope, and ended up at the same level. Then Payo Rodríguez charged fiercely against him and delivered a blow with his lance at a man called Afonso Esteves, which pierced his mail through the side; entering his body, the lance cut through two of his ribs reaching his lungs, and he fell dead to the ground.

Gil Eanes, the cousin of Gil Fernandes, fixed his lance under his arm, came upon Payo Rodríguez from the side and knocked him off his horse. The men of Payo Rodríguez rode up to help him and knocked Gil Eanes to the ground.

At this point, with the battle raging fiercely, the men of Payo Rodríguez began to flee. Gil Fernandes told two squires to hold Payo Rodríguez prisoner while he pursued the others. Then Martim Vasques, one of the squires, who had been made captive with Gil Fernandes, when he saw Payo Rodríguez standing there, spoke to him in this way:

'What is this, Payo Rodríguez? Now you will pay for what you did to Gil Fernandes and his kinsmen.'

'Do not be harsh towards the meek', he said, 'for I am very meek at the moment.'

From this point such words went on being exchanged between them until Martim Vasques killed him and cut off his head; he did the same to Nuno Fernandes Cogominho and another squire called Álvaro Rodrigues, and then left for Elvas, taking the heads with him. When Gil Fernandes returned from pursuing the fugitives and learned how Martim Vasques had killed them and in what fashion, he inquired after him in order to punish him. When he could not find him, in great distress he said, 'Let it be, since that is how it is; the fewer enemies, the better.'

Then he ordered that some who were prisoners be gathered together and he made his way towards Elvas. In all there were, what with prisoners and the dead, not more than about twenty-five, of whom one was Pero Fernández Viscaino, the squire who had advised Payo Rodríguez not to fight with Gil Fernandes.

Chapter 109

Concerning some Genoese *naos* that the Master took under his control, and how Alenquer was attacked but not taken

Y ou are all listening, yet no one asks, after Nuno Álvares headed into the Alentejo, and those things that we have related were done, what the Master was doing in the meantime in Lisbon, or on what he was spending his time for the defence of the realm and the city. Since no one asks about it, we want you to know that after the Master took his leave of Nuno Álvares in Coina, as you have heard,[124] and returned to Lisbon, three of his galleys and three barges, not far from the port of the city, went out to capture two *naos* laden with cloth and silver and many other items being transported in them. They also captured a barge from Galicia, laden with timber.

Bernabò Dentudo and Niccolò di Parma, who were the masters of these *naos*, protested that they were from Genoa, giving many reasons in proof of this, which was evident. The men of the city protested much more than they, always insisting that they were from Castile. In this uncertainty, which could easily have been avoided, the Master ordered that all the merchandise be placed in the customs house, from which they afterwards derived much profit, and which was extremely helpful to him for paying wages and other expenses. That was because in the ships were found more than 3,100 rolls of cloth from Ypres and Bruges, and scarlet, and other cloths of lesser value, over 1,000 lengths of serge and also more than 1,000 *varas* of French linen-cotton blend,[125] and silver, gold, lead and quills and many other things of which it is not necessary to write.

Seven days later a barge arrived at the city and brought news that the English were ready to set out in force and come to the aid of the Master and the kingdom. At this point the men of Alenquer sent word to the Master that he should send fifty men-at-arms there; the men of the town would join their efforts to take the castle, and would declare loyalty to him. The Master was very pleased at this, and certain men from Alenquer came by night to accompany the men whom the Master was sending there. Then the Master had two galleys fitted out, and appointed Admiral Master Manuel [Pessanha]

---

[124] In Chapter 89 above.

[125] '*Lenço*' in the original text. The term appears to mean a mixed linen and cotton fabric, possibly what the Romans called 'Carbasus lina'.

as the captain of those who were to go; he was the son of Lançarote, who had been killed in Beja.[126]

These galleys went upriver as far as the bridge of Marinha, which is a league from the town [of Alenquer]. When they came in to put the men ashore, it was already so late that it was broad daylight, and the men of the town could see them from all sides. Nevertheless, they captured the gates of the town as they had planned, and entered without further hindrance. They went directly to the castle, both those who had come from Lisbon and the inhabitants of the town; they began to attack it very fiercely, telling the governor to give up the castle to his lord, the Master. Seeing that he did not wish to do so, they began to shout for fire to be brought to burn down the gates. The fire was quickly made ready and just right for burning, for some brought wooden bars and lumps of lard, and others firewood and oil, each as best he could, so that the fire would not die down for lack of good fuel. Since the place where the gate was located was very well sheltered from any wind that might have helped the fire, however, and moreover because of the large amounts of water that those who were defending the castle threw onto it, all that labour was expended in vain.

The battle having lasted from the hour of prime until close to vespers,[127] during which time several were wounded, news came that the King of Castile, who was encamped 4 leagues away in Bombarral, was sending men in haste to come to the aid of the town, at the request of Vasco Peres de Camões, the governor of the castle. Others said that the king himself was coming with his men.

The men of the town agreed to depart at once, when they realised that the castle could not be taken as quickly as they had believed, and that the King of Castile or his men might be coming, which inevitably would turn out badly for them, because of the way into the town that they had opened up. Then all the leading men of the town left with their wives and children and the few possessions they could take along. No one remained behind except a few poor people who were not harmed afterwards.

Although Vasco Peres called out when he saw them leaving that they should come back and not be afraid of the king or his men, even if they should come, they all ignored his assurances, boarded the galleys and went back to Lisbon, extremely perturbed about what they had started, since it had not been carried through. Many of the moveable goods they owned had been left behind, and their houses full of furnishings which the men of the castle later stole before other men arrived.

---

[126] See Chapter 42 above.

[127] Approximately from 6 am to 5 pm.

The next day Garcí Fernández de Villodre arrived in Alenquer at the command of the king, with many men to assist him, believing that those who had come from Lisbon were still there fighting.

Chapter 110

How the Master ordered several galleys
to be fitted out in Lisbon

The Master and those of his council realised how the King of Castile was coming with all his forces, and were aware of the great fleet of *naos* and galleys that he had ordered to be fitted out to descend upon Lisbon, in order to blockade its port so that it could not be relieved by supplies from anywhere. For these reasons they agreed to fit out the *naos* and galleys that there were in the city, so that they would be ready. If a small number of ships should come in the meanwhile, they could prevent their arrival, and obtain supplies from the Alentejo without hindrance, both to supply the city, and to protect those who came from that direction to aid in its defence. When once they learned that the Castilian fleet was coming in full force, the *naos* and galleys would go to Oporto and join up with the others that were already there. Then they would all come together to do battle with the Castilian fleet.

The responsibility for fitting out the galleys was given to Dom Lourenço, who was at that time the Archbishop of Braga, and who accepted it very willingly. He began at once to order the vessels to be put in the cradles and launched. He applied so much effort and so many people to this task, that most of the galleys were launched by hand, without a capstan. He rode through the city on a horse, wearing two coats of mail and his rochet over them, and a lance in his hand, with the blade always pointing forward.

Even though the men of the city volunteered with goodwill for that work, he still urged them on, not sparing anyone, regardless of his status; thus no priest or friar was left out, nor any other person, but all were obliged to show up there. If anyone said he was a priest, the archbishop responded that he was just as much of a priest; if anyone said he was a friar, he would say, 'And I am an archbishop, which is better than a friar.' He made such haste in fitting out the galleys, that in a few days twelve were ready for battle; in addition, another galley and a galliot came in from the Algarve.

Since there were no shields or javelins, which had been lost in the flotillas raised by King Fernando, they made shields from barrel staves and sawed up sycamores to make javelins.

Chapter 111

How the standard was entrusted to Gonçalo Rodrigues, and how the fleet departed for Oporto

With seven *naos* fitted out, as well as the galleys, and supplied with all that was necessary, the Master named Gonçalo Rodrigues de Sousa, who was Governor of Monsaraz at the time, as captain of the fleet. The Master came to the cathedral well accompanied, along with all the city dwellers, the Orders and the clergy; from there they all set forth in a grand and solemn procession, with the clergy leading, and the Master close by with all the rest of the people, and many trumpets located where they would cause no obstruction. Thus with great rejoicing they carried the standard with the undifferenced arms of Portugal through the middle of the city, and they arrived with it at the Oura Gate, which is next to the waterfront.

There it was given to Gonçalo Rodrigues, and placed on the largest galley of them all, which they called the 'Royal Galley'. When this had been done, the Master and all the others returned to their lodgings. There was a marvel the following night. There were Christians and Moors keeping watch over the wall on the side of São Vicente de Fora, close to where there stands the Chapel of the Martyrs, named after those killed in the taking of the city when it was recovered from the Moors [in 1147]. At midnight, these watchmen saw twenty men dressed in white garments like priests. Four of them were carrying lighted candles in their hands, and they went to and fro in procession entering the church; they spoke among themselves in very low tones, as if they were praying the Hours. When the men on the wall saw this, they were very startled, and began calling others to behold so great a miracle, and suddenly they disappeared.

Just afterwards, as the guards were speaking with each other about this, they saw flames of bright light on the tips of the lances that were on the towers, which lasted for about an hour. This was witnessed by seven Christians and three Moors who were standing watch on a tower. Already a week before this a man had arrived from Montemor-o-Velho and brought to the Master a public declaration written in the hand of Lourenço Afonso, a notary of that town, in which it was stated that on a Monday, the 11th day of that month of April, in the presence of Gonçalo Gomes da Silva, his sons and many others from the same town, it had rained wax on that place, just like that which is put into candles, and he brought a sample of it.

When the people of the city heard the next day about the miracle recounted by watchmen at São Vicente da Fora, they were very joyful about it and other similar things that it pleased the Lord God to show forth at this time. The bishop and the clergy, with all the people in procession, went to the Church of the Martyrs, giving Him many thanks and asking Him to mercifully come to their aid.

At this time there was a great storm at sea, and one day three Castilian *naos* arrived driven by contrary winds, much to their regret, and anchored in the river 3 leagues from the city, opposite Oeiras. These *naos* had been sent laden with flour, barley and other items for the King of Castile's camp, in the belief that he was already besieging the city. On catching sight of them, the crews of the galleys rowed towards them to capture them; those in the *naos*, seeing this, all put on sail to get away and escape safely if they could. Realising that they could not do so because of the contrary weather, and as the sails were already unfurled, they chose to run the *naos* aground and wreck them rather than let the Portuguese take them and benefit from them and the things they were bringing. The men saved themselves by getting into boats and by swimming, as best they could. The men of the King of Castile who were in Sintra and were active in that area helped to protect them, so that they received no harm. The Portuguese burned the [Castilian] *naos* and returned to the city. In the raging storm four galleys were in danger of being lost out of those lying at anchor before the city, but it pleased God to protect them.

When the weather was favourable for the galleys to set out, before the fleet from Castile arrived (for they had already heard that it was at sea) the Master went to review the troops they carried in a place called Amora, on the Almada bank. In the afternoon the vessels came to drop anchor in front of the city, and on 14 May Gonçalo Rodrigues departed with them for the city of Oporto.

The [other Portuguese] *naos* could not go in their company, on account of the contrary weather, and they returned to the city. The galleys reached Atouguia, a town which was on the side of the King of Castile, because of João Gonçalves, who was Governor of Óbidos and loyal to him, and who thus obliged the local inhabitants to take the side he supported. Therefore the men on the galleys went out and stole provisions and other things they found, capturing nine balingers which were left over from the time of King Fernando, in order to make use of them, because they were swift.

From there the galleys continued their voyage, and arrived in the city of Oporto, where we will let them lie resting for a time, while we go to see the King of Castile.

Chapter 112

How the Castilians skirmished with the Portuguese, and how Juan Ramírez de Arellano was captured

Before this, the King of Castile stayed a few days near Óbidos in a village called Bombarral, because of the counsel of his men who advised him not to besiege Lisbon until his fleet arrived, so that all the shoreline would be under their control, and no assistance whether of men or supplies could reach the city from the other side of the Tagus, and likewise for other reasons already recorded. Thus the king took his ease there for several days, and then approached the city through those villages where he could find the best repose, until he came to a large and spacious village called Lumiar, a league from the city, and there he proposed to remain and rest for a while.

His men installed themselves in the many fine villages that there are in that district. While the king was in the vicinity, his men did not go to skirmish against the city, except for only a few times, because they were some distance away and thus it was not convenient for them.

Nevertheless, one day some captains came with their men-at-arms, foot soldiers and crossbowmen, up from the valley of Santa Bárbara to the hill of São Gens; there they gathered in large bands with their banners, protected by a pavisade,[128] jeering at the men of the town. When they had been there for a little while, they moved against the Gate of Santo Agostinho. Count Álvaro Pérez de Castro, his son Dom Pedro, Mem Rodrigues and Rui Mendes, who were the sons of Gonçalo Mendes de Vasconcelos, were responsible for guarding that sector; they had a total of 200 lances with them, besides the men of the city who were in their company. When they saw the Castilians in that array, some of them went out to skirmish. As both sides were skirmishing with a will, a good nobleman from among those enemy captains was taken prisoner; his name was Juan Ramírez de Arellano. When he was captured, the men of the city took heart, and drove the enemy back, down the long slope to the bottom. They rode dragging their banners over the planted wheat fields on the side of the hill, where there were several wounded and dead.

The Master, hearing how his men were skirmishing, went forth on foot with men-at-arms and crossbowmen to a flat piece of ground by the Gate of São Vicente. After he saw the skirmish brought to an end he returned to the

---

[128] A sort of defensive wall made of longer and wider than usual shields or 'pavises' placed side by side in a continuous line. This strategy could be used on land or in ships to protect the crew both from projectiles and from the sight of the enemy.

city. He ordered Juan Ramírez to be kept in the keep of the castle, under the guard of those who manned it, gave him some of his own clothes and did him full honour.

On this day, which was 26 May, the Castilian fleet began to arrive. Thirteen galleys and a galliot showed up before the city, with which the king was greatly pleased, because it made it possible for him to go and blockade it.

Chapter 113

How the king came close to the city, and concerning the attack he made upon it

One day passed, and no more. On the following Saturday [28 May], quite early in the morning, several noblemen on horseback from the Castilian side arrived at the towers that stand on a high hill in the direction of São Domingos. Protected by a safe conduct, they spoke to those in the towers, saying that they should go and tell the Master that the king their liege lord, who was already on his way, wished to proclaim his edicts there, along with several claims. Therefore, he should order some knights and citizens to go to that spot to see how he would make his declarations.

They told the Master this, and he sent to tell them to go away at once; if they did not do so, they would be shot at with crossbows. When the Castilians heard this message, they departed from where they were, retreating to a distance from the wall, and there they waited for their liege lord the king, who was already on his way.

Here it is important for you to know that these edicts that the king had wished to proclaim were to accuse all the inhabitants of the city of treason, in order afterwards to dispose of their property and proceed against them by his own will, saying that he had come there in person with his banner unfurled, but they had refused to receive him as their rightful lord.

At this point the King of Castile arrived with his host all on horseback, and many foot soldiers and crossbowmen whom he had obtained from the galleys, to take a look at the city. He came up close at a high hill which is now called Olivete Hill. He spent most of the day there, and many of his men went about meanwhile cutting down trees and grapevines, and doing all the damage they could.

Now it happened that this same day in the morning, before the King of Castile came, numbers of men-at-arms and crossbowmen, and likewise foot soldiers, had gone out from the city by the Santa Catarina Gate.[129] They arranged their defensive pavisade to skirmish with the Castilians, who they were already sure were going to come. Among these was Fernão Pereira, the brother of Nuno Álvares; Doctor Martim Afonso, who later became Archbishop of Braga; João Lourenço da Cunha; Juan Alfonso de Baeza; Martin-Paul, the Gascon; Vasco Martins de Gá; Fernando Álvares, the comptroller of the Master's household; and many other very honourable men-at-arms. The Master was in the tower of Álvaro Pais to see what the King of Castile would do with the men he had with him.

The king remained where he was, without doing anything, until after the third hour.[130] Seeing how those who had gone forth from the city were in full view, without showing any fear of him, he then said to his men, 'Do you not see how those villains venture out of the city, without any fear of us? Get after them, force them to shut themselves up inside, for they are all villains.'

Some of his men who heard this declared that this should not be done, since, even if they pursued them as far as the gates, they did not have the power to do any harm to the city.

The king, hearing this, was vexed, and, without replying, he called for his bascinet, and told the Master of Santiago to ride on ahead with his banner. When he did what the king commanded, many men dismounted from their horses and, with their lances in hand, moved against the Portuguese, until they converged.

There were many Castilians, and few from Lisbon; being unable to withstand them, the Portuguese were forced to turn back hurriedly towards the city.[131] Others went into the moat, which was low at the time. There they would have been slain or captured, if not for the men on the towers and walls, who defended them with stones and bolts. At this point the king came up from behind with many of his men, and Pedro Fernández de Velasco began shouting, 'Forward, gentlemen, forward! The city is ours!' Likewise, Count João Afonso Telo, the brother of Queen Leonor, was yelling in the same fashion, 'Forward, gentlemen, forward! This is the way to my house!'

When the Master, who was watching all this, saw that the men of the city were retreating in disorder and the Castilians were advancing straight towards the gate, he came down very swiftly from the tower where he had been; he closed one side of the door with his own hand, gave orders to close the other

---

[129] Situated near the present-day Loreto Church, in the Chiado district of Lisbon, i.e. on the west-facing section of the city walls.

[130] The third hour, or hour of tierce, began at 9 am.

[131] Lisbon city walls.

one and said to his men, 'Back, back, gentlemen, what is this? I'll make you brave even if you don't want to be.'

Then the Portuguese who were outside were all left between the wall and the barbican. There the two sides began to battle against each other very fiercely with lances and, although the combat lasted for a long time, the Castilians never managed to drive them out of that entrance to the barbican, the gates of which were missing. The abundant crossbow fire likewise, both from those on the galleys and those the king had brought with him, was constantly aimed at the men on the wall, so that it was littered with crossbow bolts. Moreover, the crossbowmen from inside were shooting from between the battlements at the men outside; from the tops of the towers they threw down many stones, which the women carried up in baskets, but these did little harm because they were soft, and they all shattered into fragments. The clamour was very great, and almost all the people of the city were gathering there.

While all this was going on, foot soldiers and crossbowmen went forth from the city, beyond the towers of São Domingos. Don Álvaro Pérez de Guzmán came upon them with many light horsemen and made an attack against them; several of the Portuguese were wounded, and two horses were lost, but no one died there on either side.

The Castilians, seeing that they were gaining no advantage with the battle dragging on for a very long time, stopped fighting, some of their number already having been wounded and slain. Among those who died were the Knight of the Pages and another knight called Ruy Duque, and several more, most of them slain by stones fired from a tower. Of the Portuguese, four were killed and many wounded; among the wounded were Fernão Pereira, Martin-Paul, and others.

With this action over, the king returned with his men to the place whence he had set out. The people of the city diligently buried their dead and tended the wounded.

Chapter 114

How the King of Castile arrived at Lisbon and set up his camp to besiege it

The following day, which was 29 May, the *naos* arrived, which had been fitted out to arrive in company with the galleys. In all there were forty, between the larger and smaller ones. When the King of Castile learned that the fleet of *naos* had arrived, he set out the next day with all his host to set up his camp and besiege the city. They arrived there at the hour of tierce.[132] According to rumour, the men that he had there were probably around 5,000 lances, besides men who had remained in Santarém and all the other towns that were on his side. There were also 1,000 light horsemen of whom Don Álvaro Pérez de Guzmán was the captain, and many good crossbowmen, a total of 6,000, as some have written. There were a countless number of foot soldiers, besides the men who came in the fleet, and quite a few others who came to him by land every day.

The king commanded that the siege camp be set up next to the Convent of Santos, which is for ladies of the Order of Santiago, and at a short distance from the city, little more than two crossbow shots away. There they prepared at once for the king a tall house with a number of floors, built on four thick beams, surrounded by a drystone wall.

Near to it were pitched many very grand pavilions, both that of the king and those of the noblemen who had come with him. All the other men pitched their tents around Alcântara and Campolide and the surrounding district, in long and well-ordered rows. On top of all the tents there were banners and pennons of various coats of arms and insignia. As to how each tent was adorned by arms, which made the camp glitter, and of the multitude of trumpets and other things that made it such a splendid sight, there is no need to speak.

The camp, completely palisaded on the side facing the city, was in a small valley, where there is a well, for they had no fear of receiving harm from any other direction, since all the surrounding towns were loyal to the King of Castile. It was well-stocked with provisions that came to it from Santarém in barges down the river, and by land in great trains of pack-animals, for the protection of which the king ordered men to be always stationed at certain places along the road, where he judged that they might suffer harm. Not only from Santarém, but from all the other towns loyal to the King of Castile, the camp was supplied with all that was needed.

From Seville there came many barges and boats with provisions and weapons and whatever other things were necessary. Do not believe that there was only food, for you would also have found great quantities of spices of many varied kinds on sale there. There were physicians and surgeons and apothecaries, who had available not only the items necessary to preserve the health of the body, but also various kinds of confections, sugar and conserves were to be found there in great plenty.

Rose-water, and other distilled waters of the kind used by luxury-loving men in peacetime, could all be bought there for money as each man wished. The reason for which these and many other things were to be found in the

---

[132] See Chapter 113, note 130 above.

camp, in great quantity, was the arrival of two carracks from the Levant with cargoes for Flanders. Adverse weather forced them to anchor in Restelo, along with the fleet. The king sent word to ask them if they would be pleased to unload there and sell their merchandise in the camp, from which they would make a large profit; they would please him greatly by doing so, and he would grant them favours in return. The merchants and masters reached an agreement on the matter. Given the king's repeated requests, and the implied threat underlying them, to say nothing of the prospect of profit for themselves, they granted what was asked of them, and unloaded their merchandise, from which the troops were generously supplied.

You would have found silk and wool fabrics of various sorts on several stalls, suited to every man's needs; the camp prostitutes occupied a street as big as any to be found in large cities. In the camp there was a street in which many arms were sold and repaired, and another of Christian and Jewish merchants, in which there could be found cloth, tunics, and many other things for sale. There was a street of moneychangers, where there was much buying and selling of silver, gold, and other coins in great abundance. You would have found many other things for sale that we do not care to mention; only in footwear was the camp never well supplied. It was maintained in very good discipline, so that no man feared to sleep alone, even if he had a lot of money with him, nor were other crimes committed there for which men are usually punished.

To guard the camp during the day, when the night watch had been dismissed, there were several horsemen in certain places within sight of the city, so that no one could leave it without being seen by them. On the water near Almada there always lay two galleys in readiness, so that no supplies or men could come to the city to aid in its defence.

The fleet of *naos* lay all along the city, from Cata-que-farás[133] to the Cruz Gate, all in good order one in front of the other, and from each one to the next a thick cable was stretched, so that even if some barge or boat from the other side should try to pass with men or supplies, it could not do so by that way, on account of the obstruction created by the cables. Thus the king set up his blockade by sea and by land, which clearly showed to those who saw it that his vast and noble power was sufficient for this and for greater conquests.

Since the great lords and noblemen who were there with the king saw so many advantages on his side, both from the towns he already controlled and from the men and supplies that came to him every day, and since all this was quite the opposite for the Master and the towns loyal to him, some of them, speaking one day about this, said to Fernando Álvarez de Toledo [y Meneses],

---

[133] An embankment located where the Corpo Santo Square is now.

the Marshal of Castile: 'Fernando Álvarez, you who are an old man, and have witnessed much warfare similar to this, both in France in the company of King Enrique, and in other places where it so happened that you took part in feats of arms, does it seem to you that the Master and Lisbon can carry on with this attempt they have undertaken, and defend themselves against the king our liege lord and the greater part of Portugal, and also against men of other kingdoms who are supporting him, and of whom there would be more if he should want them?'

He said: 'Gentlemen, I have seen many things, because I am a man of great age, and I have seen great undertakings begun with great might, and many opportunities for success, yet never concluding in the way desired by those who began them. I have also seen very small undertakings, without any reason to be successful, and yet little by little they came to such a great end that no one could have imagined. So, regarding this enterprise that our liege lord the king has undertaken against the Master, I say that if fortune should happen to favour him a little, the Master and the city will carry on with what they have undertaken. I know nothing more of this matter.'

Chapter 115

How the city was put on a defensive footing when the King of Castile laid siege to it

No subject could be more germane to the chapter you have just heard than for us to set down here briefly how the city was put on a defensive footing, with the King of Castile besieging it, and in what way the Master and the men who were within guarded themselves, so as not to suffer harm from their enemies, and the strength and bravery they showed against them while they were under siege.

Here it is important for you to know that, when the Master and the city dwellers learned of the coming of the King of Castile, and expected his great and powerful siege, it was at once ordered that as many supplies as possible should be gathered for the city, both wheat and meat and any other things. Many went off to the marshes in barges and boats, after Santarém had gone over to Castile, and from there brought many cattle which they slaughtered and salted down in tubs, and other things of which they made a great store. Many farmers with their wives and children and belongings took refuge in the city, along with other people from the surrounding district, and all those who chose to do so. Some crossed the Tagus with their livestock, work animals, and whatever they could carry, and went towards Setúbal and Palmela. Others remained in the city and refused to leave it. There were some who took all that they had there, and remained in the towns that had declared loyalty to Castile.

All of the city walls were in good repair, and on the seventy-seven towers that went all round the city, there were built strong pavilions of wood, which were plentifully furnished with shields, lances, spears, windlass crossbows, and other kinds of weapons, with a great abundance of crossbow bolts. There were also in these towers many pikes and bascinets, and other arms, so many of them gleaming that each tower showed clearly that it was well-equipped to defend itself. In many of them there were cannons well supplied with stones, and banners of Saint George, banners displaying the arms of the kingdom and the city, and those of certain great lords and captains who displayed them on the towers that were entrusted to them.

The Master arranged with the men of the city for the guarding of the walls to be shared among the noblemen and honourable citizens; to these were allotted certain sections of the walls, and crossbowmen and men-at-arms to assist each of them in adequately protecting his own section of wall. In each section there was a bell to ring when they saw it was necessary. When each one heard the bell of his section, all of them rushed towards it swiftly, because at times those who had charge of the towers went to walk about in the city, and left them entrusted to men on whom they relied very much; at other times there was no one in them except the lookouts. But when the bell rang, the walls were thronged with troops, many of them being outside the walls as well.

Not only those who were assigned to the defence of each place, but also the other people of the city, upon hearing the bells rung in the cathedral and the other towers, felt their hearts stirred. The artisans left off their work, and at once all of them in arms rushed to wherever it was said that the Castilians showed signs of attacking. There you could have seen the walls packed with troops, with many trumpets and much shouting and jeering, brandishing swords and lances and similar weapons, showing boldness against their enemies.

They paid no attention then to the text that says, 'The Church aids the kingdom with its prayers more than the knights with their weapons.' There was no obedience to the canonic rule: 'Clerici arma portantes',[134] according to which it is not fitting for clerics to take up arms, even if it be for the defence of the country. Priests and friars, especially from the Monastery of the Trindade, were readily on the walls, with the best arms they could get. Each group watched over its tower by night; the entire wall and towers were patrolled,

[134] 'Clerics bearing arms or practising usury shall be excommunicated', from Council of Poitiers 1078, Canon 10; Kriston Rennie, 'The Council of Poitiers (1078) and Some Legal Considerations', *Bulletin of Medieval Canon Law* (2011), 1–16 (7).

the men going from one end of their section to the other; supervisory patrols walked along the walls, some going one way and others coming back the other.

Notwithstanding all of this, the Master, who more than anyone else took special care regarding the protection and governance of the city, giving his body very little rest, frequently walked along the walls and towers at night, with lighted torches in front of him, well accompanied by many men whom he always took with him. There were no grumblers among those assigned to stand watch, nor any who neglected anything with which he had been entrusted; rather, they were all more than ready to do everything they were told. Thus there was no shortage of diligent men to carry out all the good arrangements that the Master ordered.

Of the thirty-eight gates that there are in the city, twelve were open all day, entrusted to good men-at-arms who took care to protect them. No one who was not very well known could pass through them, entering or leaving, without it first being known for certain why he was going or coming. There they placed boards crosswise over poles for those on duty to take some sleep, so that at night the gates would still be manned, and no one with evil intent would dare to try anything.

Certain people had the keys to some of the gates by night, because of the boats that at such times came and went with wheat and other provisions, as you will read in due time. Other keys were collected every night by a man in whom the Master greatly trusted; first seeing that the gates were closed, he took all the keys to the palace where the Master was staying. Near the Santa Catarina Gate, on the side near the camp, through which they most often used to go forth to skirmish, there was always a house in readiness, with beds, eggs, tow,[135] and old sheets to tear up; also a surgeon and theriac and other things needed for the care of the wounded when they returned from skirmishes.

On the riverbank two large and strong palisades of thick and sturdy stakes had been built, which the Master had ordered to be made before the King of Castile came, to prevent an attack on that area. They were erected from the point where the river spread most widely up to the land next to the city. One was on the way to Santos, at the bottom of the watchtower facing that direction where the Master judged that the king would set up his camp. They built the other one at the other end of the city next to the wall of the lime-kilns facing the Monastery of Santa Clara. The stakes were set in double rows, and so close together that no one on horseback could pass through them; nor could men on foot without first climbing over the top of the posts, which would be a very difficult thing to do. Between the double rows of stakes, there was a

---

[135] Unspun coarse flax fibres, probably used to staunch blood from wounds.

space kept free of stones, in which a boat could fit with oars shipped, should it be necessary to take shelter there.

The men of the city did not let their being under siege prevent them from building a barbican around the wall on the side facing the camp, from the Santa Catarina Gate to the tower of Álvaro Pais, which wasn't yet finished, over a length of about two crossbow shots. The young women, without any fear, gathering stone in the fields, would sing out loud:

> This is our beloved Lisbon,
> look at her and leave her be,
> unless you want some mutton
> like they served Andeiro;
> unless you want some kid
> like they served the Bishop[136]

and other similar utterances. When their enemies tried to disturb them, they were put into the same situation as the children of Israel when King Xerxes, son of King Darius, gave permission to the prophet Nehemiah to rebuild the walls of Jerusalem.[137] For when they were attacked by their neighbours from round about, to keep them from scaling the walls, with one hand they laid stone, and in the other they held a sword to defend themselves. The Portuguese who were doing that work always had their weapons with them, with which they defended themselves from their enemies when these made an effort to hinder them from doing their work.

The other things that had to do with the running of the city were all put in good and regular order. There was nobody there who started quarrels with others or interfered with others by unreasonable behaviour; rather, they all were in friendly concord and concerned for the common good.

Oh, what a beautiful thing it was to see! Such a high and mighty lord as the King of Castile, with such a multitude of men on the river and on land, set in such good and magnificent order, laying siege to such a noble city. And the city so well provided against him with men and arms, with such preparations for its protection and defence. So much so that those who saw it used

[136] This is part of a popular song against the Castilians, with reference to the first episodes of the rebellion reported in this chronicle: the deaths of Count Juan Fernández Andeiro (Chapter 9 above) and the Bishop of Lisbon (Chapter 12 above). Fearing for his life and wishing to win over the Master of Avis, Juan Fernández insistently invited him for lunch, but was served his own death, the 'mutton' (*carneiro*) in the song, which in Portuguese rhymes with 'Andeiro'.

[137] Nehemiah 4–6. In fact, it was King Artaxerxes I of Persia, the son of Xerxes, who issued the permission.

to say that such a splendid siege as this had not been seen for many years, as far as any man could recall.

Chapter 116

How Ourém was taken by the Master of the Order of Christ, how Diogo Lopes Pacheco was taken prisoner, and how Juan Ramírez de Arellano was exchanged for him

The Master being in this situation, on 11 June a message came to him from a reliable source, saying that the Master of the Order of Christ, Dom Lopo Dias de Sousa, not by force, but rather with the advice and consent of certain inhabitants of Ourém, had taken the town, which had been on the side of Castile; he had declared loyalty to the Master, and had placed the town under his lordship. Then two sons of João Afonso (the Count of Barcelos and brother of Queen Leonor) were taken captive there, along with all the men-at-arms that the said count had for his own protection. The Master and the men of the city were very pleased at this news. Soon afterwards Don Álvaro Pérez de Castro, the Count of Arraiolos, died of natural causes and was buried in the Monastery of São Domingos.[138]

Not many days afterwards, Diogo Lopes Pacheco came to the town of Almada, which is located a league away from Lisbon immediately across the river on the other side and which was still loyal to the Master. He had been in Castile, as has been mentioned in several places, with three of his sons: João Fernandes, who was legitimate, Lopo Fernandes and Fernão Lopes, who were bastard sons. He tried to enter the town, but the men of the town community refused, fearing him because he came from Castile. He lodged on the outskirts along with other Portuguese who were staying there; he had brought with him some thirty men, of whom fourteen were horsemen.

Seeking the reason for his coming, some say at this point that ever since Queen Beatriz began to rule in Castile, he was always doubtful that he could live there in safety. As a man under suspicion is never secure, he feared that the queen would hate him just as her father King Fernando had done, on account of the attack that King Enrique had made on Lisbon and of the

---

[138] On the involvement of Count Álvaro Pérez de Castro in the 1384 Siege of Lisbon and the probable date of his death, see Chapters 133 and 138 below.

destruction that he had caused there, which it was affirmed had been carried out at the behest of Diogo Lopes. However, though he felt fearful at being subject to such suspicion, he could do nothing about it, nor did it suit him to travel about any more than he had already, for he was a man of eighty years of age. When he heard that the Master had taken on the responsibility of ruling the kingdoms of Portugal and the Algarve, he decided to leave Castile and throw in his lot with the Master in Lisbon, for the greater security of his life. With such an intention he came to Almada. Realising that he could not cross the river because of the fleet that lay there, he waited for a time and opportunity when he could do so safely.

Now, it so happened that the King of Castile, after his fleet arrived, sent word to the people of Almada that they should surrender the town to him and place themselves under his power, and that he would grant them favours in return. Among other things, the men of the town replied that they were Portuguese and did not intend to change sides, but that, whatever Lisbon might do, they would do the same.

With matters in this state, about three or four days after Diogo Lopes arrived, the king, having learned of his arrival, sent secretly at night many men-at-arms, crossbowmen and horses to cross the river in galleys and *naos*' cutters.[139] Two of the galleys went to Margueira, which is a harbour near Almada, and stayed there. The men whom the king sent passed the entire night in the other galleys and cutters, and moored by the Barco de Martim Afonso cove, which is upstream from the Mutela riverbank. When it was morning the Castilians went to the road that leads from Coina to Almada. The sentinels that the men of the town had posted outside went back to report the news of their approach.

It was a very foggy morning, and most of the horsemen and foot soldiers went forth, and Diogo Lopes and his sons with them. There were in the town, between noblemen and citizens, about 80 horsemen; and the total of foot soldiers and crossbowmen numbered about 450 men. The Castilians numbered about 400 horsemen, plus many crossbowmen and foot soldiers. In the clash between the two sides, 40 of the enemy fell, among foot soldiers and horsemen, and seven of the Portuguese. Some Portuguese fell into an ambush that the Castilians had set between the town and where they had moored. As men were dying on both sides, Diogo Lopes was taken captive; his sons fled on their horses towards the castle of Sesimbra, 3 leagues from there, which was loyal

---

[139] These were one- or two-masted ship's boats used to transport light cargo or passengers. It was common for *naos* and other ships to have a smaller craft at their service.

to the Master. Afonso Galo, the alderman of Almada, was also captured, and others with him; some others fled to Sesimbra.

The Castilians, who were numerous, next attacked Almada; being unable to do anything that would cause it much damage, they settled in for a long siege, and from then on had it surrounded. Diogo Lopes was brought to the King of Castile, who kept him prisoner in the camp, bearing a very great grievance against him.

The Master, considering how Diogo Lopes had left Castile with his sons to come and serve him, and that he had been made captive in that way in defence of the realm, arranged at once to free him from captivity. He bought Juan Ramírez de Arellano from Perrin Gascon and Diogo Esteves, whose prisoner he was, in order to exchange him for Diogo Lopes. This exchange displeased many, who attempted to dissuade the Master from doing it, saying that Diogo Lopes was already a man of more than eighty, and not one who could be useful in deeds of war. Juan Ramírez was a worthy man-at-arms, as he had shown when he was captured. Since he was a person who could do serious harm to the Master, such a trade was not equal, and should not be carried out by any means.

Certainly, what was being said was true, for Juan Ramírez was a very bold and honourable knight, and the King of Castile loved him greatly, because he had brought him up, and because he was an outstanding man-at-arms. He was the son of Madame Venancia [de Branc], whom the king trusted greatly, and who had been his nurse. The Master paid no heed to all those who spoke against him, but rather deemed it good to exchange him for Diogo Lopes, showing by this act his honourable will and proper understanding. Thus Juan Ramírez was exchanged for Diogo Lopes, whom the Master at once appointed to his council and to whom he granted 500 *libras* per month for his upkeep.

Chapter 117

Concerning the captains who invaded with the Archbishop [of Santiago] to raid Portugal, and how Fernando Alfonso de Zamora was taken captive

You have heard how, about two months ago, thirteen galleys departed from Lisbon and went to the city of Oporto, so that all of them, along with the *naos* and galleys of that town, could come and do battle with the fleet of the King of Castile after he laid siege to the city.[140] So that we may see better all that was done after they arrived there, let us first read the three following chapters concerning what happened before their arrival.

It is important for you to know that, when the King of Castile had Lisbon surrounded, as we have said, and the towns in the Minho already mentioned[141] came to his side, Don Juan [García] Manrique, the Archbishop of Santiago, joined with many Portuguese and Castilian troops to raid and ravage that entire district wherever they had declared loyalty to the Master. The Portuguese captains who went with him were the following: Lope Gómez de Lira,[142] João Rodrigues Portocarreiro, Fernão Gomes da Silva, Aires Gomes the Elder, Martim Gonçalves de Ataíde, Vasco Gil de Fontelo, and Gonçalo Peres Coelho.

The Galician captains were Fernán Pérez de Andrade, Bernardo Yáñez de Santiago, García Rodríguez de Valcarce, Martín Sánchez de la Marina, Pedro Álvarez, Pay Sorredea, Juan Rodríguez de Biedma, Gonzalo Mariño, and others. In all, they brought about 700 lances and 2,000 foot soldiers, all hand-picked men, well-prepared to fight.

Also active in that district was a Castilian knight called Fernando Alfonso de Zamora, a most high-ranking man, accompanied by eighty very good squires on horseback, both Castilians and others; he, however, moved separately and with guile, as follows: when he came to towns loyal to Portugal, he said that he was on the side of the Master; when he came to those loyal to Castile, in a few words he made them understand that he was on their side. In that way he moved about with his men, swallowing up and laying waste the land, without opposition from anyone. With this deception he came to Santo Tirso de Riba de Ave with his men, and stopped there, taking his ease, very confident that nothing bad could happen to him, and without setting any guard.

On hearing of this, Count Pedro, who was in Oporto as has already been said,[143] told the men of the city that he knew for certain that Fernando Alfonso was employing that form of trickery. When they heard that he was using such a stratagem, looting and laying waste the land, they approached him one night under cover of darkness. They came at dawn to the place where he lay without a care with all his men and caught them all still in their beds. Although he

---

[140] See Chapter 111 above.

[141] See Chapter 68 above.

[142] As seen in *CKF*, Chapter 25, Fernão Lopes included Lope Gómez de Lira among the Castilian supporters of Pedro I, who sought refuge in Portugal after the king's assassination, and were welcomed and well rewarded by King Fernando. Perhaps, in this instance, the term 'Portuguese captains' could be understood as referring not to their nationality but to their role as leaders of the Portuguese pro-Castilian faction.

[143] In chapter 82 above.

made an effort to defend himself as well as he could, as did some of his men, it did them no good: several were wounded on both sides, and seven of his men were killed, while others fled, each in any way he could. He was captured, along with his son Alfonso de Valencia, and a nephew of his was killed; they took his horses and mules and all the other things they found, and brought everything to the city. He and his son were kept captive until the fleet left for Lisbon, and he was taken in it by the Castilians as you will hear later on.

Chapter 118

Concerning the council that the archbishop held with his men regarding how they should besiege Oporto

While the Archbishop [of Santiago] was in Braga with the men we have already named, and they were spread out across the land to rob and do all the harm that they could, they held a council to discuss how they might make war as safely as they could, and with the most honour. Some report that they said to each other: 'Let's go to Oporto, which is 8 leagues from here, and lay siege to it on one side. Let's establish our camp at the Olival Gate, and in a few days we will take the city, because there is no one inside it to fight against us, nor does it have the strength to defend itself.'

When the archbishop heard this, replied: 'I am not of that opinion, for two reasons: one, because it is a city of many people, who can defend it well; the other, because it is a seaport, which can get help in many ways if such a thing [as an attack] occurred. Instead, it seems to me that it will be better for us not to get very close, but rather to patrol around it at a distance of 2 leagues and hence cut off its supplies. Since they are not mounted, they cannot come and do us any harm; meanwhile, they will be using up what they have. Perhaps by this means they will change to our side, with no further harm to us. Since the greater part of the kingdom is for Castile, the rebellion of Lisbon and this city, and a few other towns that are loyal to the Master, cannot possibly last long. Surely they will see that it is futile for them to persist in defending their cause, and they will do anything that the king, our liege lord, and his wife the queen may command them. I say to you that this would be my advice.' All the Galicians and Castilians who were there agreed to this.

But the renegade Portuguese who were there, especially Lope Gómez de Lira[144] with his relatives and friends, said to the archbishop: 'My lord, let us

---

[144] See Chapter 117, note 142 above.

go forward by all means; we have no reason to fear those who live in the city: they are only men of the city community, and there is no good leadership among them. Since the hearts of many of them are confused, not only because of envy, but also because of suspicion, which is very prevalent among them, it could be that when they see us close to them, they will all rush about in disorder. There will arise such discord among them as will be a very great help to us, and a means of bringing us great advantage. Also, if they should wish to come out and fight with us, never did a fisherman cast a better net than we could cast at that point. Or it might be that we will take the town, which would be a very honourable and noteworthy deed for us. Thus, in one way or another, we cannot but come out well from this; therefore, let us not delay any longer, but rather go there by all means. If nothing else, let us at least make a show of force, and find out what they mean to do.'

The advice would have been very good, if the men of the town had been in discord as they said, because there is no death more full of poison, nor any that so destroys cities and towns and more quickly brings about their ruin than discord among its inhabitants. But the reality was quite the opposite, for the men of the city were all of a single mind, committed to its welfare and defence; they all had one heart and desire, as was shown afterwards.

Then the archbishop, seeing himself pressed by these and other arguments, had to agree to the plan that the others were proposing. They began to make their way along the Guimarães road, and came at midday near to Oporto. They established their camp at a place called São Romão, which is half a league from the town, and there they ate and rested.

Chapter 119

How the men of Oporto went forth from the city to fight with the Galicians

When the men of Oporto learned that the Castilians were in that place, and the intention with which they had come, they all found themselves in agreement, saying to each other: 'Those men who are there are many and able, and they come with the intention of besieging this city, and taking it if they can. If we are besieged by them, either we will let ourselves stay penned up here, like cattle in a corral, and will not get out, or we will challenge them to a battle. If we do not go out, this will bring us dishonour and reproof, so we ought to go forth in any way we can. Otherwise, how could we bear our shame? Are we to see our city besieged by our enemies, who want to win honour at our expense and test our mettle, and we not care about it, and stand here watching from the wall like women? For these reasons we should not allow them to win such glory at our expense and let the shame fall on us, letting them arrive here as they please. Instead, let us go out to meet them by all means, and let no one be afraid, for God will be there to help us.'

Having come to this agreement and finished the council [meeting], they all strove to arm themselves as quickly as they could; from the oldest to the smallest who could take up arms, there was no one who did not arm himself to go forth as soon as they were ready. Of these, the principal was the aforementioned Count Pedro, with 15 well-armed squires of his and 40 foot soldiers with them. There came also Aires Gonçalves da Feira, who held the castle of Gaia, with 40 well-drilled squires, and another nobleman called Martim Correia; and other good squires with their men, so that there were in all, with the men of the city, around 700 men-at-arms, 300 crossbowmen, and 1,500 foot soldiers.

There was also in this company Gonçalo Peres, clerk of the crown in the chancery, who was the father of Luís Gonçalves and Pero Gonçalves, who was called Malafaia, whom we will mention later on. The Master before this had sent him in a barge with João Ramalho and Nicolau Domingues, honourable men of that city, to attend to matters in his service.

This man kept on saying to sundry groups: 'Friends, let us go out after them, for they are worthless. We are true Portuguese, and in the defence of our land and kingdom, we should have no fear, but always fight against them, and defend the kingdom to the death, rather than let them subjugate us contrary to all right and reason.'

All of them, ready and with great valour and will, went forth, and went to camp at the fountain of Mijavelhas, which is a short distance from the city. As they were not mounted, and it was already afternoon, they did not dare go further and waited for their enemies there. When they saw that the enemy did not show up, they returned to the city, and nothing more was done at that time.

Chapter 120

How the Lisbon galleys arrived at Oporto, and how the crews joined the men of the city to fight the Galicians

The next day at dawn, they all armed themselves and went forth through the Olival Gate, because they had heard that those men intended to come from that direction, and they went out to await them for a long while, a long distance from the city. As they waited there, the galleys arrived, which we have said had left from Lisbon, all pavisaded and well-equipped. Sounding their trumpets with great joy, calling out their greetings according to the custom of seafarers, they anchored in front of the city. Those who had remained inside and had not gone forth, when they saw the galleys, were very happy about them, and sent word to the others at once. As for the men of the galleys, as soon as they arrived and were told how the men of the city had gone forth to fight the enemy troops, then, without further delay or hesitation, they unshipped the gangplanks and all leaped ashore with the banner of the Master unfurled before them, namely: Gonçalo Rodrigues de Sousa; Rui Pereira; Afonso Furtado; Estêvão Vasques Filipe; Gonçalo Vasques, the son of Vasco Martins de Melo, and his brother [Vasco Martins de Melo, the Younger]; Antão Vasques; Aires Vasques de Alvalade; and other noblemen and galley masters, and with them around 300 lances, 500 crossbowmen, and 3,500 galley rowers.[145] Thus there were in all, with the men of the city already mentioned, 1,000 men-at-arms, 800 crossbowmen, and 5,000 foot soldiers, all with a great will to fight.

When the Galicians heard that the Portuguese galleys had arrived, and how the men they brought in them had joined forces with the men of the city, they were very perturbed at the news, so that they quite lost the hope in which they had trusted. However, since they were sure that the men of the town were not mounted, they remained quietly where they were. When the Portuguese learned of this, they reached agreement among themselves, saying, 'Since it is the case that they do not want to come to us, let us go and seek them out where they are, and let no one show tiredness as long as we are able to walk, for otherwise we would be mocked by them.'

Then they all set out on the road to Paranhos with their flags out in front: the banner of the Master that they were all bound to protect, and the other with the city's signs. Many of those who saw them marching off wept with pleasure, saying, 'Lord God, merciful King, be on our side and aid them against their enemies.'

As they were thus advancing in battle formation, with a great will to fight, four light horsemen from the Galician side came up to reconnoitre. When they saw the Portuguese approaching as they did, they turned back at once, and reported to the archbishop and the others that the Portuguese were already appearing on the hilltop of Paranhos. Then they rode off at speed, crossing the River Leça, and took up a position beyond the bridge in a location both high

---

[145] Galleys relied on a large number of rowers. The largest galleys could have up to 28 benches each side, with three men to a bench, 168 rowing at a time. Taking into account the spare or resting rowers, about 100 per galley, the total number of rowers for 13 galleys comes to 3,484, which is close to Fernão Lopes's figure.

up and strong, so that no one could do them any harm, or cross that bridge without suffering great injury.

When the Portuguese saw them in that position, it ignited in them even more the will to fight. Although they were looking for a suitable spot where they could cross in safety, in order to make their enemy come down from the said hill, they were quite unable to find one. As night was approaching, they made camp near the Memorials in Leça. From there they sent a message to the archbishop by a friar of the Franciscan Order, Brother Vasco Patinho. He came to him and said, 'My lord, those captains who are there with yonder troops have sent me to beg you to kindly withdraw from here, so that they can cross the bridge without hindrance, and [request you to] position yourself in a place where they can set up for battle and fight you.'

'My friend', said the Archbishop, 'these men are here together as you see: if they wish to come to us, here they will find us ready to fight; but otherwise, we will not move from where we are, except when we consider that it suits us. Take this answer to them.'

The friar went back with this message. After a while, night fell, and they posted their sentinels on the roads, so that they would not suffer harm from any direction. They built many bonfires in the camp, and the rest watched all night, for they were no further than a crossbow shot away from the enemy. The Castilians did not refrain from extending their camp and dispatching their pack-mules off towards Braga.

Chapter 121

How the Portuguese skirmished with the Galicians, and how the archbishop went away

The night passed quickly, for it was in the month of May; in the early morning as soon as dawn broke, all the Galicians were ready, both horsemen and foot soldiers, with their unfurled banner bearing the insignia of Saint James. The Portuguese, when they saw them, sought a place where they could cross [the river], but could not find one; they showed plainly by their outward demeanour the great desire they bore in their hearts to fight.

Upstream they had to push through a very dense thicket, and they found a ford, though not very well suited for crossing. But they laid on top of it many sticks and tree branches, and began to get across that way as well as they could, up to about 300 of them, including crossbowmen and foot soldiers, and some horsemen. With them was a citizen of Oporto who was leading them, named João Ramalho.

When the Galicians saw that they were crossing at such a bad spot, they were amazed, and said, 'Let's allow as many to pass as can do so; once they are on this side, before they have any leadership and are lined up as they should be, we will take them by surprise, and thus defeat them.'

The Portuguese realised this, and [then] went further downstream to look for another, better place where they could all go across together. Before they could cross, the Galicians, on horseback and on foot, all in a rush, came to attack with great ferocity those few who were already on the far side. The Portuguese, notwithstanding, did not scatter, but kept together, and the two sides began to strike each other vigorously; the crossbowmen did much harm to the Galicians, a horseman and two foot soldiers immediately falling dead, and the Galicians perforce were driven back.

The archbishop then spoke to his men saying: 'My friends, do you not perceive how these men come at us, like men who do not fear death? Certainly we would be put in a very difficult spot, and it does not seem right to me that we should get entangled with them. This is because they have many crossbowmen, which gives them a great advantage over us. If our horses were killed, we could quickly be defeated. Therefore let's leave them and get safely away while we can. For, even if two kings were about to do battle, and the men of thirteen galleys arrived to help one of them, such an arrival would give him so great an advantage, and would place the other in such a quandary, that he would surely believe that such a battle was to be avoided. Think how much more powerfully it would affect us!'

Then they all agreed with what the archbishop was saying and moved off at once. As they were going, a number of Portuguese followed close behind barking insults at them; some of the Galicians turned around, and one of the Portuguese was killed. Then they left off following the Galicians and kept watch that day and the next night, thinking that their enemies were attempting a ruse, and that they might perhaps come back. After learning that they were very far away, the Portuguese returned to the city with great pleasure.

Chapter 122

How Rui Pereira spoke his message to the people of Oporto, and concerning the reply that they gave him

After the people of the city had been restored to calm, and likewise the men of the fleet, Rui Pereira told the city dwellers that they should all gather together, for he wished to inform them of several things that the Master had sent him to say. The next day, a Friday, they all assembled to hear the message he brought, which he, having first shown a letter of credentials, began to deliver as follows: 'Gentlemen, friends, the Master, our ruler and defender, wishes you all good health and praises your loyalty. He says to you that you well know how all this kingdom is currently in turmoil caused by differing political objectives, and how the Castilians wish to subjugate it and obtain it for themselves with all their might, which God will never grant them. You also know that for the good of the kingdom and its defence, he took on the responsibility of being its ruler and defender, as there is no other [liege lord] to stand and defend and protect it, and that he offers himself in its defence, to the extent of putting his body and life at risk of death. Moreover, you know well that the King of Castile is now very close to the city [of Lisbon] with all his men and might, intending to lay siege to it; they are raiding and laying waste that entire district which they already claim as their own, waiting until the fleet arrives so that they can then encircle the whole city by sea and land. Therefore he implores you as good and loyal Portuguese, and as people who have always shown loyalty to the House of Portugal, that you agree to the immediate fitting out of the *naos* and barges that are here in this city.

'Likewise, he asks that you have the galleys launched and fitted out at once, so that they, along with these others that have recently come from Lisbon, can all go to do battle with the Castilian fleet when it arrives. We trust in God and in the Virgin Mary His mother that He will help us against them, and He will enable us to gain such a victory as will be to the great honour and advantage of the kingdom, and service to our lord the Master, and redound to the good name of all of us. Moreover, he also says to you that, because of the great need in which he is placed, and for the defence of this kingdom, for which it is so needful, you should come to his aid with a loan, because money will be essential in meeting those inescapable expenses which, you can all see, are bound to follow. He has no pledge to give you for this loan, except for himself, if God protects him from harm, from which may it please God to preserve him. He promises you, as the son of a king that he is, and by his entire good faith, that he will well repay all of it to you. For this, I bring you here his signed pledge with all necessary powers, as you can well see, in order for me to take on this obligation in his name, in whatever way you please.'

A man responded then, a worthy citizen called Domingos Peres das Eiras, who had been chosen by the people of the city as their spokesman, as they had received prior notice of what was going to be proposed to them. He spoke as follows:

'Rui Pereira, you have delivered your message very well, and everything that was entrusted to you. I declare, for my part and on behalf of all these people who are here, that we are ready to serve the Master, our lord, with a good will, and to do all that he commands for his service and the defence of the kingdom. Even if he were a stranger whom we did not know, and he undertook such toil and danger to defend and protect us, we would serve him with our lives and possessions; all the more so since he is the son of King Pedro, and there is no one else to look after us except for God and the Master. It is very fitting that we should do anything he might wish, especially for the defence of this kingdom of which all of us are natives. Therefore we will make available for this enterprise our gold, silver and coin, and everything else we own, for it cannot be spent on anything more appropriate than the defence of our country, and never being under the power of the Castilians.

'We will all go along with his intent, for it is very appropriate, and there is no one in this city who holds a contrary opinion. If any such were to be found, God forbid, he would not be permitted to live among us. For this purpose, the *naos*, barges and galleys, with all the other things that he might need, we offer to him with great good will. You will have supplies of all sorts of flour, meats, fish and wine that may be needed for the fleet. All the people of the city who may be useful for such employment will all embark upon it very willingly. Therefore, appoint whichever agents you wish, and all will be done at once unstintingly. Send your letters through the districts, telling all that are loyal to Portugal that they should come quickly to sail in this fleet. It is certain that all those who love the honour and the good of the kingdom will be here quickly. Among those to whom you still ought to write is Count Gonçalo, who holds Coimbra. For three reasons: first, we will secure Coimbra, which is a town from which many obstacles could come for our cause; second, the men he has with him, who will be of great help to us; third, if he comes to sail in the fleet, none of the others will have anything which could greatly hinder our cause.'

Then they agreed that it would be good to send a message to the count via Dom Martim Gil, the Abbot of Paço [de Sousa];[146] they wrote their letters to other people in that district, letting them know what their full intention was. They asked them to make ready at once and come to Oporto, and told them that they would be given, unstintingly, all the things they might need.

[146] The Monastery of Paço de Sousa, near the present-day city of Penafiel.

Chapter 123

Concerning the message that the people of Oporto sent to Count Gonçalo, and the reply he gave to them

This having been agreed, they wrote their letter of credentials to the count, and gave it to Dom Martim Gonçalves,[147] the Abbot of Paço [de Sousa], who afterwards became Bishop of the Algarve. He arrived in Coimbra where the count was, and was well received by him, because he had been protected by him and had obtained his post as abbot through him. The count asked him publicly what had brought him to those parts. 'My lord', he said, 'what made me come here is a message that I bring you from the worthy men of Oporto.'

Then they withdrew alone and, when the letter of credentials had been read, the abbot said: 'My lord, those worthy men of the city of Oporto, and likewise the captain of the fleet that has arrived there from Lisbon, with all the men who are in it, send you their greetings. They say that you well know how this kingdom, for our sins, is split into two parts, so that the coming of the Antichrist could not cause greater division than that in which this country is at present. For all the Castilians are against Portugal, and the greater part of the Portuguese, as you can plainly see. But this notwithstanding, the Master with all his heart is dedicating himself fully to defending the kingdom, enduring great toil and danger in the process, since there is no other who will protect it. He is in Lisbon, about to be besieged, as you will have heard already; and the King of Castile is moving against the city with all his troops and fleet. The Master is very fearful of the great harm that he could suffer from the Castilian fleet, if it takes the control of the river from him, so that he cannot obtain the supplies and aid he could otherwise get from certain towns in the Alentejo, because he has been blockaded by water. Therefore he sent several galleys to Oporto to join forces with the *naos* and galleys that are there. All of them duly armed, they will go and do battle with the Castilian fleet, in order to break the blockade of the river, and relieve the city on that side. For this purpose the fleet of *naos* and galleys is being armed as fully as possible; they have already written to many people regarding this, bidding them come quickly to join it.

'As it is fitting for the fleet to be well armed, and placed under the leadership of a worthy captain, and as there is no one as worthy as you in this district, they decided to write to you about this matter. They send me to ask that you help them in this endeavour, and that it please you to take charge of the fleet and

[147] Also known as Martim Gil; see Chapter 122.

be its commander. They all promise to obey you and go under your protection and leadership, and give you in abundance all the things that both you and your men may need. For this reason, if you were to do it, it seems to me that you would achieve very great honour, and show your merit in doing so. All will esteem you greatly for helping to defend the land of your birth, according to the extent of my understanding, and of this matter I know nothing else.'

After these and other words that the abbot said to the count, the first thing that he said in reply was this: he asked why Gonçalo Rodrigues de Sousa was not going as captain of the fleet, just as when he had come from Lisbon.

The abbot said: 'My lord, it is the case that Gonçalo Rodrigues, when he arrived in Oporto, left there a few days later, and it is said that he came to talk to you, and also talked to Gonçalo Gomes da Silva and to the master, his nephew, and afterwards to Gonçalo Vasques de Azevedo. Regarding this matter they were all discontented, saying that he was not behaving loyally in the service of the Master, but rather that he wanted to sell the galleys and the fleet to the King of Castile. For this reason there was great turmoil in the city, and he was nearly arrested. Therefore they do not trust him in anything, whether to sail as captain or for any other honourable role.'

Upon hearing this, and after a long conversation that took place between them, the count finally said in reply that, if the Master would grant him the lands that had belonged to his sister Queen Leonor, he would declare his loyalty to him, and would serve in the fleet and in any matter that might be for his service.

The abbot then returned with this answer. When it was seen by Rui Pereira, Gonçalo Peres and others of great consequence in the service of the Master, they wrote to him immediately about the matter.

When he saw this, the Master did not know what response to make to it, inasmuch as he had granted the lands to Nuno Álvares, who had previously asked him for them. In order to win the count to his service, however, he informed Nuno Álvares of what they had written to him, and the state of affairs. When he saw his letter, Nuno Álvares, whose whole desire was to work for the Master's service in any way he could, sent one of his squires at once from Évora, where he was at the time, with a reply to the Master. He said that, despite his having promised the lands to him, and granted them to him initially, he was very glad for him to give them to the count to win him for his service. He was referring not just to those lands, but to everything that he owned, which the Master could give to whomever he favoured, in order to improve matters pertaining to his service. For he hoped in the Lord God that He would increase the Master's honour and standing so much that he, the Master, would reward him later for everything and, better than he, Nuno Álvares, would know how to request of him.

The Master, when he saw this reply, regarded it as an act of great generosity. Then, to win the count's service, which was so necessary to him at such a time, he wrote at once to him, promising the lands that had belonged to his sister. Moreover, he sent him a further letter, saying that he could take for his own, and for those who were with him, all the rights and revenues that the Master would receive in Coimbra. He also confirmed for the count's son, Dom Martinho, the towns of Bouça and Lordelo that he had formerly held. The count immediately joined his side, and began to prepare to serve him and embark with the fleet.

Then Gonçalo Peres arrived there, and asked the count to order that he be handed over the ship's dry biscuit that was stored in Coimbra and Montemor[-o-Velho]. The count was pleased to do so, and they carried away much ship's biscuit and many weapons, with which they loaded two balingers bound for Oporto. The Master sent the count many coins as a gift, and lengths of cloth for himself and his men. This was the way he joined forces with the Master and declared allegiance to him.

Chapter 124

How the galleys went to raid the coast of Galicia, and what happened to them during their voyage

In Oporto was to be found Don Pedro, the Count of Trastámara, who had escaped from Coimbra when the King of Castile went there to take the city, as we related earlier,[148] along with two of his brothers. One of them was Alfonso Enríquez, the chief huntsman of the King of Castile; the other was Alfonso Enríquez, the Younger, who was the son of a Jewish woman. He had already gone to Lisbon to tell the Master that they were ready for his service, and he remained there with him. All three were sons of the Master of Santiago, Don Fadrique, who was the son of King Alfonso and Leonor Núñez de Guzmán; this Don Fadrique was later killed by King Pedro of Castile, as we have told in its due place,[149] if you recall.

In the meantime the people of the city, at liberty and free of other worries, not with small but rather with large expenditures, were hastily arranging any things that were suitable for such an important business and service to the Master, without whom they did not believe the kingdom could be

---

[148] In Chapter 82 above.
[149] In *CKP*, Chapter 20.

defended. With each of them working to achieve all that their goodwill wished to accomplish, they agreed among themselves that since the galleys were already armed, and men were gathering to board the *naos*, they could go and raid the coast of Galicia.

Once their departure was arranged, the fleet was given supplies for several days. The masters of the Lisbon galleys were those who had come [to Oporto] with them, except in the case of the Royal Galley, in which Gonçalo Rodrigues de Sousa had come, for it was captained by Count Pedro, whom they all obeyed. In the galley named *Santa Ana* went Gonçalo Vasques de Melo and his brother Vasco Martins, who later died in the battle [of Aljubarrota]; in the *Bem Aventurada*, Afonso Furtado; in the *Santa Clara*, Estêvão Vasques Filipe; in the *São João*, Lourenço Mendes de Carvalho, knight-commander; in another, the *São Jorge*, Master Manuel, the son of Lançarote Pessanha, the High Admiral who was killed in Beja; in the *Santa Vitória*, João Rodrigues Guarda; in the *Santa Maria de Cacela*, Antão Vasques; and also Gil Esteves Fariseu, Aires Peres de Camões and others in galleys, both from Oporto and from Lisbon, which we do not care to name further.

Raiding the coast of Galicia, they came first to Bayona de Miñor, a small and weak castle; they were given 400 francs not to burn the fishing village. Next they went to Muxía, which is a fishing village without a fortress, and burned there two ships that lay in the shipyard. From there they sailed for La Coruña where they were given 600 francs so that they would not burn the fishing village. Some of the galleys remained there, and six went off to Ferrol; this was completely burned down, so that nothing was left of it except the church. Then they arrived at Neda, which was ransomed for 400 francs.

Afterwards these six galleys returned, they left with all those from La Coruña, and sailed to Betanzos, a strong fortified town, because they had received word that there were several *naos* there with siege engines that were bound for Lisbon. They found one *nao* loaded with engines that was bound for the camp, and they set it on fire. They burned another new *nao* belonging to Pero Ferreño of La Coruña. They captured a galley called *Volanda*, near the wall of the town, in which encounter several men were wounded, and they took it away with them. Then they began to attack the town, approaching the walls very closely, for there were very valiant and bold men there, such as João Rodrigues Guarda, Antão Vasques, and other noblemen of formidable prowess.

When they were on the verge of taking it, with the men of the town so beset that they were beginning to abandon the walls, Count Pedro, the captain, ordered that the trumpets be sounded for them to fall back, saying that it was not good for any of them to die for the sake of capturing a town such as that one. Rather, he proposed the pledge that if no help came to it the next day, it should be surrendered to him without further fighting. The Portuguese agreed to do this very reluctantly, not without feeling rather suspicious about it.

That night Fernán Pérez de Andrade came and entered the town with so many men that the pledge was void. The count was much censured for this, it being said that, because he knew about this aid that was to come to the townspeople, therefore he had told the Portuguese not to fight any more, giving them to understand that it was safer to allow for more time than to take it by force.

Then they ranged along that coast, and replenished their provisions abundantly, doing all the damage and harm they could, so that from the booty they took then, the crews of the galleys were paid three months' wages.

Once back at Oporto, which was rejoicing at their coming, they organised a tournament on Saint John's Eve,[150] a day on which the inhabitants of that city habitually hold a great celebration. The tournament was conducted with bascinets and very sharp swords, according to the custom of the time. Alfonso Enríquez, the chief huntsman, accidentally slashed his brother's right hand, leaving the count maimed. For that reason he did not sail with the fleet when it left Oporto for Lisbon.

Chapter 125

How Nuno Álvares should have joined the fleet, and the reason why he did not do so

While the galleys were in Oporto as we have said, the *naos* were being made ready as quickly as possible so that they could soon go to the aid of the Master and the city, because news was coming that they were in need of supplies on account of the Castilian fleet, which was preventing them from being sent in by sea. But, for the [Portuguese] fleet to be provided with what it needed, in spite of the great urgency of the situation, it was taking them longer than it should to meet the needs of the people who were waiting for their aid and support.

When the Master realised that the fleet was being delayed, and how the city was short of supplies, having great faith in his most loyal servant, Nuno Álvares Pereira, who would be sure to serve him honourably in this matter, he hastened to write to him in Évora, where he then was, telling him to assemble

[150] 23 June.

his men and go to Oporto to embark in the fleet and come to fight against the Castilian fleet, which had the city besieged.

When Nuno Álvares read the message, on finding out that Count Gonçalo and Rui Pereira as well as a number of other noblemen would be joining the fleet, he wrote to them urgently, asking them to wait for him as he would be joining them very soon. Then he shared out among his men a small amount of gold which the Master had sent to him, and they were very pleased when Nuno Álvares told them that the Master had written to him, telling him to go to Oporto. When the count and Rui Pereira and a number of others to whom Nuno Álvares had written saw his message, they were full of envy and evil intent, according to what has been said, and did not wish to wait for him. Instead, they decided to leave with the fleet, which is indeed what they did. Knowing nothing of this, Nuno Álvares went on his way hurriedly, taking with him as many as 200 lances, and anyone who writes that there were fewer is mistaken.

When he arrived in Tomar, where the Master of the Order of Christ was present, on a certain day he had a meal with him. The master asked him what he thought of these events, showing that he thought they were strange and did not expect them to turn out as Nuno Álvares and others believed. In reply Nuno Álvares said that, by the grace of God, they appeared to have started well, and he hoped that through Him the outcome would be even better. On this note he bade farewell to the master and set out for Coimbra. When he arrived there he learned that the fleet was already in Buarcos.[151] He wrote again to the captains of the fleet, beseeching them to wait for him, as they were obliged to do in the Master's service, and not to leave without him, as he would be there with them presently.

When they saw his message, they decided, still out of the same envy, to leave immediately, not wishing to stay there waiting for him. When Nuno Álvares had it confirmed that they had left, he was deeply perturbed. He understood the situation fully, saying that he hoped it would be God's wish to protect them; he added that, if some of the men were eager to leave earlier than they should have done, so that he should not go with them, he hoped God would not punish them, but guide them to safety in accordance with their wishes.

Let us leave the *naos* and galleys to sail the seas at this point. While they make their voyage, let us take Nuno Álvares to the Alentejo; and, when he returns to Évora, where he set out from [initially], we shall resume the account of how the fleet arrived in Lisbon and what happened to it there.

---

[151] Buarcos is on the coast, to the north of the estuary of the river Mondego, about 2 miles (3.2 km) from the centre of present-day Figueira da Foz.

Chapter 126

How Nuno Álvares decided to leave Coimbra, and what happened to him there

While Nuno Álvares was in Coimbra, the countess and wife[152] of Count Enrique Manuel, who was holding Sintra on behalf of the King of Castile, was staying there. Owing to the hatred she felt towards Nuno Álvares since the time when he had raided the outskirts of that city, and being most devoted to the queen as well as wishing to do service to the king, she decided to arrest him. Secretly, she assembled many soldiers, squires and other men, for she was surrounded by enough relatives, friends and *criados* to carry out such a task.

When Nuno Álvares's men, in one way or another, found out about this situation, they began to rise up, gathering together to go to the palace, where it was said that the countess was assembling her soldiers. They were determined to find a way to treat her badly. Nuno Álvares knew nothing of this and, when he found out, he rushed to where they were and saw to it that none of what had been planned should happen. In this way God saved Nuno Álvares from prison and the countess from serious danger.

Then, when Nuno Álvares wanted to return to where he had come from, he had nothing either for himself or to share with his men for the journey. It went to the point that some of them pawned their weapons for food. When he saw how his men were in great need, he ordered all the silverware that he had with him to be sold and shared out the money between them so that they could redeem their weapons. But in spite of this there was no alternative for him but to speak to the good citizens of Coimbra, and beg them to help him by lending him money for his departure. They agreed to do so and lent him a certain amount of money, out of which he ordered seven *libras* of this to be given to each of his men to cover their expenses during the journey.

Then he left and began by going to speak to Gonçalo Mendes de Vasconcelos, who was holding the castle of Coimbra, and spoke to him from the outside near a postern. When Gonçalo Mendes saw some of Nuno Álvares's men and how they were not equipped in the way he would have expected, he was very surprised and, after Nuno Álvares had gone, he remarked to his own men, 'I am amazed that men such as these are able to defend this kingdom

---

[152] This is Dona Brites de Sousa, who was the half-sister of João Lourenço da Cunha. See *CKF*, Chapter 65.

from the King of Castile, who is such a mighty lord, unless they have God for their captain!'

From there Nuno Álvares travelled to Tomar, and there, with his council, he decided to go to Torres Novas to speak to Gonçalo Vasques de Azevedo, who was a good friend of his, and was holding the town on behalf of the King of Castile, to see if he could persuade him to serve the Master. Indeed, he travelled there and spoke to Gonçalo Vasques about this matter in the manner he thought was most suitable. After lengthy discussions between the two of them, the only response he could obtain from him was that Gonçalo Vasques could not see any way or basis for the Master to attain the goal Nuno Álvares desired, so giving the impression, though not very clearly, that, if he could only see such good and reasonable grounds on which to base his hopes, he would be very willing to serve the Master.

That being so, Nuno Álvares took leave of him and returned to Tomar.

Chapter 127

Concerning what happened to Nuno Álvares with Dom David Alguaduxe regarding money that he wanted to give him

It appears that somehow Gonçalo Vasques de Azevedo heard about what had happened to Nuno Álvares in Coimbra and how he was short of money. He wrote immediately to the King of Castile, saying that he thought it would be a good idea to offer him some money to ascertain how he would respond, and if he would change sides because of the dire financial position in which he found himself. Furthermore, if the king had him on his side, then not only would a great burden be removed from his concerns, but he would also be sure to achieve everything he had hoped for.

The King of Castile's response to this was that it did not seem right and proper to him that such a thing should be proposed to Nuno Álvares in his name, because, if it happened that he did not accept his offer, he might go around boasting and saying that the king had tried to plead with him and entice him with a bribe, for which everyone would hold the king himself in low esteem. Instead, Gonçalo Vasques should arrange for the offer to be made to Nuno Álvares in a different way, as though on his own initiative. If Nuno Álvares were persuaded to accept something and gave any sign that, if he received as much as he wanted, he would go over to the king's side, then

Gonçalo Vasques should promise him whatever he wanted and should let the king know everything that had happened right away.

Then Gonçalo Vasques spoke to a Jew by the name of David Alguaduxe, the brother of the wife of Dom Yehuda, who had been treasurer to King Fernando. The Jew went to see Nuno Álvares in Tomar where he was staying and told him that he had heard that he was badly in need of money, and that he, Dom David Alguaduxe, had in his possession certain monies belonging to the King of Castile and, if he was willing to accept some of that, then he would let him have 1,000 *dobras* to begin with, and the time would come, some day in the future, when he could pay the king in service.

Nuno Álvares understood what the Jew meant and was well aware of this stratagem. So he spoke to some of his council to see what they would advise him to do in this situation. There were some who told him that they thought it was a good idea, since God had given him this opportunity to receive that money without him having to ask for it, and that he should accept the offer, as he needed it so badly for his expenses.

Nuno Álvares said that he did not consider it wise or proper for them to receive money from anyone but the person they intended to serve. Since they were in the service of the Master, with the aim of defending the kingdom of Portugal, then they should not accept money from anyone else. Thus far they had always acted honourably, without being reproached for anything; now, if they accepted this money in order to dupe its owner, they might be censured by some people, claiming that they had already taken money from the King of Castile and accepted benefits and favours from him, which might bring discord and suspicion among them. So Nuno Álvares did not accept any money, although the Jew very persistently lured him with it.

Chapter 128

How Nuno Álvares fought with some Castilians and overcame them

Nuno Álvares left Tomar where he had been staying and went to Punhete,[153] on his way to the Alentejo, the region that he was in charge of. There he found out that a number of Castilians were in Crato preparing to leave for Santarém, and that there were others who wanted to leave Santarém for Castile. These people were travelling with a great number of mules loaded

[153] Present-day Constância, which lies some 11 miles (*c.* 18 km) south-east of Tomar.

with things such as bedding, clothing, agricultural tools, and other items that might prove useful, which had been plundered by certain Castilians in the Santarém area and other places. It was decided that he should wait for two or three days for one group or the other on the road along which they were to pass, so that, with God's help, he would be able to fight against whichever group should happen to come along.

With this plan he left Punhete, and came to the road along which the Castilians would have to go in order to reach Santarém, or from Santarém on their way to Castile, and stopped at a little stream called Alperraiam[154] and had a meal close to it, under some young ash trees. Before he sat down to eat, he stationed his lookouts at a distance of a crossbow shot and further away, on various hilltops, so that no one would be able to pass without his knowing it. It was his habit never to stop on the way unless he had lookouts during the day, and guards and scouts at night, posted both at a distance and close by.

The lookouts were in their position and he and all his men were eating, when suddenly one of his scouts approached swiftly and very quietly, saying that he had seen clouds of dust on the road to Santarém, and that he thought there were people approaching, some on horseback and some on foot. Nuno Álvares was very pleased at this news and immediately gave orders for the meal to be cleared away and the mounts saddled quickly and quietly. He told all his men to join him at once and do so quietly, which they did, as there was no reason for any delay, since they were armed at least with their helmets, and their mounts were saddled and ready for that which they were waiting for.

Nuno Álvares was at some distance from the road along which the Castilians were approaching, and between him and the road there was a high stretch of moorland, like the ridge of a mountain, and from that ridge there was a track down to the road. He told his men to make their way on foot as quietly as they could, up to the top of the moorland, which they all did. When they were there on the top, he gave the order for the trumpets to be sounded loudly, and they all rushed pell-mell down the hillside to the road along which the Castilians were travelling. There were only eight of them on horseback and about 100 foot soldiers, sturdy *almogávares*, all with lances, spears and daggers, and with them went a number of crossbowmen.

When the Castilians saw Nuno Álvares and his men rushing down the hill, they were confused, but not for long, for they immediately started to defend themselves bravely; but their defence was of no use, as they were quickly

---

[154] This stream has proved impossible to identify, though it is probably one joining the Tagus near Alpiarça, a village some 7 miles (11 km) to the east of Santarém, through which the Castilians would inevitably pass. The name given in the text is probably a corruption of Alpiarça.

overcome. Taking into account the dead and the prisoners, there were little more than eighty left behind. Some others hid themselves in the undergrowth, so as not to be found.

Nuno Álvares's men took many pack-mules and other animals, as well as gold and silver, money, clothing and other things, and set out for Évora.[155] We shall leave Nuno Álvares there, guarding his frontier, and let us see if the fleet that left Oporto, heading for Lisbon, has arrived and find out what has become of it.

Chapter 129

Concerning the council held by the King of Castile to discuss how he should fight against the Portuguese fleet

While the fleet was making preparations in Oporto, getting ready to sail as you have heard, the King of Castile had spies positioned along the road, so that every day he was informed of what was happening in that city. A few days before the fleet was due to leave, he was told on which day it would come out of the estuary. He sent for Fernán Sánchez de Tovar, his High Admiral, and Pero Afán de Ribera, captain of the *naos*, and spoke to them, saying, 'I want you to get all the commanders of the galleys and masters of the *naos* assembled here tomorrow, for I wish to discuss with you and them a few things that concern my service.'

The next day they did as the king had asked and assembled the commanders of the galleys and the masters of the *naos*, whose names were on the roll. The king went with them into the Monastery of Santos, taking with him some knights, such as Pedro Fernández de Velasco, Fernando Álvarez de Toledo, the Count of Mayorga and a few others. The king ordered the guards to close the gates and move people away from the area around the monastery so that no one could hear what was being said inside it. The king sat down on the steps of the high altar, which had been arranged appropriately. A missal was placed there and, when everyone was seated before him, on both sides, the king addressed them, saying: 'I have summoned you here in council in order to consult you all about something. But before you hear what I am going to tell you, you must swear to me on the Holy Gospels that not a word of what

---

[155] This thread of the narrative is picked up again from the end of Chapter 142 below.

I shall talk to you about here will be revealed until such time as is necessary for it to be made known.'

When they had all sworn, he went on to add: 'In spite of the oath that you have all taken, I forbid each one of you, on pain of treason, to speak of any matter which will now be mentioned here to either a relative or a friend, or anyone else whomsoever. You must not disclose anything or give the slightest inkling to anyone, unless I order you to do so, or when it is set in motion.'

They said that they would do as he wished.

The king said: 'Now, I want you to know, that the reason why I have assembled you here is that I have it on good authority that the Portuguese fleet is already equipped and ready with an appointed date to set out from the estuary. I think that Nuno Álvares is on board, with many men from the Alentejo. At this point it behoves us to discuss the best way to fight the fleet unscathed: should we fight it here on the river or off the estuary? To this end, Fernán Sánchez and the commanders of the galleys, and you, Pero Afán, with those masters of the *naos*, should take your respective groups apart, whereas I shall discuss the matter with these noblemen. The course of action with the greatest support among us is the one we will follow.'

Then off they all went separately, each to his own place, and when the king reached an agreement with his nobles, he summoned the others and asked Fernán Sánchez what he had decided.

The admiral said: 'My lord, on this matter this is what seems to me and the commanders here: that it would be much better to fight with the fleet out on open water, off the estuary, rather than here on the river. The reason for this is as follows. Either their fleet is well armed, or it is not. If it is not, its defeat is a foregone conclusion; but if it is well armed, we shall be better than they are. We will position ourselves behind Berlenga Island,[156] and from there we will come out to fight them. We believe that with God's blessing and good fortune on your side, we will overpower them without any of their vessels getting away. If we fight here on the river, even if we get to grapple with all the vessels, some of them may get away. What's more, they have some *naos* and barges in front of the city, which they can arm well and will go to their aid, and cause us considerable damage. Therefore, our opinion is, at all costs, to fight them in the open sea.'

'And what about you, Pero Afán?' the king asked, 'What is your conclusion?'

He replied: 'Sire, we think that it would be much better for us to fight here, on the river than on the open water, for a number of reasons. Firstly, this is the time of year for prevailing north winds in these parts, and if we

---

[156] We assume this is a reference to the Berlenga Grande, the largest island of this small archipelago off what is now the peninsula of Peniche, Portugal.

wanted to go out to sea, the *naos* could not keep up with the galleys, and if they could, the only way to make this possible would be by sailing against the wind. This would mean that the fleet would have to spread out and could not remain all together, which would not suit us, because our opponents would all be grouped together since they have a following wind. If they found us dispersed they could pick us off, one by one. Even if we all went together and wanted to close with them, seeing that they have a following wind, they would cut through, past all of us, into the river,[157] especially as their fleet has very good sailors who are well experienced in warfare.

'For these reasons, it will be better and safer for us to fight them on the river than elsewhere. We will prepare our *naos* very carefully and station ourselves beyond Restelo with all the galleys upstream of us. When they approach, we will let them go past us and then engage them right away; and the wind that is with them will then be with us and we will fight them. With God's help and your good fortune, we shall well and truly defeat them. If, God forbid, things should turn out otherwise, the land on the other side [of the river] belongs to you, and likewise on this side, so whichever direction we went, we would find help and support and be able to find armed men to fight alongside us, as many as we needed.'

'Indeed', said the king, 'that is very good advice, and it is what I and these noblemen have agreed to do.'

At this juncture Fernán Sánchez said: 'In truth, my liege, this will look very cowardly, you being here with the whole of your army and fleet, and us not moving out of the river if only to greet them with a salvo from our cannons. Please, sire, we beg you, at least let us go as far as Cascais. As for the advantage we might have here on the river, where the wind is as favourable to us as it is for them on the open water, we will also benefit from it, even more so in Cascais, so my advice is that we should go out and meet them on the open sea.'

'But suppose', said the king, 'it were to happen that you were defeated out at sea, what would you do then?'

'If such a thing were to happen', he said, 'God forbid, we would rush back in the galleys at the greatest speed to fetch men that you would have ready to supply the fleet with.'

The king said: 'Admiral, you have spoken very well, but when once a wrestler has been forced to the ground, he will not willingly go back for more. Likewise, once you started to feel defeat, you would not want to return.

---

[157] The Portuguese fleet would go past the Castilian fleet, even if their ships were clustered together, and get into the river, thus succeeding in delivering supplies to the besieged city.

Therefore, it is better to fight the fleet here on the river than anywhere else;
for I will have so many men prepared that, in the event of a possible defeat,
they will at once be aboard the barges and boats.'

'Sire', said Pero Afán, 'this is what we think, because if anything should
happen to us, we will be best helped from nearby than from afar.'

'And I', said the king, 'am pleased with it and order that it be done thus.'

Chapter 130

Concerning the reasons Pedro Fernández de Velasco gave in order to show that it was not a good idea that his fleet should fight against the Portuguese fleet, and what the king said in reply

When these words had been spoken and the discussion was over as has
been described, Pedro Fernández de Velasco stood up, went to kneel
before the king, and spoke in this manner:

'Sire, you have taken advice and decided to fight against the Portuguese
fleet here on the river rather than beyond the river mouth, contrary to the
wishes of the admiral and the galley commanders who came with him. It seems
to me that it does not make much difference whether you attack it in one place
or the other, since both sides put forward very good reasons which, as they
understand it, support their opinion. Therefore, wherever it is your wish that
it is to be done, it is right that it should be done, without discussing the matter
further. However, as to whether we should fight against the Portuguese fleet
at all, then speaking by your leave and with all due respect to yourself and to
all here, I have to say that this does not seem to me to be so sound a project
that no better plan might be devised – and this for the following reasons.

'It seems to me, sire, that you think that by fighting and defeating this fleet,
you will thereby defeat and seize the whole kingdom. But things are not like
that, because in the fleet there are many of Portugal's noblemen, as well as
squires and citizens, and also many men of lowly estate, all of whom have
many close relationships in this city and throughout the kingdom, whether
relatives, *criados* or intimate friends. If those men die here, you will forever
have the enmity of their blood relatives, as they may well be holding a good
number of the castles in the kingdom. When they see that you have slain their
sons, brothers and other relatives, and the lords on whom they depended, they
will have no wish to obey you and will always give you as much trouble and

do you wrong in whatever ways they can. Even if you rule over their bodies you will never win their hearts and their love, which is the best thing that a king can have when he wants to take possession of a country for the first time. If not, what does a lord profit from owning the bodies of his vassals if he does not win their hearts? Unless you have their goodwill, you will never be lord of a quiet and peaceful land, which is something that would not befit you.

'Moreover, you said that you think that Nuno Álvares is approaching aboard that fleet with a great number of men from the Alentejo, and ostensibly the fleet is well armed. Both sides having more or less equal numbers of men, with only a few more on our side, no one has the advantage, except in the successful outcome of the venture to whomsoever God wishes to grant it, which is something that will remain very uncertain until that outcome is actually seen. Furthermore, I would think that they are all united in the determination to do or die. Even though they may be vanquished, they will kill so many of your men before they are themselves slain that this will cause great sorrow and damage to you as well as great loss to the kingdom of Castile. If, on the other hand, they should be victorious, which is something that could happen, then greater would be the loss and sorrow, and weakening of your men, and the valour of his men the greater.

'In order to choose the most certain of all these possibilities, I think it would be best for you to negotiate with the Master so that he retains his standing in this land and you become lord of the kingdom, rather than fighting their fleet or waging another war. He is so placed that one can imagine you will negotiate with him as you please. In this way you will set all their hearts at ease and not make them more inflamed against you than they already are.'

The king said that he did not wish to accept such advice, nor did he wish to propose any pact with the Master for, as Pedro Fernández could see clearly, the majority of the towns and noblemen of Portugal had declared for him, the king, and were on the side of the queen, his wife. Whoever had such advantages over the Master on land and at sea and offered him any kind of settlement or pact would show great weakness and cowardice. Rather, the king intended to carry on with his plan to fight against the Master's fleet and keep besieging the city until he took it as well as the entire kingdom, which was his by right.

If some people, at this point, write that the king answered that he had already made several attempts at negotiation, stating in which terms and in what manner, and the replies that the Master gave, you should consider such writing to be a fabrication and should not believe it, for it is very far from true. Since it is clear that up to this time the king had not put forward any agreement to him, nor did he have reason to do so, he in fact regarded with scorn the position that the Master and the city of Lisbon had taken and believed that soon he and all his faction would be lost.

Chapter 131

How the fleet from Oporto arrived at Cascais, and concerning the way in which the Master ordered it to proceed

Once the king had decided that his fleet should fight on the river, as we have said, he ordered two galleys to go beyond the mouth of the river to act as lookouts, and wait there; they were to let him know as soon as they spotted the Portuguese fleet approaching.

While the galleys lay 7 leagues from the city, at a place called Mata-Palombas, the whole Portuguese fleet came into view together. It was made up of seventeen *naos* and seventeen galleys, as you have heard.[158] As soon as the two galleys saw them, they went to deliver the news to the King of Castile and the men of his fleet. When these men were informed that the Portuguese fleet had appeared, all the crews of the Castilian galleys rose to their feet and started to brandish their unsheathed swords and other weapons, jeering and shouting, with great excitement, thinking that they would vanquish the fleet the following day, and that once they had done so the city would be taken immediately. This took place just over an hour before sunset. The people in the city could see the men of the fleet making such a display of their merriment, but they did not know why they were so excited. At this point the [Portuguese] fleet reached Cascais after their [noon] meal on that day, which was Sunday, 17 July of the year already mentioned.[159]

With the [Portuguese] fleet at anchor in that place, which was 5 leagues from the city, its captains discussed how they would enter the Tagus and how the fight should proceed. Some said that, since the King of Castile had many men and a much larger fleet than they did, they ought not to pull too far out into the open sea because there were many landlubbers on board who were not used to the sea, and who might get seasick; but if the Castilian *naos* followed them, they could turn round and attack when they saw fit, and this would greatly help them overcome the Castilians. They talked to one another

---

[158] In Chapter 125 we were told that the fleet left Oporto heading for Lisbon, but the exact number of *naos* and galleys in it is never stated before the present chapter.
[159] 1384.

about this and many other possibilities, but they could not come to a final decision. They agreed to send a cockboat to inform the Master that the fleet was there, to ask what his orders were for them on entering the river and request that he send them help.

The cockboat set out well after dark, with good rowers and well pavised, and hugged the Almada bank so that the men in the Castilian fleet should not be aware of them. On board, to speak to the Master, came João Ramalho, who was a wealthy merchant from Oporto and a hardened sailor. He reached Lisbon late at night but he went to inform the Master that the fleet was off Cascais, at what time they had arrived there, and that he had come to find out what the Master would have them do the following day. The Master extended a warm welcome to him, as well as to the others who were there, and was very pleased to hear the news. Everyone realised that the cause of the joy shown by the men in the Castilian galleys was the arrival of the Portuguese fleet, when they found out that it was approaching.

Then the Master went with João Ramalho into a separate chamber and asked him how well armed and in what shape his fleet was. He replied that the galleys were well armed but, as for the *naos*, some carried the usual number of armed men, but others were short of men-at-arms. He also said that the reason why the galleys were well armed was that Count Gonçalo was acting as their captain and he had many good squires.

The Master was very troubled at this, but he said: 'João Ramalho, you will do as follows: I have here many large barges which I have had fitted with gunwales like the ones in foists;[160] and also some *naos* and barges which are lying at anchor here and will be ready to sail early tomorrow morning. Since the wind is favourable for making the voyage, you will set off immediately with the tide, with the galleys [sailing] all along the river, and the *naos* as close to them on the Almada side as possible, or as you think best. Do not make any attempt to fight. You must all come up before the city, and then we will supply the *naos* with valiant men and will also arm the ships and barges that are here. Then, all of you together, and I with you, will go and fight them. However, if the Castilian *naos* should happen to close with any of yours, let them defend themselves as best they can. I will have the vessels ready with enough people to come to your aid, or maybe you will find me already out at sea. That is the way in which you are to enter the river.'

---

[160] A foist, 'fusta' in Portuguese, is a smaller, lighter and faster version of a galley, often used for reconnaissance operations. One of its distinguishing features were rowlocks fitted on the gunwales such that each rowlock could serve as guide to two oars. This meant that the oarsmen had to sit close, side by side, and more of them could work in a relatively small space, hence the light weight and speed of the foist.

Then João Ramalho bade him farewell, and the cockboat returned the way it had come, without being seen by the [Castilian] fleet, or encountering any other setback.

Chapter 132

How it was known in the city that the fleet was approaching, and what the people did on that account

When João Ramalho bade farewell to the Master, though it was already very late at night, it was soon known throughout the city that a message had arrived from the fleet that it was already lying at Cascais, and that the next day it was to enter the river and fight against the Castilian fleet. When this news was heard and spread throughout the city, it is not easy to describe how full of anxiety and hope the hearts of its citizens were. They were very happy with the hope that, when their fleet fought against the Castilian fleet, it would defeat it, and the city would be rid of the seaward blockade, and they would be able to receive supplies, of which they were very much in need. Also, if the Castilian fleet were defeated they would be able to seize part of it, and that would bring such a loss to the Castilians that perhaps it might be a reason for the King of Castile to raise the siege from the city.

On the other hand, they felt fear and anxiety when they took into account how the Castilian fleet was much bigger than theirs, and armed with many good men, and the great help which could come from the king's camp, which was so near, if they needed it; and if the Portuguese fleet were to be defeated, they considered the great loss of fathers, sons, husbands and brothers, and other relatives who would perish there. Apart from this, it is worth noting that another great misfortune was in store for them. The city would be under such distress and anguish that not only would they lose all hope of being able to defend themselves but also, if such a thing were to happen to them, within a few days they were bound to fall into the cruel hands of their mortal enemies to be dealt with as they deemed fit.

These inevitable fears made everyone rise from their beds at once, men and women alike, for they could no longer sleep. Talking to each other out of the window about these matters and the next day's battle, a great noise and commotion of people conversing began to spread throughout the city, and this, which went on for a long time, caused the church bells to toll early for matins, especially as the nights were short then. At this point the people began to go to the churches and monasteries with lighted candles in their hands, having Masses said and indulging in other devotions, with fervent prayers and many tears.

What condition or way of life was then exempt from such anxiety at that moment? Certainly none at all, because everyone, including not only lay people but even the religious, was drawn under the huge mantle of such thoughts, namely that they all expected to receive their due portion, whether of victory or its opposite.

What heart could be so merciless that it would not be softened by gentle compassion on seeing the churches full of men and women, carrying their children in their arms, all crying out to God to come to their aid and to help the House of Portugal? Surely not a single one, unless it was not truly Portuguese.

Thus they spent most of the night, until morning came, some people weeping and praying devoutly, and others making preparations and getting ready to do battle with the enemy.

Chapter 133

How certain Portuguese *naos* fought against those of Castile, how three of them were seized and the worthy Rui Pereira killed

The Master got very little sleep that night, and likewise the city folk, as we have said. But before daybreak he attended Mass as usual, and went to the river bank, accompanied by many of his men who had been waiting for him, to arm the ships and barges which were to support the fleet. As the men were embarking, the Master wanted to get aboard a *nao*, but a friendly contest arose between them: the city-folk told the Master not to board any of the ships, since they would never allow him to expose himself to such a hazard and endanger his life, but that they would go and fight the enemy, whereas he should remain in the city and not desert them.

The Master said he was grateful for their thoughtfulness and loyal goodwill, but there was no reason in the world why he should remain in the city, and he would be personally taking part in the combat; also, he trusted in God that he would come out of the fight with great honour to himself, the city and the kingdom of Portugal. When they saw that this was his only course of action, they told him to do as he wished.

After this was done, when it was full morning, all the ships in the King of Castile's fleet, which was made up of forty *naos* and thirteen galleys, hoisted their topmost yards and were filled with many brave men. As the tide was going out and there was little wind, the galleys towed the large *naos* and the smaller *naos* were pulled by the skiffs ahead. They all proceeded to Restelo o Velho, which was barely a league nearer to where the Portuguese fleet would be approaching, and they all lined up, with their prows pointing towards Almada, each one moored by its hawser so that it would not drift with the tide. This was how they drew up their battle formation. Furthermore, the king ordered mounted men-at-arms to attack the walls [by the gates] of Santo Agostinho and São Vicente de Fora, so that the people in the city should be kept busy defending that part and not be free to help the fleet unhindered.

Now it so happened that it was soon after tierce, and the tide already coming in, when the Portuguese fleet appeared near the Point of São Gião, which lies 3 leagues from the city. This is the order in which they came:

Five *naos* sailed in front and, in the largest of these, which was named the *Milheira*, was Rui Pereira with sixty men-at-arms and forty crossbowmen; in another, the *Estrela*, there was Álvaro Pérez de Castro;[161] in the *Farinheira* came João Gomes da Silva; in the *Sangrenta*, there was Aires Gonçalves de Figueiredo; in another, Pero Lourenço and Rui Lourenço de Távora. Likewise, the other ships also had their captains, such as Gil Vasques and Lopo Vasques da Cunha, João Rodrigues Pereira, Lopo Dias de Castro, Nuno Viegas, Gonçalo Eanes do Vale and others. But we have mentioned those four by name, because these were the only ones that went into attack. After these five *naos* came all the galleys together, pavisaded and bedecked with pennants. Then, behind the galleys came twelve *naos*. An onshore breeze was blowing up the river, giving favourable conditions for entering.

When Rui Pereira, a very eminent man whose extraordinary heart overflowed with courage, saw that the Castilian *naos* stood moored to land, as we have said, and not knowing why they had not yet set their sails, he came very close to them meaning to challenge them; the other four *naos* went with him. When he saw that the Castilians showed no inclination to fight, he changed his course and made for Almada.

So it was that although the morning light had not yet begun to brighten up the land fully, the walls and high places were already packed with men and women who wanted to watch. Since daybreak men and women had done

---

[161] In Chapter 116 above, we read that Count Álvaro Pérez de Castro died not long after 11 June 1384. In the present chapter, he enters the Tagus with the Oporto fleet, which engages in a naval battle with the Castilians on 17 July, just over a month after the beginning of the Lisbon siege. As Chapter 138 below states that the count and his son Pedro were responsible for the defence of a section of the city walls, this seems to indicate that his probable date of death was some time that July, which is coherent with the statement in Chapter 116.

nothing but run to the walls and high places to find somewhere from which they could behold the battle. Mindful of their fathers and brothers who were about to fight there, beating their breasts and kneeling on the ground, they tearfully petitioned God to come to their aid. Mothers encouraged the innocent infants whom they carried in their arms to raise their hands to Heaven, teaching them how to pray and petition God to come to the rescue of the Portuguese. Others uttered their supplications in many different ways, calling on the Holy Mother of God and Saint Vincent the Martyr[162] to go to their rescue.

Elsewhere, the Master and all the city folk were busy making preparations to board the larger ships and barges which were being armed in order to go to the aid of their fleet; so that not only the young men but white-haired men were arming themselves for the fighting. Then the Master boarded a large, handsome *nao*, which was one of those that, as we have related, they had seized from the Genoese, with a cargo of lengths of cloth.[163] With him there went on board over 400 men-at-arms, but because the *nao* had insufficient ballast and more men went aboard than should have done, it was not possible to steer it properly.

So many people had boarded the other ships, as well as the barges modified as foists, that they were in danger of capsizing. One such, aboard which was Gonçalo Gonçalves Borjas, set sail bound for Restelo, but the head wind forced it to head towards Sacavém,[164] and the same happened to another, carrying Mem Rodrigues de Vasconcelos.

The Master had also wanted to put out but, watching the tide and the head wind, and seeing how conditions were worsening for unfurling the sails, he went ashore and so did the men. The barges were small crafts, incapable of causing damage to the larger vessels, especially with the weather against them, and so they were derigged as well as the ships.

Now with Rui Pereira's *nao* and the other *naos* on a course for Almada in the way we have described, and all the Portuguese galleys rowing in line against the enemy fleet, when the Castilians saw that now they would be able to take them on their leeward side, all at once they got under way in order to attack them. The first one to cast off was a large *nao* named the *Juan de Arena*, which had a cockboat [with the sail] at half-mast, garrisoned by men-at-arms.

When Rui Pereira saw that the Castilian *naos* were heading to attack the Portuguese galleys and that the wind was freshening, fearing that they would harm them, and so as to hinder them, he made a wise move rather than acting

[162] Patron saint of Lisbon.

[163] In Chapter 109 above.

[164] This means that they were pushed up-river, as Sacavém is a town on the Tagus river, just under 7 miles (*c*. 11 km) north-east of Lisbon.

with foolish bravado, as some would have it, and changed tack in order to attack the *Juan de Arena*. Five Castilian *naos* and a large carrack fought with three Portuguese *naos*. The opposing crews were not slow to attack each other, forming one whole mass and fighting quite pitilessly. So it was that they were pushed by the tide and the wind towards the cliffs of Almada near Cacilhas. Rui Pereira's attack on the Castilian *naos* was a great help to the Portuguese galleys, because the leading [enemy] *nao* wanted to fall upon them, but while Rui Pereira attacked them and grappled with them, the galleys sailed past without any of the other [Castilian] *naos* being able to impede them or get near to them. But, by a cruel stroke of fortune, the fighting having gone on for a long time, Rui Pereira met his death in the following way.

While he was fighting as bravely as a bold and courageous knight could possibly fight, he lifted up the visor of his bascinet, which was causing him considerable trouble, and he was struck in the forehead by a bolt. As a result, shortly afterwards that nobleman, who should not have met his end so early in life, gave up his spirit.

Oh noble and valiant man and a true Portuguese! How you were then reproached by many, who said that you could well have avoided the battle and kept yourself out of danger like the other *naos*, but that through your foolhardiness you put yourself in such mortal danger! Yet it was not so, but was rather as the common people explained, saying that just as Jesus Christ had died to save the whole world, so had Rui Pereira died, to render salvation possible for the others. His death was felt deeply by the Master and everyone in the city.

The twelve Portuguese *naos* that were behind the rest moved up as fast as they could towards the city, and the Castilian ships went after them, but they could not cause them any damage because of the strong wind that favoured the Portuguese. The *nao* carrying Aires Gonçalves had weighed anchor when the Portuguese had begun to yield, and five galleys went in pursuit, staying close to it and trying very hard to seize it, particularly near a place called Cuba because of the wind which becalmed them there, in the lee of the high ground. The Castilian galleys attacked it so fiercely with their crossbows that the whole *nao*, the sails and all the gear were riddled with bolts, so that it was a strange sight to behold. When the *nao* came out of the shadow of that hill, it moved away from the galleys with the tide and the following wind, and safely escaped.

Oh, what a wonderful sight it was to behold: in such a small space across such a narrow river, to see fifty-seven *naos* and thirty galleys, all armed and well equipped, craving to cause damage to one another! Oh, what a day it was, so full of uncertainty! Especially for those who put most of their hopes in this battle, since desire imagined one thing, and fate decreed another!

The Castilian galleys did not succeed in catching up with those of the Portuguese, nor did the Portuguese try to close with the Castilians, because every Castilian galley had behind it a *nao* full of armed men ready to come to their assistance whenever this should become necessary. In fact, no other *naos* fought except those we have mentioned. Of these, three Portuguese ones were taken; some men from both sides were killed, and the rest of the Portuguese were all taken prisoner, many of them wounded. The Master walked along the riverbank, armed and accompanied by many of his men, welcoming the members of the fleet, which moored close to land and stretched from the shipyards to as far as the Sea Gate.[165] Meanwhile, the Castilian fleet headed back to Restelo.

Chapter 134

How they brought to the king one of the squires who had been taken prisoner, and the conversation he had with him

When those three [Portuguese] *naos* had thus been captured, and all the others had reached safety, the fighting ceased on both sides. The Castilians began to put the Portuguese they had found in them into the ship's boats, both those who were wounded and those who had no injuries. The king commanded that one of those who had been captured should be brought before him, but not a person of low rank.

When those who had been sent for this purpose arrived at the shore, they saw Vasco Rodrigues Leitão, one of the worthy squires who had come there, approaching the shore in a boat with others who were being brought to land. They said that he would suffice to give news to the king regarding what he wished to know. Then they took him into the king's presence. The first thing that the king asked him was whether Nuno Álvares was with the fleet; the squire answered that he was not. Then he asked him who were in the galleys and the *naos*; the squire named them all, and described how they had fought, how Rui Pereira had been killed, and other related things.

While he was speaking with the king, the queen came into a room near the one where the king was. Vasco Rodrigues, when he saw her, went to kiss her

---

[165] Gate on the old Moorish city walls not far from the riverfront, situated on what is nowadays the Rua dos Bacalhoeiros.

hands. She, who knew him well because he was a *criado* of Gonçalo Vasques de Azevedo, looked at him and said, 'Oh, Vasco Rodrigues! You are here?'

'Here, my lady', he said, 'at God's mercy and yours.'

The queen then went out of the room; left alone, he returned to where the king was. The king, smiling, said to him: 'Confound you! This is pretty hand-kissing! You come with lance in hand to deprive your liege lady of the kingdom that is hers by right, and then you mock her by kissing her hands! You deserve no better than to have your lips and tongue cut off for kissing her hands the way you do.'

He said: 'Sire, this was not the way it was explained to us; rather, we were led to believe that, considering the cause of this war, and how you entered the kingdom before the time that was stipulated in the treaties, and violated the clauses that were contained in them, you had lost any claim you had to the kingdom; and that we were in the right and should defend our land as we are doing, since you wished to take it from us in this way.'

When Pedro Fernández de Velasco and other knights who were present heard this from Vasco Rodrigues, they said to the king, 'See there, my liege, what they say to you! This is what we have told you again and again, and our advice was not heeded, and you did what you liked.' As they were speaking of this, the squire was removed from the king's presence and taken to join the other prisoners who were coming forth from the *naos*. Some of them were later ransomed, and some exchanged; others escaped into the city; and others were carried to Seville in the galleys.

Chapter 135

Why the Portuguese fleet did not fight further with the Castilian fleet, and how the king ordered that Almada be attacked

Just as the Master had seen the need and taken care to man his fleet in the best way possible to fight with the Castilian fleet, for the reasons already noted, he began to arrange with the men of the city for its defence and protection, considering everything that was necessary for so great an undertaking, and to leave whatever contrary things might happen in the hands of fortune. As he was waiting for a good time to put all this into effect, there arrived for the King of Castile an increase to his fleet: twenty-one *naos* and three armed galleys, when a week had not yet passed since the battle with the other [Portuguese] *naos*.

Thus the king had in total in his fleet sixty-one *naos* besides the carracks, sixteen galleys and a galliot, which he ordered to lie at anchor all along the city from Cata-que-Farás to the Cruz Gate according to the formation that you have heard about.[166] When the Master saw how unevenly matched the fleets were, and the great advantage that the king had in that regard, he decided to abandon what he had intended to do.

At this point, the town of Almada having been besieged, as we have said, for about two months, since that day when Diogo Lopes was taken prisoner,[167] the town was hard pressed by the attacks of its enemies from the landward side, where they were encamped. On the seaward side, nothing could trouble them because of the great height of the hill, except depriving them of water. This was more dangerous to them than arms or mines, or even a powerful bombard, with which several shots were fired at them. Thus those who were within, who remained loyal to the Master, began to experience things which were very hard to endure, which it is well that you should be told about briefly, since they have not yet been mentioned.

So it was that when the Castilian fleet descended upon Lisbon, the inhabitants of Almada all took refuge in the castle. As for two balingers that they had, in which at times provisions were taken to the city, the galleys attempted to capture them on land beneath the castle where they were pulled up on shore. In their defence at that time many were wounded, but the enemy were unable to seize those balingers. Afterwards the people of the town burned them so that the Castilians would not get them. In the town there were plenty of men who could defend it, as well as other foreigners who took refuge in it. They had come to join forces with the Master but could not do so because of the fleet.

Those people had provisions of bread, wine, meat and other things for six months and more, but they had no water other than what was in a small cistern. A strong guard was placed on this, and each person was given two and a half pints per day, and no more.[168] In spite of this, the men of the town went forth to await the Castilians in certain spots; the latter were wont to go foraging through the land, even as far as Sesimbra, and the Portuguese killed and wounded some of them, so that they no longer dared to go unless there were many of them together. Likewise, the Portuguese waited for those who went off in ship's boats to Arrentela and Amora to pillage, so that one day

166 In Chapter 114 above.
167 In Chapter 116 above.
168 In the Portuguese text: 'one *canada*', an ancient measure equivalent to roughly 2.4 pints (*c.* 1.4 litres). See: Luís Seabra Lopes, 'Sistemas Legais de Medidas de Peso e Capacidade, do Condado Portucalense ao Século XVI', *Portugalia*, New Series, 24 (2003), 155.

they killed more than thirty, all on a mudbank, as they were trying to get back into the ship's boats, not knowing the harbour. This going out and returning, whenever they wished, was done through the gate by the cliff, called Meijão Frio, which faces the sea.

After the town had been attacked many times, and nothing could be done against them that could cause them any great harm, the king ordered that a mine be dug underground. They began it at some distance away in the outskirts, and it headed straight towards the tower that is above the castle gate, in order to undermine it by placing stacks of wood under it and burning it down, as is usually done. Those within got word of this. So, when the Castilians believed that they were going deep underground, they emerged through the mouth of the tunnel where it met the ditch around the barbican, which those inside [the castle] had dug much deeper than it was before. There they fought with each other, and the master sapper was killed, with some wounded on both sides, so that the Castilians could gain no further advantage from it. This mine is still there today and can be seen.

The king was greatly vexed when he learned of this, and he went in person to the said town with some of his men and captains, in order to have it attacked as he wished. In the bell tower of the Church of Santiago, which is close to the castle, he ordered a strong wooden scaffold to be built for him, from which he could see the entire town, and how it was being attacked.

When the day for the attack arrived, the king stationed himself on the scaffold and had all of his men attack the town all around the landward side, since from the seaward side it was impossible, given the great ruggedness and height of the hill. It was attacked by men-at-arms and foot soldiers, cannons, crossbow fire, staff slings, mantlets[169] and other artillery equipment, from the hour of tierce until after midday. The men of the town, realising that the king was on the said scaffold, even though there was no attack from there except with arrows, decided to fire at him with a cannon. Wearied, the king left to eat and was already down in the church when the cannon was fired, hitting the scaffold, killing two men and wounding three. The king ordered his men to fall back, and not to attack further at that time. Some Castilians were killed and wounded, and two Portuguese were killed, a son of João Lobato, and Diogo Domingues, the son of Domingos de Santarém; others were wounded by stones and arrows. As for the cannon fire that the enemies targeted to fall inside [Almada castle], it caused no harm. This was because all the missiles passed over and fell into the water, on account of the narrowness of the town. Then the king ordered a bombard to be brought up, that fired a stone that

---

[169] A movable shelter or screen used to protect soldiers when attacking or besieging a fortified place.

weighed well over 500 pounds.[170] The first stone to be fired went very low, and did no damage; on firing the second shot, which caused no harm, the bombard split open in such a way that it could no longer be used.

When the king saw that nothing would get them to surrender, he promised never to negotiate with them, but rather pledged that they would all be put to the sword. He left Pedro Sarmiento and Juan Rodríguez de Castañeda besieging the town with a great number of men and ordered that they should attack them every day, whereas he decided to leave the place.

Chapter 136

Concerning the things that the people of Almada endured because of the lack of water

The king returned to his camp, swearing and promising that he would never give them respite from attack until the town was entered by force, with no terms of surrender.

Now it is important for you to know that within the town there were some forty horses, besides other beasts of burden. When the water began to run short, they decided not to give the animals anything to drink. Their thirst was so great that, whenever the men urinated, the animals would go to suck and eat the damp earth. Then they decided to get rid of them to avoid watching them die. So that the Castilians should not get any use out of them, they pushed them all over the edge of the cliff down into the sea. Each man pushed his own animal, and thus all were killed. Because of the lack of water, they kneaded their bread with wine, and boiled their meat and fish in it. They ate the bread while it was hot, for when it was cold no one could eat it, and they did the same with other foods.

At one point the water of the cistern ran out, and they were forced to drink other, most loathsome water which had collected in the ditch from the rain that had fallen in the winter, in which the women, before the siege began, used to wash filthy clothes and infants' nappies. This water was green and very dirty, and dead mules lay in it, as well as dogs and cats, so that it was a sickening thing to see. By night men would descend on ropes from within to make off with the said water. When the Castilians found out that they were taking it in that way, they endeavoured to guard it. Many times it happened

---

[170] In the Portuguese text, 'five *quintais*', roughly equivalent to 566 lbs (*c.* 257 kg), where each *quintal* is roughly 113 lbs (*c.* 51.4 kg).

by night and by day that men were killed and wounded on both sides over it. They would boil the water and, once it was boiled, they would drink it and make bread with it.

After this water became scarce, they tried to get it from the river, and from big tubs they had set up on the riverbank to collect fresh water. They would descend the cliff by a path they had made to get that water. The first day they brought as much as they wished; but when the Castilians found out, they set a guard on it. The townspeople went there and found the Castilians guarding it. The Portuguese numbered no more than seventeen, but their enemies, who were lying hidden among the boulders, totalled 100. As they fought over the water, three of the Portuguese were killed, and the other fourteen were badly wounded with arrows and spears. They carried away no more than two wineskins half full of water, and the Castilians broke their tubs.

By then the people were dying of thirst, men, women and little children alike; some of those who had taken refuge there went forth from the town by night and fled to save their lives. All night they sent many signals by beacon to the Master, by which they gave him to understand the grievous plight in which they were placed, for there was no other way in which they could let him know, being besieged by sea and by land.

The Master and the city folk well understood the great distress which they were under, but they could not give them any help. Nonetheless, one night the Master sent a swift barge with a very powerful cannon, gunpowder, crossbows, and other defensive weapons. By chance it came into port where Castilian barges lay at anchor; it was captured with the weapons, and all those who were manning it were taken prisoner.

At that time a Gascon knight, called Monsieur Iman, a very worthy man and valiant man-at-arms, held as his captive Afonso Galo, who was the alderman of the town and who had been taken prisoner in the first skirmish when Diogo Lopes Pacheco had been seized. This knight led Afonso Galo, bound with a rope, close to the castle. He said to those inside that they knew well that that town and the entire kingdom belonged by right to the King of Castile, that many towns of the kingdom had given themselves up to him, and that they, in their stubbornness, were refusing to do what the others were doing. So, he entreated them, they should act in such a way that they would not be traitors, and should give up the town to the King of Castile, who would grant them many favours in return. He said that he was bringing before them that very Afonso Galo who was alderman of the town, and that they should do what he told them, for, if not, Afonso Galo would in all certainty die. They should not want to witness his death, and the deaths of the others who were prisoners, for the king would order them all to be killed.

The townspeople responded that the king could kill the prisoners if he liked, but that they would not surrender the town for anything, and that he should withdraw from there with his honour intact, and leave with his prisoner. As he insisted in his arguments that they should give up the town to the king, they prepared a small cannon and shot at him from between the battlements. Such was their luck that they knocked him dead to the ground, and Afonso Galo remained alive, there where he stood. The king was much aggrieved by the knight's death and swore that they would all die by the sword.

Chapter 137

How the people of Almada surrendered the town to the King of Castile

Finding themselves so hard-pressed because of the scarcity of water, which they could not obtain, the men of Almada agreed to send a message to the Master, but they knew of no expedient or plan by which they could get it to him. The Master likewise, who had a good sense of the tribulations which they were suffering, was very keen to learn at what point their affairs had reached, but he had no means and knew of no way in which he could arrive at any certainty about it. Then a man from Almada who had come in the fleet from Oporto said that he would take the message by swimming over, if the Master wished to send him.

The Master was very pleased at this, and told him by word of mouth the things he should say; moreover, he wrote to them in a letter what he considered to be apt for his purposes. One night the man reached the shore by the hill and climbed up the cliff called Meijão Frio by the hidden path, which he knew well. He called to the men of the castle who were on watch, and they were startled when they heard him; but, on recognising him, they opened the door, delighted to see him. When they realised that he had swum his way there, they considered it a great achievement. After the message had been delivered orally and in writing, they concluded that the Master wanted to receive word on what their plight was, and tell them that they should hold out as long as they could. They informed the man of all that they had endured up to that point and told him that they had no water at all, nor did they know of any way of saving their lives. With this message, the man swam back at once by night.

The Master, in view of their sufferings which could not be remedied, after three days sent the man there again with a message, to tell them that he was deeply grieved by what they had suffered and, since things were as they were, they should surrender to the King of Castile on the best terms they could,

and give him the town. Then they decided to send two worthy men with a
message to the king, saying that they wished to be his subjects and give him
the town. Before this, however, that man [from Almada] had swum across the
river between Lisbon and Almada six times, carrying messages and bringing
replies, always by night.

The king already knew from a man who had been captured, one of those
who were fleeing from the town, that they had no water at all, that many
children had died, and were dying every day, also that they had no choice but
to surrender or all die. His will was not to negotiate terms with them, which
answer he gave to the two men who had been sent to him. At the end of
waiting for three days, the king still refused to see them. As they were about
to return, the queen had them summoned; with them present, she asked the
king for mercy, to pardon them and negotiate their surrender.

The king was pleased to grant this. The terms of surrender were that the
king guaranteed the safety of their lives and possessions, and that each man
might remain in his house and retain ownership of it, without anything being
taken from him; and so it was done. Two days after the pact was made, the
first day of August, the king and queen went in galleys to Almada; the town
was given up to him with its keys, and he was received as its liege lord. This
came after they had first suffered, as we have said, so many trials and tribulations, the like of which no other town in Portugal suffered in the service of
the Master, or as a result of declaring loyalty to him.

The king and queen dined in the town. The king summoned the townspeople, and told them to be loyal to him, and he would grant them many
favours. Some of the men asked him for certain things, and he granted their
requests. He ordered that the notaries should write in his name, and should
call themselves his men; he left as judges those who had been judges before.
He named as alderman of the town a knight called João Bravo; as its garrison,
he appointed the men and captains who had previously besieged it. That same
day he returned to his camp.

Chapter 138

How it was revealed to the Master what Dom Pedro had decided to do, and the approach he took in the matter

The Master gave many thanks to the Lord God in acknowledgement of His
favours at the beginning of his worthy deeds, among which one of them
was to reveal to him certain acts of treachery that were being planned against
him by people whom he trusted greatly. For there were many who came to

him with mischievous desires and perverse hearts, both high-ranking people and those of other stations, showing him signs of love and good service, and yet who did not persevere for very long, as you will see when the time comes.

Regarding others, he did not have a good opinion of them, but nonetheless granted them great favours in order to change their evil intent; abandoning the initial deception bit by bit, they afterwards displayed serious shortcomings and deserved shameful reproach. Among those who were blemished by such an error, it is told, was Dom Pedro, who was the son of the Count of Arraiolos Dom Álvaro Pérez de Castro, who by now had died, as you have heard,[171] and who was married to a daughter of Count João Afonso Telo and Countess Guiomar, by name Dona Leonor. Regarding how the Master got word of this, however, there are varying accounts.

Some say that after Dom Pedro de Castro had conferred with the King of Castile, in a conversation in which João Lourenço da Cunha took part, that he agreed to give him entry into the city through his section of the wall; then he spoke of it with Rui Freire, because he was Galician like him. He believed that he would keep it secret, but Rui Freire revealed it to the Master. The latter, when he saw Dom Pedro in the presence of many noblemen, told him openly what he had been informed of and by whom. Dom Pedro said that Rui Freire was lying, and that he would challenge him in combat. As Rui Freire replied that he was quite willing, and other related things, the Master told them to be quiet, and he paid no further attention to it; and thus the matter was dropped.

Nevertheless, that written account is quite mistaken, for two reasons, briefly stated. First, it is not to be believed that a great lord, as wise and discreet as the Master, hearing a thing of such great importance, which could be the downfall of the kingdom, and could also cause his own dishonour and endanger his life, would make public in this way what had been confided to him in secret. Second, it is not to be believed that he would pay no further attention to it, and that he would let it go unpunished in that way, as if it had been done in jest.

Others say that João Lourenço da Cunha and certain others were plotting to murder the Master with poison, or in some other way, and to hand over the city to the King of Castile; and that Dom Pedro was privy to this betrayal and was their leader, as it was his duty to guard the Santo Agostinho section [of the walls] and the gate through which the king or his men were to enter.

Another author, however, whose words we are more inclined to accept, speaking of this part of the story, states as follows: Count Álvaro Pérez and his son Dom Pedro de Castro, being with the Master during this siege, were

[171] In Chapter 116 above.

responsible for guarding the city walls from the Santo André Gate to the Gate of Santo Agostinho, and had with them a little over 100 lances, besides other men-at-arms of the city, as the guard of that sector.[172] When the count died as we have said, Dom Pedro remained with his men and those of his father at that same post. That author writes that the Master learned through Rui Freire everything that Dom Pedro was preparing to do in this matter and when, but not that the Master revealed it. There was a very strong reason for Rui Freire to mention this to the Master, for he was the son of the Master of the Order of Christ, Dom Nuno Freire, who had been the guardian and mentor of the Master of Avis when he was a boy, for which reason the Master bore great goodwill towards him. He also states that at this point João Lourenço da Cunha, who had been the husband of Queen Leonor, fell into a sickness from which he later died. When he confessed his sins, he said to the abbot that he knew many things which could harm the city and the Master, and even the entire kingdom. The confessor said that he would neither absolve him nor give him penance until he told the Master what he knew. Then the Master was called and spoke with João Lourenço, who revealed many things to him that put the Master on his guard.

Among these was that Dom Pedro de Castro and all his vassals, in exchange for a large amount of gold and silver that he was to receive from the king, had sold him the city. On the 15th day of that month of August, on the evening of the feast of the Assumption of the Blessed Virgin, he was to let in the king's men, and they were to climb up on ladders suitable for the purpose set against the walls. Moreover, it was in Alenquer that the hooks for the ladders had been made. The signal for the time when they should come was to be a lamp placed in an arrow-slit in the city wall. When the Master learned of that signal, he ordered men to be stationed on guard near that spot; they received the Castilians with arrows, stones and the like when they arrived, at which they were not very pleased. Dom Pedro was taken prisoner immediately that evening, and all his men with him.

The next day, when it became known throughout the city how this had happened, everyone cried out to the Master that he should order Dom Pedro to be cruelly put to death. He pacified them with gentle words, with no further harm being done to Dom Pedro. A week later, he ordered all Dom Pedro's vassals and relatives, along with certain other Galicians and Castilians, to be banished from the city, taking away from them their arms and everything they had. Dom Pedro remained a prisoner under lock and key.

Inasmuch as we have pen in hand, and so as not to disrupt later the order of what we have to tell, let us at once recount another clever ruse of Alfonso

---

[172] See Chapter 133, note 161 above.

Enríquez [the Chief Huntsman], who came in the fleet. He was the brother of Count Pedro [of Trastámara][173] who had stayed in Oporto, and was frequently in the company of João Rodrigues de Sá, showing him great friendship. One day Alfonso Enríquez, wishing to join the Castilians, suggested to João Rodrigues that they go and look at the King of Castile's camp. João Rodrigues agreed, and they both mounted up, João Rodrigues on a good chestnut horse and Alfonso Enríquez on a mule. As they were both looking on, Alfonso Enríquez said to João Rodrigues, 'My dear brother, lend me that horse and I will go and speak with my relatives there. So that I can speak with them in greater safety, I would rather ride it than this mule.'

João Rodrigues, having no idea of what he meant to do, dismounted at once, and Alfonso Enríquez mounted the horse. As soon as he was in the saddle, he said to João Rodrigues, 'My dear brother, God be with you, for I intend to join my relatives.' Then he gave the horse a good kick and fled to the camp of the Castilians. João Rodrigues was left there in astonishment and considered that Alfonso Enríquez had made a fool of him. He went to the Master, whom he found in the dockyards, and told him what had happened to him, offering the excuse that he had known nothing about the matter. The Master, who knew João Rodrigues well as a good and true Portuguese, burst out laughing, and said that he considered him blameless.

Now, you should know that Alfonso Enríquez, when he went over, did not take along any of the men who were with him, which everybody took amiss. His men wept because he had gone off in that way. His brother[174] threw down the gauntlet in the presence of the Master, saying that he would challenge anyone who might say that he had known anything about the matter. The Master, laughing, said that he should not worry about Alfonso Enríquez's departure, for he was under no suspicion at all.

At this point the Master called together all the city folk, and they decided to impose a levy of 100,000 *libras* in old coin to pay the wages of the men-at-arms, from which neither clergy nor friars were exempt, nor anyone else, no matter how honourable. Beyond what each clergyman had to pay in his own right, according to the income of his benefice, all the churches and monasteries contributed silver in the form of crosses, chalices and other ornaments to be used in minting that money.

This was followed on the 19th of that month, at noon, by an eclipse of the sun,[175] which was then in the sign of Leo. It lost its brightness, which caused everyone a great fright. The astrologers said that it meant great mortality

---

[173] See Chapter 124.
[174] Alfonso Enríquez the Younger.
[175] By modern reckoning, this annular eclipse occurred on 17 August 1384.

would be inflicted upon honourable people in a royal house. So it came to pass afterwards among the great lords of the King of Castile, as you will hear later on.

Chapter 139

How the Castilian galleys tried to capture those of Portugal, and concerning what ensued

With the Castilian *naos* thus lying at anchor, and the galleys close to Santos, the Castilians often rowed past the city, along the river towards Xabregas, firing many cannons and bolts at the Portuguese fleet, which was beached near the city walls: the [local] *naos* lay alongside the wall of the Paço da Madeira,[176] with masts crosswise and other defences forward, because of the cannons that were being fired at them; the galleys were quite close by. Nevertheless, it pleased God that not one was harmed, nor the men inside.

The King of Castile sometimes went in his galleys, to examine and reconnoitre the city; then the galleys would return, and the king would go back to his siege camp. When the king saw how the Portuguese galleys floated up with the flowing tide, and were left stranded at low water, and likewise the small number of men who manned them as guards, he thought of a way in which he could capture them all. He summoned masters, galley commanders and others who were expert at this, and revealed to them all what he intended to do and what his thoughts were in this regard.

They all praised the king's words, recognising that he had given thought to this, and considered the galleys as good as captured, in the way that the king had said. They asked him if he wanted them all to be burned, or to be brought away just as they were found. The king said that they should not burn those galleys, but bring them to him as safely as possible. 'For the galleys are mine', said the king, 'and I've no wish to lose them like that.' He said this in order to make it clear that the galleys, and the entire realm and everything in it, belonged to him.

Then those masters and seafaring men with whom the king had discussed this decided on the following: that on 27 August, when there would be a spring tide, and high tide coincided with dawn, the men of the galleys should all arm themselves at night and, taking along a few galley-oarsmen, many

---

[176] This was a department of the Customs House, dealing mainly with timber (*madeira*) but also other goods.

crossbowmen and men-at-arms, all the large boats from the *naos* should be fitted out and made ready. All this should be done so quietly and secretly that it could not be seen or heard by the people in the city. The Count of Mayorga, with 400 men-at-arms, as well as foot soldiers and crossbowmen, should attack the area between the Santa Catarina Gate and Cata-que-farás, and, if they could, should seize the stockade along the shore. At the said gate 500 or 600 lances should attack, with many men armed with shields and crossbows, indicating that they meant to attack on that side, and in fact they should attack vigorously, to harass the city folk, and send them running off in different directions. The strategy would have been very good, if the city defenders had been few and scattered over many areas; but there were so many companies of men, and so numerous were the forces to defend the city, that, even if it could have been attacked from all sides, which was not possible, there were enough men to thwart their attack.

The Saturday that they had chosen for the attack arrived, and very early in the morning, as the sun was coming up, the Castilian galleys began to row from Santos, where they lay by the shore, along with the boats pavised and armed as appropriate. The Count of Mayorga likewise approached by land, with many men poised to attack along the city wall, and many other troops at the Santa Catarina Gate as had been planned; all this was done very swiftly.

When the sentries of the city saw this, they began at once to ring the cathedral bells, as they did in the wall sections where there were any bells; however, they had no notion of what the galleys were going to do. Rather, they thought they were just rowing along the river, as they had been in the habit of doing. Because of the men who were approaching by land, they rallied to the city walls in that area, where the enemies gave every sign that they meant to attack, while many of the city folk were still asleep.

The Portuguese galleys lay very close together, and all had their oars out of the rowlocks; each one was under the command of a nobleman, who always deployed men to guard them as they thought best. The Castilian galleys, heading for the city, all rowed vigorously towards land. Then, with their anchors astern, they began to grapple with the Portuguese galleys from the prow, and the armed ship's boats among them too, with the intention of suddenly and without warning capturing them all, but they were unable to grapple with all of them.

The way that they were grappling, with the abundant crossbow-fire and the many men-at-arms they were carrying, did great harm to the few soldiers and galley oarsmen who were in the Portuguese galleys, unprepared to defend themselves. Thus, although they defended them as well as they could, with many of the men already wounded, though others were uninjured, they began to abandon the galleys. The city folk rallied quickly to help them, but the closed gates near the galleys hindered them greatly, and they could not get to the shore, except through a gate a long way from there.

When the Master, from his palace, heard the bells ringing and saw how the enemy galleys were grappling with his own, he rode very swiftly to the shore, with many good men following him. He passed through the dockyard gate, much against the will of Count Gonçalo, who with a cowardly heart told him not to go out until he saw what was happening. The Master paid no attention to what he said, and rode along the shore, telling his men to board the galleys, encouraging them as much as possible. The number of men kept growing, gaining strength from his presence, and for that reason they became bolder in defending the galleys as well as they could. One galley, which Afonso Furtado boarded, lay broadside on rather than lengthways. Two Castilian galleys approached to grapple with it, but he careened it to landward, so that the seaward side was raised, and the two galleys struck the waist of his galley with their prows. The galley defended itself very well, because of the advantage of its raised side; it did plenty of damage to the other galleys, and was not captured.

At this point a Castilian galley was grappling with a Portuguese galley commanded by Fernão Nunes Homem, Commander of the Order of Avis, which was forcibly boarded by the enemy, but only after Alfonso Gutiérrez de Padilla, a valiant Castilian knight who followed the Master's cause, was wounded and brought down; because as long as he was in the prow [of the Portuguese galley] with a lance in his hands and a bascinet with no visor, no one could board it, no matter how hard he tried. With four bolts embedded in his face, yet fighting on, he raised his arm to deliver a blow, when a chance bolt, finding its way in under his upraised arm, pierced him through the mouth. Disabled by such a wound, he was left exposed to others, and could not stop himself falling back from the prow into the water. Then the Castilians boarded the galley against the will of those who were defending it, forcing their way as far as amidships.

When the men on the shore saw that no other galley than this had been boarded, and that it was on the verge of being lost, they began to shout at the men on the city wall to throw axes down to them so they could break it up and prevent the Castilians from taking it away, and the axes were duly thrown down.

As they began to chop at the galley, João Rodrigues de Sá, a man of noteworthy fame and a very valiant man-at-arms, was close by [in another galley]. Seeing such a fierce combat taking place in the galley and being a very ready and remarkably bold knight, he got over the oars to come to its help. Crawling on hands and feet, with his lance clutched under himself, he left the galley where he was standing and, with one of his foot soldiers, he boarded the one the Castilians were trying to capture. With lance in hand, he made his way along the central gangway and began to perform such deeds that it was both a great pleasure for the Portuguese to watch and difficult for their enemies to endure. He made all the Castilians who were aboard abandon the galley, leaving some wounded and some dead, while others were unwilling to await his blows, and thus the galley was cleared of those who had captured it by force.

At this point the struggle became more and more heated, being very fiercely fought and accompanied by loud clamour on both sides, with the shouts of men, the blaring of trumpets and the ringing of bells, as well as the loud cries of 'For Portugal and Saint George!' and, on the other side, 'For Castile! Saint James!' They were no less hard beset than if the city had already had numbers of its enemies within the city walls, and others were trying to get in.

The Master kept shouting at them to do things that he saw had to be done urgently, but the great noise of the men and the clanging of the weapons with which they were fighting drowned out his orders, so that it seemed he was giving commands in vain.

Two things made this fight especially fierce and disproportionate on the part of the Castilians: first, the great desire to capture the galleys they had come for, which they expected to take easily according to the charge they had been given by their liege lord the king; second, the limited time in which the galleys could fight, which could not be prolonged beyond that in which they could remain afloat. As for the Portuguese, they too were fighting fiercely, considering themselves to be disgraced if they lost the galleys in that way through ill-preparedness.

Even though we have praised João Rodrigues and Alfonso Gutiérrez because they accomplished such fine deeds, you should not assume that they alone were defending the galleys, without anyone else fighting to protect them. These and certain other noblemen whom we do not name here, however, were as superior to the other men-at-arms as wild bulls put in a corral in the company of docile cattle.

The Master was riding along the shore as we have said, urging his men to board the galleys, wading into the water with determination. While he was in the water a bolt was fired and struck his horse on the shoulder. Feeling the wound, the horse immediately fell over with him into the water. The Master was submerged, armed as he was and wearing a bascinet with no visor. The men were all occupied, each man fighting where best he could, and they did not see him; with no help from anyone, when he found himself underwater and off his horse, he levered himself up by pressing against his knees and rose to his feet. He was in so deep that the water came up over his chin, and when he saw his predicament, he waded out of the water. Some who saw him thus rallied to him at once, and brought him a mule, which he mounted. Then he returned to his primary task of encouraging his men and urging them to board the galleys to defend them.

Now, it chanced that the Castilian galley whose master was Vasco Pérez de Meira, the one who invaded the Portuguese galley freed by João Rodrigues, when it was closing in to grapple, the fluke of its anchor fell through the anchor ring, also known as the shackle, of the Portuguese galley with which it was grappling. The latter was opposite the Butchers' Gate and was hitched to a cable that went through a wide drainage hole right inside the city walls. While they were fighting, a man saw how the anchors were entangled, got onto a tender fastened to the side of the galley, and tied one anchor securely to the other.

The fearless and doughty João Rodrigues, although he was badly wounded, was not satisfied with what he had already done, which was extremely praise-worthy, in retaking that galley which the Castilians had captured. Rather, he tried to force his way onto their galley and seize it. He fought in such a way, supported by others, that against the will of his enemies he leapt onto their galley. The Castilians, seeing how it was being taken, tried to unhitch the galley but could not, for that spot was very well defended, and all their efforts were of no avail, nor were they aware of the hindrance that we have described. Then the Portuguese began to shout at the men on the wall to haul on the cable of their galley. When they began to do so, there were so many men and women for that task that they found no room for their hands, and they hauled both galleys up on land. By then the Castilian galley was nearly defeated, with many crewmen throwing themselves into the water, rather than be killed or taken prisoner. Vasco Pérez, when he saw that the galley was entirely lost and could not be saved by any means, went down from the poop, in full armour as he was, stepped onto the edge of the tender, and plunged forward with it into the water, where he drowned. Many others did the same who, after the tide went out, were left on dry land and were dragged away with nets.

The other Castilian galleys kept fighting until weariness and despair of not being able to carry out what they had undertaken made them retreat. They rode at anchor on open water, extremely vexed at what had happened to them, tending the wounded. Many Castilians were captured and killed, and ten men of the city; João Rodrigues de Sá sustained fifteen wounds, two to his face. In the galley that had been captured as described, they found Portuguese prisoners below decks, and letters that some had sent from Seville asking their friends to bring them back Portuguese[177] girls who were good servants.

---

[177] The word used is 'chamorras', a disparaging term implying that the Portuguese,

The men who had come there to attack by land and along the shore, as we have said, did not create any real difficulties for the defenders. Indeed, they did it more to bring confusion to the people than on account of any advantage they expected to gain. Besides, the hail of stones and arrows from the city wall were so abundant that they had to fall back for their safety, as also from the stockade on the shore.

The Master went around visiting those knights and squires who were wounded, encouraging them with kind words and bestowing favours on them, and everyone gave thanks to God who had thus aided them to defend themselves against their enemies.

Chapter 140

Concerning certain things that happened to the besieged city folk at the hands of those in the siege camp

When that day of great toil, both by sea and by land, had passed, and the Master and the city folk saw how all this had so cunningly been done to them, without their having any suspicion, they set a better guard and watch on the galleys and other things. As the king had the city surrounded with a great multitude of men, and likewise the river along it fully occupied by his *naos* and galleys, with which he prevented them from getting any aid or supplies, the city began to suffer a greater drain on its resources than it had experienced before because of the men who had come in the fleet. Therefore, being well aware of all this, the king was of the opinion that he was poised to take the city by starvation.

Now, while the city was maintaining itself as well as it could, there were not at that time more than twenty horsemen in it, for as soon as they realised that they were going to be besieged, they immediately sent all the horses to the other side of the river, because they could not feed them if the siege lasted for a long time. Those twenty included Juan Alfonso de Baeza, Gómez García de Hoyos, Vasco Martins de Gá, Luís Henriques and others like them.

Even for those few horses that were there, they could not obtain fodder; instead, they bought pillows full of straw, emptied them, and gave the straw to the horses to eat. At times these horsemen went out with foot soldiers and

---

being clean-shaven, and with short hair, were geldings or eunuchs. Applied to women, it was also offensive, and 'good servants' may have had a similarly sexual implication.

crossbowmen to skirmish with their enemies. The men in the siege camp
came forward to meet them, and they fought with one another as is customary.

If we were to recount in detail all the things that happened to them on both
sides in battles and skirmishes, this entire day would not be enough; you would
get tired of listening, and we would get weary of writing. Nonetheless, leaving
aside those deeds that could plainly be told, just consider what typically occurs
in similar encounters: fortune, which cannot please both sides, sometimes
decreed that the enemy would force the men of the city back to the gates;
sometimes the Portuguese would force the Castilians back to the stockade of
their encampment near the Santos Well. On these occasions, on both sides,
sometimes there were men captured, killed and wounded, and other times not.
Since these skirmishes took place fairly near the city, many came out to watch
without carrying any weapons. The Master did not approve of this, because
they could suffer harm from the enemy. He ordered that any man who went
to watch and did not take along defensive and offensive arms should have
his clothing taken away. From then on, they behaved with caution, and all
went forth duly armed.

At this point it happened one day that word spread in the city, it was not
known by whom, that the king had removed to Almada because of the plague,
and that there were only a very few men in the camp.

They all swiftly became excited, and wished to go out and attack the
camp, not only the men, but even the women, saying that they wanted to
carry firewood out to burn it. As they were already assembled at the Santa
Catarina Gate, the Master studied the situation, and said that it was not wise to
go forth in such a disorderly way, for matters might turn out differently from
what was being proposed, and there could be very grave danger. Instead, the
few horsemen who were there should go to find out for certain how things
were, and then they could reach agreement on the approach they should take.

The horsemen went out through a different gate, called Santo Antão,[178] so
as not to be seen by the men of the camp, making their way up through a
valley close to the tents of the enemies. The Castilians, when they saw them
nearby, began to shout, 'To arms! To arms!' and blew their trumpets loudly.
There was a great commotion in the camp, with many horsemen rushing to
their mounts, as they always had their horses ready, and those on foot made
ready as well, each as best he could. They set out after the Portuguese and
tracked one down, a Galician squire who fell with his horse; his name was

---

[178] This was situated near the present-day Church of São Luís dos Franceses (Saint
Louis of the French). This church stands very near a street in Lisbon still called 'Portas
de Santo Antão'.

Vasco González, who later became high steward of the granary. They captured him, but he was released on ransom.

While they went out and came back, the Master remained constantly at the gate, preventing the people from venturing out. When the Portuguese were seen retreating, Fernão Rodrigues, the Commander of Juromenha, who later became Master of Avis, and was in charge of guarding the gate that day, went out with the men-at-arms who were with him to assist the horsemen who were fleeing from the Castilians who were following close behind. In this way many people of the city would have been lost at that time if the Master had not restrained them with his prudence and sound judgement.

Chapter 141

How the king sent to propose an agreement to the Master, and the words that were exchanged about it

We do not care to speak further of such things that happened during the siege. Mournful death began to display its ire more harshly against the troops in the siege camp, and likewise against those in the Castilian fleet; not only did it take squires and noblemen and others of lesser station, so many that it was an extraordinary thing to behold, but also it began to attack the lords of high rank, so that it caused great terror among everyone.

The Castilians, seeing themselves thus beset with plague, which flared up increasingly among them, well understood that their stay there could not last long, and that they would perforce have to lift the siege and depart soon. Among the many and varied considerations they put to the king, they told him that it would be wise to offer to negotiate with the Master, so as to come away with some honour from his invasion. The arguments that each of them stated seemed valid to the king, so he sent to ask for safe conduct from the Master so that Pedro Fernández de Velasco could go and speak to him on his behalf, for he was a man whom the king greatly trusted. The Master agreed and, on the day that had been designated for Pedro Fernández to come and speak, the Master sent several knights along the road to remain as hostages with the contingent that accompanied Pedro Fernández, until he had spoken with the Master and returned, in line with what had been requested by the Castilians. The hostages were Juan Alfonso de Baeza, Álvaro Gonçalves Camelo, Afonso Eanes Nogueira, Mem Rodrigues, Rui Mendes de Vasconcelos and others. Pedro Fernández arrived before noon, on a good horse, accompanied by a page with a lance and skullcap, who remained behind with the contingent.

The Master came forward on horseback wearing a haubergeon, vambraces, a sword girded on and a short tabard over the top. When they saw each other, they bowed and embraced each other. This meeting took place between the barbican and the city wall, at the gate of Santa Catarina.

Regarding what was said in that place, bias has made some writers state things in favour of the King of Castile in such a way as never happened,[179] saying that the Master proposed to Pedro Fernández that, if the king would approve of his remaining as governor of the realm until the King of Castile should have a son by his wife the queen, holding the governorship as Queen Leonor was to have held it, as had been set down in the treaties between the King of Castile and King Fernando, then he [the Master] would declare loyalty to Queen Beatriz and rule the kingdom for her. Provided that the King of Castile went back to his own realm and did not think of entering this realm [of Portugal] again, following the form of the clauses agreed upon in this regard, he [the Master] said that he would consent to any allegiance and written documents that might be appropriate for such a case. They further add that Pedro Fernández replied to the Master that his liege lord the king would not agree to such an arrangement in any way, shape or form. He would, however, go as far as to appoint two governors: the Master as one of them, and as the other any Castilian knight that the king might choose. They also claim that the Master said in response that the kingdom of Portugal would not consent to a Castilian knight being its regent or governor, and that thus Pedro Fernández took his leave, not having reached agreement with the Master in that negotiation.

Anyone who wrote such things, however, moved by bias in favour of another, did a great disservice to the truth. For no human understanding, even if we had not written this, could accept that Pedro Fernández would have come to negotiate an agreement with the Master on behalf of his liege lord the king, and that the Master would have spoken first, before Pedro Fernández put forward his demand. Moreover, they keep very quiet about what ensued from the visit paid by the Prior of Crato [to speak to the Master]. Therefore, all such accounts are to be rejected, and the exchanges that did take place, in brief summary, went as follows.

Pedro Fernández told the Master that he had come to apprise him of things to his advantage, if he were pleased to go along with them. He said that the Master could plainly see how he was besieged by sea and land by his liege lord, the King of Castile. Moreover, supplies were so scarce in the city that it could not maintain itself for long, as he well knew. Inasmuch as he was

---

[179] The account referred to below was written by Pero López de Ayala (*Crónica del rey don Juan*, 1384, Year 6, Chapter 9).

the son of a king, he should not let himself be lost in such a way, but rather should come to an agreement with his liege lord the king, from whom he would receive many favours and much preferment in anything benefitting his honour. He also said, regarding any pact that he might reach with the King of Castile, that he and Pedro [Ruiz] Sarmiento, and any others he liked, would offer him their solemn pledge that the King of Castile would honour any agreement and compact which they might conclude between them. If the king did not do so, they themselves would abandon the service of the King of Castile and help the Master against him in anything that could be of service to him.

To this the Master replied that he had spoken like the good knight he was, for which he thanked him very much, but that Pedro Fernández could be sure that whatever might happen to him [the Master], in this undertaking that he had begun, he believed that he was not losing, but rather that he was winning. For this kingdom had belonged to his father and his forefathers, and now the King of Castile wanted to subjugate and possess it unjustly, in violation of the promises he had made in the treaties. Therefore many *criados* of his father King Pedro and of King Fernando, his brother, had come to him to help to defend the realm; with them and the truth on his side, he believed that by the grace of God he could defend it, not only against the King of Castile, but against any other who might wish to do it harm. Even if matters were not to have the outcome that he desired, as Pedro Fernández said, he believed that he was not losing thereby, but rather winning, with great honour both for himself and all those who followed him.

Regarding this, many words were exchanged, but the Master never gave any response that would open up the possibility of an agreement. For, had he given any such reply, as some have written, bear in mind that the terms imposed would have been very harsh, and the King of Castile would not have agreed to them, in view of the plague that was raging among his men, and his own wish to gain some honour from his invasion.

The people were on the walls watching from afar, praying to God that He might bring them to some accord by which the city would be released from the siege, because of the great scarcity of provisions.

Pedro Fernández, seeing that, no matter how many good arguments he put to the Master, they were not leading to any talk of agreement, took leave of him with his good wishes, and went back to his men who were waiting for him; the Portuguese knights returned to the city. When Pedro Fernández entered the presence of the King of Castile, the latter asked him what message he had received from the Master. He replied, 'The devil take him, my liege, for I could never get any other words out of him, for all that I said, nor any other answer that he would give me, except "No, no, no, no!"' The king was vexed by this and said that he paid it no heed, for it might happen that the

Master would ask him later for an agreement, at a time when it would be very hard for him to get one, and other such arguments.

Dom Pedro Álvares, the Prior of the Order of the Hospitallers, who was present, a close adviser of the king and a very confidant and kinsman of the Master, said that he would like to go and speak to him. He believed he could persuade him and ascertain his full intentions. The king would not consent to this, either at that point or for days afterwards; but eventually, given the persistence of his men and also the worsening plague, he was induced to give the prior his permission. Twenty-two days after Pedro Fernández had come to speak to the Master, the prior went to talk to him. The Count of Mayorga also went with him, but not to take part in the conversation.

When all the arguments that the prior could put to him on such a matter had been set forth, he still could get no answer from the Master except the one he had given to Pedro Fernández. He took his leave and went away. The king was outraged at this, and swore by God that he would never again offer to negotiate, nor lift the siege of the city, no matter what might happen, until either through starvation or force of arms he should capture it as he wished. Then everyone, both the city folk and those in the siege camp, realised that this new and great war was not to be resolved by negotiation and agreement, but by cold steel and the shedding of blood.

The prior, having understood this, in order to undermine the loyalty of his brother Nuno Álvares and cause discord between him and the Master, wrote him a letter in which he informed him that the King of Castile was negotiating an agreement with the Master, a circumstance that very much pleased him. He was very aggrieved, however, because in the terms they had negotiated, there was no mention of Nuno Álvares at all, even though he had given the Master so much good service.

When he saw the letter, Nuno Álvares understood very well that its only purpose was to lure him away from serving the Master. He replied to it with another, saying that if his liege lord the Master were considering any agreement with the king, of any kind whatsoever, he knew him to be a man of such quality as would negotiate no terms except those in keeping with his honour and with that of all his men. He said, however, that he was astonished at the prior's having spent so little time with the Castilians, yet having already learned so many Castilian tricks.[180]

It is important that you should know that on the day after the prior spoke to the Master, which was the last day of August, after dinner the Count of Mayorga came from the siege camp, well accompanied by worthy men, and

[180] The chronicler makes up a noun, derived from the word 'Castilian', whose irony becomes all the more effective.

received as his wife Dona Beatriz,[181] the daughter of the deceased Count Álvaro Pérez de Castro. The Master was present and led her horse by the reins together with [her brother] Count Gonçalo, who joined their hands, and many other knights and noblemen. Then they conducted the bride to the camp, accompanied by her mother.

Chapter 142

How the Master decided, with those of his council, to do battle with the King of Castile

With no hope on the horizon and ill fortune having prevented the arrival of the human assistance that the Master sought from those places and people able to supply it, as you have heard,[182] and since he did not value any agreement that the King of Castile might offer him, he took the resolute decision never to consent to any terms of agreement that might be offered to him. Rather, he would either put the realm and his honour, life and status in the hands of destiny, or he would work for its defence in such a way that it would never be subjugated by Castile.

Seeing that the provisions were exhausted, and likewise the other things that have been mentioned, as well as others that you will hear of in greater detail later on, he resolved to do something that would not befit any but a great and strong heart: before the famine became more acute, and other things might come to pass, they should all assemble and go to do battle with the King of Castile. If the king were defeated by them, as they trusted in God he would be, they would win such great honour as had not been heard of for many years. If matters turned out differently, which was possible, they would die valiantly and honourably, rather than be subjugated by one who had no right over them. Although they beheld the numerous cavalry of their adversaries, and many and notable dangers facing them in such an attempt, they agreed nevertheless that the last resort in this situation was to do battle with the King of Castile, accepting whatever fortune God wished to give them, hoping that it would be good. Regarding the battle, however, they argued in various ways.

---

[181] She was last heard about in Chapter 79, regarding her part in the marriage proposal of Count Pedro with Leonor Teles.

[182] Chapter 47 above. This is a reference to the hope of receiving English assistance which, in the event, only arrived on 2 April 1385, as related in *CKJ2*, Chapter 4.

Some said that Nuno Álvares should come from the Alentejo with his men, and they should all go out together to do battle with the king. But that was difficult to do because there were no means by which they could cross the river [Tagus] in secret other than in a few small boats, which could not hold very many men at one time. Even if there had been enough boats in which to cross, it would be with great fear and in great peril, because of the Castilian fleet, which controlled the river.

Others believed that it would be better for the Master to cross with the men he had in the galleys to the other side and then immediately set fire to them all, so that the Castilians could not capture them. He would join up with Nuno Álvares, and all of them would return circling around [the estuary of the Tagus][183] to do battle with the King of Castile. Many rejected this proposal, however, saying that meanwhile the city would be left in very great uncertainty and danger.

After many suggestions, which you can understand would have been put forward in such a situation, it was finally agreed that the best plan for such a great undertaking was to send a message to Nuno Álvares, saying that on a certain day and at a certain time, as quietly as possible, he should come with his men to attack the siege camp; then the Master would come forth with all the men from the city. In this way they trusted in God that they would have a much better chance to defeat their enemies.

Then the Master wrote to Nuno Álvares, telling him how the fleet from Oporto had arrived in Lisbon, and how it had not been able to do battle with the Castilian fleet because the latter was so much larger and better armed, and because the weather had been unfavourable for going to its aid. He also wrote that the city had been besieged on the seaward side as it had been before, for which reason, if at first it was short of provisions, now it was much more so and would continue to be, especially on account of the many men who had arrived additionally with the fleet. Since from day to day the hope of being able to defend themselves dwindled, he had decided and agreed with his council to go out with the men of the city and do battle with the King of Castile. Furthermore, Nuno Álvares, beyond the 320 lances that he had with him at the time, should assemble as many more as he could, and make a large circle round to approach the city on the day and at the time that they both would choose to put their plan into effect. The Master had mustered the men he had with him, and found a number of paid lances amounting to 1,600 men-at-arms; and, among the city dwellers, 400 lances, and many foot soldiers and crossbowmen. Therefore he was informing Nuno Álvares of everything

---

[183] This would involve a march of over 75 miles (*c.* 120 km), and still requiring a river crossing by boat.

so that he could respond to him about it and set in motion the plan they were to follow in this matter.

If some recount that the Master wrote and told him to come to Montijo[184] with all his men, because he wanted to cross over the Tagus to assemble men and return to do battle with the King of Castile, and that Nuno Álvares came to meet him there, this was purely in order to discuss the plan they would follow in the battle. He had no intention of abandoning the city and leaving it in the power of many men regarding whose service he was not fully sure. In any case, that [meeting] proved impossible to bring about.

Nuno Álvares was pleased at this message, as a man who was very desirous of performing honourable deeds. He told his men that the Master had written to him about everything that had happened up to then, and the point at which they now found themselves; that the city was besieged by sea and land, and could not be resupplied with provisions, and for that reason it was very doubtful that it could defend itself for very long; and that, if Lisbon were taken, the entire kingdom would be lost. Therefore it seemed to him that they should leave behind all the baggage that could be dispensed with, and not take along more provisions than what would suffice as far as Lisbon. One day, in the early hours they should appear suddenly at the encampment of the King of Castile and take no heed of any guards they might encounter, nor any other obstacle, but rather go together, everyone straight to the king's lodging. Should the men of the camp make an effort to defend him, they should do battle with them. He would send word to the Master so that on that day and at that time he might come forth with the men of the city to help them. He hoped in God and His precious Mother that they would carry out their enterprise with much honour to themselves. If it were to turn out otherwise, with God disposing matters to the contrary, it would be much better for them to die there honourably, at the coat tails of such a noble king,[185] than for him to hunt them down from place to place, like young partridges, and hang them up one by one from the cork-oaks.

When they had heard what Nuno Álvares proposed, all of his men responded that it was a very good and well-reasoned plan, but that Lisbon was not yet in such a plight that they should put themselves at such great risk; rather, they should wait a few days, until they saw what God wished to do in this

---

184 Montijo lies on the south bank of the Tagus, some 7 miles (c. 11 km) to the east of Lisbon.

185 Nuno Álvares is referring to the Master of Avis as if he were already king, although at this point he was still Regent and Defender of the Realm. He was acclaimed king only in April 1385.

matter. If and when the city came to be in such dire straits that it had no other recourse, they still had as a last resort an attack on the camp.

Although Nuno Álvares very much wished to put his plan into action at once, nonetheless, because it was his custom to agree to any good and well-grounded arguments made by his council, he went along with them in this, especially because, for such an enterprise, it is understandable that it would not do for anyone to go forth except with a positive and active will. In this regard Nuno Álvares would later say at times that when he reflected that they were so very few and the others so many and well-equipped, it seemed to him a difficult feat and very daunting to attempt. On the other hand, when he trusted, with his firm faith in God, that they were going to defeat the King of Castile, it seemed to him that he could see their enemies fleeing towards Sintra and Cascais and those other places that had declared loyalty to the King of Castile. Then he wrote to the Master about the conclusion he had come to with his men, and everything they planned to do in that matter.

Thus was the city hoping for the day of God's good grace, for no longer did it expect aid or assistance from anyone else. Let us leave it with that hope, without speaking further of its affairs for now, and go and learn what Nuno Álvares did after he departed from Punhete and arrived at the town of Évora.[186]

Chapter 143

How Nuno Álvares arranged to take Monsaraz by guile, and the manner in which it was seized

While Nuno Álvares was in that town, ready to go anywhere where the enemy wanted to wage war, he learned that Gonçalo Rodrigues de Sousa, who held the castle of Monsaraz[187] and had thrown in his lot with the Castilians, had ordered the person who held the castle in his stead to declare support for the King of Castile and hold the castle for him. Nuno Álvares was very disturbed at this because the place was on the frontier, from which he planned to undertake actions in the service of the Master as the occasion arose; and furthermore, because such a good nobleman [as Gonçalo Rodrigues], and others whom the Master trusted and to whom he granted favours, were no longer acting genuinely in his service, as could be seen by the behaviour

---

[186] See Chapter 128 above.

[187] Situated some 45 miles (*c.* 72 km) to the south-east of Évora.

of some. The suspicions that people formed about him[188] in Oporto when he went as captain of the fleet now seemed to be well founded.

You should know, since we have not yet mentioned it, that this Gonçalo Rodrigues was the son of Rodrigo Afonso de Sousa, a great nobleman, born to him by an unmarried woman, Constança Gil, at a time when he himself was a married man.

Wanting to gain that castle, Nuno Álvares proceeded in the following way. He received reliable information that the squire who was acting as governor had with him only his wife and a few men, and that he was short of provisions. Nuno Álvares spoke to one of his trusted squires, and gave him about ten to twelve men to accompany him, and make their way during the night to the outskirts of the town. He, from the other side of the castle, would arrange for five or six cows to be driven down into a nearby valley, as if they were abandoned and left behind from some pillaging carried out by the Castilians. He reckoned that the governor would go out after them through the gate called Colorquia,[189] and would not bother to close it so as to herd the cows into the castle. The squires were to keep watch on the governor so that, when they saw him go out of the castle, they would all immediately dash inside and close the gate promptly behind them.

The squires made their way there, and some hid inside a group of houses that were closest to the castle, while others positioned themselves behind a nearby formation of rocks and gullies. When, before dawn, the cows were driven into the place agreed on by Nuno Álvares, the governor arose and saw them wandering in the valley. As soon as he saw them, he thought that God was bringing good fortune right to his door. He went out immediately and, in his haste to get to the cows, did not bother to close the gate, nor did he order it to be guarded, thinking to return with them straightaway.

When the squires who were on watch saw him go out, they immediately rushed to the gate, entered the castle and expelled the governor's wife and those inside with her. They informed Nuno Álvares that the castle had been taken, which made him most happy. He ordered a suitable garrison to be installed, and then sent word to the Master, who was very pleased.

[188] See Chapter 123 above.

[189] This corresponds to the present-day 'Porta Falsa', literally the false gate, or postern gate. See Adelino de Almeida Calado (ed.), *Estoria de Dom Nuno Alvrez Pereyra: edição crítica da "Coronica do Condestabre"* (Coimbra: Universidade de Coimbra, 1991), p. 76, note 15.

Chapter 144

Concerning the message that Juan Rodríguez de Castañeda sent to Nuno Álvares, and the consequences

While Nuno Álvares was in Évora, he received a message informing him that a great and most notable knight called Juan Rodríguez de Castañeda, who captained 300 lances, together with García Fernández [de Villagarcía], the Grand Commander of the Order of Santiago, and other knights and most valiant men, had arrived at Badajoz, saying that he wished to come and seek him out. Some say that he was sent by the King of Castile. As soon as he heard this, Nuno Álvares set out immediately for Elvas before Juan Rodríguez could leave Badajoz, in order to spare him the effort.

When Juan Rodríguez learned that Nuno Álvares was in Elvas, 3 leagues away, he sent one of his trumpeters to tell him that he was well aware that his liege lord the King of Castile was King of Portugal by right, and that, if Nuno Álvares were pleased to serve him and be his vassal, he would arrange with the king to increase his estate and grant him many favours. Also, that if Nuno Álvares did not want to do so, he would come to him; Nuno Álvares should wait for him there, because he would be with him the following day to engage in a battle, should he wish to enter it. He ought to see full well that it was wrong to wage war on the king in his own domain.

Nuno Álvares received the trumpeter courteously and gave orders for him to be comfortably lodged. Then he replied to the effect that he should tell Juan Rodríguez that he himself was fully aware that, in the treaty the King of Castile had made with King Fernando, when he had married the latter's daughter, there were certain clauses which he had not respected, and he had entered the kingdom in contravention of the oath he had sworn. Also, that Juan Rodríguez should send word to the King of Castile to raise the siege on Lisbon and return to his country, maintaining the terms of the treaty as they had been set out. Thus they could all be in agreement, otherwise not. As for the part where Juan Rodríguez said that he would seek him out and join battle with him, he would be very pleased at his approach, and would have a good dinner waiting for him. With this reply, the trumpeter departed the next morning. He had gone no further than the vineyards, a little more than two crossbow shots' distance, when Nuno Álvares ordered the trumpets to sound, and those in the town, men-at-arms as well as foot soldiers, set forth with him as joyfully as if going to a wedding.

In all, those with Nuno Álvares would number up to 400 lances, together with foot soldiers and crossbowmen. Juan Rodríguez would have a good 500 men-at-arms, 300 light horsemen, and a good number of foot soldiers, those whom he had brought with him as well as inhabitants of Badajoz.

While the trumpeter was conveying Nuno Álvares's reply to Juan Rodríguez and the other knights accompanying him, who laughed the whole thing to scorn, they saw where Nuno Álvares was advancing with his men. They were amazed at this, so hurriedly mounted and rode out of the town, with the intention of blocking off the landing-place of the Guadiana River that flows close by. Nuno Álvares passed across much against their will, and there a major skirmish took place, very fierce and well-fought, in which up to twenty of Juan Rodríguez's squires were taken prisoner and many were wounded. He was forced to turn back with his forces and take refuge inside the town, ordering the gates to be closed.

Nuno Álvares remained for a long time in the environs of Badajoz, at one crossbow shot's distance, waiting to see if anyone would come out again to avenge any grudge they had. But nobody was daring enough to attack him, so with his troops in good order he made his way back to Elvas, whence he had set out.

Chapter 145

How Nuno Álvares received a message that forces were gathering together to come and seek him out, and the manner in which he acted

The King of Castile was greatly enraged on account of the fighting and aggravation caused by Nuno Álvares in that region where he was guarding the frontier; he was also much affected by the death of the Master of Alcántara, who had been killed in the Battle of Os Atoleiros, as you have heard.[190] So he ordered a great captain of his army, one Pedro [Ruiz] Sarmiento, the chief provincial Governor of Galicia, who was well renowned for his feats of arms, to take as many of his men as he wished and go to the Alentejo in search of Nuno Álvares, with orders to take him either dead or alive. Speaking to the king on this matter, Pedro Sarmiento promised him that he would give his arse a good whipping, as one does to a boy.

Others write that Dom Pedro Álvares, who was the Prior of the Hospitallers and brother of Nuno Álvares, and the said Pedro Ruiz Sarmiento entreated

---

[190] In Chapter 95 above.

the king to give them permission, because they wished to go and avenge the death of the Master of Alcántara, and that the king granted it.

While Nuno Álvares was in Elvas, a message arrived for him that many Castilians were in Crato,[191] and that, from the camp around Lisbon where the King of Castile lay, the said Pedro Sarmiento and the Prior of the Hospitallers, Nuno Álvares's brother, would come to join them there with 600 lances.

As soon as Nuno Álvares heard this, he immediately discussed in council about going to bar their way at Ponte de Sor,[192] before they could join up with the other Castilian forces. He departed speedily from Elvas and travelled 7 leagues[193] with his forces that day. He lodged at the Fonte da Figueira which is at the edge of the alder grove on the road to Cano,[194] and at nightfall set his guards and sentries as was usual.

When it was already far into the evening, some thirty lances of his company detached themselves from the encampment, in the direction of Cano, so that their exhausted animals could be better rested. They took with them a trumpeter who was in the company of one of those who had moved away. When it came to midnight, the trumpeter, lacking all good sense, began to play and was heard in the encampment where Nuno Álvares was resting. They thought it was the Castilians, whom they were seeking to encounter, heading in their direction. Immediately, Nuno Álvares ordered the trumpets to sound and put himself and his troops, all armed, in battle formation. Then, by torchlight, he walked serenely up to where the trumpet had sounded. When he found out what it was, he returned to where he had set out, and forbade henceforth anybody to be so bold as to move away from the encampment for whatever reason.

When morning came, Nuno Álvares set out for Ponte de Sor. On the other side of Avis,[195] he received a definite report that Pedro Sarmiento and the prior his brother, and the other men who had set out from the [Lisbon] camp for Crato, had passed through that place a day earlier. This displeased him greatly, as it did those who were with him. From there, he turned back to Cano, where they were well nourished with figs, due to a total lack of other provisions there on account of the war; this, and the fact that they hadn't

[191] This village is located some 13 miles (*c.* 21 km) to the west of Portalegre.

[192] Ponte de Sor lies some 44 miles (*c.* 71 km) due north of Évora.

[193] 7 leagues is roughly 21 miles (*c.* 33 km). The distances offered in this chapter allow the reader to form an idea of the radius of action of the Castilian forces and the speed of response achieved by Nuno Álvares and his men.

[194] Cano is located 12 miles (*c.* 19 km) to the north-west of Estremoz.

[195] This village lies halfway along the road from Ponte de Sor to Estremoz.

brought any with them, prevented anyone from lingering there. From there they proceeded to Évora.

Chapter 146

How Nuno Álvares set up battle with Pedro Sarmiento and other captains, but they refused to fight him

While Nuno Álvares was pondering these matters in Évora, a message arrived from his liege lord the Master in which he was informed that 600 lances had left the King of Castile's encampment to join up in Crato with the other troops who were already there, to go and do battle with him, and that he commended him to God. The Master also sent money for a month's wages, which were very much needed at that time. Immediately after this message, another arrived for Nuno Álvares to the effect that his brother the prior, along with Pedro Sarmiento, Juan Rodríguez de Castañeda and the Count of Niebla, plus the Master of Alcántara, who had become master after the death of his predecessor who died in the battle of Fronteira,[196] and Martim Eanes de Barbuda, who styled himself Master of Avis, as well as other noblemen and squires, in all 2,500 lances, 600 light horsemen and many foot soldiers and crossbowmen, had all gathered in Crato. There they were, taking care of all arrangements needed to enter the Alentejo, to come and seek him out, and to challenge him to battle. Hence, they planned to rob and raid the entire Alentejo region, in the worst manner that they could.

Nuno Álvares immediately sent word throughout the district to gather more troops. In all, there were 530 lances, and 5,000 between foot soldiers and crossbowmen. In the meantime, the said Castilian lords departed with all their forces from Crato, ravaging the land, until they arrived at Arraiolos[197] which, according to some, was attacked and taken by force. But those who speak with greater accuracy about this say that it was delivered to them by some unworthy Portuguese, among whom the principal figure was Gonçalo Mendes de Oliveira, a kinsman of the queen [Leonor Teles].

From there, Pedro Sarmiento sent a knight of his company, one García González de Herrera, bearing a most intemperate letter to Nuno Álvares, of which the latter took no notice and to which he refused to reply. He also

---

[196] This is another name by which the Battle of Os Atoleiros is known. See Chapter 145, note 190 above.

[197] This village lies some 10 miles (c. 16 km) to the north of Évora.

brought him a two-handed sword and said that he was to give it to Nuno
Álvares as a gage, and to challenge him on his behalf to come to battle because
he intended to give his arse a good whipping as one does to a boy.

Without displaying any anger, even though the words were discourteous,
Nuno Álvares received the knight politely, took the sword and accepted the
challenge. He ordered him to be comfortably lodged and said that he would
give him his reply later. He gave immediate orders for guards to be set in the
town, and for everything else that he deemed necessary. He summoned his
council, and it was resolutely decided to advance towards them before they
should come to him.

Early the next day, Nuno Álvares attended Mass, sent for the Castilian
who had brought the said rude letter with its challenge, and said in a pleasant
manner, 'My dear sir, go with God now and tell my friend Pedro Sarmiento and
those captains who are in his company that they may come my way whenever
they like, and there they will find me ready, as they wish.'

García González departed right away, much amazed at his temperance
and boldness.

At this point, as Nuno Álvares was about to eat, it was confirmed that the
Castilians were coming as fast as they could. When he learned this, he broke
off and had the trumpets sound the order to ride out. His men took their drink
while standing, each as best he could, and they all gathered together with him
in great haste. He left immediately with everyone, in good order, and went
beyond the farm of Oliveira, a little more than a league from the town, and
there stopped and waited for the enemy.

Nuno Álvares would have had something to eat while there, had there been
anything, but he had not given orders to bring pack-mules or any other supply
transport, thinking that battle would take place shortly after he arrived, because
the Castilians were many, and they were very few in comparison. Besides, he
thought that the victor in the field would find whatever he needed. A search
took place among the troops to find something for him to eat, but the only
viands found were a half-eaten loaf of bread, a small radish and a little wine
that a foot soldier carried in a gourd. Such was his repast for that whole day,
during which he remained with his forces drawn up near the road, waiting
until nightfall for the Castilians.

Very early next morning, he departed and went up to the [River] Divor,
a league from that place.[198] There, he disposed his troops on foot as before.
He placed his vanguard, rearguard, and wings of men-at-arms, foot soldiers
and crossbowmen as he well knew how to do, with himself in the vanguard.

---

[198] That is to say, the spot 'beyond the farm of Oliveira'.

Then Pedro Sarmiento and the prior arrived there with their captains, and disposed their mounted troops in the vanguard, rearguard and wings, all very close to each other, and remained motionless, giving no sign of wanting to fight. The enemy's light horsemen surrounded all the Portuguese, so that no one would be able to come from Évora to join Nuno Álvares's company, nor would any of his men be able to leave for the town without being captured. The light horsemen carried out a number of assaults on the foot soldiers and elsewhere, as they thought best, but they found everything ready for defence, thus making it impossible to harm them in any way.

After a long while, the Castilians, fearing to begin the battle, sent word to Nuno Álvares that he could clearly see that his scheme had fallen apart and that he should abandon his intention, whatever it was. It was quite obvious that he could not possibly defend himself, so he should by all means return to the service of the King of Castile, who would increase his estate, granting him many favours, such as he well deserved; this was saner advice than bringing himself and all those with him to ruin.

To these and other such arguments, Nuno Álvares briefly told the messenger that he would do better to disregard those words and go safely back, but he should tell those lords, who had sent him, that it did not seem right to him to let time pass in vain like that. In sending to challenge him, they added little to their honour since they were so many and well mounted and he and his men to the contrary, and they delayed so long in joining the battle that they had sought, despite their being so ready, as he could well see. As they were mounted and coming to seek battle, they should be the ones to begin first. Failing that, they should arrange their forces for battle on foot, and he would attack them. Therefore, he entreated them, in one way or another, to join battle.

The Castilians made no reply to these words, but remained thus with their battle order set and during the night they withdrew a little and set up camp.

Nuno Álvares saw that the Castilians were doing this astutely in order to starve him and his men, since it was already two days and one night that they had been out of the town [of Évora] without provisions, and that, on their retreat, the Castilians could kill them while keeping themselves safe and avoiding battle. He thus decided that they should all return that night to Évora, in order to go back the following day well provided with food, should the Castilians wish to join battle. That night there was a great storm of torrential rain and fog, and the retreat was perilous, so that some mistook the terrain and, not knowing how to get to the town, stumbled upon the Castilians' camp, where they were seized and taken prisoner. Others remained in the vineyards eating grapes, where they were found by their enemies and then seized and killed.

Nuno Álvares reached Évora at dead of night and, when morning came, he learned that the Castilians had struck camp and were making their way to Viana [do Alentejo], 2 leagues from Évora. As they were well mounted, they overran the country, took as much booty as they could, and went to Arraiolos. From there they departed, some to Crato, while Pedro Sarmiento and Juan Rodríguez de Castañeda and other knights, up to 700 lances, took the road to Lisbon through Almada, and thence to the King of Castile's encampment.

They went to speak to the king, who did not give them a warm welcome on account of their not fighting with Nuno Álvares, whom it had been agreed they would fight. They made their excuses with feeble arguments and incurred the king's great displeasure, for he told them that Nuno Álvares could not have done more, by challenging them in the field and waiting two days for battle, whereas they, out of cowardice, had not dared to fight him. Pedro Sarmiento and the prior felt greatly pained at this, seeing how much they had been found wanting.

Chapter 147

How Nuno Álvares arranged to go to Almada to fall upon Pedro Sarmiento, and concerning what happened in relation to this

Nuno Álvares was infuriated by the way the Castilians had treated him in making him come to the field twice without wanting to join battle, and thus seeking to defeat him by astute cunning rather than by real courage, because they were far more numerous and better equipped. Moreover, the way they looted the land with which he had been entrusted as Officer of the Marches made him feel he was the object of their scorn. He pondered on how he could arrange a similar ploy, or better, if possible.

Through spies that he sent to Almada, he learned what Pedro Sarmiento, Juan Rodríguez de Castañeda and a few other noblemen, were doing. Hoping to take them by surprise, as he saw that the time was right, he gathered his troops, who numbered over 300 lances apart from foot soldiers and a few crossbowmen, and went with them to Palmela. There he stayed and arranged his sortie. If anyone here says that Nuno Álvares took the castle of Palmela at this time, we do not credit it, nor is there any reason to believe it, because the places belonging to the Order of Santiago always supported Portugal after the Master, Dom Fernando Afonso de Albuquerque, came to Lisbon, as we have said.[199] If he did take it then, what happened to the Castilians and to the governor who was present and who supported Castile? For, in all the places that supported him, the king placed governors and troops who defended them. To prove this, it would have been appropriate at the least to name the governor and say very briefly how it had been taken, considering that it was such a strong place and so difficult to seize, but it seems there was no authority for saying it.

The next day, for relaxation, Nuno Álvares went hunting not far from the town and killed a large, splendid boar. He had it placed on top of a fine mule, with four foot soldiers to accompany it, as well as a squire named Gonçalo Martins Frazão, whom he charged with presenting it.

Here, some write that Nuno Álvares sent this boar as a present to Pedro Sarmiento; that he sent word to him that he would come and see him in a few days; that Pedro Sarmiento was very pleased with it and dispatched it straightaway to the King of Castile in his camp, sending his warm thanks to Nuno Álvares but not replying to the rest. Others go further and relate that when Nuno Álvares had the boar conveyed to him, he sent an accompanying message saying that he wished to come and dine with him; to which Pedro Sarmiento replied that he would be welcome whenever he wished to come because he would find the sauce good and ready.

But if we examine such opinions according to what one historian writes, they are unsatisfactory to any reasonable mind. It is clearly shown to be so, because if Nuno Álvares's gift had been presented to Pedro Sarmiento with such words as these, they would have pressed him on to prepare immediately for his arrival, and so it would have been extremely difficult for Nuno Álvares to carry out any plans he might have in mind. Neither do those who tell this story in this way make mention of Pedro Sarmiento upon Nuno Álvares's arrival at Almada, nor of anything that took place between Nuno Álvares and him. But how can you expect them to mention someone who was not there, nor was presented with any boar or sow?

Instead, leaving aside the historian's erroneous statements, and according to the arguments of an author who has very carefully scrutinised the substance of such doubts, it is important you should know that on the morning of Wednesday, 31 August, the foot soldiers set out with the said boar on the road for Almada, a good 5 leagues distant. When they arrived, at noon, they did not find Pedro Sarmiento there because he was on the other side of the river in the King of Castile's camp. They deposited the boar at Cacilhas, the port for Almada, to await Pedro Sarmiento's return.

[199] See Chapter 47 above.

Having dispatched the boar, Nuno Álvares told his troops to carry out certain tasks on their arrival, each in his due place, as follows: some should go to the barricades and palisade that were erected at the entrance of the streets, and they should demolish them before the Castilians could turn up; others should position themselves between the outskirts and the town to seize those who wanted to dash from the outskirts into the town. With these should go his banner; and, if they found the gate open, the banner should be taken inside with those men-at-arms who accompanied it, or they should force their way in pell-mell with those who might be fleeing, and thus would take the castle. Others were to go to the port of Cacilhas, in order to hinder any Castilians from the fleet, who might happen to pass, from gaining any ground.

Nuno Álvares was certain that in Coina, 3 leagues from Almada, there were thirty light horsemen on guard, so that if any of his companies, or from anywhere else, were to come, they would send the news to those in the township [Almada], because that was the logical route they were expected to follow. For this reason, he left Palmela with such an intent as we have said, with the sun already long set, and took the road through the heath over Azeitão towards Sesimbra, about a league away from those sentries, thinking at all events to be in Almada at sun-up. Throughout the night, he travelled a good 7 leagues, the greater part of them off the road. As the guides were not quite certain of the terrain, the night being very dark, they judged that they were already close to Almada, so Nuno Álvares stopped there a little while, and all of them got some sleep. When they woke up, and it began to get light, they realised that they were farther from Almada than they thought.

Then Nuno Álvares made ready to push on more swiftly. As the sun rose, he came to a place called Sobreda, which is about a league from Almada. Since they arrived so late, he told his troops to advance at the trot and the gallop, according to the stamina of their mounts. That they did, so that although the whole land was already enveloped and bathed in sunlight, they still arrived at a time when many of the Castilians were lying in bed in a morning sleep that proved to do them no good at all. The first one to reach the barricades was Nuno Álvares, with three squires who quickly dismounted. With them, he passed through the barrier of the outlying area facing Coina, attacking with lances a number of Castilians who sought to impede him. At this point, his banner arrived, being close at hand, with all those who were guarding it, and they took the main road that goes to Cacilhas, each one doing the best he could.

Little did the Castilians foresee such an action, for some of them were asleep and others lazing around. When they heard shouts coming from the castle and surroundings, 'To arms! To arms! For Castile! Castile!' some of them rose from their beds to find out what was going on. Others dressed, trying to put their armour on in haste, and those who were already outside their lodgings prepared themselves to defend the streets. However, such was the disarray that their defence was worth very little, because the main concern was to try to escape with their lives. Nevertheless, some grouped together and, taking heart, attempted to confront Nuno Álvares in the street along which he was advancing, already knowing that it was himself. One of the latter's foot soldiers, a certain Lopo Álvares, came out of a side street between Nuno Álvares and the enemy, hurled a javelin at a Castilian and struck him down dead. The others fled as best they could. Unwilling to wait around to be similarly dealt with, Juan Rodríguez de Castañeda went in among them, having risen hastily from bed in the lodgings where he lay, and failing to don his doublet properly.

Nuno Álvares's banner, with its escort, arrived at the gate of the castle, its bearers thinking to find it open as they had expected. However, those inside the castle had shut the gates, first gathering in those they could. As for the rest, some threw themselves onto the barbican,[200] and others over the barricades, each one as best he could.

With the Castilians shut inside the castle, and the Portuguese unable to hinder them any more, a number of men-at-arms remained on the spot while others returned to the surrounding area, where they killed and seized many Castilians. Some of the latter fled over the rooftops; others hid in obscure places, so that very few escaped who were not seized or killed. Had it not been so far into the day, nobody would have escaped. In addition, like confused men whose only thought was to flee, they could not take their belongings with them. All their horses and mules, their weapons and personal treasures were seized, from Pedro Sarmiento as well as from all the others who were lodging outside the castle.

After the surrounding area was completely plundered, Nuno Álvares ordered trumpets to sound, calling all his men to gather round him. Those who had been ordered to guard the port of Cacilhas found the boar that Nuno Álvares had sent to Pedro Sarmiento on the shore, waiting for him to return from the camp. With his troops gathered together and everyone close at hand, Nuno Álvares made his way to a mound overlooking the sea and had them line up with his banner unfurled in the middle, the trumpets sounding, and with whooping and other signs of joy. This was in view of those in the city [of Lisbon] and of the Castilian siege camp. When the latter saw them in that manner, they thought it was the troops of the town who were being mustered in order to get their pay, while those in the city thought that they were the enemy's troops.

[200] The outer rampart.

The king, who knew that he had not ordered such wages to be paid, truly thought that it was something else, and thinking that perhaps Pedro Sarmiento had ordered it, he sent for him. He asked him who those troops were who were on the said hill. 'To be sure, my liege, I do not know', he said, 'but my instinct tells me it is Nuno Álvares.'

'A fine reply, upon my word!' said the king. 'You, the Officer of the Marches for that place, being insulted by a squire and five nags!'

'You may say so, Sire! But give thanks to God and to this river that is between you both, for if this water were not here, he would come and seek you out wherever you were.'

Then Pedro Sarmiento departed at speed without having finished dressing and embarked in one galley, while the king ordered the others to be supplied with oars and men-at-arms. However, it could not be done so quickly because they were unprepared for this.

Nuno Álvares remained there as long as he wished, the sight of which caused the king great disgust, and those of the city great pleasure when they found out that it was he.

The galley conveying Pedro Sarmiento arrived before the others at the port of Cacilhas, and when he set foot on land he began to cry out, 'For Castile! Castile! It is nothing, it is nothing!' while shouting in haste for a horse.

One of the Castilians who had been robbed said: 'I do not know how you can say "It is nothing, it is nothing". The devil take whatever is left to me out of everything I had, animals as well as weapons, because they took everything. It was only by great good fortune that I escaped prison or death, and the same applies to all of us here, yet you ask for a horse! What good is it to bring you a horse, even if there were one here, because Nuno Álvares has already left with all his men at his pleasure, just as he wished?'

'That's of no account', he said. 'Bring me a horse if there is one, so at least I can see them go.' But nothing more was done about this.

Nuno Álvares went to Coina to eat, and there he shared out the booty among everyone, keeping nothing back for himself. Then he took his horse and went to Palmela. When it was night, he ordered beacons to be lit such as could be seen from Lisbon, so that those of the city would know he was there and take heart from it.

Indeed, it was so, because, when the Master saw those beacons in Palmela, he clearly understood that it was Nuno Álvares who was there with his forces, and was immensely pleased, along with all those who saw this. He ordered many torches to be lit on the large terrace of the king's palace where he was then lodging, so they could be seen from Palmela, to let them know that they saw their beacons and were answering with their own lights, since no other communication was possible between them. Thus the Master remained a good while talking to his men about the deeds of Nuno Álvares with that gentle discourse and praise with which so loyal a servant deserved to be spoken of. Then he retired to his chamber.

Nuno Álvares also put out his fires in order to regain his lost sleep. Let him have a good night while we return to the much tormented city of Lisbon to see how it is coping with the situation.

Chapter 148

Concerning the tribulations suffered by Lisbon on account of the lack of food

With the city thus surrounded in the way that you have already heard, the provisions were being used up more and more because of the many people dwelling there, including the men from the surrounding villages with their wives and children who had gathered within the city limits, as well as those who came in the fleet from Oporto. Every so often, some of them made for the creeks on the Ribatejo bank in boats, setting out at night and in secret. There, they loaded on board various quantities of wheat that they found there, all of it ready in response to messages they had sent beforehand. They would go out at night, rowing hard, and when one or other of the galleys heard the sound of oars they would speedily row after them. Both sides were put to much hard work: the boats to make their escape and the galleys to try and capture them.

Those waiting for the wheat walked along the shore near Xabregas, watching for its arrival. If those on the lookout saw the galleys rowing towards them, they immediately sounded the bell to summon help. When those in the city heard the bell, they left off their sleep, and many people took their weapons and went out to defend the boats with crossbows if necessary, wounds sometimes being inflicted on both sides. However, they were never caught, except once when a few boats were on the Ribatejo side with wheat and were betrayed by an Almada man and captured by the Castilians. He was later seized, bound, dragged through the streets, mutilated and hanged. Although this wheat was of some help, it was so little and so infrequent that it would have been necessary to multiply it as did Jesus Christ with the loaves, with which He fed the 5,000.[201]

---

[201] Matthew 14. 14–21; Mark 6. 41–44; Luke 9. 10–17; John 6. 5–14.

The city exhausted its reserves and was in great straits, so that public alms began to fail, and none of the poor found anyone to give them bread. In this manner, the common loss overcame all compassion and, in view of the great lack of provisions, it was decided that destitute people, unfit to defend the city, should be expelled. This was done two or three times, until all the prostitutes and Jews, and others like them, were thrown out. It was said that such people were not able to fight and therefore should not take the food out of the mouths of the defenders. But this did not bring any significant advantage.

At first, the Castilians were pleasant to them, giving them food and shelter. Then, when they saw that it was because of famine, the king, in order to exhaust the city further, gave orders that no one from inside should be taken into his camp, but that everyone should be thrown out. Those who did not want to go would be whipped and made to return to the city. This was very hard for the latter, to be forced to go back to such a place where, despite their tears, they could not expect to be received. In the camp were those who went out of the city of their own free will and into the encampment, much preferring to be captives rather than perish through starvation.

How would they not expel the poverty-stricken and those of no use, when the Master ordered an accurate investigation to be made throughout the city as to what grain there was in all, whether buried or anywhere else, and they found that it was so little that it was necessary to take counsel about it?

There was no wheat for sale in the city and, if there was any, it was so scarce and expensive that the poor people could not get hold of it, because it fetched 4 *libras* a bushel.[202] Millet was worth 40 *soldos* the bushel, and 1 *canada*[203] of wine fetched 3 or 4 *libras*. People suffered mightily for there were days when, even if people could give 1 *dobra* for a loaf, they could not find it for sale. So they began to eat bread made from olive-must, cheeses made from mallow and roots of weeds, and other strange things, inimical to nature. There were those who survived on sugar dough. In the place where wheat used to be sold, there were men and boys scratching away at the earth and, if they found some grains of wheat, they put them in their mouths without any other sustenance. Others ate their fill of grasses and drank so much water that men and boys were found lying swollen and dead, in the squares and in other places.

Similarly, there was a great lack of meat in the city, and anyone who raised pigs lived on them. A small slice of pork was worth 5 or 6 *libras*, the same as 1 Castilian *dobla*; a hen, 40 *soldos*; a dozen eggs, 12 *soldos*. If drovers brought in any oxen, each one fetched 70 *libras*, the equal of 14 crossed *dobras*,

[202] One bushel was 8 gallons (just over 35 litres).
[203] See Chapter 135, note 168 above.

each *dobra* at that time being worth 5 or 6 *libras*. Head and tripe fetched 1 *dobra*. Hence, the poor, lacking money, could not eat meat and suffered badly. They began to eat the flesh of beasts of burden; and not just the poor and the indigent, but grand people of the city suffered cruelly, not knowing what to do. With their faces altered through famine, they clearly showed their hidden suffering. Children of three or four years of age went through the city begging for bread for the love of God, as their mothers taught them to. But many people had nothing to give them, apart from tears to share with them, which was a sad thing to see. If they were given a piece of bread the size of a walnut, they thought it a great fortune. From lack of food, the milk dried up in those women with babes at the breast and when they saw the suffering of their children whom they could not help, they frequently cried over them as if they were dead, before death deprived them of life. Many looked upon the prayers of others with tearful eyes, to fulfil what pity demands but, having nothing with which to help them, fell into redoubled sadness.

The whole city was given over to distress, full of petty complaints, being unable to take any pleasure there might be, some because of their great suffering, others being grief-stricken at those who were afflicted. This was not without cause, for if the heart concerned by the contrary things that may happen in the future feels sad and wretched, just consider what those people would feel facing them continually in the here-and-now. However, despite all this, when the bells tolled, nobody showed that he or she was starving, but rather that they were strong and determined against their enemies. Some people made great efforts to console others, to relieve their great distress, but words could offer little comfort, nor could such pain be assuaged with sweet reason. Hence, as it is a normal thing for the hand frequently to go to where the pain is felt, so men, speaking with one another, could not talk about any matter other than the lack suffered by everyone.

Oh, how often did people order Masses and sermons that they might devoutly pray to God for the state of the city! On their knees and kissing the ground, they clamoured to God to help them but their prayers were not answered! Some wept to themselves, cursing their days, complaining that they were still alive, as if they were saying, along with the Prophet, 'Now let death come before time, and the earth cover our faces, so that we may not see such sadness!'[204] Thus, they asked for death to carry them off, saying that it would be better to die than to face each day with renewed and multiple sufferings. Others complained to their friends, saying that they were unfortunate folk in that they did not deliver themselves to the King of Castile, rather than suffer

---

[204] The source of the quotation seems to be not the Prophet Jeremiah, but Job 3.21–22 or 7.15.

new miseries each day, reckoning completely on the worst things that fortune might yet bring to pass.

The Master and those of his council knew of this and they were very pained to hear such news. But seeing that they could not remedy these ills, they closed their ears to the murmurings of the people.

How could you not expect various men and women to curse their lives and want to die, for there is as much difference between hearing of these things and being those who have endured them, as there is between life and death? Fathers and mothers who saw their beloved children withering away with starvation tore at their faces and breasts over them, having nothing with which to help them apart from lamentations and the shedding of tears. Above all this was the great fear of the cruel revenge that they thought the King of Castile would take upon them. Thus, they suffered two great wars: one from the enemy who besieged them, the other from the lack of provisions, and so they had the worry of defending themselves from two forms of death.

Why should one speak any more of such distress? Such was the dearth of necessities that a rumour went through the city one day that the Master would drive outside all those who had no bread to eat, and that only those who had it would remain. But who, without groaning and crying, could hear such a decision taken about those who had no bread? However, when it was known that it was not so, it was already some comfort.

You should know that the famine and dearth that the people suffered in this way was not on account of the siege being protracted, because Lisbon had not been surrounded for very long. It was rather on account of the many people who had gathered inside from all the surrounding villages, and also of the fleet from Oporto when it arrived, and the provisions being so inadequate.

Now look, as if you were there, upon such a city, so dejected and with no sure guarantee of its liberation. How would its people live, with so many different worries, suffering waves of afflictions like these? Oh, you generation that came afterwards, fortunate folk, because you have known nothing of such evil, nor have you received your portion of such sufferings! These it pleased God in His mercy soon to curtail in another way, as you shall hear shortly.

Chapter 149

Concerning the plague that raged among the Castilians, and concerning certain captains who died of it

It is superfluous to strive to praise the many valiant soldiers that the King of Castile had with him when he was moved to enter Portugal. For, certainly, you may be assured that the House of Castile was at that time one of the noblest houses in the world, a house of many fine gentlemen, great lords and noblemen, as well as knights and squires well mounted and furnished with arms, and with other lesser troops, including a great number of crossbowmen and foot soldiers.

After the king entered the kingdom and as he was advancing towards Lisbon, lodging in villages 2 or 3 leagues away, a few people of lesser rank in the encampment began to die of the plague. When some worthy knight or squire happened to die, his men took him to Sintra or Alenquer, or to some of the other places that supported Castile. There, they opened and salted their corpses and placed them on catafalques in the open air, or burned them and kept the bones, to take them later to their place of origin. For this reason, the king moved from one village to another with his troops until his fleet arrived, when he launched himself upon the city as has already been said. With his siege in place, many deaths began to occur in the fleet, and also among those in the siege camp, so that both the one and the other were deeply perturbed. They repeatedly advised the king to leave there for the moment: then he would have the opportunity to come and surround the city any time he wished. But he rejected their good reasons and was very much inclined not to raise the siege, whatever might happen. He well knew that the city was severely short of provisions and that it could not be long before it became unable to resist and he could take it at will.

Now it is true that, among all the things in which we see Divine power most resplendent, it is in those that, being desperate in every aspect, He brings to an advantageous result when it pleases Him. Thus, then, He acted in His mercy concerning this city, where, being greatly afflicted by famine in many ways, everyone was losing any hope that might come from other sources, except that which they had in God Most High and in His precious Mother who would help them. While they were prepared to die or win some day, as we have said, indeed, it pleased that Lord Who is Prince of hosts and Victor in battles that there was no struggle or fight other than His. So He commanded the angel of death to stretch out his hand further and run harshly through the horde of those [Castilian] people.

Despite the fact that many had died before, the plague began to flare up so fiercely among them, at sea as well as on land, that there were days when 100 died, or 150, or 200. There could be more or less, as the case might be, so that for the better part of the day the troops in the camp were occupied in burying their dead. This was an alarming thing to see for those who were sick, and strange to hear for those who were surrounded. That was because, from the day when the Master of Santiago, Don Pedro Fernández Cabeza de Vaca, died of the plague, up to this moment,[205] so did more than 2,000 men-at-arms of the best that the King of Castile had, apart from many captains whom we are not able to name, although we can give the names of some. Men like Don Ruy González Mejía, whom the king made Master after the death of Don Pedro Fernández; Don Pedro Rodríguez de Sandoval, his Grand Commander, who thought he would be master;[206] Pedro Fernández de Velasco, the king's lord chamberlain; Don Fernán Sánchez de Tovar, his High Admiral; Fernando Álvarez de Toledo, the Marshal of Castile; Pedro Ruiz Sarmiento, the Chief Provincial Governor of Galicia; Don Pedro Núñez de Lara, the Count of Mayorga, who only shortly before had married, as you have heard;[207] Don Juan Alfonso de Benavides; Don Fernando Alfonso de Zamora, the Master of Santiago, and counting him, that made three masters who died; Juan Martínez de Rojas; Lope Ochoa de Avellaneda; thirteen of the king's knights from the city of Toledo; and many other knights and squires of Castile and León.

It was a great marvel, decided by some power unknown to us, that in the intensity of such a plague, not one of the Portuguese noblemen who were there, neither prisoners, nor those present in any other capacity, died of plague, nor was afflicted with such pain. In a spirit of malice and revenge that did them no credit, the Castilians put the Portuguese prisoners they kept with them alongside those who were ill with swellings, so that they would be infected and die of the plague. The Castilians fell sick and died, but none of the Portuguese perished, neither inside the city, which was so close to the camp, nor in the city limits outside.

It seems very hard to believe that a king, thus accompanied and served by so many noblemen and of such distinction as those he had brought with him,

[205] Presumably, this refers to the end of August or beginning of September, when the siege was lifted. Although neither Lopes nor Ayala mention the date of Pedro Fernández's death, Spanish scholars give it as 22 March 1384. For Ayala's account, which Lopes is using here, see the former's *Crónica del rey Don Juan* (1384, Year 6, Chapter 11).

[206] In fact, he was not appointed Master of Santiago as expected, because he died shortly after Pedro Fernández Cabeza de Vaca.

[207] See Chapter 141 above.

would see so many die before his very eyes, bootlessly, as well as the great number of other lesser troops, yet would not change his mind about what he had set in train, despite so much advice given to him, as if he deliberately wished to offer them to death!

Chapter 150

Concerning the arguments that Don Carlos put to the King of Castile, and how the king struck camp and lifted the siege of the city

The kingdom was in great torment, as you have heard, and Lisbon bore the brunt of such storms. The surrounding district was devastated by fire and other destruction; all the villages and farms from the outskirts to as far as Cascais, a distance of 5 leagues, were already razed to the ground, as well as the villages and townships of the Ribatejo region. On top of that, the continued famine and no certain hope of delivery from it resulted in the city's inhabitants having very little trust in being able to escape, except that trust in God which they had, in the way that we have said.

Likewise, the King of Castile who, despite the clear evidence confronting him in the mortality of his troops, which ought to have made him understand that it was not pleasing to God to stay there any longer, remained firm in his intention to persevere until he should take the city. Hence, the besieged and the besiegers both suffered serious affliction through two contrary hopes. Those inside the city hoped each day that the king would soon strike camp, owing to the persistence of the great plague; the Castilians, in their turn, thought that those in the city, constrained by famine, would petition to surrender the city, on conditions of great honour to them. Thus, with both sides maintaining their opinion, they suffered the two greatest evils that could come about in similar circumstances: namely, the one group from severe famine through shortage of provisions; the other from mortal pestilence among all conditions of troops in the siege camp.

Prince Carlos, the heir of Navarre, who was married to Princess Leonor, the king's sister, who was with him in this siege, saw the enormous death rate among them, and that it was getting forever worse. He told the king on various occasions that he should be good enough not to wish to tempt God by remaining any longer in that place, and that he should raise the siege on the city and go back to his own kingdom. After all, even if the king left the place, he would leave in Portugal sufficient knights and other forces, who held many towns and castles, from where they would wage war on the Master, and on those who wanted to continue to support him. When it was God's pleasure to put an end to that plague once and for all, then he could return with his forces and take the kingdom at his pleasure.

Prince Carlos added that the king should not be like his grandfather King Alfonso [XI]. When King Alfonso besieged Gibraltar and his forces were dying of the plague, he was advised by the lords and great captains of the army that he should depart from that place because of the many troops who were dying, and he was endangering his own life, yet he refused to do so. His reply to those who advised him was that they should not speak to him of such a thing. He considered that town, which he greatly valued taking, to be so afflicted and with no prospect whatsoever of any help that in a few days it would be his and he would take it. With that intention, he refused to raise the siege however much urgent counsel they gave him. Thereupon, he developed a fatal swelling, from which he died a few days later, and so lost the town and many of the men he had brought with him.

The prince said: 'So, my liege, do not prolong your stay in like manner, nor tarry amid so much peril. For, even though I and the other members of your Royal Council might not say it to you, your reason would give you full understanding of the situation, especially since nobody is advising you to abandon this war altogether, nor the quest that you have begun. You can return to it at any time you please. But what they tell you stands to reason: since it pleases God that this plague causes so much harm among your forces, you should postpone this matter until the appropriate time; otherwise by wishing to persist in it further, it seems to me that this will lead to the camp soon losing the greater part and the best of those who came with you.'

The king answered: 'In truth, you are giving me very good advice, and it is my wish to follow it. You say that my grandfather besieged Gibraltar and, despite the plague among his forces, since at that moment the town that he wished so much to take was so afflicted and with no prospect of help and could be his in a few days, he refused to raise the siege although many of his troops were dying. And then, death deprived him of life. He did all this to take a rocky hill of little value. Now, what should I do to take such a city as this, because once it is taken, as I hope, from here I expect to take the whole kingdom? I already have it so afflicted with famine that those inside are suffering so greatly, according to the certain news I have, that they will offer it to me within days without combat or any other fighting, and will fully do my bidding. So, I wish to follow my grandfather's counsel and not yours, nor that of anyone else who tells me that I should depart from here. I am very sorrowful that my troops are dying, but I wish to believe that, with me, they embarked upon a combat in which they would perish honourably in the defence of my kingdom, and let no one tell me otherwise.'

Despite these words, the king clearly saw the arguments that the prince and the members of his Royal Council gave him were just and well-reasoned. But his great and brave heart despised and held in little account all doubt and fearful caution that some people might conceive in relation to such deeds. So, although he suffered such a severe penalty, he hardened his heart against raising the siege, obdurate in continuing what he had started.

At that point, the queen was afflicted with two swellings although they were not very serious. In view of that, the king made up his mind to abandon the siege. Thus, he struck camp on a Saturday after eating. On that day and on Sunday, his men set fire to everything that could be of no use to them, according to the custom of those who raise a siege. Burning through the night, it was one of the greatest fires that people had ever seen. He went to lodge on the other side of the city, near the Monastery of Santo Antão, which is close to it, and there he stayed for a day.

When Nuno Álvares, who did not know any of this, saw such fires at night from Palmela, where he was still staying, he became quite alarmed as well as greatly disturbed, thinking that the Master had suffered deceit and disloyalty from some of the people of higher rank who were with him, and whom he suspected of not being faithful in his service, because the fires were so big that it seemed as if the whole city were burning. This upset and concern remained with him until the next morning, when Lisbon appeared clearly, intact and undamaged by the fire.

On the morning of Monday, 5 September, the king left the city, taking the road to Torres Vedras with all his troops. Yet many men had begun to travel during the night, each as best he could. Had there been any horsemen in the city who dared to attack the king, they could well have caused him great harm. The king began his journey with much greater sadness than the joy with which he had come to the siege. When he got to a place where the city was disappearing from view, he turned his face towards it and is reputed to have said, 'Oh, Lisbon! Lisbon! May God grant me the great favour of seeing you under the plough one day!'

Then the king began to organise his troops who continued to be persecuted by the angel of death, some dying on the road and in the places that he later reached. That day, he went to sleep at Sapataria, 5 leagues from the city. The next day, he stopped in Torres Vedras, 3 leagues from Sapataria, where the queen, his wife, came close to death from the two tumours that she developed in the camp, although it pleased God that she regained her health.

The siege, therefore, lasted four months and twenty-seven days, if we calculate from the king's arrival at Lumiar until he raised it on 3 September.

We are not counting the time that the Master of Santiago [Pedro Fernández Cabeza de Vaca] and Pedro Fernández de Velasco, and many other forces with them, began to encircle the surrounding district before the king came, as we have related it in its due place.[208] But if, as others do, we are to count from that point, we shall say that it was seven months, because from then onwards, and even before, all the people of the district were already sheltering in the city out of fear of the Castilians and consuming its provisions.

The king departed from Torres Vedras and arrived in Santarém with his wife and the forces he led. There, let him carry out his deeds and organise his garrisons in the border areas, while we go and see what the Master and those of the city did after the king raised the siege.

Chapter 151

How the people of Lisbon organised a procession to give thanks to God, and concerning the sermon that a friar preached

When the Master and the people of Lisbon saw that the King of Castile had departed with his people and had raised the siege at the moment of the city's greatest tribulation, which was the dearth of provisions, as there were none to be had, their joy at his departure was such that it is not possible to express it in writing. They gave many thanks to the Lord God, Who had taken mercy on them in that way.

Then they went out of the city to see the area of the siege camp that had already been burned, and found many sick people in the Convent of Santos that we have mentioned.[209] They treated them with charitable compassion, even though they were their enemies.

The following day, they organised a great and devout procession, in which everyone went barefoot to the Monastery of the Trindade which is within the city wall. The Most Honourable João Escudeiro, who was then bishop of the city, set out barefoot from the cathedral church of his see, in pontificals, with the Host in his hands, as decently and honourably as could be, accompanied by a great number of regular and secular clergy, and also by the Master with all the other people.

[208] In Chapter 71 above.
[209] See Chapter 114 above.

When they had all arrived at the monastery, and devoutly said their prayers, a great and notable preacher, Master Rodrigo de Sintra of the Order of St Francis, who was well versed in theology, began to preach. He gave a long and solemn sermon, fully illustrated with texts from the Holy Scriptures, which he brought to bear to his purpose in a very learned manner. We cannot give more than the broad lines which it followed, according to what some have written very briefly, which was as follows.

At the beginning of his sermon, he took as his theme '*Misericordiam fecit nobiscum*', repeating it in the vernacular, 'The Lord has been most merciful to us'. Next, he expounded what mercy and pity were, and how mercy proceeded from the laws of nature, and lay in man's duty to relieve his neighbour from the misery he suffers, and how all the perfection of the Christian religion lay in mercy and pity. Then, he dealt with what had moved the King of Castile to leave his great and powerful kingdom, in contradiction of the solemn oath he had promised in relation to the treaties, and to come most unworthily to occupy the kingdom of Portugal, which was not sanctioned by law at that point. He said that this arose from foolish greed and delight in conquering; also, from the bad advice of some of his privy councillors which, after great efforts and the death of many, would turn out to be fruitless.

Master Rodrigo said:

> Take heed and open the window of your hearts, and observe how days came upon this kingdom, and especially upon this city, when its enemies surrounded it and caused it to suffer great anguish. For our sins, Portugal is set against Portugal, so little of it remaining that it has seemed almost naked and abandoned. So, all evil in this time of great darkness has sprung and does spring from corrupt intentions in one and all alike.

Then he brought in notable examples: of the great city of Samaria that was besieged by Ben-Hadad, the King of Syria, in the time of the prophet Elisha. During the siege, the hunger was so severe that people gave 80 silver *reais* for an ass's head, and a little dove's guano for salting meat was worth 50. Such was the great famine that some people ate their children. The king was so grievously stricken at such want and predicament that he tore his clothing, revealing the hairshirt that he wore next to his skin.[210] With everyone in total despair, the Lord God had taken mercy on them, inspiring such terror among those in the siege camp that it seemed to them a great host of people was pursuing them, making them flee without bothering to take anything at all.

---

[210] II Kings 6. 24–30.

He told how the city of Jerusalem had been besieged by Sennacherib, King of Assyria, when Hezekiah was its king, and how God wished to take mercy on its state of siege. One night, the angel of God had struck those in the siege camp, and killed 185,000 of them. The king had fled with just ten men, owing to the great fear and alarm that he felt.[211] He further spoke of Prince Holofernes, how he had besieged the city of Bethulia, and had severed the water pipes that came into the city, thus depriving the inhabitants of the benefit of two springs that were nearby. With the great lack of water people began to complain to each other, saying that it would be better to serve Holofernes than die of thirst like that. While they were in this predicament, God had so arranged it that the holy woman, Judith, in an act of deception, would go outside the city so that Holofernes would see her, and desire to sleep with her. So it happened: he saw her and desired her. She was brought to his tent, but he sated himself with wine, and immediately fell asleep on the bed. Then she cut off his head with his sword and went back to the city. The next day, when those in the camp found that their lord was dead they were greatly disturbed and began to flee, and so the city ceased to be surrounded.[212]

Then Master Rodrigo turned to comparing in detail the dearth and famine of Lisbon and the other shortages and sufferings, firstly to those of the city of Samaria, and then to the other cities, and the great mercy that God had shown to it, in freeing us in that way. Such similarities and comparisons were heard not without loud cries, sobs and the shedding of many tears, so the impression was that of a fervent lamentation made for some great lord, with everyone raising their hands to heaven and giving many thanks to the Lord God, who had been pleased to grant such great mercy to them. He said:

> Now with this city in the fire of such tribulation and feeling its intensest heat, which was the torment and suffering of a great siege and widespread famine, God extinguished the blaze by dispelling the enemy.
>
> Human reason was no use, nor anything else that people could do against the King of Castile's power. It was no good holding Masses, nor was there any benefit from prayers that devout people could offer, clamouring to God to have mercy on us and to decide to free this city from the hands of its mortal enemies. It seemed that the Lord God had closed his ears to us, and turned His face against wishing to free us.
>
> With us in uttermost grief and anguish, the most high and heavenly King, the father of great mercies and God of all consolation, spoke in the

---

[211] II Kings 19. 35–36.

[212] Judith (the Apocrypha), especially 7. 6–17; 10. 17–20; 12. 15–20; 13. 1–10; 15. 1–4. The references are to the Latin rendering of Judith in the Vulgate, Fernão Lopes's biblical source.

consistory of his wisdom, 'It is time to have compassion on the oppressed city and let it suffer no more', just as if saying, 'Oh city of Lisbon! Your prayers have been heard! Because I have loved you, I wish to liberate you out of pity for you. This will be through my strong hand, and your trust henceforth will be in me.'

But because that great King of Castile had so hardened his heart against raising the siege from this city for anything whatsoever, until he could take it through famine or force of arms, God, in order to show His great power, wished to deal with him in the same way that He dealt with the Pharaoh, whom He commanded so frequently to let His people go and make sacrifices in the desert. Although God persecuted him with great and strange plagues, the Pharaoh had no wish ever to let them go, until God smote him with the tenth plague, killing all the first-born sons, from the son of the greatest lord of Egypt to the son of the lowliest slave-girl that was among them.[213] But none of the sons of Israel died at that time. Thus the Lord God began to afflict the King of Castile with pestilence before he could reach this city, which was a sign and warning that it was not pleasing to Him that he should come here. But, despite this, he did not refrain from coming. After he had the city surrounded, many of his people began to die, those of high estate as well as others of lesser condition.

With the increase in mortality, his first-born, noblemen and lords, began to die, such a multitude in a short space of time, as you all know. Even with all this, the king remained steadfastly opposed to raising the siege, despite so much advice given to him on the matter. Then, God smote the one who was his best-loved first-born, in the person of the queen his wife, who developed two pestilential buboes. Fearing her sad death, his hard heart broke and he raised the siege of this city, in which outcome God treated us with great mercy. Despite the fact that God touched the king with that pestilential plague, as you have seen, still he departs with the intention of returning to this kingdom to destroy and subjugate it. When he returns he will suffer the same as did the Pharaoh with the people of Israel. After he let them go into the desert, he set after them with a very great host, thinking to pursue and kill them. But all those he took with him were killed and destroyed instead, and he did not fulfil his desire.

The same will happen to the King of Castile, if he returns to this kingdom with the intention he carries away with him. God will kill so many of his first-born, who are the great and honourable personages of his kingdom, with whom he broke the vow that he had taken, that he will never want to return to this land. He puts his hope in a vast army of men, so as to destroy us without a reason, but we shall put our hope in one God, Who will free us from his hands. He has allowed us to suffer many trials and tribulations,

---

[213] Exodus 6–12.

as you have seen, so that we should have a reason to love Him better upon His delivering us from them.

Thus let us place our trust in the Lord God, Who brings all things to a good outcome, according to His pleasure. Such things are done through His sure judgement and will, which are not revealed to us. Wanting to scrutinise His ways and reasons merely inflicts war and weariness upon the spirit. Since that is so, let us therefore confess that we deserve what we suffer on account of our sins, and let us approach God through penitence. Let us sing to the Lord God a new song, as the Jews sang when they saw what God had done for them, killing their enemies before their eyes, and let us all speak with a pure mind and desire: 'Blessed be You, most Almighty God, Prince over earthly kings, sweet Comfort of the afflicted. Let us give You many thanks, for You chose to listen to us, and through Your sweet kindness You have distilled upon us such great mercy, curtailing the days of our tribulation so that they might not be further prolonged. For, had they lasted longer, it would have been very doubtful that we could bear it. All creatures praise and bless You, and we bless and praise Your Holy Name now and for ever, Amen.'

These and many other arguments were advanced by the good friar in his sermon, at which the people cried out mightily, all raising their hands to Heaven, and giving many thanks to God on high Who had delivered them thus from the power of their enemies.

With the sermon ended, Mass was said very solemnly, and the procession returned to the cathedral with the Host, in the same way as everyone had set out, and then they all departed very devoutly and much consoled.

Chapter 152

How Nuno Álvares crossed the river to Lisbon to speak to the Master

Nuno Álvares, who was in Palmela, learned how the king [of Castile] had raised the siege and was in Santarém, which news pleased him greatly. He received confirmation that there the king had mustered but a few, poorly equipped troops to assign to his border garrisons. When Nuno Álvares, who was very astute and bold in all things, found this out, as well as the fact that there would be many corpses and sick people from the king's army going with him, he thought that they would be spread out along the road without too many precautions. So, with a great and brave heart, he was entirely seized with the desire to come out on the road ahead of the king and, with God's help, to attack and rout him together with all his men.

Some say, when giving a brief account of this story, that he sent for permission from the Master to do this; that the latter replied he was very pleased about it, but asked Nuno Álvares to wait for him since he wanted to join with him in that action; that because the matter was delayed, and the Master did not set out in time, the King of Castile went his way without hindrance from anyone; that Nuno Álvares was much aggrieved at this and at the fate of his request for permission. But another compiler of these deeds, from whose writings we insert longer passages into this work as appropriate, relates it as follows. He says that when Nuno Álvares was in Palmela and learned the above-mentioned news, and how the king was departing with a powerful desire to return to the kingdom with greater forces to subjugate it through warfare, he decided to go and speak to the Master, as much about his plan to do battle with the King of Castile, as about other things that were very necessary to the former's service, despite the fact that the whole [Castilian] fleet was still lying off the city exactly as it had lain beforehand.

For this reason, he went to the promontory of Montijo in the Ribatejo, which is 2 leagues from the city, where he had a small boat in readiness to take him across the water.

When he was about to embark, one of his trusted squires, called Vasco Martins do Outeiro, took Nuno Álvares aside and said: 'Nuno Álvares, I beg you kindly not to board this boat, nor to make the crossing to the other side. Last night, I dreamed that I was crossing with you in this boat, and that the Castilian galleys captured you and all of us with you. This upset me so much that I wanted to kill myself when I saw such loss. On that account, I think it best that you put off this journey for now.'

At this, Nuno Álvares replied very gently, saying: 'My friend, I thank you for your good counsel, but God will work things better than you say. For you not to see the things you dreamed about, I order you to stay behind and not go with me. Thus, you will not see your dream fulfilled, nor will it please God for things to turn out that way.'

Taking no notice of this, the squire said that he wished to go with him at all costs, but Nuno Álvares would not consent, and thus he stayed behind, much against his will.

Despising all dreams and vain omens, Nuno Álvares did not change his mind about what he proposed. He embarked on the boat with some of his people at midnight and, although he could have taken a detour, he decided to make his crossing through the fleet that lay before the city. When he was right in the middle of it, he immediately gave order to sound the trumpets. On hearing this, the men in the *naos* began to be alarmed, all shouting, 'To arms! To arms!' Some jumped into their ship's boats, others rushed to the side of the ship, not knowing what was happening. However, men in some of the *naos* asked those in the boat who went there and received the reply that it was Nuno Álvares. Seeing that they could not obstruct him, they ceased taking any action against him. This took place in the last week of September.

Chapter 153

How Nuno Álvares spoke to the Master, and the discussion between them

Nuno Álvares reached land before dawn, and those who saw him were very pleased at his coming. They brought him a mule to ride on, with his page behind him with the sword that Pedro Sarmiento had sent him as a gage when he was to have joined battle with him at Évora.[214] All his men went on foot around him, along with many others accompanying him.

He went straightaway to the Monastery of São Domingos to attend Mass in [the Church of] Santa Maria da Escada,[215] for whom he had special veneration. When Mass was over, he went directly to the palace where the Master was lodging. Having already heard that he had come, the Master was making ready to receive him. While doing so, he was told that Nuno Álvares was about to arrive, so the Master went down to the gates of a large and spacious courtyard that lay before the palace. When he saw him, he was seized with great pleasure and rushed to embrace him. Not only did the Master do this, but his men also did the same, embracing those accompanying Nuno Álvares, kissing their cheeks, as if neither group could take enough pleasure in the other.

Nuno Álvares went down on his knees before the Master in order to kiss his hands, but he did not wish to allow that. He remained on his knees before him, trying to kiss his hands, and the Master trying to raise him up, the latter saying that it was not for someone such as Nuno Álvares to be given his hands to kiss, but rather he should receive many marks of favours and preferment. 'Especially', said the Master, 'from one such as myself, who remained here, penned up in this courtyard, unable to do anything of any consequence.'

---

[214] See Chapter 146.

[215] Saint Mary of the Stairway to Heaven (Santa Maria Scala Coeli, as the church in Rome). There was a strong devotion to this representation of the Virgin Mary during the Middle Ages, especially on the part of the Avis dynasty.

To that, Nuno Álvares replied with such fine and decorous words, that the eyes of many who were there, seeing such an amiable contest, were filled with tears of joy, which ran down their cheeks.

Even at the end of his speech, Nuno Álvares still did not want to rise until the Master allowed him to kiss his hands. Then, he got to his feet and both of them went to the chamber where, during the days that he was there, they spoke of many things concerning the provisioning of the war in which they were engaged and expected to go on being. Among their discussions, Nuno Álvares mentioned to the Master that Pedro Eanes Lobato, whom he had sent to the Master with a message about the taking of Monsaraz, had affirmed to him that, in speaking with certain of the noblemen whom the Master had with him, he had understood many of them were not serving him loyally. Hence, Nuno Álvares thought it was desirable for the Master to tell them they should all pay him homage and receive him once more as their liege lord, both those who had received him before as well as the noblemen of the Minho, so that they should remain his vassals in order to serve him in the forthcoming war. That was because, if they returned to their homes without first doing this, the Master could not afterwards be so sure of them, nor would he have them so bound to him, nor so ready for his service. This had been the main issue that had moved Nuno Álvares to come and speak to him, and he asked him to be so good as to see it done.

The Master thought this was wise advice, and arranged for it to be undertaken. On 2 October, all the noblemen and people of the city gathered together in the Monastery of São Domingos. The Master addressed them, saying that they well knew how he had been ready to leave the kingdom for certain reasons, of which they were all aware, but, owing to the insistent requests and prayers of the inhabitants of the city, and likewise of certain noblemen who were present, he had taken on the responsibility of ruler and defender of these kingdoms,[216] for whose defence and support he had suffered, and intended to bear whatever misfortunes and labours might befall him, to the extent of risking death.

Furthermore, as they saw the present disposition of the kingdom, and the intention with which the King of Castile was leaving, there were many greater labours ready for him to undergo, even more than those undergone until then. Capturing the places that supported Castile, and further defending those that supported him, could not be achieved unless everyone was of one mind and one will; also, they had to determine where they could find funds to support such undertakings. This was why he had arranged to talk of these things, while

---

[216] Portuguese monarchs started using the title of 'King of Portugal and the Algarve', when King Afonso III took over the latter territory in 1249.

everyone was gathered together. For they were well aware that the kingdom was close to being lost, and that it was no lesser effort to recover it than when it had been taken from the Moors. Therefore, they should discuss the best way to go about these things, because he was ready to give his consent to every good solution they could organise.

Chapter 154

How the nobility and the people paid homage to the Master, and concerning the privileges that he gave to the city

With many and various projects discussed, both by the nobility and the people at large, and the good and the bad that could ensue from such deeds laid out before their eyes, after long debates which we wish to leave aside so as not to detain you, their final conclusion was this: although everyone in the city and certain noblemen among those who were present had already received the Master as their liege lord, and although he had adopted the title of ruler and defender, they should all receive him as their lord once more, noblemen as well as citizens, and pay him homage as to the ruler and defender of the kingdoms of Portugal and the Algarve; also, they should consider themselves bound to serve and aid him with their lives and possessions, since they saw they were at a juncture where that was necessary. Furthermore, they should summon the districts that maintained support for Portugal; and everyone in Coimbra, together with the noblemen and clergymen who were gathered there,[217] should discuss the provisioning of the war, and where the necessary funds could be obtained.

With this decided, when it came to 6 October of the aforementioned year of 1384, the following gathered in the royal palace where the Master was lodging: Count Gonçalo, Brother Álvaro Gonçalves [Pereira], who was the Prior of the Hospitallers, Nuno Álvares Pereira, Diogo Lopes Pacheco, and other lords with all the noblemen, knights as well as squires, and all the inhabitants of the city and of other places whose presence on such an occasion was fitting.

All together, and one by one, they swore by touching the Holy Gospels and pledged fealty and homage to the Master as their liege lord, to serve and

---

[217] At this point, the Master's authority to convene *cortes* is questionable, given that he is not yet king. However, in listing the several estates to be summoned to Coimbra, Fernão Lopes may be hinting at the future significance of the proposed assembly.

help him with all their might, against the King of Castile as against any others who might wish to cause him harm, and kissed his hand as their lord. Some did so heart and soul, while others pretended to do so but were insincere, as afterwards was shown. He vowed and swore to them to guard all the privileges and freedoms they had, and to maintain the kingdom in law and justice.

When this was over, their lord the Master saw how the city folk showed such a desire to serve him as could not be greater. They were ready to carry this action forward in any way, despite the siege and famine they had endured and despite, too, the destruction of property they had experienced and were expecting to suffer, to the point of laying down their lives in his service and for the honour of the kingdom.

As a noble lord of royal heart, not only did the largesse of great gifts abound in him but it could also be said that he was a flowing river of pure and virtuous magnanimity. With a firm purpose, without delay, he immediately made up his mind to sprinkle their hearts with the sweetest water of gratitude. So he called the members of his council, such as Count Gonçalo; Brother Álvaro Gonçalves [Pereira], the Prior of the Hospitallers; Dom Lourenço, the Archbishop of Braga; Dom João, the Bishop of Lisbon; Dom Paio de Meira, the Bishop of Silves; Nuno Álvares Pereira; Diogo Lopes [Pacheco], the Lord of Ferreira; Doctor João das Regras; Doctor Martim Afonso; and several others that are not named here.

He put it to them, saying that they were well aware how the city of Lisbon was the greatest and best in the kingdom, and how it had been the first to give support and commitment to defend these kingdoms from the subjection under which the King of Castile had wanted to place them, without having any reason or right in the matter, and how Queen Leonor, wanting to place them totally under his subjection, had made every effort to do so. To that subjugation, Lisbon's people had never wished to consent, and they took him as their lord, ruler and defender, like other towns and places of the kingdom, which, following Lisbon's example, later did the same. Also, on account of that, Lisbon had been blockaded by water and by land, as everyone saw, and, in the siege that thus ensued, many of them lost their property and shed much of their blood. Through their defence of the city and with the Grace of Almighty God, the kingdom remained in part free, and out of the reach of such subjection, a freedom which it would not have retained, if they had consented to the city's subjection. Furthermore, he was looking at the great expenditure that they had made up till then, and which it would be incumbent on them to make for the honour of his rank and the betterment of the kingdom. He thought it behoved those who wished to undertake such a great quest, as that of defending the country from the vast might of its enemies, to endure such dangers and labours as could hardly be rewarded with favours.

However, as a reward for such a deed, and to maintain it evermore in the memory of those who came after, he had decided to bestow certain privileges and to grant a number of favours to the said city, in recompense for such great services. Even though these were not equivalent to what it deserved, at least his desire was to make it free and exempt from the exaction of certain dues of lesser importance that until then the kings had enjoyed within the city and in the outskirts, out of law and usage. This was so that everyone could live unencumbered by base subjugation, making free use of what was theirs. There was no one who contradicted him when he said what they were and how they would work, but everyone said that it was very little in comparison with such notable services, such as those that the city provided and would continue to provide. There were many arguments put forward about this action, and they said that, although other towns of the kingdom, large and small, maintained their support for him and his cause, everything was due to the wish to help and favour Lisbon, and it should be borne in mind that, whatever it did, the others would follow. This was so much so that the honour and loss of the kingdom rested entirely with the city, and this should not fail to be noted. So everyone praised the great worthiness of the Master, for having taken such a virtuous decision. They said that God would henceforth guide his actions, with such honour and increase of his state that he would reward the city better and better, with an abundance of generous favours.

Then he exempted the city from those customs and duties that were habitually levied, as follows: the royal monopoly on the sale of wine;[218] duties on land tilled for wheat and vines; stewardship tax;[219] militia levy;[220] market sales tax;[221] tax on baked bread;[222] municipal grain tax;[223] *lombos*;[224] and value added tax on total sales revenues. He also granted the city ownership of the Houses in which such duties were levied, such as the House of Wheat which is under the toll gate where formerly there were butchers' shops; the House of Wholesale Flour, and the House where now the butchers cut up meat. He also handed over to the city sixteen booths that stretched from the arches

---

[218] This monopoly on the sale of wine from the royal demesnes applied only to certain dates in the year.

[219] A tax paid by those who kept a household administrator, such as a steward.

[220] A tax levied locally to finance a company of crossbowmen or horsemen.

[221] A market sales tax paid on a wide range of products: meat, poultry, fish, fruit, vegetables, bread, pots and pans, etc.

[222] A tax levied on bread baked in the ovens of the court or of an archbishop's palace.

[223] A tax levied by the municipality on each measure of grain brought to be sold in the market.

[224] An ancient tax the nature of which remains unclear.

where the ironmongers traded up to the Butchers' Gate, eight on one side, and eight on the other. He ordered these to be demolished, to make the city square more beautiful.

Furthermore, he gave the city two notaries' offices in Oeiras and in the royal demesne of Ribamar, so that there should be no other notaries within the area around the city who administered justice in their own right. Not only did he exempt it from these duties and customs but also gave the following privilege to all those dwelling in the city and its surrounding area at that time and in the future: that nowhere in the kingdoms of Portugal and the Algarve should they pay tolls, usufruct, customary tributes, or any other duty or tax on any of the merchandise that they might take to any given place in the said kingdoms, or that they might bring from other places to the said city, either for their own sustenance or to sell.

He had all this drawn up in the most rigorous terms, which pleased the city people very much, and brought him great praise and repute. The people asked if he would be good enough to give immediate orders for the city castle to be demolished. When he granted this, it was razed to the ground without delay.

That day, Nuno Álvares spoke to the Master about his firm desire to intercept the King of Castile on the road to Chão de Couce once he had departed from Santarém, and to attack him one morning. He thought that with God's help he would rout him, and therefore he asked as a great favour the permission to do this. He said that contrary to fighting him when he came back with many well-equipped forces, they should be able to fight them better, now that he had just a few badly organised companies. The Master replied that it pleased him very much and he wished to be his companion in such action. For the moment, Nuno Álvares should return to Palmela and await him there. He himself would cross to the other side with as many men as he could, and from there they would go out to seek the king and do battle with him.

Then Nuno Álvares returned the same way he had come by boat. While he waited for the Master to do what we have explained, the King of Castile departed earlier than they expected, so they knew nothing about it. Thus the plan Nuno Álvares had devised against him could no longer be put in motion, and he made his way to Évora. Let him rest there awhile, until he is ready to take Portel. In the meantime, we shall usher the King of Castile out of the kingdom.

Chapter 155

How the King of Castile reached Santarém and placed governors in a number of towns

The king departed from Torres Vedras as you have heard,[225] and reached Santarém with his wife. Not yet completely recovered, she was conveyed in a litter, with the Prince of Navarre leading the draught-horses by the reins. There, the king started to plan how the places that supported him should remain secure and defended. On a Monday, there was a muster in Valada [do Ribatejo], to see what people he had to assign, both those who were to remain in each place and those he was to take with him. The muster yielded but a few people, poorly equipped as men in retreat after a siege; also, most of them had lost to death the lords with whom they had come.

In Santarém, the king removed the governor Lope Fernández de Padilla in order to take him back to Castile, and left Diego Gómez Sarmiento, his brother,[226] in the town as Officer of the Marches; whereas he ordered Gómez Pérez de Valderrábano to remain in the fortress with a good 800 lances and 300 crossbowmen. In Sintra, he left Count Enrique Manuel; in Torres Vedras, a Castilian knight whom people called Juan Duque; in Alenquer, Vasco Peres de Camões; in Óbidos, João Gonçalves Teixeira; in Leiria, García Rodríguez Taborda, who had been King Fernando's chief justice; and in Torres Novas, Alfonso López de Tejada, a native Castilian who was a grand commander of the Order of Santiago, in order to take with him Gonçalo Vasques de Azevedo, on whom he played a good trick, which we shall recount in this chapter.

He left the Count of Viana in charge of Penela and Miranda [do Corvo], and in other towns he kept there those who already held them, as we have explained where appropriate, or put others in their place, as was the case with Prior Pedro Álvares when he left with the king, and the latter placed a number of men in the fortified places within the lands of his priory to guard them. Also, in Castelo de Vide, [the king left] Gonçalo Eanes; in Vila Viçosa, Vasco Porcalho, a grand commander of the Order of Avis; in Portel, Fernão Gonçalves de Sousa; in Monforte, Martim Eanes de Barbuda; in Campo Maior and Ouguela, Payo Rodríguez Mariño;[227] in Olivença, Pero Rodrigues da

---

[225] See the end of Chapter 150 above.

[226] Fernão Lopes is mistaken here. Diego Gómez Sarmiento was the brother of Pedro Ruiz Sarmiento, who had died in the plague. See Chapter 149 above.

[227] It is strange to find Payo Rodríguez Mariño's name here, as his death was reported in Chapter 108 above. Perhaps his name has been added here because he had

Fonseca; in Moura, Álvaro Gonçalves; and in Mértola, Fernão de Antas, a grand commander of the Order of Santiago.

In Guimarães, Aires Gomes da Silva; in Ponte de Lima, Lope Gómez de Lira; in Braga, João Lourenço Bubal; and likewise other governors in the places that they held. In these as well as in all other places the king left behind as many squires, crossbowmen and foot soldiers as he deemed suitable for each place. He spoke where possible to the governors in person, and told others in writing that they should stand firm and defend their fortresses well, for if it pleased God he would return very soon, and repay it all to them with great rewards and favours.

It was said that the king was so lacking in money to pay wages to the people he was leaving behind that, before departing, he ordered his great dinner service of gold and silver that he had brought with him to be dismantled. It was cut up with shears and given in eight-ounce pieces to each man.

Now, at this juncture, you should know that although some people blamed Gonçalo Vasques de Azevedo for having advised and motivated the surrender of Santarém to the King of Castile, he was not, however, in the siege with him, nor did he participate further in his deeds. He merely remained all the while in Torres Novas, not making up his mind which side to take until he saw the outcome of this great matter. But others argue to the contrary, saying that, while in Torres Novas, he sent letters and messengers to the Master, asking to be pardoned for all that had taken place, and saying that he would serve him well and loyally against the King of Castile and against any other people. To this effect, he sent him his pledge by word and in writing, which greatly pleased the Master, who gave him and his people wages in coin, and also in jewels. This version seems more accurate, because Álvaro Gonçalves, son of this Gonçalo Vasques, then declared for the Master's party with certain of his own and his father's squires, and came to Lisbon in the Oporto fleet. There, the Master showed him great favour and goodwill, until he fled with Gonçalo Rodrigues de Sousa and went over to the Castilians.

This time, when the King of Castile arrived at Torres Novas, Gonçalo Vasques did not come out to receive him. Gaining the impression that the governor did not want to do so, the king did not lodge in the castle. With the latter lodging in the town, no Castilian entered the castle; instead, when they wished to give him some message, he came to speak to them at the gate. Although the king requested Gonçalo Vasques to come and speak to him, he always made excuses not to, fearing what indeed did happen to him afterwards. The king was very perturbed at this, believing that, as soon as he should depart,

---

been the Governor of Campo Maior, and that is one of the castles in the list of those that the King of Castile manned with people faithful to him.

Gonçalo Vasques would immediately turn coat and go over to the Master's party. He thus determined to take him with him, and it was in this manner.

The liberty that men allow their wives, which often brings the former dishonour and ruin, led Inês Afonso, the wife of Gonçalo Vasques, to go and see Queen Beatriz, her relative,[228] and the king as well. Both informed her that the lack of courtesy shown by her husband in serving them resulted in their not having any trust in him, enumerating the many good reasons he had to love the king's service, and hence for the king to grant him favours and preferment. Rather foolishly, she formed a picture of all these in her mind and promised the king and queen that she would bring him back to their service in every respect. When she returned to her husband, she began to rehearse all the arguments that the king and queen had put to her and the great honour and increase that they were minded to give him, principally because he was their uncle, but also because of having his support, which it was his duty to give. Therefore, he should hand over the castle to the king and join his company. She reinforced this advice by saying that the Master's design was a baseless fabrication, into which certain ignorant folk of little understanding were falling, while the prudent were guarding against it. Since Queen Leonor had renounced the regency in favour of the king, Queen Beatriz was heiress to the kingdom, something no one could deny. In particular, with so many places already declaring for her, and Portugal divided against itself, it was quite obvious that all the rest was just hot air, as he would soon see. For the Master did not have the power to equal the great might of the King of Castile, even if he had twenty times the number of men he had.

Gonçalo Vasques heard everything attentively, but his reply was not such as could please her, because he was weak-willed, like many others, when they saw that the king was returning to his kingdom without finishing what he had come for, which occasioned very great uncertainty.

Seeing that she could not induce her husband with sweet words to hand over the castle and go with the king, Inês Afonso arranged that, at a time when he was not likely to ask for her, she would secretly go out through the postern gate, saying that the king was calling for her and, thus, she went to the palace to speak with him. After the king had her with him, he sent word to Gonçalo Vasques that he should come and speak to him. The latter excused himself with various reasons, but the king replied that he would not press him to go or not to go; since he already had his wife in his power, Gonçalo Vasques could stay with God's blessing because he was taking her with him to Castile.

---

[228] Gonçalo Vasques de Azevedo was first cousin once removed of Leonor Teles's mother. Thus, in medieval terms, Queen Beatriz was his niece.

When Gonçalo Vasques heard this, he was out of his mind at such news and asked his people about her. They told him how she had gone out, at which he was most amazed. Moved then by a feminised heart – the kind that women call soft-hearted – he went to speak to the king, to beg him not to take his wife away. As soon as he was with the king, the latter sent the wife and daughter-in-law back to the castle, and took with him Gonçalo Vasques and Álvaro Gonçalves, his son. On departing from Torres Novas, he left Alfonso López de Tejada to defend the place, with the men that he deemed necessary.

When news reached Lisbon that the King of Castile had departed for his kingdom, which was on 14 October, the Master ordered that a man named João do Porto should have his feet and hands cut off, be dragged through the streets and hanged, because this man, a clerk of King Fernando's privy council, had falsified letters from the said king when he was alive and also from the Master after he had become regent. Seven days later, on 21 October, the Castilian fleet departed in the morning, *naos* as well as galleys. In the evening, every one of them returned owing to the unfavourable weather they encountered. Then, on 28 October, they all left without coming back again. Whoever says that this fleet lay before Lisbon until the king later returned to do battle should be told that he was dreaming when he wrote that.

Chapter 156

How the King of Castile departed for his kingdom, and the manner of his going

While the King of Castile was in Santarém, he was joined by all those whose lords had died [in the campaign], and who now sought to take their remains back to their homes in Castile according to what we have previously said.[229] They left Óbidos and Alenquer and the other places that supported Castile and all gathered together with him in that town. When the king left Santarém, everybody departed with him, disposed as follows.

The mourners all went in front, separately from the other men-at-arms, and each group bore their lord on a bier covered with black cloth and carried on a mule, escorted by all those on foot, dressed in deep mourning. Behind came those on horseback who used to attend that lord during his lifetime, with the banner of his arms right next to him. Thus everyone marched in due order, one in front of the other, along a great stretch of road, and such a procession was painful to see.

[229] See Chapter 155 above.

The King of Castile followed at the rear with his companies in a very sad frame of mind and unattended by the lords and noblemen whom he had brought at the beginning as befitted his royal estate. How could there be any pleasure in the heart of a king who had brought with him so many honourable vassals, well equipped and joyful to serve and help him, and in such a short time saw their corpses being borne before him, with their having added nothing to their honour? You may well believe that, given the great distress that the king was suffering at the time, on account of these and other troops whom he had lost, a distress shared by those travelling with him, and given the great heartbreak of those who accompanied the dead, any small group of men, who happened to come along strongly determined to harm him, would not take long to inflict all the damage they wished.

In the way we describe, the king made his way until he arrived at the frontier, where everyone shouldered the responsibility of taking their lords for burial in the places where they belonged, while the king went to Seville. There, he ordered that Don Pedro Muñiz de Godoy, who was the Master of the Order of Calatrava, should become Master of the Order of Santiago, and that Dom Pedro Álvares Pereira, who was the Prior of the Order of the Hospitallers in Portugal and who was there present with the king, should become Master of the Order of Calatrava, even though many people were displeased with this change that the king made. But the friars of these orders did what the king commanded them, and the Pope called Clement, for whom the king had declared,[230] confirmed these changes.

When Dom Pedro Álvares was made Master of the Order of Calatrava, the king immediately made the Count of Barcelos Count of Mayorga and made Gonçalo Vasques de Azevedo Provincial Governor of Old Castile.

Some say that the king began to do this because he feared those of his party might later change sides, which would mean his honour would be damaged, depending on how things might develop. For that reason, under the pretence of prompt reward, and showing a great desire to elevate those who joined him, he had wanted to deplete Portugal thoroughly of those honourable personages by whom he might later be obstructed, and give the honours and dignities they had held in their own kingdom to his fellow countrymen, in order to secure his estate.

Furthermore, up till now we have named two priors of Crato[231] but not said how this could be. First of all, you should know that they were styled in this way: Álvaro Gonçalves Camelo, for his great worth in the time of

---

[230] In 1383, Clement VII conceded by papal bull to Juan I the prerogative of directly appointing the masters of the military orders.

[231] At the time, the priory of Crato was the seat of the military Order of the Hospitallers in Portugal.

King Fernando, was nominated by the Grand Master of the Order to the priory in Portugal. The king, who preferred Pedro Álvares, the son of Prior Álvaro Gonçalves [Pereira] to have it, instigated that he should be approved by the one called Pope Clement, for whom the king had declared; he said that the Grand Master supported Pope Urban VI, and so he paid no heed to the appointment he had given to Álvaro Gonçalves [Camelo]. This is how Dom Pedro Álvares had the priorship, and the other remained without it. When the Master began his good deeds, and Álvaro Gonçalves came over to him to serve him, the Master, considering Dom Pedro Álvares to be his enemy and Álvaro Gonçalves to be a good servant, gave the latter the title of prior even though Dom Pedro would retain the income. Meanwhile Álvaro Gonçalves Camelo received great favours from the Master, until he later received the priorship.

But now let us leave the king in Seville as we have said, gathering his people together, and equipping a fleet to return to Portugal, and let us relate how Nuno Álvares took Portel, and what happened afterwards to Lisbon and to the Master up to the time when he was declared king in Coimbra.

Chapter 157

How Nuno Álvares took the town of Portel with the help of some who lived within

Among the places in the Alentejo that maintained support for Castile was the town of Portel,[232] the governor of which was a great Portuguese nobleman called Fernão Gonçalves de Sousa, married to Dona Teresa de Meira,[233] who had been governess to Beatriz, the Queen of Castile. It is said that, owing to his wife's counsel, he declared against Portugal and became a Castilian, as did Gonçalo Vasques de Azevedo and others.

As well as the people that he had with him, there were in the town as Officer of the Marches, Don García Fernández, the Lord of Villagarcía, who later became Master of the Order of Santiago, with 120 lances and other Castilians. The town thus being for Castile, Fernão Gonçalves, for fear of its inhabitants, impounded the weapons of all of them and placed them in the castle. It happened one day that men from Évora attacked Portel and carried off a number of cattle and prisoners. García Fernández went out to them with

---

[232] Portel lies 25 miles (c. 40 km) to the south-east of Évora.

[233] See *CKFI*, Chapter 65, in which Queen Leonor Teles arranged their marriage and gave the castle of Portel to Fernão Gonçalves de Sousa.

a company of troops as well as men from the town, but the latter had nothing to take along except capes over their arms and stones in their hands.

When García Fernández saw that, he took them for honourable men and said to Fernão Gonçalves that he did not think it right that they should be weaponless in that way; because, even though they might wish to carry out some worthy action, they did not have the wherewithal, and they cut very poor figures going with him with capes over their arms and stones in their hands. On account of these and other words that he spoke on the matter, Fernão Gonçalves was moved to return their weapons to them.

In this town of Portel was a priest called João Mateus, who very much wished that the town should support Portugal and declare for the Master. He considered in his heart that this could readily be done by having keys counterfeited in order to open the gates at a time of his choosing. So he took wax and inserted it in the locks, and went secretly to Évora where Nuno Álvares was. He spoke to him of his idea, and how he wanted to arrange counterfeit keys with which to open the gates at night. Once he had the keys ready, he would let him know. Nuno Álvares thanked him warmly, as one who was greatly displeased that Portel supported Castile, because it was a town within his border region, and much of his action took place round about. He said he should endeavour to put it in hand, and that the Master would grant him many favours for it.

The cleric had the keys made in Évora and took them back to Portel in great secrecy and made sure that they unlocked the gates. He returned to Évora to speak to Nuno Álvares and reported that the keys would open one of the gates, and that he had spoken to João Longo and others who were watchmen at that gate, and who were much pleased at the plan.

Nuno Álvares rejoiced at such news, and they agreed that on a certain day he should set out with his people in the evening, and travel the intervening 6 leagues, so that when dawn came they would be near the town [of Portel], but the night would hide them from the view of those in the town. The agreed signal for them to get up to the gates undetected would be this: given that the Castilians patrolled along the walls checking with the watch for anything untoward, it could happen that upon arrival at the said gate they might be there at that very moment, which represented a great danger. So the moment that the patrol approached that gate, those on watch would yell loudly and hoot, 'There goes the fox! There goes the fox!' and then Nuno Álvares and his men would keep quiet and not move at all; but, when they shouted out without mentioning the fox, they should then move speedily and would find the gates open.

With this arranged, Nuno Álvares forewarned a number of his men but without revealing where he planned to go. One day, he left Évora in the afternoon and took the road to Évoramonte, a good league from the town. Then he followed a brook downstream, keeping away from any path, until he came out on the road leading to Portel, at a place called Torre dos Coelheiros, which is 3 leagues away. There they rested a little and some of them slept. Then they mounted and proceeded so that a good while before morning they arrived near the place. The night was still dark, and they moved so quietly that the townspeople heard nothing. There they all dismounted and stood firm, wearing their bascinets and armed as usual, lances in their hands. They began to walk as quietly as possible.

When the watch, who were very much on the alert for them, sensed that they were nearby and saw the patrol coming along the walls, they started to shout and hoot, 'There goes the fox! There goes the fox!' which was the agreed signal between them. As soon as the patrol was at a fair distance, they began to sing and to talk of other things.

The priest João Mateus, who was more concerned to open the gates than to say Matins, immediately went very softly to the gates and opened them. Nuno Álvares's men began to enter but a few Castilians, who were with the watch, heard the sound they were making and began to shout, saying, 'To arms! To arms! For Castile! Castile!'

When Nuno Álvares saw that he had been discovered, he ordered the trumpets to sound. García Fernández and all his men saw how things were and withdrew to the castle, as hurriedly as they could, some of them in undershirts and others barely dressed. Many were taken prisoner. Nuno Álvares would have dearly liked this García Fernández to have been taken prisoner, if he himself had not been discovered so soon. His men took all the weapons and mounts from the Castilians and everything they had there, for the latter were unable to save anything.

Chapter 158

How the castle was delivered up to Nuno Álvares, and how Fernão Gonçalves went to Castile

Fernão Gonçalves, who was in the castle as we have said, was the most humorous man in Portugal, and very coarse in his language. When he saw that action, he was amazed, fully understanding that the people of the town had brought it about, but he knew no remedy for such a deed. When everyone was calm once more, and everything that had been found had been plundered, Nuno Álvares sent to him to say that he should hand over the castle for the

Master, his lord; if not, he could be sure that he would soon fight for it and rend it into three parts.

Although Fernão Gonçalves was somewhat angry, he carried on behaving in his usual way, and immediately replied to the messenger: 'Tell Nuno Álvares that with his great pride and threatening words he cannot please God. For even if the castle of Portel were a pair of breeches of French cloth, of the sort with three holes, they would not rend as quickly as he says he will rend this castle. Now go and tell him that I shall discuss terms.'

That day, Nuno Álvares's troops and a number of men from Beja who were with them, after taking their supper and without anyone ordering them, began suddenly and in a disorderly manner to attack the castle, shouting that somebody should set fire to the gates. When Fernão Gonçalves saw this, he said to his people in jest, 'Did you ever see such a strange thing as this, Portel fighting Portel?' He said this because of the abundance of excellent wines there are in that town, giving to understand that they had drunk more than they ought, and that was what had moved them to do that.

Then Nuno Álvares ordered them not to attack any more, since some could perish without being able to do anything very advantageous. Then Fernão Gonçalves sent to ask Nuno Álvares if it pleased him for them to talk under safe conduct. Nuno Álvares said that it did, so they spoke at the outer wall of the castle near the Beja Gate. In order to bring him back to the Master's service, Nuno Álvares told Fernão Gonçalves in that parley that he was quite amazed at him, being such a good nobleman, of such great lineage and also a genuine Portuguese, as he was. Furthermore, being lord of that town as well as of Vila Alva and Vila Ruiva, to abandon everything to give Portel to the King of Castile, and to leave the certain for the uncertain, it seemed to him that he had been ill advised on the matter. However, despite this, if he were to be so good as to declare support for his liege lord, the Master, he would so arrange matters that the Master would give him all those towns and others as well and grant him many favours.

Fernão Gonçalves replied that God knew well that he regretted what he had done, but that he had no alternative now but to carry on as he had begun. But he asked him to offer some reasonable guarantee of security to him and the Castilians. Nuno Álvares said that he should speak to Don García Fernández and the others, and he would let him have an answer, depending on the kind of pledges they were looking for.

Fernão Gonçalves returned to his castle, and immediately the next day he sent him their proposal: that he should allow them to go in safety to Castile with all their belongings, after being given back what the Portuguese had seized, and they would deliver the castle to him. However, Nuno Álvares and certain people who were with him should swear an oath to this.

Nuno Álvares was pleased at this, and took the oath that was asked of him. Among those who swore it was his brother Fernão Pereira, who was there with him. Then Nuno Álvares ordered to be handed over to Fernão Gonçalves and to Don García Fernández and to all the others whatever was found to be theirs; the exception was a coat of mail and a sword belonging to Don García Fernández that Fernão Pereira hid without Nuno Álvares's knowledge.

With this done, Fernão Gonçalves and his wife, with all the others, made themselves ready to depart. To see them safely into Castile, Nuno Álvares sent with them a good squire of Évora who was called Diogo Lopes Lobo. When Fernão Gonçalves and his wife were about to leave the town, although he was little pleased, he began to say that they should call the horns to sound, saying to his wife, 'Come along here, good lady, and let us dance, you and I, to the sound of these horns, you as a wicked old whore and I as a silly old bugger who's been well and truly buggered, just the way you wanted it. Or better still, let's sing it like this:

> Since Marina has danced,
> let her take what she's earned.
> Better by far Portel and Vila Ruiva
> than Zafra and Segura.
> Let her take what she's earned,
> that old whore of a lady.'[234]

He said this because he was losing Portel and Vila Ruiva and was being given Safra and Segura in Castile. Besides, it was reputed that he had given his support to Castile because his wife persuaded him to do so.

These and other bawdy quips Fernão Gonçalves carried on saying as he proceeded through the town and the outskirts. Then they mounted up and took the road for Castile. Following that, Nuno Álvares established order and security in the town, as necessary, and returned to Évora.

---

[234] The verse sung by Fernão Gonçalves is in the style of a *cantiga de mal-dizer*, a satirical genre much cultivated in the 13th and early 14th centuries. See Josiah Blackmore, 'Singing the Scene of History in Fernão Lopes', in Michelle M. Hamilton and Núria Silleras-Fernández (eds), *In and Out of the Mediterranean: Medieval and Early Modern Iberian Studies* (Nashville, Tennessee: Vanderbilt University Press, 2015), pp. 143–55.

Chapter 159

Concerning the names of certain people who helped the Master defend the kingdom

As this work is being compiled by the application of our limited skills, it seemed to us to be a good and worthy gesture that those who were the Master's companions in his great and virtuous labours should share in some commemoration, even if it is only to be set down in writing. For, if the slipping away of great epochs erodes the fame of excellent princes, so much more do long ages bury with them in their tomb the names of other people.

Since, at the start of his good deeds, the Master had nobles and citizens who served him well and loyally, laying down their lives and possessions for the honour of the kingdom, it seems to us that an injury would be done to them if they were allowed to fall into perpetual oblivion. For, just as the great lord of whom we speak, with his immense largesse in distributing special gifts, rewarded them all without leaving anybody out, so past authors should have made some mention of them, which in our view should have been like this: first by naming those of noble birth who at such uncertain times rallied to the Master and remained to serve him; then the governors of castles who voiced their support for Portugal without changing sides; and finally the residents and the sons of Lisbon citizens who always acted in his service.

In our attempt to be of assistance in this as in other shortcomings where past authors do not fulfil our expectations, we have found that it is no longer possible to fully succeed in this endeavour because, as the names of such people have aged, the brightness of their nobility has also died. Who would you now expect to drag out of the obscurity of so many years the names which can scarcely be found of those who have no other witness except ashes and oblivion? Who would you think would not grow weary of perusing cartularies of rotting documents whose age and decay deny a man what he wants to know? Who would be able to find, among so many ancient inscriptions written on tombs, any evidence of who lies in them? Who would assuage other people's feelings and the varied opinions of men, so that everyone should be pleased with what we want to say? It would be quite impossible.

Therefore, after some toil, though not as much as it ought to be, only enough to restore accounts as closely as possible to how they ought to have been presented, the process of writing this down will be very short. First, we shall name certain nobles who stayed with the Master; then certain citizens of Lisbon, since the city was the mother and source of these deeds. Although we have set down their names in a few places in this book, here you will find them all written down together, those whom we managed to recover, in the same way in which at the start of this work we named a number of nobles who helped Count Henrique to capture land from the Moors. Thus in this second volume we will give an account of a few of those who were the Master's companions in defending the kingdom from its enemies.[235]

Not writing in order of nobility but as the hand wills the quill to move, let the first in this litany be the very noble Nuno Álvares Pereira, praise and glory be to all his lineage, whose brightness in excellent service was never eclipsed; nor did it lose its lustre. Not only Nuno Álvares, but he along with his companions, in a brief and pleasing comparison, should be placed first. For just as the Son of God, after His death which He endured to save the human line, ordered His apostles to preach the Gospel throughout the world to all creatures, placing them for the same reason at the start of the litany, naming Saint Peter first,[236] so did the Master, after he readied himself to die if necessary for the salvation of the land that his forefathers had won, send Nuno Álvares and his companions to preach the Portuguese gospel throughout the kingdom. This Gospel was that all should believe in and hold firm to Pope Urban [VI] as the true pastor of the Church, outside of whose obedience none could be saved. Moreover, they were to uphold that belief which their fathers had always held and which consisted of using their possessions and whatever they had to defend the kingdom from its enemies and, in order to maintain this faith, shedding their blood even unto death. Nuno Álvares and his men preached this by word and deed so completely that some of them, as you will see later, were slain defending it, such as Fernão Pereira and Antão Vasques and others whom we do not care to name.

Therefore, leaving aside those whom we already mentioned when Nuno Álvares left Lisbon, and many whose names it would be superfluous to write down, let the following suffice for now:

From the kingdom of the Algarve, from Tavira and Faro: Rodrigo Afonso de Aragão; Vasco Eanes, the father of Vasco Eanes Corte Real; Gonçalo Arrais; Martim Arrais; Nuno Velho; Pedro Afonso da Âncora; João Fernandes Garganta; Gonçalo Vasques Baião; and Paio Pereira.

---

[235] These last two sentences refer to the full sequence of royal chronicles written by Lopes, going back to the conquests of Count Henri of Burgundy (d. 1112), the father of the first king of Portugal, Afonso Henriques. All the earlier chronicles have been lost. 16th-century copies of older chronicles of the same kings appear to be partially connected with them, but they are the result of subsequent interpolations and no longer represent Lopes's texts. There is still considerable scholarly debate about this. See also *CKP*, Prologue, note 2.

[236] Matthew 16. 18; Acts 1. 2–8.

From Loulé and Silves: Vasco Afonso, the chief governor of the place, and his brother João Vasques; Gonçalo Nunes Barreto; and Lopo Esteves de Sarria. From Albufeira: Rodrigo Álvares Banzão; Fernão Peres Banha; Gonçalo Navarro; and João Delgado.

From Beja and Campo de Ourique: Martim Gomes, the Grand Commander of the Order of Santiago; Rodrigo Eanes Frandino; Álvaro Afonso de Negrelos; Vasco Lourenço, a bailiff; Gonçalo Nunes, the chief provincial governor of the place; Mendo Afonso de Beja; and João Afonso de Brito.

From Serpa and Moura: Diogo Nunes de Serpa; Vasco Lourenço da Coutada; Egas Lourenço Raposo; Pero Rodrigues and Lopo Álvares, the sons of Álvaro Gonçalves de Moura; Pero Lourenço de Arraiolos; João Gomes, a vicar; and Estêvão Eanes Mangancha.

From Portel and Mourão: Pero Esteves, the father of Paio Rodrigues; Lopo Soares; and Soeiro Álvares.

From Elvas: Pero Martins Alcoforado.

From Juromenha and Alandroal: Vasco Afonso, the Commander of Juromenha; Pero Rodrigues do Alandroal; and João Gomes.

From Vila Viçosa and Estremoz: Lourenço Gonçalves; Gonçalo Gonçalves; Afonso Peres 'the Black';[237] Lopo Gonçalves de Alcanena;[238] Fernão Lourenço; Gil Nunes; Gonçalo Eanes Frandino; Mendo Afonso; and Álvaro Martins de Alvarenga.

From Évora: Fernão Gonçalves da Arca, the Elder, and his son João Fernandes; the four brothers Diogo Lopes Lobo, Fernão Lopes Lobo, Martim Lopes Lobo and Estêvão Fernandes; Álvaro Peres Carvoeiro; Rodrigo Álvares Pimentel; James Lourenço; Afonso Peres, a nurse's son; Martim Cotrim; Fernão Martins Brandão; Gomes Martins Zagalo; Afonso Lourenço do Vimeiro; João Afonso da Regueira; João Farto; Martim Vicente de Vila-Lobos; and Fernão Gonçalves Façanha.

From Portalegre and Montemor[-o-Novo]: Martim Gonçalves de Tavares; Martim Afonso da Aramenha; Martim Gonçalves, the count's uncle;[239] Nuno Fernandes de Morais; Lourenço Mendes; Lourenço Eanes Azeiteiro;[240] Vasco Gil, a former chief justice; and João Lourenço Carvalho.

[237] He later became Governor of Vila Viçosa. See Chapter 100 above.

[238] Possibly the same person as Lopo Gonçalves de Estremoz, referred to in *CKJ2*, Chapters 152 and 154.

[239] Martim Gonçalves do Carvalhal, brother of Iria Gonçalves do Carvalhal, Nuno Álvares Pereira's mother. By then Nuno Álvares had already been made Count of Ourém. See Chapter 36 above.

[240] Nuno Álvares Pereira's squire, later also rewarded for his service in the war. See *CKJ2*, Chapter 152.

From Alcácer [do Sal] and Setúbal: Rodrigo Eanes Carvalho; Martim Anes Serrão; Álvaro da Aguiã; Pero Fernandes and his brother, Gomes Fernandes.

From Lisbon: João Vasques de Almada; Pedro Eanes Lobato; Vasco Leitão, the son of Estêvão Leitão and grandson of the Master of the Order of Christ, Dom Estêvão Gonçalves [Leitão]; Afonso Peres da Charneca; Antão Martins; João Álvares de Faria; Estêvão Eanes Borbeleta; João Esteves Correia; Lopo Afonso da Água and his brother Lourenço Afonso; Afonso Domingues de Saavedra; João Lobato and others whom we mention in their place so it is not necessary to repeat them further.

We can say well and appropriately that, just as Our Saviour Jesus Christ founded His Church on Peter, giving him authority that what he might bind and loosen on earth would be bound and loosened in Heaven,[241] so the Master who founded the defence of that region [the Alentejo] on the bravery and courage of Nuno Álvares, gave him free and full power so that he could appoint governors, accept or reject oaths of allegiance, grant goods and land, award and take away endowments and all other things with as much power as the Master would have himself over them. Those grants that Nuno Álvares issued through his charters should not afterwards be given to others by the Master. This was done without hesitation in such a manner that, whenever it was proved that a grant by Nuno Álvares had been issued first, the Master would immediately order his own to be halted, saying that it was not his will to go against any donation that Nuno Álvares had made to someone, but, rather, to confirm and uphold it. Thus he did for Nuno Fernandes de Morais, to whom Nuno Álvares gave the property of Gonçalo Mendes de Oliveira which Nuno Rodrigues de Vasconcelos had held in Évora and Arraiolos, and for many others whose names it is not necessary to write down.

Other honourable disciples arrived afterwards at Nuno Álvares's side to help him preach this Portuguese Gospel, whose perseverance made them and their lineage grow in great honour and increase. Thus were the Admiral Master Carlos,[242] Álvaro Pérez de Castro, Martim Afonso de Melo, Afonso Vasques Correia, Gonçalo Eanes of Castelo de Vide and others who are not written down in this book.

[241] Matthew 16. 19.
[242] Also a son of Lançarote Pessanha, he succeeded his brother, Manuel, in the post of Admiral.

Chapter 160

Concerning the names of certain nobles,
both Portuguese and Castilian

Through a similar comparison we can on another list nominate as martyrs the residents of Lisbon and those who were in the Master's company while he was besieged. This is just and right because the name of 'martyr' is not given only to those who suffer for not adoring idols, but also to those who are persecuted by the schismatic heretics for not abandoning the truth they believe. If by 'martyr' we mean 'witness', the inhabitants of Lisbon are good witnesses to those who died in the city's siege and in their trials and tribulations. For that reason, since Lisbon is like a city widowed of her king, at that time having the Master as her defender and bridegroom, we can interrogate her, saying,[243]

'O city of Lisbon, famous among cities, sturdy prop and column that supports all Portugal! Who is your bridegroom? Who were the martyrs who accompanied you in your persecution and your painful siege?'

Responding, she could say,

> Are you asking me from which ancestors he descends? He is the grandson of King Afonso IV. As for his bodily height, he is of good and rightful stature and the composition of his limbs is very well balanced with a gracious and honourable presence. He has shown great courage and a strong mind in the deeds that relate to my defence, and all my well-being and protection are placed in his hands alone.
>
> The martyrs who accompanied him were of two kinds: some, seeing the good intention and just quarrel that I took on to defend the kingdom from its mortal enemies, were publicly converted, receiving such a belief in their heart, coming to me so that I could be helped by them, or so it seemed. Yet after a few days, deceived completely by the spirit of Satan and the evil counsel of some false Portuguese, little by little they abandoned their noble purpose, going back to making sacrifices and adoring the idols that they had believed in before.
>
> Among those who did this, not bearing the fruit that would have been expected from the leaves shown in their words, are those who were not so much to blame since they were distorted shoots born of the wild olive tree.[244] Thus were Count Enrique Manuel; Count Pedro and his brother

---

[243] The extended metaphor of Lisbon personified as wife and mother (in Part 2 of the chronicle) seems to justify the use of 'she' and 'her'.

[244] Meaning those born in Castile. The extended fruit metaphor is inspired by

Alfonso Enríquez; Vasco Peres de Camões; Lopo Gomes; Juan Alfonso de Baeza; Gonçalo Tenreiro, who later was known in Castile as Master of the Order of Christ, and his brother Afonso Tenreiro; Lope Gómez de Lira and other such people.

Yet there were some straight shoots, whose birth traced their ancient beginnings from the good and gentle Portuguese olive tree, that strove to sever themselves from the tree that raised them and change its sweet fruit into bitter liquor; this causes pain and makes one weep! Thus were Master Lançarote, the Admiral; Dom Gonçalo Teles, the Count of Neiva;[245] Dom João Afonso Teles, the Count of Barcelos; the Count of Viana, the son of the old count; Dom Pedro de Castro and his brother Dom Afonso; Dom Pedro Álvares, the Prior of the Order of the Hospitallers and his brother Diogo Álvares; Martim Afonso de Melo, a high ranking nobleman, and his son Fernando Afonso de Melo; Fernão Gonçalves de Sousa; Gonçalo Rodrigues de Sousa; Aires Gomes da Silva; Fernão Gomes da Silva and his brother Afonso Gomes da Silva; Gonçalo Vasques de Azevedo and his son Álvaro Gonçalves; Pedro Lourenço Bubal,[246] who called himself Archbishop of Braga; Pero Rodrigues da Fonseca; Gonçalo Eanes da Fonseca; Martim Gonçalves de Ataíde; García Rodríguez Taborda; Fernão de Antas, the Governor of Mértola, who in Castile was called Master of the Order of Santiago in Portugal, and his brother Vasco de Antas; Martim Eanes de Barbuda; Gil Vasques de Barbuda; Álvaro Mendes de Oliveira; Gonçalo Mendes de Oliveira; Payo [Rodríguez] Mariño; Gonzalo Mariño; Diogo Botelho; Vasco Botelho; João Rodrigues Portocarreiro; Fernão Vasques Pimentel; Martim Correia who held the castle of Feira; Álvaro Gil de Carvalho; Gil Álvares de Carvalho; Fernão Gonçalves de Meira;[247] Vasco Porcalho; João Gonçalves Teixeira; Vasco Gomes de Abreu;[248] Rui Vasques Michão; Vasco Gonçalves de Vieira; Gonçalo Rodrigues de Bornes and his brother Manuel Rodrigues; Nuno Garcia de Chaves; Pedro Mendes, the commander of Almada;[249] Vasco Madeira; Estêvão Eanes de Beja the

---

numerous biblical references to agricultural and tree images. The wild olive is used for the rootstock onto which is grafted the sweeter domesticated olive. Suckers can at times shoot forth from below the graft: these are the distorted shoots whose loyalties are always questionable.

[245] Gonçalo Teles, Count of Neiva and of Faria, was the brother of Queen Leonor Teles.

[246] Appointed Archbishop of Braga by the Avignon Pope Clement VII in 1383, but he was never consecrated.

[247] Former Governor of the Castle of Torres Vedras, who had handed over the castle to the King of Castile. See Chapter 86 above. At this point of Lopes's narrative, he was already deceased.

[248] Lope Gómez de Lira's father-in-law.

[249] The castle of Almada was entrusted to the military Order of Santiago.

Younger; Álvaro Fernandes Turrichão; João Martins de Outel who, while
with the king in the battle,[250] switched to the Castilian side; and many others
who would form a great chapter in themselves.

If some would say, in order to excuse them all, that if these and the
aforementioned others had received from the Master due honour mixed
with favours, which forms bonds in noble hearts, then both the distorted
shoots and the new growth would have brought forth pleasant fruit, they
can be well answered: such gracious generosity or sweeter company could
not be found in any other man. Concerning the granting of great favours,
according to each one's status, the Master could be blamed for excess, but
not for granting too little. In fact, it seemed more likely that he had been
elected for the liberal distribution of the goods and lands of the kingdom
than in order to be its defender. Good witnesses of this would be the ledgers
of grants issued at that time if it were necessary to look for them. Therefore,
nothing that related to the forming of bonds in noble hearts was lacking,
everything was done to all of them, but the suckers would not let themselves
be grafted and the true shoots changed their nature, as happens sometimes
when scions of good stock turn into something quite the opposite, without
blame falling on those who planted them.

Therefore, I would not have wanted to put such martyrs as I have named
in my calendar[251] if it were not for the fine fruit that they put forth, with
which the Master my lord was afterwards well-served and attended, and the
kingdom defended and protected from its enemies and rivals.

Chapter 161

Concerning the names of certain nobles and citizens who helped the Master defend the kingdom

The other kind of martyr who accompanied me, whose commemoration
should last forever, were those who remained strong and very firm,
with pure intention and without duplicitous words, not being moved from
what they had begun by any dangers or threats. The names of many of these
can no longer be found in order to commemorate them, and even if they

[250] This is actually Gil Martins Doutel, who left the Portuguese side to join the
King of Castile at the Battle of Aljubarrota.

[251] The reference to a calendar is the continuation of the religious language encountered earlier. These martyrs, followed by the confessors below, are listed as in a
calendar of saints at the beginning of a medieval Book of Hours.

could all be found it would create such a great procession that it would be excessive rather than necessary and well ordered. Therefore, these few are put here, not in order of their nobility, as we have already said, but made into a little sheaf, as if for easier harvesting, and are representative of themselves and all others.

The Master of the Order of Christ, Dom Lopo Dias de Sousa, who, being the nephew of Queen Leonor and having more lands in Portugal than the Master of Avis, as a true Portuguese and seeing that the King of Castile had broken the treaties, declared himself for Portugal and served the Master as a magistrate until he was captured while trying to besiege Torres Novas, which had declared for Castile.

The Master of the Order of Santiago, Dom Fernando Afonso de Albuquerque, the bastard son of Dom João Afonso de Albuquerque, who came to the Master and offered him the lands of his office as Master [of Santiago]; Dom Lourenço, the Archbishop of Braga; Doctor Gil do Sém; Doctor João das Regras; Doctor Martim Afonso, who later became Archbishop of Braga; Lourenço Eanes Fogaça; Diogo Lopes Pacheco, who in such uncertain times came from Castile with his sons João Fernandes, Lopo Fernandes and Fernão Lopes to cast their lot with the Master; João Rodrigues Pereira, the son of Rui Vasques Pereira; Rui Pereira, who died in the naval engagement;[252] Fernão Pereira, and Rodrigo Álvares, the brothers of Nuno Álvares; Gil Vasques da Cunha; Lopo Vasques da Cunha; Mem Rodrigues de Vasconcelos and his brother Rui Mendes, who left their father Gonçalo Mendes in Coimbra and came to the Master; Lopo Dias de Azevedo, who left all his property and came to the Master to serve him; João Gomes da Silva, who left his father in Montemor-o-Velho where he lived and went to Oporto to join the fleet and came in it to the siege on behalf of the Master; João Lourenço da Cunha, who came from Castile to the Master and his son Álvaro da Cunha;[253] Álvaro Pérez de Castro; Aires Gonçalves de Figueiredo; João Rodrigues de Sá; Fernão Vasques de Resende; Rui Freire and his brother Gomes Freire; Pedro Lourenço de Távora and his brother Rui Lourenço; João Lourenço de Penela; Vasco Martins de Gá; Sancho Gomes do Avelar; Lourenço Martins do Avelar; Vasco Rodrigues Leitão[254] and his son Álvaro Leitão; Fernão Rodrigues

---

[252] See Chapter 133 above.

[253] He was born of João Lourenço da Cunha and Leonor Teles, before their marriage was dissolved and she married King Fernando of Portugal. He and his father eventually returned to Portugal to serve King João. Álvaro da Cunha took part in the 1415 expedition to Ceuta, was knighted by Prince Henry, and inherited his father's estate and title of Lord of Pombeiro.

[254] Former Governor of Santarém for Gonçalo Vasques de Azevedo; see *CKF*, Chapter 176.

de Sequeira; Gonçalo Vasques de Sequeira; Lopo Vasques de Sequeira; Fernando Álvares de Almeida; Gómez García de Hoyos; Rodrigo Eanes de Buarcos;[255] João Afonso de Santarém; Rodrigo Eanes de Barbudo; João Rodrigues da Mota;[256] Gil Esteves de Outiz; Pero Fogaça; Pero Vasques de Pedra Alçada; Nuno Viegas, [the Younger]; and Álvaro Vasques de Góis.

Some citizens who resided in me, both knights and squires, were as follows: Martim Afonso Valente; Estêvão Vasques Filipe; Gil Esteves Fariseu; Afonso Eanes Nogueira; Antão Vasques; Álvaro Pais and his son Diogo Álvares; Gonçalo Peres, who afterwards governed the High Court of Justice; Afonso Furtado; Geraldo Martins de Lemos and his son Gomes Martins; Aires Vasques de Alvalade; Rui Cravo; Gonçalo Gonçalves Borges; Fernão Gonçalves da Ameixoeira; Pedro Afonso do Casal; Vasco Queimado; Afonso Esteves de Azambuja and his son João Afonso, who later became a cardinal;[257] Gonçalo Vasques Carregueiro; João Domingues Torrado; Lopo Afonso do Quintal; Estêvão Eanes da Grã; Lopo Afonso Donzel; Francisco Domingues de Beja; João da Veiga, the Elder; Silvestre Esteves and his brother Afonso Esteves; Martim Lourenço, the father of Doctor Gil Martins, and his brother Afonso Lourenço; Martim da Maia; João Peres Canelas; Diogo Afonso Alvernaz and his brother João Afonso [Alvernaz]; Martim Alvernaz; Estêvão Eanes de Barbudo; Afonso Martins de Gorizo; Nuno Fernandes de Chaves; Pedro Afonso do Casal;[258] Martim Gonçalves Rombo; Gonçalo Eanes do Vale; Álvaro Vasques da Veiga; João Peres da Veiga; Diogo Lourenço da Veiga; Fernando Álvares [de Almeida], the father of Doctor Rui Fernandes; Álvaro Gil de Pedroso; Lourenço Martins Pratas; Martim Taveira and his son Lopo Taveira; Lopo das Regas; Afonso Domingues do Pau; Rui Portela; Gonçalo Domingues Barrufo; Rodrigo Afonso Barateiro; Estêvão Eanes Lobato; and Diogo Álvares de Santo António.

Many other martyrs declared for the kingdom and upheld my cause faithfully. Of those who came to help the Master at the time of my suffering during the siege, it was my intention to put just a few down in writing even if the memory of many of them will be lost completely.

Yet since a good intention often slips away and does not last, and just men fall down seven times each day, getting themselves back up just as many times, it is no wonder if some noblemen among those I previously mentioned, after the most excellent deeds they had done for the kingdom, fell from their honourable estate, leaving what they had begun through human weakness and the contrariness of the times. Those who were true

---

[255] Former squire of Gonçalo Vasques de Azevedo; see *CKJI*, Chapter 67 above.

[256] Also a former squire of Gonçalo Vasques de Azevedo.

[257] See Chapter 27, note 38 above.

[258] We have not been able to establish whether or not this is a different person to the Pedro Afonso do Casal named above.

Portuguese and loyal servants of the Master both then and afterwards were granted great honours and preferment, as could well have been written down.

Whoever in the tale of these martyrs and apostles does not find their father, brother or some well-beloved relative should not blame this work for that reason, for it has been put together with great labour. It cannot satisfy everyone, just as a wind cannot please all the various sailors. Instead, have the patience of those saints who are named neither in the litany nor in the prayers said at Mass!

Chapter 162

The names of a number of places that declared for Portugal

Leaving aside the names of such apostles and martyrs, it is appropriate for us to question the city of Lisbon again, saying: 'O most noble city of Lisbon, life and heart of this kingdom, purged of all the dross in the crucible of loyalty! Since we already know of certain martyrs among those who suffered for you, let us now see: who were the confessors who made you renowned among the people, adhering always to your cause without failing in their faith?' Answering such a question, she could reply as follows:

Among those that declared with me that Pope Urban [VI] was the true pastor of the Church, and the Master the ruler and defender of these kingdoms, it was the good and loyal city of Oporto that laboured much with me in this very serious business, providing great help and expenditure to support the truth of the cause I defended. With her were: Coimbra, Évora, Guarda, Viseu, Lamego and the town of Silves. Also together with them, in the Algarve, were: Castro Marim, Tavira, Faro and the other places in that kingdom. Others were Sines, Santiago do Cacém, Mourão, Serpa, Elvas, Monsaraz, Portalegre, Arronches, Fronteira, Portel, Évoramonte, Estremoz, Castelo de Vide, Avis, Montemor-o-Novo, Palmela, Setúbal, Almada, Amieira, Sertã, Penamacor, Pinhel, Monsanto, Trancoso, Linhares, Lousã, Celorico, Moncorvo, Miranda, Freixo de Espada à Cinta, Vila Flor, Castelo Branco, Nisa, Almourol, Marialva, Celorico de Basto, Abrantes, Tomar, Soure, Pombal, Alcanhede and other places similar to these.

All the others abandoned me, some through failing courage and some because the Portuguese were disloyal; others through the force of torment which they could not bear, some making a mockery of me and the cause that I fought for, in order to escape the subjection which our enemies against all reason wanted to impose on us by force. Those that are named here were the confessors that always supported my cause, being my companions in the trials and tribulations that I set myself to suffer to defend the kingdom.

Living thus widowed and disconsolate, having no one else to support me except the Master my lord and bridegroom in whom lay my great trust and hope, everybody came together in the city of Coimbra and there publicly received me with him, giving him to me as liege lord and king as you will later hear. I intend always to serve and love him and to be very obedient not only to him but to all who descend from him in whatever things they graciously order me to do and which my goodwill can achieve.

Chapter 163

Concerning the Seventh Age that began in the time of the Master

Following our account, in order to put an end to what we have started, you should note at this stage that those who wrote about the passage of time, such as Eusebius in *De temporibus*[259] and Bede[260] and certain others, assigned six ages to the world.

The first was from Adam to Noah and lasted for 1,656 years, in which ten generations were contained, and all perished in the flood.

The second was from Noah to Abraham and lasted for 296 years, in which there were another ten generations.

The third was from Abraham to David, in which there were fourteen generations, and it lasted 940 years.

The fourth was from David to the Babylonian Captivity, in which there were another fourteen generations, and it lasted 373 years.

The fifth was from the Babylonian Captivity to the coming of the Saviour, in which were contained fourteen generations, and it lasted 589 years.

The sixth is the one in which we live now, which has lasted 1,443 years.[261] There is no certainty about the number of years or about the calculation of

---

[259] *De temporibus* (*Concerning the Times*), the title by which the second part of Eusebius of Caesarea's *Chronicon* was known in the 15th century.

[260] Bede, the Venerable, in his *De temporibus: sive de sex aetatibus hujus seculi liber* (A.D. 703) on Christian chronology.

[261] Writing in 1443 (sixty years after João I's rise to power in 1383, as is indicated at the end of the chapter), here Lopes makes an exception to his use of the Era of Caesar, which can partially be explained by the independent nature of this chapter in the narrative sequence.

generations, but some think that it will end when the world ends, which they say will last 6,000 years, of which there would have already passed, in this way, 5,297; thus there would remain 703 years until the end of the world.

As to the existence of another age in this present life, none have ventured to speak of it save some who have said that, just as God created the world in the space of seven days and on the seventh day rested, so the refreshment the souls of the blessed would have in Paradise would be the Seventh Age.[262] Yet such views are best rejected among the wise, for since Jesus Christ said in the Gospel that as far as the Last Day was concerned none knew, not even the angels of heaven, but only the Father,[263] it follows that such words hold little truth.

Yet with daring words as if in jest, by way of comparison, we make this the Seventh Age in which another new world and a new generation of people rose up. Our reason is that the sons of men of such low status as is unsuitable to relate were at this time made knights for their good service and work, immediately taking on new lineages and surnames. Others so took a fancy to long forgotten ancient titles of nobility that, through dignities, honours and offices of the kingdom granted by this great lord, first as Master and afterwards as King, they rose to such prominence that their descendants today are called 'Dom' and are held in great account. Thus, just as the Son of God summoned his Apostles, saying that he would make them fishers of men,[264] so many of those raised up by the Master fished so many men for themselves, thanks to their great and honourable estate, that some of them continuously had in their entourage 20 or 30 horsemen, and in the war that followed they were accompanied by 300 to 400 lances and some hereditary nobles.

Thus this age, which we say began with the deeds of the Master, and which we date in this chronicle with reference to the Era of Caesar, has now lasted for sixty years.[265] And it will last until the end of time, or as long as it pleases God, creator of them all.

---

[262] This is a reference to the doctrine of *refrigerium*, a happy state in which, according to the early Christian writer Tertullian, the souls of the blessed are refreshed while they await the Last Judgement and their entry into Heaven.

[263] Matthew 24. 36.

[264] Matthew 4. 19.

[265] A date referring to the Era of Caesar seems to be missing from this sentence.

Chapter 164

How the Master went to take Sintra and could not get there because there was too much rain

In so far as we were able, in these more recent times, we have set down the names of a number of places that declared for Portugal and also those of certain people who helped in its defence, not because of some spiritual benefit that might accrue to the dead from such remembrance, but to provide an opportunity for those who hear this to follow the good and honourable deeds through which those of their lineage won great and noteworthy fame. That is because there are no surer nor better lessons to be had regarding deeds of chivalry than for men to consider the works through which former people excelled or had some setback, whereas if men ignore them they will be nearly blind as to how to act in the future. Therefore, without prolonging this explanation even further, you should briefly know that, with certain nobles and citizens from among those whom we have named, plus another group of worthy people, the Master began his great military campaigns.

The first thing that he strove to do after the King of Castile raised the siege was to capture the places around the city [of Lisbon] that had declared for Castile. He held talks with a number of people from Sintra – where Count Enrique Manuel was stationed as Lord of the Marches – some 5 leagues from Lisbon, asking them to give him the castle of that place, a great fortress on a high craggy mountain with a town at its foot without any circuit of walls to defend it. On Monday, 24 October, which was the day arranged between them, a little later than the hour of vespers, the Master ordered those few horsemen that he had and other armed men and foot soldiers to sally forth from the city to a square nearby that is called Santa Bárbara, indicating that he wanted to muster the troops.

After they had all assembled, the Master took aside some nobles such as Count Gonçalo and Archbishop Lourenço and as many other troops whom it pleased him to take; the others returned to the city. The Master left this place with them, none knowing where they were going save those with whom he had spoken. The majority went on foot, owing to the lack of mounts, which was a result of the siege they had been placed under.

While they were on their way, not far from the city, light clouds surrounded by darkness formed in the sky, dampening the ground with a light drizzle. This grew heavier until the sky was so filled with a rainy blackness that the night showed its deepest gloom before its due time. Torrents of heavy rain began to pour down the mountains. Coursing down on to the roads, their speedy flow greatly impeded the troops who wished to keep to their route. In this way the tiny brooks, scarcely big enough to house a single frog, turned into such great streams that they put fear into those wanting to cross them. Each moment the harshness of such an intractable winter worsened, as in the sky it seemed that new kinds of rain were born to destroy the world once more with a deadly flood. Thus, with the rivers exceeding their normal bounds and submerging the familiar bridges, the men barely mustered enough courage to attempt the frightening task of crossing them.

Despite this, the Master kept to his route step by step, for no other course was suitable for those who came with him on foot. He hoped that soon the bad weather would cease, as it usually happens, and that he would finish what he had set out to do. At this point, the darkness having completely descended on everyone with an infernal obscurity, suddenly there burst forth the mighty roar of a great wind, mixed with fog and hail. The wind blew itself out, and the whole sky unleashed thunder and lightning beyond the bounds of normality, as if deliberately sent to obstruct the Master's journey.

Then the guide who was leading them lost all sense of the terrain, which he knew very well, and the troops began to lose touch with each other and did not know what to do; nor did they know where they were, being already some 4 leagues from the city, according to what the morning light later showed them. Some chanced to end up near some houses and got their owners to come out and show them which way they had to go; but none could say or show them anything that was of any use to them. Some collided with others, unable to see the way or where they were, and came to a standstill, shocked by such an extraordinary night.

What is the use of dwelling on this since it is not possible to describe it adequately in words? The blackness was of such density that not even a lightning flash allowed them a clear view that was of any help. Yet, just as with sailors to whom in the final despair in the face of a great storm there appear coronas and luminescence on the bulwarks and rigging of the ship, which are called corposant [Saint Elmo's Fire], thus on this awful night there appeared three lights on the tips of the lances of some who were near the Master. When he saw such a fell event, he spoke to those whom he found near him and declared that, since it did not please God to end the bad weather – rather, it became worse with each moment – they should not continue forward, but each one should try hard to turn back, if he knew how to locate the path, or go wherever he was best able.

It is important for you to know that those were the heaviest rains that men had ever seen or heard of. They lasted until around dawn, waning little by little as they had begun. The volume of water was so great that it could not be contained in the town gutters, along which it was customarily dispersed when it rained, and it became dammed up against the wall in such a quantity, that, coming out of the Gate of São Vicente, the water rose to half way up the postern and destroyed the nearest houses. It brought down the wall around the Monastery of São Domingos and flooded inside reaching a height of nearly nine feet;[266] it devastated the brothers' cells on the ground floor and a very noble library where it damaged many very fine books. The water flowed so violently through the church door that it brought down the wall of the porch from where the friars preached. The whole Rossio was a great sea, flooding many houses around it. The wine barrels floated in Rua das Esteiras and Rua Nova, a galley floated in the dockyard, while many other things happened that seem impossible to believe.

The Master arrived back the next day in the afternoon without the company that he had left with, and it was fascinating to hear each one telling of the things that had happened to them.

Chapter 165

How the Master went to Almada and took the town in accordance with the wishes of its inhabitants

Four days having passed after this, the Master ordered the payment of wages which were immediately paid for a month. Wishing to take Torres Vedras and other places we shall mention, he first of all sent João Fernandes Pacheco with men-at-arms, crossbowmen and foot soldiers to begin to besiege the town of Torres Vedras, which Juan Duque, Lord of the Marches, held for Castile. As soon as he got there, they came out to skirmish with him, but João Fernandes, and those accompanying him, by force of arms made them retreat behind the town's gates and corralled them inside against their will. In this way they were besieged until the Master arrived there later.

Well, it so happened that when the King of Castile decided to leave the siege of Lisbon, before he moved his camp, he summoned some of the honourable men of Almada and told them that he wanted to return to Castile in order to deal with certain matters pertaining to his interests. He promised them that, if they were good and loyal vassals, holding that town for him as he hoped they would, he would take care always to defend them and grant them many favours. However, as it could be the case that through the inducement of certain others their goodwill might change, he wanted them, as insurance

---

[266] In the original text the height of the flood was measured at 4.5 *côvados*. A *côvado* equates to just over 2 feet or 66 centimetres.

against such a possibility, to give him as hostages the children of the most honourable of the townsfolk, in order to send them, with the fleet, to his kingdom. If on his return he found that they were good and loyal servants, he would bring up their children diligently, and arrange marriages for them as well as grant them many favours. As they could do nothing else, they said that, since that was his gracious demand, then it pleased them to give him their children. Up to twenty of them, both boys and girls, were then handed over as hostages, all of them offspring and relatives of the most honourable men in the town. Some of them were so young that they were under four years of age. These children were all handed over to the admiral of the fleet.[267]

The fleet stayed for some days after the king raised the siege and left Lisbon, and then departed.[268] It reached Sesimbra where the men on board looted whatever they could seize. Returning again to the port of Lisbon, four galleys headed straight for Almada and the men went ashore very boldly thinking, as was reasonable, that the town was theirs. When the Almada townsfolk, who were then starting to harvest the grapes, saw the galleys come to shore at Cacilhas, which is very close by, they quickly rang the bells, and those who could get themselves ready immediately rushed over there in a group. The Castilians were already going through the outskirts of the town, trying to take away the grapes that they found. The Portuguese started to prevent them doing so, throwing themselves among them, wounding and killing until they reached the waterfront, in such a way that when the Castilians retreated back to the galleys, where many of them died, they were forced to cut the cables that held them to the shore. The masters of the galleys swore that because of this they would kill their children whom they had taken on board as hostages; thus they left without returning.

When the Master heard about this, such news pleased him a lot, and he praised the people of Almada as true Portuguese. He immediately held talks with them, which resulted in their inviting him to come and receive the town; they would hand it over and declare themselves for him, despite having surrendered their children as hostages, and knowing that the Castilians would kill them. The Master ordered a number of barges to be made ready, suitable for this purpose, and, no more than three days after the Castilian galleys had left Almada, the Master arrived there with Count Gonçalo and 200 lances.[269] The townsfolk all came out to receive him in a procession and thus they accompanied him into the town, which they joyfully handed over to him telling of

---

[267] Juan Fernández de Tovar, the son of the late admiral of the Castilian fleet, Fernán Sánchez de Tovar, killed by the plague at the siege of Lisbon. See Chapter 149 above.

[268] On 21 October. See Chapter 155 above.

[269] Presumably on 31 October.

the trials and tribulations which they had suffered because of declaring for him. The Master duly promised to grant them favours.

Chapter 166

How the Master left Almada and went to attack Alenquer

While the Master was in Almada as we have said, there arrived a message from certain people in Alenquer with whom he had been discussing matters, urging him to leave immediately to besiege it, if he thought this to be in his interest, and asking him to go before dawn if he could. That same evening immediately after supper, he embarked with those he had with him on board thirty-five vessels, both barges and cutters. The Archbishop [of Braga], Afonso Furtado and others went by land. Although the tide was coming in, and thus favourable for reaching Alenquer more quickly, since the wind was against them they took all night to arrive at a place called Piquete, between Vila Nova and Castanheira, about a league from Alenquer. There the Master disembarked with those he had brought with him and set off on foot fully armed, in the bright morning sunshine. When they got close to Alenquer, the townspeople saw them and, ringing the bells, came out immediately through the gate as far as the stockades.

When the Master arrived at a church called Santo Espírito, which is on a level field next to the river that runs around the town, he collected his men around him. They then went up a long paved street and found lodging at the Monastery of São Francisco. There the Master sent a message to Vasco Peres [the town governor] setting out all the good reasons why he thought he should bring himself to hand the town over; the latter's final answer after long exchanges was that he did not intend to do so.

The Master then sent to Lisbon for cannons and two siege engines, which were brought to him by barges up to where he had disembarked; then they were drawn by oxen to the town. When they arrived in the outskirts, where the oxen could go no further, men took ropes to drag them to where they were to be set up. As the shaft attached to one of the engines was very heavy, and they could not make much headway with it, no matter how hard they pulled, the Master then spoke out, 'My friends! Make an effort, in God's name, and pull hard. Remember your wives and households, and the children and lands to which you belong. Strive to cast these enemies of ours out of this place.' They renewed their efforts with these fine words in such a way that they put each of the engines in the place where it needed to be.

One morning, it happened that the Master and Count Gonçalo, along with a number of troops, went to see a house where the Master had ordered [his men] to begin digging a tunnel. This was intended to sap the tower next to the Gate of Santa Maria da Várzea, also known as the Carvalho Gate, making it collapse by burning the stays used to prop it up. They also went to see a siege engine he had ordered to be set up in a vegetable garden near the town. Some of the defenders sallied out in arms from the town gate and the Master's men, including Aires Gonçalves de Figueiredo, moved against them. The men from the town rushed to shelter inside a low stockade where they were well defended by those on top of the walls. As a valiant man-at-arms, Aires Gonçalves entered through the gate of the stockade to the consternation of those inside, and got close the town gate where, wishing to show his prowess, he struck the wall three or four times with his dagger.

In this respect you ought to know that Alfonso Enríquez, the brother of Count Pedro, was a man small in stature but good-looking. He was very much in love with Dona Beatriz de Castro, the widow of the Count of Mayorga,[270] who had stayed in Alenquer when the King of Castile left for his kingdom. One day, when these nobles were speaking in the Master's presence about the skills of good men-at-arms, Aires Gonçalves began to express the view that men who were small in body did not have the strength to be the equals of those who were taller. While some defended each side of the argument, Alfonso Enríquez said to Aires Gonçalves that, if it pleased him to be his companion in arms, he would always find him at his side in whatever fine deed he put his hand to. Aires Gonçalves said that it would please him a great deal, and they shook hands in token of such brotherhood. People said that Alfonso Enríquez did all this for his beloved Dona Beatriz, so enamoured was he.

Consequently, when Aires Gonçalves made his way in through the gate of the stockade, as we have said, Alfonso Enríquez went with him. One of the many stones thrown from above hit him so hard that he fell to the ground and rolled over several times. Not being able to endure any more stones, Aires Gonçalves drew back and returned.

Alfonso Enríquez was much blamed for this fall by his men who said that he wanted to get himself into dangers for which he was unfitted, especially with one such as Aires Gonçalves who was a man of such great physical size and strength as no other in that camp, and that their declared mutual parity was inappropriate, and other such comments. He answered by giving them to understand that he did not intend to give up the endeavour he had undertaken. News then very quickly reached the place where the Master was lodging,

---

[270] The count died of the plague in the siege of Lisbon, shortly after marrying Dona Beatriz. See Chapter 149 above.

about how the town was under powerful attack, although that was not the case. All who were there [with the Master] and in the outskirts of the town, armed themselves and made their way to the Soure Gate in order to fight on that side, which was a long way from where the Master was to be found. When they got there some said that such a combat was not sensible: on the one hand because the gate was very strong; and on the other hand because they were very few and the townspeople very many.

Doctor João das Regras, who had gone with this group, then answered with these words: 'My friends! That is the true fight, where one Portuguese does not fight with one Castilian but with three or four whenever necessary. Therefore, there is nothing else to do here but to fight with all goodwill even if the gate is strong and the enemy are many.'

They then came closer and set fire to the gate of the barbican but, because of the many stones thrown down from the towers atop the gate, as well as from the stockade, they were forced to withdraw without burning any part of it that could be of use, or inflicting on it any other damage. Even if it had burned, and they had opened it at will, it would not have benefited them because the town gate was extremely strong. At this point, the Master came from the other side, where they had been skirmishing; those there [attacking the gate] left off what they had started, and they all went back to their lodgings.

Chapter 167

Concerning the battle between those in the siege camp and those in the town, a battle in which Alfonso Enríquez and others were killed

On this day after their meal, the men from the town came out to dismantle and cut down a bridge of thick poles over which the assailants crossed the stockade ditch, and where they had previously tried to set the gates on fire. When those in the camp saw this, they sought to prevent them from cutting it down, and many troops went there to this purpose. Those from the town came out to the stockade to defend their men, and there was great uproar and fighting, to the extent that from skirmishing they began to battle in earnest. At this, Alfonso Enríquez the Younger, who was with the Master in the monastery, on hearing the great clamour, asked permission to put on the Master's armour as he was not at his lodgings. The Master said this pleased him, and Alfonso Enríquez armed himself with a coat of plates mounted on green silk cloth by which the Master was recognised whenever he wore it. Then he went to the gate of the stockade where they had started to fight and, arriving there, he went forward and struck the town gate with his lance to show his boldness. One of the many stones which hailed down from the towers above the gate struck him, and he fell dead to the ground. Those from the town saw him fall and recognising the arms he wore as those of the Master they thought it was he. They then set themselves to throw many more stones at him until he was completely covered.

When Aires Gonçalves who was present saw this, he took a pavise from the stockade to shield himself from the stones as best he could, seized Alfonso Enríquez by a small part of his leg that was visible and dragged him out of there by force, despite all the stones that were thrown at him. In this way Alfonso Enríquez died, carrying out brave deeds that did nobody any good, and at whose death the Master showed himself to be saddened because, according to what he led him to believe, Alfonso Enríquez had been very keen to serve him.

In this conflict João Afonso, the son of Afonso Esteves de Azambuja, sustained a crossbow bolt in the face from which he died the same day. Gil Afonso, a *criado* of the Master, and others [also] died or were wounded. It happened also that two crossbowmen, one from the town and one from the siege camp, took aim at each other, and their first shots found their mark and both were killed. This battle, which had started out as mere provocation but ended in a real fight, lasted until almost sunset.

Chapter 168

How the Master made a pact with Vasco Peres and raised the siege from Alenquer

After the Master had besieged Alenquer for some days, Count Pedro arrived, the brother of the aforesaid Alfonso Enríquez who had died there. He had stayed in Oporto with a hand injury when the fleet had left, as we have related.[271] He brought a few men with him, and the Master received him very well and made him feel welcome.

At this point the town began to lack water because a paved conduit that was under construction did not reach far enough up the hill to channel the water [from a nearby spring] for people to collect, and although it was wintertime it did not rain enough to be of any use. Aware of the mines that were being

---

[271] In Chapter 124 above.

dug and the great trebuchet they were setting up to launch stones at them, and aware also that the Master had sent to Lisbon for supplies, Vasco Peres understood that he intended to continue this siege.

Therefore Vasco Peres and his father-in-law, Gonçalo Tenreiro, sent a message informing the Master about a settlement by which they agreed to the following terms: Vasco Peres would expel the men-at-arms and crossbowmen from Castile who were present and who were to go to Santarém with all their possessions; he would declare for the Master and serve him in war and peace; and, if Queen Leonor who had given him that castle [to guard] should return to the kingdom under her own free will without the company of Castilians, in order to help defend the kingdom, he would hand it over to her so that he would not lose face.

They made this agreement on 10 December in the Monastery of São Francisco where the Master was staying; this took place at night by torchlight with many of those who were in Alenquer in attendance. It was laid down in the agreement that the Master would leave men-at-arms there to guard the town, those whom Vasco Peres wished to choose. Having done homage to the Master, Vasco Peres chose, to stay with him, Rui Cravo, Gonçalo Gonçalves Borges, Fernão Gonçalves da Ameixoeira and others who were his companions and friends. The Master left there and went to besiege Torres Vedras, having spent six weeks besieging Alenquer.

Chapter 169

How the Master left Alenquer and went to besiege Torres Vedras

Once this pact had been agreed and Alenquer was his, the Master left for Torres Vedras where João Fernandes Pacheco had already begun the siege. The Master had siege engines and cannons carried there so that they could fire upon the town. The man who held Torres Vedras for the King of Castile, Juan Duque, was a Castilian nobleman, well-accompanied with men-at-arms, foot soldiers and crossbowmen, quite enough to defend the place. The Master billeted his people in the area outside the walls where he could lodge them best; in the royal palace where Count Gonçalo and João Fernandes Pacheco were staying, a guard post was set up night and day, and another was placed on the other side facing the castle.

Torres Vedras has a fortress set on top of a beautiful hill which nature has created in such a regular shape that it was as if it had been contrived by human hand. The land within its boundary, close to the town and round about, comprises cornfields, vineyards and other crops, which at that time were stripped bare, owing to the war. The town's walls encircle the hill, on the highest part of which is the castle. So few people lived between the castle and the town that they are not worth mentioning. All the population lived outside the walls in an urban settlement with many fine houses in well-ordered streets at the foot of the hill.

The Master wanted very much to capture and keep this town, and Juan Duque was very keen to prevent him doing so. For this reason, there were several skirmishes between those outside and those inside about which it is not worth telling, except for the long preparations the Master made to take it. He ordered the digging of one huge mine not to mention other saps he also had dug; this was to come out in the square of the Church of Santa Maria which is inside the walls between the town and the castle.

This mine was wide and roomy so that three men-at-arms could comfortably walk along it abreast. It was started as secretly as possible in a very secluded tent well away from the town, to the extent that, not only did the townspeople not get wind of it at all, but also many in the camp knew nothing of what was being done there. The earth that was excavated every day was left in the tent and then at night cast out in such a place that the enemy would not realise what they were doing.

The Castilians had sentries on top of the church and, when they saw that the Master frequently went to that tent, which had not been his custom previously, they suspected what it was. In order to allay such suspicions, the Master stopped going there by day and went at night to see what was happening. This being so, all the attentiveness and suspicion of the Castilians would have been in vain, were it not for certain people who accompanied the Master but little loved his service. Through signs and other secret methods they enabled the Castilians to know all about what the Master was planning against them.

They not only revealed all the secrets that had been spoken of in council, but they also hindered whatever things the Master ordered to be performed for the destruction of the town. Thus in the engagement of the siege engines, which the Master said were to be aimed at the wall and the towers to destroy and demolish them, they told him to order that they be aimed at the foot of the town wall and that through there they would make a gateway so that they could enter to take the castle. The man who was in charge of firing with the engines spoke vehemently against such advice and, despite what he was told, he shot at [the top of] the town wall and at the tower of the keep. Under pressure from the said false counsellors, the Master had so much cause to complain against the man that he told him that if he did not shoot at the foot of the wall as they ordered him, he would have him thrown by the engine's sling into the castle. Seeing that the reward promised for his good service was one that he greatly feared, the man fled that night and went to Leiria.

Chapter 170

How the Master of the Order of Christ was captured and taken to Santarém

In this same season, in the month of November, when we said that the Master had gone to besiege Alenquer, the Master of the Order of Christ, Dom Lopo Dias de Sousa, departed from the town of Tomar. With him went Dom Álvaro Gonçalves Camelo, who called himself Prior of the Order of the Hospitallers, Rodrigo Álvares Pereira, who was the brother of Nuno Álvares, and others. He went to lay siege to Torres Novas,[272] taking around 100 lances, as well as foot soldiers and crossbowmen, and he brought along a small siege engine which he ordered to be used to fire on the town, battering it every so often but causing little harm.

Alfonso López de Tejada, who had been left as governor of the town, defended it as best he could. As there followed a period of days under siege, he began to run out of water and fish so that every day they ate meat and expected to suffer worse.[273]

Diego Gómez Sarmiento was in Santarém and became aware of the shortage of provisions in Torres Novas. He ordered a raid to be made in that direction in order to kill two birds with one stone: to take some victuals to the town, if it were possible to get them in through the postern gate, and to try as hard as he could to lift the siege. With this aim the raiders left Santarém at midnight with 200 horsemen, both men-at-arms and light horsemen. They travelled the 5 leagues that lay between the two towns, reaching Torres Novas as the sun rose.

When the Master of the Order of Christ, who knew nothing of this, suddenly saw them so close to him, he assembled all the men he had there and prepared them to fight. Seeing them to be so few, the Castilians also summoned up the courage to fight them. The master was defeated and taken prisoner, and with Álvaro Gonçalves Camelo and others was taken to Santarém. They thus lay there until the Battle [of Aljubarrota] was won, as you will hear later. While a prisoner he sent word to the Master, who was at Torres Vedras, to

---

[272] Torres Novas is about 11 miles (c. 18 km) south-west of Tomar.

[273] Truly pious medieval people were not supposed to eat meat every day; Wednesday, Friday and Saturday were meant to be fish days.

request the favour that Martim Gonçalves, the Commander of Almourol, would meanwhile administer the Order of Christ for him. The Master was pleased at this and thus ordered it by charter. He ordered good defences to be installed in all the towns belonging to the territory of the Order.

Chapter 171

How Nuno Álvares went to Elvas and expelled some of the people from the town

We described previously, where we spoke of the capture of Portel, how after Nuno Álvares had left it suitably secure he returned straight to Évora.[274] While the Master is besieging Torres Vedras and digging a mine in order to capture it, let us see what Nuno Álvares has been doing in the meantime, since everything took place at the same time.

According to one historian, while Nuno Álvares was in that town [Évora], a message came to him from the town called Elvas that some of the worthy men of the place wanted it to rebel and declare for the King of Castile. Nuno Álvares left for there, taking some of his men with him in order to restore calm to the town, depending on what he saw to be necessary. Others say that [his brother] Fernão Pereira had arrived in Évora a little earlier on his way to see his mother who was in Elvas, and that Nuno Álvares set out for there in order to marry him to a daughter of Gonçalo Martins, the former governor of the said town, and invest his brother as its governor.

Anyway, whatever the reason was, while going along the road with his men, Nuno Álvares saw his brother Fernão Pereira dressed in the coat of mail that had belonged to García Fernández and belted with his sword, things that he had hidden in Portel when García Fernández had to leave.[275] When Nuno Álvares saw him approaching thus attired and recognised whose things they were, he felt very angry. He then told Fernão Pereira that he had done a great wrong to have fallen short of his oath, saying he hoped it might please God that no great harm would come to him for breaking his sworn word in such a fashion. Fernão Pereira made excuses for himself, to which Nuno Álvares chose not to reply, and thus they continued their journey till reaching Elvas. They had been there for only a few days when, in the name of the Master, Nuno Álvares ordered that Gil Fernandes, Martim Rodrigues and other local

---

[274] See Chapter 158 above.
[275] As also told in Chapter 158.

notables were to leave the town and go to Torres Vedras which the Master was besieging, in order to serve him. This annoyed them very much, for they considered themselves to be true Portuguese and loyal servants of the Master, as their actions had well shown so far. However, they obeyed his order and left.

When they arrived at Torres Vedras the Master received them well, showing his great pleasure at their arrival, bidding them a warm welcome and giving other signs of a hospitable reception. Gil Fernandes, outspoken in his speech, said immediately in front of everyone, 'But we are not welcome at all, my lord, since we have done such great service for you, and yet you throw us out of Elvas as if we were traitors.' Then he and the others each stated what they understood to be their honourable due.

The Master apologised, answering that he had known nothing about it and that it was not done by his order or consent. Rather, he considered them to be true Portuguese and worthy servants, or even worthier servants than they told him they were. He would grant them many favours and rewards as they would well be able to see. With these and other kind words he calmed them down, and thus they stayed with him for a number of days.

Chapter 172

How Nuno Álvares went to capture Vila Viçosa, how his brother was killed and how he besieged the town but could not take it

It has been related so many times and has so often been heard that, when Nuno Álvares went to capture Vila Viçosa, which Vasco Porcalho had given to the Castilians, his brother Fernão Pereira died when entering the town, that no one doubts this at all. But, concerning why he went there in the way he did, the divergence among historians places on us a burdensome task.

Some say that Nuno Álvares knew that the commander[276] had organised the wedding and provided a household for one of his *criados* called Álvaro Machado, arranging a great feast and entertainment to take place on that day. Nuno Álvares thought that, while the bride and groom were in the church and most of the people with them, he could suddenly take the place by assault. It was because of this that he left for Vila Viçosa.

---

[276] Vasco Porcalho, Grand Commander of the Order of Avis, to whom Juan I of Castile had entrusted Vila Viçosa. See Chapter 155 above.

Others recount that certain worthy men of Vila Viçosa had sent word to Nuno Álvares that, if he went there, they would ensure that he could avail himself of a town gate by which he might enter. Being very happy with such an embassy, he immediately planned to put the idea into action. He left with his men at night, pretending that he was going somewhere else. While leaving by the town gate [of Elvas] the standard-bearer [accidentally] broke his banner-pole. Everyone present took it as a bad sign, telling Nuno Álvares that he should in no way leave and that he should decide against travelling to where he wanted to go. He did not heed anything they said, ordered the banner to be placed on another pole, and went on with the plan that he had begun. Having travelled the 4 leagues between one place and the other, he arrived near Vila Viçosa and lodged nearby in a place called Orelhal, noiselessly and with everyone keeping very quiet.

The following morning, Nuno Álvares decided to take the town, in accordance with the information that had been sent out to him. He sent ahead his brother Fernão Pereira and Álvaro Coitado, along with certain others, all of whom went off on horseback, armed and wearing bascinets as such a deed demanded. They swiftly reached Vila Viçosa and dismounted from their horses in order to charge their way in through the gate called the Tower, the strongest the town had, as described below.

This is a very wide tower, with a vault above the entrance to the gate. Nobody can arrive at the gate without passing under the whole vault, which has an opening halfway along, through which great blocks of stone can be passed to be thrown down on whomsoever they want to hit. As Fernão Pereira and the others were charging through that vaulted entrance in order to get to the town gate, a great block came down from above and hit Fernão Pereira, crushing his bascinet and his whole head, killing him outright. In the same way they also killed his squire Vicente Esteves, who was following him.

As for Álvaro Coitado, he arrived at the gate without delay or hindrance and while trying to enter was injured, taken prisoner and taken inside the town. They also brought in the body of Fernão Pereira, who was one of the most daring and handsome figures of a man in the entire realm, he at that time being twenty-four years old. Nuno Álvares arrived with his banner and his men and, when he found out that his brother was dead and Álvaro Coitado taken prisoner and wounded, he could not have been more grief-stricken. Unable to do anything else, as the gates were closed and such an entry very dangerous, he returned very sadly in the direction of Borba which was on the Master's side and about a league away.

It is important for you to know that another historian's tale of why Nuno Álvares left for Vila Viçosa at that time does not provide the same explanation. He says that Vasco Porcalho deceived Nuno Álvares by writing that letter in the name of three or four of the worthy men of the town, saying that, if he managed to arrive there with his men as best he could in order to take the town and however many were in it, they would give him entry. Believing such a thing to be true, Nuno Álvares made the plan that we have related and met with the aforementioned great misfortune and deception.

Certainly, such a story seems more reasonable than any of the others. For if those of the town had in great secret planned such a thing to the loss and harm of the commander and those who were in the town, would they not have been killed by those seeking vengeance against any who had committed such a misdeed? We do not find an account that says that anybody received punishment for this; rather, they were all agreed and very ready when Fernão Pereira arrived, which seems to imply that they knew all about it. Others state, regarding this episode, that the guards had called to arms once they had seen them, and this is why they were all there ready.

The following day, Nuno Álvares, deeply aggrieved at receiving such a loss, sent word to Vasco Porcalho, requesting him to send him the body of his brother; it was duly brought to him. He ordered it to be taken for burial in the Monastery of São Francisco in Estremoz, which is a league away, feeling strongly and believing that all that misfortune which had befallen his brother was because of the coat of mail and sword of García Fernández, which he had taken against his oath. However, in spite of this, as is the way of great lords, he did not show so much grief on the outside as he kept in his heart, as much because he had not carried out what he had started, as because of the death of his brother. As a man of great courage, he consoled himself and his men, summoning from the surrounding places more companies of men besides those he had with him.

Nuno Álvares sent to Elvas for a siege engine and went off to besiege Vila Viçosa, staying there for some time and launching stones at it day and night with that engine. He skirmished and fought but could not harm it as much as he wanted, for in the town there were valiant Castilian and Portuguese troops who defended it well, with a great abundance of provisions. To prevent any deaths among the valiant men who were with him, whom he loved greatly, and also to assist in other things that had sprung up in that region, to which it would be suitable to turn in order to serve the Master, he struck camp and turned back towards Estremoz.

Furthermore, according to what is said, his mind was little disposed to continuing sieges or remaining in a siege camp because of the great danger which sometimes ensues. He declared that he would rather be met in open battle and encounter any chance incident; whoever conquered in the field would easily capture the besieged townships.

Chapter 173

How the men of Oporto took the castle of
Vila Nova de Gaia and destroyed it

Leaving aside certain things that happened in Oporto at this time, we shall briefly recount just one matter, in order to keep on track. This concerned Aires Gonçalves de Figueiredo, who had been entrusted with the castle of Vila Nova de Gaia by Count Gonçalo [Teles]. Aires Gonçalves's wife was in the castle with some squires and foot soldiers as guards. These guards were so unneighbourly in the surrounding villages, stealing and seizing by force anything that they were minded to take, that everybody felt most maltreated. The people of Oporto felt very strongly about this and desired to avenge it as best they could.

One day it happened that the wife of Aires Gonçalves sent word to a local village, demanding that the villagers should supply certain things for herself and for those she had with her. They refused to do it, saying that even if that castle had declared for Castile they could not have received worse neighbourliness than they had up to that point. The villagers did not want to allow the men to take what they wanted. When this message reached the wife of Aires Gonçalves, with little sense and much complaining she went to the said village, taking with her as many men as she had in order to take vengeance on the villagers and bring away everything she might wish.

When the city dwellers found out about this, they joined together immediately and went there [to Vila Nova de Gaia], taking and stealing from the castle whatever they found there. They brought down the wall and towers, leaving it all in ruins.

When Aires Gonçalves found out about this in Torres Vedras, where he was, he became very angry, saying to Count Gonçalo whom he accompanied, because he had been mentor of the latter and steward of his household when he was a boy: 'Take notice, my lord! Just see what kind of lord we serve, and from whom we expect benefits and favours! A man goes off in his service and spends bad nights and arduous days serving him, endangering his own life, and he has us honoured in the way you see! It's clear that the people of Oporto didn't dare do such a thing unless he told them to. If they've declared for him, we have too, so why therefore would they decide to dishonour me in such a way, unless, as it seems, he suspects us of some evil intent and ordered us to be "honoured" like this?'

The count did not show as much anger as Aires Gonçalves; but under pressure from him he went to the Master and told him about their reason for complaint, and other reasons besides, and their conclusion that the Master did not have entire confidence in them and that he had, therefore, ordered the said attack to be carried out. The Master apologised as much as he could, saying that he had known nothing about it and that it had been done neither at his command nor with his consent. The men of Oporto had declared for him and they had served him, and would continue to serve him well in all they could. He did not know why they had brought themselves to do it. However, he suspected that they did it in his service, as those of Lisbon had done when they had demolished the city castle. Since it had been done, he went on, it could not be undone, but he would give back to the count his own castle and another, better castle, and for his good service he would grant him many favours as was only right. Yet, for all his fine explanations, the Master could not placate them, and thus they left him, still feeling much aggrieved.

This is where we set aside their complaints for now; let us turn to see the mine that was being dug and what stage it had got to while these things had been occurring.

Chapter 174

How the Master attacked the town [of Torres Vedras] with the mines that he had dug yet could not take it

They had dug the mine that we told you about over the space of many days, until it had reached beyond the wall between the town and the castle. In order to be able to estimate where they were, they brought up two very stout augers suitable for this task and with one of them they made a hole through to the surface, so that they could see for certain where they had got to; with the other one they filled the hole in with mud so it would not be discovered. Thus they broke in with the mine so close to the church that the bell tower was already in sight.

With great pleasure the Master thought that he would seize the town the next day and had those he judged to be suitable for such work made ready, such as João Gomes da Silva and others, telling them they were to emerge in the churchyard and thus make their way into the town where their enemies were. Juan Duque had already been warned where the mine was and where it would come out by the Master's aforementioned disloyal counsellors. Knowing everything about what was being done, very early in the morning the Castilians raised a tent over the spot where the Portuguese planned to gain entry, starting to block it in such a way that the two sides started to come to blows. Each side in order to get its way was put to great toil, so that they grievously wounded one another.

Those above prevented any exit with boards and planks, and those inside set fire to them; in turn water was thrown down to put out the fire. The Master then ordered a cannon to be set up in the mine, but although missiles did hit the wooden boards, splitting them and inflicting damage, it was not enough for the Master's men to achieve the objective with which they had started out. After much labour and injuries on both sides, they stopped fighting.

Seeing that, however much work had been done during all that time, it had all been in vain, the Master was most distressed. He ordered a mine to be dug under the wall of the town. They worked on it for a few days and propped up a stretch of the wall and its towers on timber stakes; one day he ordered his soldiers to set fire to the mine. When it was on fire, the wall and the towers fell to the ground. Those inside the town, who were already prepared and knew what to do, had got some barrels and vats and had built up such barricades at that spot, that when the Master thought that a great gateway would be opened up there, through which they could enter at will, they could not. The reason was that the place sloped upwards and ended up stronger than it had been before, so that nobody could attack it or inflict any damage on it.

When the Master saw this, he ordered his people out, not suspecting that such deception and disservice could have come from anyone in his company; instead he thought that it was the good organisation of those inside the town, who in such deeds had shown themselves to be very sharp.

At this stage those in the town began to run out of water in the two cisterns they had inside the walls; they were also short of meat. The Master knew nothing of this when, one day, Juan Duque sent him a shameful present in two chamber pots: it consisted of an ass's penis cooked with two oranges and bearing a ditty, the gist of which was that he was sending him the daintiest meat he had. But he asked him as a favour to send him some fresh meat which he had much desired for days; for it was not his fault that he was defending the place, because his lord had left him in charge of it.

The Master started to laugh and ordered meat to be sent to him, as much as would be plenty for one day; as to the part where Juan Duque refused to accept any blame, he answered that he did not blame him but thought well of him because that was how a good nobleman was bound to behave. He told him to strive to defend himself because he would do all he could to capture the town. Juan Duque, seeing how the provisions were used up, decided he should go to speak to the Master. However, during their discussion, they put forward proposals on which they could not agree and parted without reaching an agreement.

The Master was very sorry that in so few days there had been so many setbacks befalling those on his side. There had been the rout and capture of the Master of the Order of Christ, the death of Fernão Pereira and Nuno Álvares's siege which had not gone well. There were also the two armed Castilian galleys that had arrived at Lisbon in the middle of the night, nobody knowing they were coming. They had captured a [Portuguese] *nao* from Oporto loaded with merchandise as well as two galleys lying unarmed in the water, and had burned them in the middle of the river, and the *nao* likewise, because the city folk had not given them time to make away with it.

In spite of these things that secretly gave the Master much to distress him, his strength of heart covered it all up, not giving anything away, but rather displaying a joyous and cheerful countenance to everyone. When they spoke of this, he said, among other such statements, that it was customary for wars to cause both grief and pleasure to those who were much involved in them, giving his people to understand that none of those things disturbed him and that he had the heart to match any great travail.

Chapter 175

Concerning those people who were not faithful vassals of the Master

We are compelled when dealing with certain matters to make our tale rather long, since we are accustomed to recite the opinions and parts of the text of certain authors who, before us, have already written about these things. We do not do this out of any pleasure at being long-winded, which great lords find boring, but because not finding such explanations in this volume would be counted as imperfection. Moreover, whoever desires to read many works of history, especially authentic and authoritative ones, will find that their writers have praised [certain] great lords and their good usages and have described the character of others as ugly and their deeds as equally wretched. Saint Augustine, whose work and authority are beyond criticism, has written like this in the book entitled *The City of God*. In this part of our work, following his lead, we are forced to censure some people, speaking against them in certain sections, especially as the tale of their excesses had already been broadcast by others before us in such accounts. However, their stained reputations, according to written law and evangelical doctrine, have not blemished their lineage when their descendants chose not to follow in their perverse footsteps.

We said that when the Master had besieged that town which he desired so much to take, there were faithless vassals whom he had brought with him who, by written messages and various other means, had informed the besieged defenders about his every undertaking, causing it to be in vain. Therefore, it is only reasonable for you to expect us to tell you who they were, what status they had, whether the Master knew anything about it and when and how he knew. Before we say what made them do this and make known what others first divulged, let us see immediately which men they were. Searching through all the books that make mention of these events, the accounts refer to four men: Count Pedro,[277] Dom Pedro de Castro, Juan Alfonso de Baeza and García González de Valdés.

You have already heard of Count Pedro when we spoke of what happened to Queen Leonor when she went to Coimbra; how this Count of Trastámara, a first cousin of the King of Castile, had wanted to cast his lot with her while there, and how he had fled and gone to Oporto, and thence in the Portuguese galleys to Galicia. He had aroused severe suspicion at the Battle of Betanzos and had been wounded by his brother in the tourney at Oporto.[278] Afterwards he had come to the Master, who at that time was besieging Alenquer as we have said, and he was with him in that siege.

You already know that Dom Pedro de Castro was the son of the Count of Arraiolos, Don Álvaro Pérez de Castro, and that during the siege of Lisbon he was accused of wanting to allow the Castilians to enter through the Santo Agostinho Gate, which was his responsibility to guard.[279] He was imprisoned and afterwards pardoned, and here he was in the company of the Master.

Juan Alfonso de Baeza was one of the Castilian noblemen who, along with others in the time of King Fernando, had escaped to Portugal after the death of King Pedro of Castile.[280] When Cardinal Guy de Boulogne had arranged peace between the monarchs of both kingdoms, one of the people whom King Enrique named to be sent out of Portugal, among the twenty-eight he then listed in writing, was this Juan Alfonso de Baeza. When the English came after the Earl of Cambridge had arrived in Lisbon, some of those who had been living in England with him returned [to Portugal], among whom was this Juan Alfonso de Baeza. He stayed in the kingdom and accompanied the Master.[281]

---

[277] Pedro Enríquez of Castile, Count of Trastámara, second son of Don Fadrique Alfonso of Trastámara, and grandson of Alfonso XI of Castile. He was also the brother-in-law of Dom Pedro de Castro.

[278] See Chapters 81, 82 and 124 above.

[279] In Chapter 138 above.

[280] See *CKF*, Chapter 25.

[281] See *CKF*, Chapters 82 and 128.

García González de Valdés was an Asturian squire, tall and strongly built, who had fled to the Master when the King of Castile besieged Lisbon, offering him his service and remaining as his vassal.

Although the crossing over of such men in the hard times of war from one side to the other was something that prudent lords should very much fear, because everyone finds it easy to believe whatever is most agreeable to them, especially the service of worthy nobles at a time when they are needed, the Master was not suspicious about this man, nor did he recall the tainted past of the others.

Well, what brought them to this [betrayal at Torres Vedras], as the history books tell us, was that the King of Castile had sent letters in great secret via a Jew to his cousin Count Pedro, reminding him that he should be fully aware of their close family ties, yet the worst enemy the king had in the world was the Master of Avis, whom Count Pedro accompanied; moreover, he added, he ought to help him against this enemy because of the close family relationship between them. If Count Pedro wanted to do the best he could in this respect, he should talk to some of those who loved the king's service and would kill the Master without endangering themselves, which was an easy task to carry out; in this he would render the king great service and pleasure, greater than anything else that was possible. For this he would be forgiven any errors of the past, and the king would increase his estate in such a way that in the kingdom he would have no equal. Those who helped him in such a deed would be given great preferment and the king would grant them many favours. Seeing the words of the letter, and what the Jew said, who knew how to present it to him, the count was delighted and more than willing. He spoke about this with the three whom we named and with some of his squires, all of whom, on hearing the great promises, each one being intent on the betterment of his own standing, nurtured this abominable secret in their hearts, determining to kill the Master as soon as they could.

Lord Jean, the Duke of Brittany and father of the present duke,[282] speaking on one occasion with his nobles about the disloyalty that vassals commit against their liege lords, asked each of them to express his own thoughts on this issue. Some said that they would rather be cuckolded than descend to treason; others said they would rather die than commit such an evil act; others [that they] would rather be arrested and imprisoned forever. Thus each one named the evil that they would prefer to undergo, rather than commit such a grave crime. Noting every man's opinions, the duke smiled and said, 'You don't know what you're saying, because each one of you would commit a

---

[282] This is a reference to Jean V (sometimes known as VI), the Wise, and to his son François, who succeeded to the dukedom in 1442.

betrayal, and I too if the occasion arose, for a more trivial reason than any of those.' They asked why this would be so, and he answered them, saying, 'to avenge a little bit of spite, or out of greed for greater honour.'

Certainly, those we describe here as having plotted this did it for this second reason. This view is supported by Christophorus, the doctor in canon law, when speaking of the deeds of the Master in a treatise that he composed, in the chapter that starts with the words 'However, after ...', where he says 'They were thus promised many benefits, because of it.'[283]

Chapter 176

In what way they had arranged to kill the Master and how their secrets were revealed

Despite what is said here, and which long experience teaches, some however are of the opinion that both the things we mentioned, namely desire for honour and vengeance arising from hatred, were involved in this plot. They say that Dom Pedro [de Castro] consented to this conspiracy, when he was told about it, more out of vengeance for a grudge that he had against the Master, who had had him imprisoned, than because he was greedy to increase his honour, as some write. Yet we cannot speak of what is concealed, but only of the kindnesses, favours, honour and pleasant treatment that each one of them, according to his station, received from the Master. For, although the Master imprisoned Dom Pedro for that error which the chronicles recount, he straightaway in a very few days ordered him to be released. Later, while besieging Alenquer, a little more than two months out of his prison, the Master confirmed him in the permanent grant of all the towns, villages, and castles that the kings had given to his father Count Álvaro Pérez, both by inheritance and by grant and by whatever other means, except for the property of Diogo Lopes Pacheco which King Fernando had given to the said count his father. Everything else the Master granted to him was firmly fixed in writing, as Dom Pedro had wanted it to be done. Therefore, it is hard to believe that it was through hate that he acted against a lord, from whom he had received such remarkable favours.

---

[283] This is a lost Latin source for Lopes's chronicles. The opening words of the chapter are *Postquam autem* in the original, and the full quotation is *Eis propter hoc, multa bona promitentis* (probably meant to be *promittentes*).

Well, whatever were the reasons, the plan took this form: each one of them if he could kill the Master without endangering himself would do it, but Juan Alfonso and García González were specially charged with this task and were to dash immediately and quickly into the town when the deed was done. Since Juan Duque already knew about this, he would always be keeping watch, so that when he saw tumult break out across the camp he might immediately open the gates and go out with his men to rescue those who were running away. The death was to have been in one of two ways.

Juan Alfonso de Baeza was a great horseman and very agile, especially when riding with short stirrups.[284] When the Master went out riding with some of his men, Juan Alfonso always went well ahead with a lance in his hand to accompany him like the others; and he would spur on the horse, coming at a gallop brandishing the lance. As he drew near the Master he would pretend that he was going to throw the lance at him but would veer away at the last moment, and then laughing he would immediately return, making everybody think that he did it for fun, so that neither the Master nor any of the others might have any suspicions about him. This he intended to do as many times as necessary to lower the Master's defences until the moment came when he might throw the lance and thus kill him.

Here one should know, and it is not without reason that it is noted, that the Master had a *criado* and comptroller of his household who was called Fernando Álvares, the commander of Vila Viçosa, a wise and very prudent man, who very much loved the Master's service. He always rode out with the Master in such a way that near or far he never left his side. Seeing that Juan Alfonso often played that trick and especially that he never did it with anyone else than the Master, Fernando Álvares disapproved of it very much, without, however, having any possible suspicion. One day, when Juan Alfonso was galloping fast with the lance in his hand to act out his customary show, Fernando Álvares placed himself in front and diverted him with his lance, saying, 'Away, away with your lance! Are you not ashamed of doing this so many times, coming in such a way against the Master, my lord? Be aware that you do not come across well; rather, it looks wrong to those who see you do it.'

Juan Alfonso said that he was doing it as a joke and for fun and not to displease the Master. 'Go and play this joke on someone else, but not on the liege lord with whom you live', said Fernando Álvares. After this they began

---

[284] Riding 'à geneta' or ('à gineta) with short stirrups and the legs tucked up was a style learned from the Arabs. This method, and the other principal style of riding with straight legs, and the appropriate saddles for each, are described by King Duarte of Portugal in his manual of horsemanship, *O Livro da Ensinança de Bem Cavalgar Toda Sela*, which dates from the 1430s.

to argue and the Master told them to be quiet and to think no more about it. After that, Juan Alfonso no longer dared to play that pretend joke again. He lost hope that by such means he could bring off what he had planned.

The other way was that when the Master went to inspect the siege engines, as was his custom, while he was sparsely accompanied and with few troops around him, they would get an opportunity to fulfil their ill intent. Thus they went on biding their time until they could commit and carry out such a malicious act. While all this was going on, they gave the Master much bad advice with a serene countenance and false reasoning, while making known to Juan Duque both in writing and through signals whatever the Master ordered to be carried out against the town. It was done in this way, as was afterwards discovered: they split crossbow bolts and put in them quills of paper or parchment, writing on them whatever they wanted him to know. Moreover, they let him know that, wherever any of their men positioned themselves and started insulting the townsfolk and waving their hands, that was where the mine ran. This they did in fact, for they called the townspeople cuckolded bastards and vassals of the Devil, while making certain signals to them by which they warned them of everything. Indeed, by this means and by the bad advice that they gave the Master in everything that he did against the town, he gained little from his labours.

Chapter 177

How the treasonable plot against the Master was discovered, and how García González was burned [at the stake]

We have already explained how Count Gonçalo and Aires Gonçalves de Figueiredo came to complain a great deal to the Master because of how the castle of Gaia was taken, as you have heard, and the discussions that they had about it. From then until this time they both always showed in their manner that they were unhappy with the Master, so much so that their withdrawal and frequent conversations, in secret and apart from the others, caused people to assume that they wanted to plot something against the Master. Indeed, for this reason there were some who said to the Master: 'My lord, you should know that there is a rumour that Count Gonçalo and Aires Gonçalves de Figueiredo are not loyally working in your service and want to go over to Coimbra with their men in order to oppose you in the things that you decide to do. Order a warning to be issued about this so that you are not obstructed by them, before they dare start something.' The Master heard what they told him and worried about what could be happening, but kept quiet without revealing that he knew anything. At this point it started to be claimed that these captains, Diego Gómez Sarmiento, who was in Santarém with 400 lances, Vasco Peres in Alenquer with 150, João Gonçalves in Óbidos with 100, and Count Enrique [Manuel] in Sintra with another 100 lances, were all in league with Juan Duque and with the very Count Pedro [de Trastámara] whom we have mentioned, so that one night they would suddenly all fall on the Master and, whether killed or imprisoned and defeated, he would not be able to escape.

That doctor already alluded to in the chapter that we cited[285] says that the agreement held between them was of this kind: that if they were not able to kill the Master as they had planned, they would one day all go over to the town. Six days after they had cast their lot together in the town, those captains would arrive and to help them Juan Duque would come out with his men in order that they might all accomplish what they had planned.

Well, when the Master heard what was being said, on 8 January 1385, knowing nothing about what had been planned against him and thinking only to be prepared and truly secure, he decided to hold a council on that day and ordered, moreover, that all the captains should appear before him with their men so that he might see how many men-at-arms he had with him. It happened that among the first who came to the council were Count Gonçalo and his son Dom Martinho and with him Aires Gonçalves. As soon as they were all inside the Master's tent he ordered all three to be taken prisoner, even though the son was a young boy, and handed them over to Vasco Martins de Melo.

When Count Pedro, Juan Alfonso de Baeza and Dom Pedro de Castro, who were out in the countryside talking about horses, heard that Count Gonçalo and Aires Gonçalves had been taken prisoner, they were convinced that their secret and agreement had been discovered. In their great fear, without other counsel or delaying any longer, they began to flee in haste. Count Pedro rushed inside the town while Juan Alfonso de Baeza and Dom Pedro de Castro fled towards Santarém. Wanting to run into the town with Count Pedro, García González was seized by the Master's men, thanks to the guard commanded by Antão Vasques.

There was a great tumult in the camp, as the flight of such men was so sudden and unexpected. The Master was shocked and did not know what to say. He greatly rejoiced when they told him that García González had been captured, as he could find out the truth from him. When he was brought before the Master, the latter asked him about his reason for running away. Thinking to save his life, García González gave excuses that were not well thought

---

[285] Christophorus, see Chapter 175 above.

out and which nobody wanted to believe. The Master then ordered him to be flogged so that he confessed in detail all that you have heard, named the guilty men, and how, when the King of Castile had besieged Lisbon, he had at his order crossed over to the Master in order to kill him together with the others.

When the Master recognised this great evil, he gave thanks to God who through His great mercy had wanted to protect him from so much danger, as he had lived so unguarded among them. On the other hand he was filled with rage against García González, out of unusual and justified anger. He did not want to order him to die a simple and honest death but a cruel death by fire that caused real suffering. So he ordered him to be burnt at the stake. If somebody at this point writes that the Master was absolutely sure that these people plotted his death and never revealed to them that he knew anything about it, waiting to find out the manner in which they had intended to do it, you should not believe any such thing. For whoever could not tolerate a slight suspicion, like the one the Master felt about Count Gonçalo, holding him prisoner for so long, as you will hear later on, would certainly find it very hard to endure learning about it in theory and then wait for it to be put into practice.

Therefore, on the day when they were to take García González to be delivered to the flames, the Master ordered him to be brought before his tent. There he ordered him to confess again, in everyone's presence, what he had said in private under torture. García González begged the boon of not being obliged to repeat what he had already confessed. Nevertheless, the Master ordered that he should say it. He answered that it was more painful than the death to which he had been condemned.

He then began to recount at length the notable crime of which he and those who had fled and other people were guilty. His confession ended, they took him to the fire that was already prepared. They tied him to a stake, and, as he burned, his life was brought to an evil end.

Chapter 178

How the Master distributed the property of those who were guilty [of acting] against him

After that well-deserved justice had been meted out to García González, the people could not speak of anything else other than the treason that he, along with others, had plotted against the Master. They made various comments on it, gave examples and, talking angrily among themselves, they criticised the Master as follows: 'So let him get on with it if that is the way he wants it! What Dom Pedro did in the siege of Lisbon was not enough for him, when he wanted to give the city to the King of Castile so that the kingdom and all of us would be lost. He had him taken prisoner and then released him again so that he could afterwards deliver death to the Master as a reward for his release! He did not immediately order him to be killed or to be put in a prison from which he would never come out, in order to remove this threat from the kingdom, but released him after a few days as if it were a trivial matter that had caused him little hindrance. So now they can truly say the same as the old proverb, that whoever saves his enemy should die at his hands. The Master thinks that forgiving wicked men is a good thing to do; yet they carry out ever more evil deeds and play this game against him as you can all see.'

They told so many more of these proverbs and stories and in so many ways that they could not get tired of it.

Others said that the Master had done well, ordering such men to be pursued, caught and submitted to the justice they deserved. Yet this had availed him nothing because they had the best and swiftest horses that there were in the whole army, with the result that no one had ever been able to catch up with them.

Indeed, the Master, publicly and in everyone's presence, told of the great treason and evil against him, according to what the dead man had confessed, saying that now he was aware of it all and understood why Juan Alfonso used to brandish his lance, why each one of them had spoken in so many ways of how devoted they were to his service, and how all of them had been based on disservice and harm towards him. He recounted what had transpired with each one of them during the siege of Torres Vedras, and in other matters, and how, in consequence, it had not been taken and he had wasted so much effort on it in vain.

Yet at this there was no shortage of those who answered with many arguments, blaming the Master for the pardon that he had given Dom Pedro, saying that whoever placed his life and honour in the hands of someone who on some occasion had set out to do him wrong took a great risk. Moreover, they said that trusting any Castilian was very damaging to him, especially such a one as Count Pedro, who was first cousin to the King of Castile, and about whom the Master should have understood that he would not be loyal to his service.

The Master answered everybody and concluded by saying: 'I am not the first to be deceived by false vassals, nor will I be the last. But I had great trust in all their counsel, as they were men of such authority and also because they claimed with great earnestness to be my devoted servants. So much so that at times they made me say harsh words to men who desired to serve me loyally, words such as I uttered to the siege engine master, who fled from here through fear of me, and to many others without cause.'[286]

When Juan Duque saw how they had burned García González, feeling great bitterness about it, he ordered six or seven Portuguese labourers whom he had imprisoned, to be brought out and to have their hands cut off and their noses slit; then all the hands were put around the neck of one of them. He sent them thus to the Master who, when he saw such disproportionate cruelty, was about to order the Castilian prisoners whom he held to be thrown into the town on the trebuchet. He then chose mercy over zeal for vengeance, took pity on them and ordered that it should not be done.

At this point Nuno Álvares arrived, whom the Master had summoned from where he was, in Évora, so that he could talk with him. He brought with him some sixty mules bearing coats of mail and vambraces. Hearing in Lisbon how the captains of the places that we spoke of were banding together to attack the Master one night, he borrowed enough arms for those accompanying him and hurried to Torres Vedras.

The Master learned of his approach and was very pleased with him, going out to welcome him, and ordering him to be well lodged. For three days after the flight of those whom we mentioned, the Master waited to do battle with the troops who it was said were due to attack him. Neither then nor afterwards did anybody come who might do him harm.

The Master ordered Count Gonçalo and Aires Gonçalves to be taken to the castle of Tomar and handed over to its governor. Afterwards they were taken to Évora.

The Master then gave to Vasco Martins de Melo all the lands and property that the Countess [María], the widow of Count Álvaro Pérez, their son Dom Pedro de Castro and their son-in-law Count Pedro held in whatever part of the kingdom (for Count Pedro was married to Dona Isabel de Castro, the daughter of Count Álvaro Pérez and this Countess María), both fortified places as well as open land, except the lands and townships of the Count of Viana and those that had been given as part of his county to the aforementioned Count Álvaro Pérez. He commanded the following explanation to be put on the charter granting the favour: 'For the said Count Pedro plotted to deliver us to death and treason, and the said countess consented to it.' This Countess María went to Castile with Countess Beatriz, who was the wife of the Count of Barcelos Dom João Afonso Telo, the brother of Queen Leonor, when Countess

---

[286] See the end of Chapter 169 above.

Beatriz left the kingdom.[287] The Master then gave their property to Afonso Gomes da Silva.

Moreover, the Master gave to Lopo Dias de Azevedo all the lands and property that had belonged to Juan Alfonso de Baeza, both those that he had granted to him as well as any others that he held. He ordered the following words to be written on the charter: 'For the said Juan Alfonso, while living with us and receiving many favours from us, being an evil and disloyal man, plotted to deliver us to death and treason and fled to Castile.' He not only gave away his property but also that of his concubine Maria Anes Leitoa, who lived in Lisbon, if it were found that she had fled with him or had conspired in that evil, and the same applied to others who were his *criados*.

It is important for you to know that at this time, while the King of Castile was in Seville arming *naos* and galleys in order to send them to Lisbon and bringing together many people to invade Portugal, the message reached him about the rout of the Master [of the Order] of Christ, his imprisonment and that of the Prior [of the Order of Hospitallers], and such news pleased him very much. When they told him what had happened to these nobles whom we named and how they were already on his side he was also very happy, thinking that his plans were working out well. If these things very much pleased the king, his mother-in-law Queen Leonor was equally pleased about both the imprisonment of her brother Count Gonçalo and the rout of her nephew the Master of [the Order of] Christ. In the case of her brother, it was because he had not wanted to do her will when she went to Coimbra with her son-in-law the king. As for the imprisonment of her nephew, it was because he had not rescued her on the journey when she had been taken to Castile as a prisoner, as she had told him to do in a letter, and which he had been well able to do. Speaking at that moment of the deeds of the Master of Avis, she said, 'Master, Master! How greatly you are betrayed and do not know it!' Those present asked her why, and she then answered: 'because of all the teeth there are in his mouth, all but one are loose'. This one, she said, was Nuno Álvares.

[287] The grammar of the sentence makes it possible that María and Beatriz might have left the kingdom with Queen Leonor, but this is most unlikely, given that the queen was taken to Castile as a prisoner.

Chapter 179

How Vasco Peres again declared for the King of Castile

We have recounted how the Master, while besieging Alenquer, negotiated with Vasco Peres de Camões that he would give him the town, subject to certain conditions on which they agreed, Vasco Peres and his father-in-law Gonçalo Tenreiro receiving cash from the Master.[288] Having thus declared for Portugal, Vasco Peres learned how García González had died at the stake and how that malicious conspiracy of theirs had been discovered, which he and the others had kept secret among themselves. Vasco Peres sent his father-in-law Gonçalo Tenreiro to the Master with a message about certain things, and when he returned from Torres Vedras it seems that Vasco Peres was not happy with the answer that he brought; or perhaps he had in mind to do what he did and sought thereby an opportunity to do it with less blame attaching to him.

Vasco Peres then ordered all the notables in the town to be summoned, both those of highest status as well as those of other ranks, giving them to understand that he wanted to take counsel with them. Moreover, he did it to find out what they intended to do. Consequently, in the presence of them all, he proposed the following: 'My friends and lords, in view of the things that you see have happened, I would like to know from you what your wishes are or what you want us to do. Does it please you that we take the side of the King of Castile, or should we maintain our support for the Master? This is what I think: I see that the best captains that he brought with him have left the Master: such as Count Pedro, Dom Pedro de Castro, Juan Alfonso de Baeza, Count Gonçalo, whom he ordered to be imprisoned, and Aires Gonçalves as well. Thus, with him no longer remain men who are of any account or value, the fact being that without [such] men he is not able to defend himself from his enemies and adversaries. Moreover, all these towns around and about are for the King of Castile, of whom I have reliable news that he will be here in a very few days with all his might in order to take possession of this kingdom, which he says is his by right. So be advised of these things and see what you think would be best for us to do. Give me your answer soon, or whenever it pleases you to be agreed thereupon.'

As they understood from such words exactly what he wanted to do, they said that he should do as he thought best for the benefit of their lives and possessions; for they were ready to do whatever he commanded and thought to be beneficial.

---

[288] In Chapter 168 above.

He then answered, saying, 'Friends, let me tell you that I have already given much thought to this. For the safety of us all, I think that it is best for us to take the side of the King of Castile.' Having discussed the matter they got up, and he went into the castle and ordered a banner [of Castile] to be raised on the tower of the keep. He told those who remained there on the side of the Master that, if they wanted to stay with him, Vasco Peres, and declare for the King of Castile his liege lord, he would grant them many favours, and, if they did not want to stay, they should quit the town and go immediately.

After that, there remained with him his cousin Aires Peres de Camões and Sir Lello Francês,[289] a *criado* of Count Álvaro Pérez. But Rui Cravo, Fernão Gonçalves da Ameixoeira and others left to go to the Master, who was at Torres Vedras. This was on the eve of the Feast of Saint Vincent on 21 January of that year [1385]. Vasco Peres ordered a proclamation to be put out that all those who were there in support of the Master should leave immediately under pain of death. Their followers left with them; all the others remained. He then killed many of the animals from the herds that were put to graze around the town and requested that the Castilians whom he had sent to Santarém should come and join him. He put together provisions as best he could and announced he was for Castile.

Talking about this, he said something publicly that made people speak ill of such a nobleman: 'Look here, for God's sake! What a fine agreement the Master wanted to make with me! I sent my father Gonçalo Tenreiro over there on some affairs but he brought me nothing; at least if he had brought me 1,000 *dobras* wrapped up in a little old rag I would have kept to the agreement, but as he brought me nothing, I don't care to keep to it.'

When the Master heard that Vasco Peres de Camões had rebelled with Alenquer and had declared for Castile in the way he did, he smiled, showing that he did not worry about it, and said to the others, 'Those vassals of mine are determined to come to a bad end!' He then discussed with Nuno Álvares and others how it made sense to raise their siege [from Torres Vedras], since the town was so difficult to take that they would need to remain there for a long time, and especially as it was most necessary for him to reach Coimbra where all the noblemen and representatives of the town communities of the kingdom had assembled to talk about the state of the war and how they should

---

[289] The surname *Francês* usually translates as 'Frenchman' and generally refers to a foreigner, as does the title 'Sir' (*Miçe*). However, Lello is not a normal French name of the period. It was a medieval version of the Welsh name *Llwelyn*, and therefore this could plausibly be a Welsh mercenary soldier in French employment, who at some point in his career was knighted.

act in order to continue it. Their departure was to be in a fortnight's time, and Nuno Álvares was meanwhile to summon his men.

Chapter 180

How the Master left Torres Vedras and reached Leiria

The Master decided to raise his siege and make his way to Coimbra, where it was already certain that at his order all the bishops and proctors of the towns and cities who intended to take his side had come together. According to their summons, it was in order to decide with them how they were to pursue this war into which they had been thrust out of sheer necessity. As some engines of war were there, including two trebuchets, for which the conditions were not right to take them to Lisbon, the Master ordered them to be burnt so that the enemy could not make use of them.

Here it should be known that at this time the region around Lisbon was much ravaged, with a desperate lack of provisions, owing to the arrival and encampment of the King of Castile. This also applied to the territory around Torres Vedras and other places in that area. Seeing how they were left so impoverished while in the power of the Castilians, how constrained they were by such necessity and how they did not know what would happen to them afterwards, many farmers and other people who lived there, when they learned that the Master intended to leave, came to him with their wives, children and many infants. Thus there assembled all those who lived in the outskirts of Torres Vedras and its surrounding area, along with people from some other places.

When the Master saw so many people in such conditions and how they all cried out that he should have mercy on them and allow them to accompany him so that they could have some provisions and not remain in the power of their enemies, he was worried about what to do with them. It would have pleased him more to have that many men-at-arms who might help him, than to take along with him men, women and children, all wracked with want. They were so many and of such a kind that they might well then call him the father of all men.

Even a blind man who lived in the outskirts, hearing how the Master was leaving accompanied by all these people, started to call out with loud cries, pleading in the name of God to take him with them and not leave him in the power of such evil people. When Nuno Álvares heard this, moved by pity and compassion for the wretched man, he ordered him to be put on his own mule behind himself, and in this way he went with the others.

The Master then left with them like Moses when he brought the children of Israel across the desert.[290] They took this order: the country folk all went in front, and he and his men came behind. There were up to 600 lances, of whom around 150 were on horseback, and the others all on foot wearing coats of mail and gambesons with their bascinets over the poleaxes suspended round their necks. Thus they travelled in weary stages, the Master seeing to it that each day's journey was no longer than those poor people could manage at a slow pace, which was a distance of 2 or 3 leagues and sometimes a little more. Having gone 4 leagues, the blind man stayed in a place where he was content to remain. At times the Master went with his men on foot to keep them good company as was his custom. So they passed between Óbidos and Cadaval, and in the town of Óbidos, Álvaro Fernandes Turrichão, who was the Commander of Montemor-o-Novo, and others went off to join the Castilians.

From there they went to Alcobaça where the castle had been declared for the Master along with the other places of the [Cistercian] Order. The abbot at the time was Dom João de Ornelas who always served the Master well.

When the Master arrived at Leiria, where he thought he would find a warm welcome from García Rodríguez [Taborda], the town's governor, the latter behaved in a wholly different way though he had reason to do the opposite. Indeed, the Master thought the town was his, according to what García Rodríguez had given him to understand in his letters, and he had granted him great favours, both in the siege of Lisbon and while besieging Alenquer, as to a man of whom he expected good service at such a time. This was what the Master said in public and in the charters granting favours, ordering such reasons to be set down as follows:

> Seeing and valuing the very distinguished service that until now we have received and expect to receive in the future from García Rodríguez Taborda, the governor of our castle of Leiria, and desiring to reward him with favours as a good lord should do for good service, we grant him in perpetuity our township of Porto de Mós with its surrounding region, income and rights, etc.

Thus he said in the charter when he gave him by right and inheritance the duty collected on tilled wheat land in Leiria, and when he bestowed on him the land of Nespereira and other places in the region of Viseu, as well as in other charters granting favours which it is not necessary to mention. Consider, then, whether the Master was right to think that the town [of Leiria] was his and that he would have on his side a man to whom so many favours had

---

[290] Exodus 13.18–19.

been given. Yet with all of this he could never get an answer from him when he reached there, other than that he had paid homage on behalf of Leiria to Queen Leonor, and that it was to her that he intended to hand it over and to none other. After they pressed him a great deal he said that he would not wage war over the town with anybody until God put an end to these events, according to His grace. Thus if all the Master's teeth were loose, as the queen had said in Castile, this one was really loose and rotten, until at last it fell out completely, as others did.

Chapter 181

How the Master arrived in Coimbra and was welcomed by everyone in the city

The Master left Leiria and made his way to Coimbra without further delay; meanwhile Afonso,[291] the brother of Dom Pedro de Castro, entered Leiria, to join García Rodríguez [Taborda].

Now, concerning the intentions the Master had, some writers are in disagreement and so here the lack of certainty gives rise to several assertions. Some write that the Master was going to the *Cortes* to decide whether or not he would take the title of king, this being a decision that he was required to make. Others say that his intention was no more than to govern and defend the realm until Prince João was released, so that he could then deliver it to him, and that this was the most honourable deed that any man could do and for which he would be greatly praised by all those who would learn of it.

Some of the writers also say that he ordered the assembly only for them to organise the prosecution of the war and how to provide for the expenses and all things necessary for it. Others state that all the [proctors of the] town communities were gathered there only to make him king, and that he was willing to accept that. Once this was achieved, then they would speak about the conduct of the war and matters related to it. This reason, as it appears to us, seems to be closer to the truth than the others. That is because, in the power of attorney document that Lopo Martins, at that time a magistrate in Lisbon, and João da Veiga, Afonso Gonçalves, Silvestre Esteves, Álvaro Gil, as well as many others from the city, had duly granted to Pedro Afonso Sardinha, the son of Afonso Eanes, and to Martim Lourenço, both of whom

---

[291] Afonso de Castro, son of Count Álvaro Pérez de Castro.

were Lisbon citizens, when they sent the two of them to these *Cortes*,[292] they specifically used the following words and conferred the following powers, saying that, 'on their behalf and in their name they could elevate and receive as king and liege lord of these realms the very noble lord Dom João, Master of the Chivalric Order of Avis; and pay him respect and allegiance as their king and liege lord; and receive from him the promise and pledge to keep and maintain their privileges, rights and customs'.

So stated the mandate granted by the town community of Évora and by all other towns and cities of the realm that were then gathered together, which clearly shows that he [the Master of Avis] went there for this specific purpose.

While the Master was on his way to Coimbra and before he reached it, Gonçalo Gomes da Silva, who was in Montemor-o-Velho, which had already declared for him, went out with all his men to welcome him, and the Master received him with great honours and kindness. However, Gonçalo Mendes de Vasconcelos, who was in the city and held the castle, did not go out to welcome him. He said, just as García Rodríguez had said, that he had declared for Queen Leonor, to whom all allegiance was due after the death of King Fernando, and that he should obey her. However, some say that he wanted to declare for Portugal, inasmuch as the King of Castile had broken the treaties by entering the kingdom before the due time, and because, as you have heard, two of his sons had been with the Master for some while. Others claim that Gonçalo Mendes was taking this stand, supporting neither Portugal nor Castile until he had seen who was gaining the advantage; then he would back that party, as the others were doing. However, he did not wait so very long because a few days later he went over to the Master and was one of those electing him when he was proclaimed king.

People from the city hastened to go and welcome the Master, the clergy going in a procession, the lay people with their games and tumbling, and likewise the nobles and town communities who were there, all mingled together and mounted, in their best manner. While they were all preparing themselves, a number of boys began to rush out of the city, without anyone telling them to do so, along the road where the Master was coming, with hobby horses each one had made, holding rods with banners, all running and crying out, 'For Portugal! Portugal! For King João! Welcome our king!' In that fashion they continued for a very long distance, for about a league.

---

[292] It may be noted that this is the first use by Fernão Lopes of the formally correct term for the forthcoming meeting of the estates of the realm in Coimbra. In contrast to Chapter 154 above, the term is now needed because it was the *Cortes* of Coimbra which, in the exercise of its authority, was to make the Master, formally, a king.

The Master and Nuno Álvares and many who were riding along greatly marvelled at this, considering it a strange event, just like a miracle, saying that God had moved them to do that and was speaking through those young boys as if through the mouths of prophets. Thus they went ahead of him to the city, where he was welcomed with great honour.

When the Master reached a spot near the city and saw the procession already drawn up, he and all the others dismounted from their horses. He humbly knelt to kiss the cross and then walked along with the procession, entering the city amid great festivity and many expressions of delight at his coming. He was taken to the Paços da Alcáçova, where he was to stay. This took place on Friday, 3 March 1385.

Chapter 182

Concerning the talks that took place before the *Cortes* started, and the names of some of those who were present

When those prelates and noblemen who intended to defend Portugal had gathered there, together with a number of proctors from certain towns and cities throughout the realm, they began to speak to one another, knights and squires as well as other ordinary folk, both in public and in private, about the governance of the land and who should rule.

Those who were in favour of Prince João, who was being held prisoner in Castile, formed a faction on his behalf; and, having no doubt with regard to that, were ready to give him the kingdom through direct line of succession and with immediate effect, saying that he alone and no other man should reign; and that the Master should rule and govern the realm until the prince was freed and released, or something else should happen to him. If he were to die, then either his brother Prince Dinis, or the Master, or whoever was deemed to be the most appropriate person to rule for the benefit of the realm, was to reign. But, they said, electing another king, seeing the juncture at which they were, was a very wrong thing to do, and it was not to be accepted. This party had the support of certain noblemen who declared themselves openly and others privately, especially Martim Vasques da Cunha and his brothers and some of their followers.

The greatest number of the other noblemen and common people were completely against this intent and gave many reasons why it should not be so. They said that one of the princes was imprisoned and would never be released.

Besides, he had come to make war against the kingdom. The other had done the very same thing at the time of King Enrique. Therefore, it behoved them to elect such a man as would rule the kingdom and dedicate himself to it, and they should not think of any other heirs there might be. They spoke about this matter so often, putting forward their conflicting opinions and sometimes using such harsh words, that it was soon well known to all which noblemen were opposed to the Master becoming king and which defended his party, so that they were ranged in two opposing parties, of which the Master had already been notified.

At this point came the day when they had to go to the *Cortes*, at which the following prelates were present, namely: Dom Lourenço, the Archbishop of Braga; Dom João, the Bishop of Lisbon; Dom Lourenço, the Bishop of Lamego; Dom João, the Bishop of Oporto; Dom João, the Bishop of Évora; Friar Rodrigo, the Bishop of Ciudad Rodrigo; Friar Vasco, the Bishop of Guarda; the Prior of Santa Cruz; the Abbot of São João da Alpendorada; the Abbot of Bustelo; Rui Lourenço, the Dean of Coimbra, a great scholar; and other high-ranking ecclesiastics.

Likewise, the following noblemen were present: Vasco Martins de Sousa, a grandee; Nuno Álvares Pereira; Vasco Martins da Cunha the Elder; his sons, Martim Vasques da Cunha, Vasco Martins the Younger, Gil Vasques da Cunha and Lopo Vasques; Gonçalo Mendes de Vasconcelos; his sons Mem Rodrigues and Rui Mendes; Diogo Lopes Pacheco; his sons João Fernandes and Lopo Fernandes; Gonçalo Vasques Coutinho; João Rodrigues Pereira; Álvaro Pereira; Gonçalo Gomes da Silva and his son João Gomes; Martim Afonso de Sousa; Vasco Martins de Melo and his sons Gonçalo Vasques, Vasco Martins and Martim Afonso; Fernão Pereira,[293] Nuno Álvares's brother; Estêvão Vasques de Góis; Fernão Vasques de Resende; Afonso Vasques Correia; Álvaro da Cunha; and other noblemen we do not name.

Present also were Afonso Furtado, the captain general of the fleet; Afonso Eanes Nogueira; Gonçalo Eanes de Castelo de Vide, who had already joined the Master; Fernão Rodrigues, who later became Master of Avis; Martim Gil, the Grand Commander of the Order of Christ; Pedro Lourenço de Távora; his brother Rui Lourenço; Álvaro Gil [de] Cabral; Lourenço Mendes de Carvalho; Gomes Martins de Lemos; Nuno Viegas the Younger; Rui Vasques de Castelo Branco; Antão Vasques, a knight; Egas Coelho; Gonçalo Gonçalves Borges; Martim Afonso Valente; Estêvão Vasques Filipe; Rui Cravo; and many other knights and squires of good repute, as well as many other ordinary people.

---

[293] This is another brother of Nuno Álvares, with the same name as the one who was killed at the siege of Vila Viçosa. See Chapter 172 above. His name is mentioned only in this instance.

Proctors from towns and cities were gathered there, those we have named as confessors of their faith in the Portuguese cause before this chapter, where it was appropriate.[294]

Chapter 183

How Doctor João das Regras spoke in the *Cortes*, showing that there were four heirs to the throne

Together with everyone in a peaceful and well-ordered assembly in the palace, there was a distinguished man, one who was highly competent, of wide-ranging knowledge and a great scholar in law: his name was Doctor João das Regras. The subtlety and clarity of his oral exposition are qualities nowadays held in high regard by learned men.

This man addressed the *Cortes*, taking care to show, through knowledge and reasoned thinking, the true nature of such an important issue as this and the benefits at stake, and then leaving it up to the people to make their own decision. But who would be able to retain, as some have written, his great speech in full and how wisely he proceeded in such an important act? About this outstanding discourse, some laymen who have left us the few scattered details of what they were able to glean and put in writing, say that he began in this fashion:

> My noble lords and honourable people now here present. As you well know, we are gathered together here, with the grace and help of Almighty God, in order to deal with and agree on things that are necessary to rule and govern these realms, especially those matters concerning our defence in the war in which we are involved and which are so pressing, as you all know too well. In addition, we must discuss whether these realms, after the death of King Fernando, who was the last to hold them, have become vacant and destitute, without a king and a legitimate defender who can and should inherit them by right, so that we can make arrangements for it in accordance with God's help, in order that the realm be kept in law and justice, and that we be protected and defended from our enemies and opponents.
>
> Since some people say that there is no rightful heir, and others affirm that we do have an obvious one, whereby you are in some disagreement, in order to save you the debate and the weariness of arguing over the reasons why

---

[294] See Chapter 162 above.

one or the other should succeed, I wish to show that there is not just one heir but many, making it possible for us to choose the one that pleases us.

But before we pronounce on this matter, I want to respond to one opinion held here by some who claim that, because there are so few of us present, we cannot elect or choose a king, since the realm is divided within itself and we are not all in total agreement. Rather, we should let these matters be and then, when it pleases God that the whole realm is in total agreement and in the tranquillity that existed before, only then should we all elect a king whom we each perceive to be of greatest benefit to this land. In this way his election will be valid, as it will be done with everyone's agreement and not just with that of the small number of us here present; moreover, no election should be carried out in any other way nor would it be valid.

Those who support this view are not to be censured for lacking both the basic principles and the teachings of law. For if the Pope, who is a greater entity, can be elected by a single cardinal, should all others die and the latter alone remain, and even if he should die, the clergy can elect the pastor of the Church, making him a true pope, then all the more reason why, in this hour of need, even though we are but few and the realm is divided within itself, we can elect someone who will rule the kingdom and defend us from our enemies. On this matter it behoves us not to waste time or create a delay with speeches, especially seeing that we include in our number a good fifty proctors from the towns and cities of the realm.

However, leaving that aside, let us return to our purpose, and, since this kingdom is helpless and in need of a king and a defender who will take up its cause, let us see if we have a successor for it, someone who can and must inherit by right. You will find that there are many, from whom we can pick one.

Let us start by considering the King of Castile, who was first cousin of King Fernando, whose relationship cannot be put in any doubt, because King Fernando was the son of Princess Constanza, who was the wife of King Pedro of Portugal.[295] This King of Castile is the son of Queen Juana, who was the wife of King Enrique; and both queens were sisters, being daughters of Don Juan Manuel. Thus they were first cousins, sons of two sisters. In addition, he is married to Beatriz, the legitimate daughter of King Fernando, who was the last holder of these kingdoms. Therefore, she is heiress to the said realms and, likewise, so is her husband the king by virtue of that marriage.

If we did not have these two, there are the princes João and Dinis, the sons of King Pedro and brothers of King Fernando who are living and are such close relatives that it cannot be said in fairness that the throne of these

---

[295] Constanza never became queen because she died before Pedro succeeded to his father Afonso IV.

kingdoms is vacant and lacking a successor to inherit it. The conclusion is that we do have heirs.

Chapter 184

Explanations given by the said doctor as to why Queen Beatriz could not inherit this kingdom

As we have enough heirs from among whom to choose one that we prefer, it now remains to go through the detailed process of explaining which of them must be chosen, so that he can rule rightfully, in accordance with the dictates of law. To spare you this task, I wish to show you through real facts and the law that the throne of these kingdoms is now truly vacant, and that not one of those I have named must or can be successor thereto, even though for some of you the opposite may seem to be true, for the reasons I have mentioned relating to them.

In order that you, my lords, can see this clearly, it behoves you first of all to free yourselves of any affection and goodwill you may have towards any of those people, as such feelings should have no voice in these *Cortes* or dwell inside any of you. According to what wise men say, affection must be totally set aside by all men, for through it the mind loses its rational judgement and judges not according to what it impartially understands but according to what it loves, thus corrupting the judgement of reason. Therefore, leaving aside ties of affection, let us all see what is most beneficial, according to what our present needs dictate, so that, with the grace and help of Almighty God, who gave our undertaking a good start, this matter may be brought to a good conclusion for His glory and service and for the honour and preservation of these realms.

Now, my lords, I said we had enough heirs from whom to choose the one we prefer, and I first named the King of Castile, pointing out that he was first cousin to King Fernando, the last king to reign over these realms; and because of this kinship as well as of the part of the queen his wife, the daughter of King Fernando, he was the rightful heir to them. I will not bother with the kinship because there are other closer relatives, namely the brothers of King Fernando. But in respect of his being able to succeed on account of his marriage to his wife, and also as a result of the treaties that were made between these kingdoms and that of Castile on the occasion of that marriage, I say to you that in no manner can he succeed. I shall now demonstrate this to you.

Queen Beatriz, who is now the wife of the King of Castile, was not born legitimate, because her mother, when she married King Fernando, could not marry him, and by law that marriage was not valid. Nor can Queen

Beatriz be their legitimate daughter, to be entitled to succeed or inherit the throne. All who are present here know full well that Queen Leonor could not marry. Indeed, before she married King Fernando, she was married to João Lourenço da Cunha, to whom she bore a daughter who has died, and a son, Álvaro da Cunha, who is present here. Although, after the king had taken her to wife, she called him Álvaro de Sousa, saying that he was the son of Lopo Dias de Sousa and a woman from her household called Elvira, all this was to pretend to be a virgin for King Fernando, claiming that her husband had never slept with her; and though the king boasted that he had found her to be a virgin, the fact is that Álvaro de Sousa was her son. That is why, when João Lourenço fell ill in Lisbon, he asked the Master, who went to see him before he died, the favour of granting his property to this young man and allowing him to take possession of it as his son, but whom he had never dared to call so while King Fernando was alive. Accordingly, the young man was given the property and is now heir to it, as everyone knows. Dona Leonor and João Lourenço had already been married some three years when King Fernando took her as his wife, later receiving her in public. However, this was something he could not do while her husband was alive and that act greatly grieved João Lourenço.

If someone should say, as is true, that, since Queen Leonor was a relative of João Lourenço, he could not be her husband and therefore she was free to marry another and that marriage would be valid, I say that this argument does not detract from my assertion, because quite the opposite was true, since they were granted a dispensation from Rome for their marriage to be valid. Diogo Lopes Pacheco and many others who are present here know this very well. The same is true of Vasco Martins de Sousa, who indeed saw and held the dispensation in his hands, because the old count[296] showed it to him when he spoke to him about these events. So she was João Lourenço's legal wife and he was her husband, for which reason she could not marry another.

I shall give you yet another reason why she could not in any manner be King Fernando's wife without first getting a special dispensation from the Pope. It was because she was a close relative of his, King Fernando and her husband João Lourenço being sons of second-degree cousins. See how this came to pass: João Lourenço da Cunha was the legitimate son of Martim Lourenço da Cunha and of Dona Maria de Briteiros, who was the daughter of Dona Maria Afonso Chichorra, the grand-daughter of King Afonso [III], who was [also] the Count of Boulogne and grandfather to King Afonso IV, the father of King Pedro, who was the father of King Fernando. Consequently, King Fernando and Queen Leonor's husband João Lourenço were third-degree cousins, being sons of second-degree cousins, and that is what they sometimes called themselves. I know that Vasco Martins de

---

[296] João Afonso Telo, fourth Count of Barcelos, Queen Leonor's uncle.

Sousa is aware of this relationship because he comes and descends from that lineage.

Now, consider how could someone who wed a married woman, with the full knowledge that she was such a close relative, have her as his legal wife and how could their sons and daughters be able and entitled to inherit? In fact, such a marriage was not valid before God or the world but was, rather, a matter that caused shame and mockery, both in these kingdoms and in Castile.

I submit one more reason, although there is no need to do so. It is this: on every woman who is infamous for being unfaithful to her husband, and where this reputation is publicly known, the law passes judgement and calls into question the legitimacy of the children she gives birth to, for they may not be her husband's. That is because, if she sleeps with two men, she cannot be certain which of the two has made her pregnant. Indeed, Queen Leonor once applied this rule to King Fernando, for she did not accept as his son the child of a married woman who had slept with him and which child he was prepared to accept without casting any doubt, as he did not care to give much thought to such a thing. The queen, who was more prudent in these matters, asked the woman how long it was from the time she had slept with her husband to when the king had coupled with her and she found that it was such a short time that she could not be sure whose son it was, and so the queen made the king reject him.

Now, to return to our purpose, there is no need to discourse further on how and in what way Queen Leonor was infamous for not being faithful to her husband. It is much better to keep silent about such things, because they are ugly, than to make them public shamefully. So, let me come back to my argument: if we had to choose an heir from those I have named, we would not select Queen Leonor's daughter, since the law casts a doubt on her legitimacy because she is the daughter of an unchaste mother. We must accept as an heir to rule over us not a person whose legitimacy is in doubt but rather one whose legitimacy is certain and beyond doubt. But how can we be sure of something the law leaves in doubt? Or how can we say that someone is legitimately born when the law has cast suspicion on that person's birth?

If someone should say that many sons and daughters of such women inherit their property and those of their husbands, without anybody opposing them, I must admit to that. It is because the law consents to some things in simple and unimportant cases and does not give its assent where there are grave doubts in the important ones, because of the dangers that can follow, such as in the case of the succession of a kingdom or similar questions; this does not happen with the few possessions of little value left by an ordinary man or a woman. Therefore, we should not have as our ruler an heir of doubtful legitimacy.

Chapter 185

Explanations given by that same doctor as to why neither the King of Castile nor his wife should be selected as rulers

Leaving aside those impediments on the part of the mother, and others concerning her own person on which we could detain ourselves, such as her being her husband's niece[297] and daughter of her first-degree cousin, and the fact that, if there was a dispensation, it had not been granted by a true pope, as well as other similar reasons which could demonstrate that the marriage was not valid, let us come to another and greater counter-argument.

It is a fact that the inheritance which the King and Queen of Castile were to receive from this kingdom was to be valid for a certain number of years and to depend on certain conditions which he, the king of Castile, and his wife swore to abide by, subject to great penalties provided for by the treaties. The king totally agreed to these treaties, before he took her to wife when he received her in Badajoz. The king gave his royal oath on the Holy Gospels, physically touching them; placing his hands on the consecrated Body of Christ which the bishop of that city, dressed in his pontifical robes, held in a paten, he swore to keep and fulfil each and every clause contained in the treaties and never to act against them partially or completely, neither by himself nor on behalf of another party, in public or in secret, neither by deed nor word nor by any other means. Furthermore, should he in any way reason or speak against any of the conditions, partially or completely, rightfully or wrongfully, in public or in secret, nothing would be valid, and he would be considered to have committed perjury, and would incur a penalty of 100,000 gold marks.

Should he incur such a penalty, he would be quite satisfied to allow King Fernando or those who had the power to do so, and all the men in the kingdom of Portugal, on their own authority and without further ado, to seize and accept the surrender of the towns and cities and property of the realm of Castile, for which reason King Fernando could make war against him and all his inhabitants until those 100,000 gold marks were paid over. For that war, the King of Castile could seize neither lands nor the property belonging to the Portuguese. Rather, however many times he might act against those treaties partially or completely, so many times he would have to pay those 100,000 gold marks. He further promised never to claim any exception, neither for himself nor on behalf of another party, nor any other legitimate reason, nor have recourse to any judicial privileges or canonical

---

[297] The term 'niece', more extensive than today, was also applied to a cousin's child. See Chapter 155, note 228 above.

decree, law, custom, precedent, or any other entitlement, subjecting himself to the pain of excommunication and interdict, placed upon him and his kingdoms, should he act against the aforementioned clauses or any one of them, thereby losing any rights he might have to the kingdoms of Portugal, in whatever manner it might be, as many who are now present here and who were present when the oath was taken know full well. In the same manner, Queen Beatriz, by the authority vested in her and with her consent, took an oath when she had the Body of Christ in her hands.

Likewise, the lords and noblemen of the kingdom of Castile swore on the consecrated Body of Christ touched by their hands, and then solemnly doing homage with their hands in the hands of Gonçalo Mendes de Vasconcelos, who is present here, that should their liege lord the King of Castile not keep the treaties in the form they were set out or if he broke one sole condition contained therein, they should rebel against him, join the Portuguese and make war against him; and, if they did not do that, they would incur the same penalty as those who betray the castle entrusted to them or kill their liege lord.[298] Now, if we had to challenge as traitors all those who have incurred such a penalty by breaking their oath and we had to demand as many 100,000 gold marks as the number of times the King of Castile has incurred the penalties after he had sworn to obey these treaties and began to violate them, the kingdom of Castile would not suffice, even if it were auctioned in its entirety to pay such a large sum.

I also put it to you that, founded on another very strong basis, neither reason nor the law consent that the King of Castile should be our king or his wife accepted as our queen, even if he had not broken the treaties nor acted against the oath he took, whereby he lost any entitlement he might have had to this kingdom; and the basis is as follows. It is a fact that we owe our obedience more to God than to men. Furthermore, no law is worthy of the name if it does not conform to the law of God and the commandments of the Church. Since the Pope, like God himself, has the power to do all things on earth, with the exception of what is sinful, and whoever ignores what he commands, is ignoring Jesus Christ, Whom he represents, therefore we must not deviate in any way from his command, neither with regard to God nor with regard to the world because he has such a great power on earth. So much so that not only over Christians but also over all the infidels does he hold power and jurisdiction because they, both the good and the bad, are all his sheep. Moreover, we should not even demand a reason as to why he can do this or not, for the Pope is the Vicar of Christ.

Since the Pope can chastise and punish Jews and infidels, there is to be no doubt that he can do the same to Christians. This Pope and pastor must exist only as one being and no more, in obedience to and fear of whom we must all live and find salvation. Outside a single militant Church and

---

[298] See *CKF*, Chapters 158, 159 and 160.

obedience to it, even if one is a martyr for the love of Jesus Christ, there is no salvation if one persists in and bases one's actions on schism. Therefore the Pope can justly order any schismatic who does not obey the Church to be punished.

If Pope Urban, our Pastor and God on earth, orders and urges us to hunt down all schismatic infidels as heretics and cut them off from the Church, having excommunicated them in the most forceful excommunication, granting us for this purpose those privileges and pardons which he grants to those who go to war against the enemies of the Faith to help the Holy Land, how could we take as our king and liege lord someone who has been and is so clearly against him, as the origin of so great an evil and of a schism? Certainly, no one could say that; because, it is well known that King Fernando took the side of our lord Pope Urban as soon as the schism started; then, after insistent entreaties of the King of Castile he declared for the Antipope, and this allegiance lasted until the arrival of the English, who made him return to the original truth.

As the King of Castile and those who follow his intention in his wickedness and ignoble purposes are condemned as schismatics and heretics by the sentence of our lord the Pope, how could we take such persons as our monarchs and liege lords? I tell you without any doubt that it would be no less than to take as our king and liege lord a Moor or someone else from outside our faith. That is why canon law states that anyone who declares himself to be a Christian and fails to obey the commandments of the Apostolic See lives in sin and the wickedness of pagans. In fact, this is not without reason, for Our Lord Jesus Christ so ordered and assembled one sole Catholic Church which does not accept within it any separation or division but must exist as one unit, forever and ever. These schismatic heretics want to cleave asunder the Church of God and tear the Lord's seamless vestment apart, so sinning against that article of faith: I believe in the Holy Spirit and in one Holy Catholic Church.

Should we indeed take as our king and liege lord an infidel schismatic heretic that canon law and our lord the Pope condemn? May God not will it that we should commit such an error but rather let us defend our land, which we can justly do; and may no one presume through erroneous and imprudent thinking that the opposite of this must be done.

Chapter 186

How the doctor showed clearly that it was never certain that Dona Inês was King Pedro's wife

Now that we have shown that the King and Queen of Castile do not possess the right qualities to rule Portugal, let us see if we can find some other close relatives who might be able to rule in their stead. Indeed, we have them on hand, and they are the Princes João and Dinis, the sons of King Pedro. Many people think it is redundant to discuss whether or not they should inherit the throne. That is because, just as any man who wants to find salvation will never cast doubt on the faith he believes in, so with regard to these princes, such people, with no further doubt, are always willing to hear that they are legitimate heirs, without finding anything that might be contrary thereto. Since some people are inclined towards this idea and lest we should make a careless mistake, let us weigh up this matter well, without being bound by any affection, and let us give it a fair judgement as reason and the law demand, so that we can see whether the truth contradicts the wishes of such people.

As all our explanations must be clearly set forth in order to arrive at certainty on this point, without other arguments or further disputes, venerable truth first requires that two things concerning this issue be known. One is whether Dona Inês was, in fact, the wife of King Pedro. The other is, even if he should marry her, whether she could be his lawful wife and their offspring could succeed. The fact that many people believe that he had taken her to wife is no surprise, for having seen the sworn statements made by the king and others on this matter and likewise the explanation put forward by the Count of Barcelos in this city at the time, as well as a letter of dispensation which was made public before everyone, it is natural to think that she was, without a shadow of a doubt, his wife.

Since all these things are well known, and there are many here who were present at those events, I do not intend to dwell further on how they came to pass. However, in response to the first point, which requires us to know whether she was his wife or not, I submit that it was never established as a fact, neither during the life of King Afonso [IV] nor later, that he had taken her to wife, even though there were many attempts here to prove it.

The fact that it was not known during the life of his father the king can be elucidated thus: it is true that King Afonso, the father of King Pedro, being alive and the then prince being married to Princess Constanza, Dona Inês de Castro, the niece of Dona Teresa de Albuquerque, was brought to the Court of the king to serve as maid of honour to Queen Beatriz. So, while she was in the king's household, and she being a fine-looking woman, Prince Pedro fell in love with her and began to change his manner towards her. The king his father found out and was much displeased with this love affair because, apart from being very zealous in such matters, as you will have heard, he loved Princess Constanza dearly and was a great friend of Juan Manuel, her father. So he immediately decided that Dona Inês be sent to her aunt; while she was with her aunt, it so happened that Princess Constanza died.[299]

The prince, not forgetting his old affection, sent messages to the aunt and her niece so that was how she came to be with him, as you will have heard. This greatly displeased his father the king, all the more so because some people said that she was his wife while others affirmed that she could not be. As the prince continued to have her in his household and had children by her, the king determined to establish whether she was his wife or not. On one of the occasions when he was in this city [Coimbra], he sent Diogo Lopes Pacheco, who is here, and Master João, both of whom were members of his Royal Council, to the Palace of Santa Clara, where the prince was then living. Through those men the king informed the prince that, since he was not disposed to marry a king's daughter and he so loved Dona Inês, he should marry her and take her to wife, and that he, the king, would be pleased by it and would honour her as his wife. The prince then replied that it was not his desire to do so, however much people insisted on it, nor was it his intention to do it as long as he lived.

When the king spoke to his counsellors about such a reply, some said that they thought the prince did not want to do it only because such a marriage was very inconvenient for him. That is because Dona Inês, when she first came to the court, was not called Dona Inês, but rather she was known as Inês Peres, the bastard daughter of Don Pedro de Castro. Furthermore, I must tell you that I have never heard or found it written who her mother had been. After the prince took her to live with him, only then was she called Dona Inês.

Thus it was never known, during the life of King Afonso, that the prince had wedded her or that he had said that he had done so. And if anyone should wish to dispute my reasoning, let Diogo Lopes Pacheco, who is present here, swear on the Gospels whether what I am saying is the truth, and I believe he will say that it was as I have said.

Their children were not even called princes until after King Pedro came to the throne; and whenever King Afonso gave something to one or other of them, he stated in the letter he addressed to them, 'wishing to grant a favour and a boon to Dom João, my vassal, son of Prince Pedro, my son.' In no other way did he address them. Nor would King Afonso, had he known that she was his legitimate wife, even if she did not fulfil the conditions to be so, ever have her put to death for whatever may have happened. But considering her his concubine, he had her put to death in the manner that you all know.

---

[299] The commonly accepted date is 1345, but a reference in the Portuguese National Archives suggests that she died early in 1349.

However, despite what I have said, the opposite party may well submit that, although this doubt was never removed during the life of King Afonso, it was immediately made clear later, when King Pedro announced to everyone in this city that he had married her. The fact that many people believed it at the time is not surprising nor can they be blamed for doing so, because lies that are hidden under the semblance of truth easily take over the unwary heart. But those who are prudent and circumspect do not accept such things lightly nor do they follow the opinion of others, but rather carefully examine what they hear to find out whether there is a basis for it or not, so as not to make a mistake.

This is how we should proceed, being faced with such an important issue as this. For I put it to you that the proclamation that was then made to show that she was his wife served more to confirm that such had never been the case than to put an end to any doubt in men's minds. Therefore, while they thought that they were making it most clear so that everyone would believe it, they left so many dubious leads that there is nobody, however rash he might be, who would not baulk at them. You will see just how.

King Pedro stated in Cantanhede, under oath, that it was some seven years before, more or less, not being able to remember either the month or the date, that he had received this Dona Inês as his lawful wife. Since there were many who did not look kindly upon this marriage, and he, through fear and dread of his father, had not dared to make the declaration at that time, when his father was alive, he was now notifying everyone to clear his conscience.[300] Moreover, the Count of Barcelos and Master Afonso das Leis, together with many others summoned by the king, came here and they questioned Estêvão Lobato and the Bishop of Guarda, who had already been summoned to be witnesses of this fact. Having seen the latters' statements and a dispensation which they immediately made public, all the gullible among those who were assembled there readily believed that it was just as they were being told. That is how the whole kingdom came to learn that the king had said that she had been his wife, and thenceforth public instruments were drawn up, for and in favour of their children.

Just consider how in God's name this could be a story for any sensible man to have to believe!

---

[300] Note the close correlation between João das Regras's account (in the present chapter and in Chapter 190 below) of King Pedro's public declaration that he had married Inês de Castro secretly, out of fear and dread of his father's reaction, and the first account of the incident in *CKP*, Chapter 27. The reiterated terms 'fear and dread' and the formula *verba de praesenti* (in Portuguese 'palavras de presente') are further evidence, according to Teresa Amado's private communication to the translators, that Fernão Lopes was working from documents he had at his disposal, the contents of which he inserted in the narrative as appropriate.

It is true that, the more weighty an action is and the more it is valued and kept secret, the longer it remains in the mind of the person who does it and of those who are present there. So, how can such an important event like the marriage, which the king[301] carried out so secretly and in such great fear and dread of his father, according to what they said, be forgotten so quickly, with him unable to remember the day and the month when it was carried out; and not just him but whoever was called in such great secrecy to witness the act? Surely reason cannot accept this, for there is no man among you who, if asked now on what date he got married, even if it was not a feast day, but an ordinary day, however many years might have gone by, would not remember the day or the month or possibly even the time when it took place, even though he might have totally forgotten the exact year when it occurred.

When Estêvão Lobato thought he was making a positive statement by saying that it had taken place on the first day of January, he actually made his statement much more dubious and too suspect to be believed, because the first of January is a great feast that everyone celebrates. Consider whether this wasn't a special enough feast day for the king to remember such an event, even though it had been 100 years before. But it seems that at this time men lost their memory very early!

As for the other reason that they then gave as to why King Pedro had failed to make a declaration [earlier], this is much weaker and much harder to believe. That is because if, during the king's life, he had been a dutiful son and had never caused his father any grief at all, there was still reason to believe that this was as he said.

But a man who caused his father so much trouble, by taking such a woman in defiance of him and engaging in a great conflict with him because of such a course of action, and for a considerable time after she died, how could he be fearful of saying that she was his wife?

He was not afraid to gather around himself all the criminals and rabble there were throughout the kingdom and with them make war against the king his father, laying siege to his towns and castles, robbing and burning the land as if they belonged to his enemies, yet he says that he greatly feared and dreaded to declare that Dona Inês was his wife! Rather, it would have been better to make a public declaration then, and the people would have said that the king his father had been very wrong in putting his wife to death, and they would have been better inclined towards him.

Consider if it was a good move, that of a son against his father, to wage war against him throughout the kingdom and to cause so much destruction that the king had his towns and castles guarded and watched over because of him, as if his enemies were advancing through his kingdom.

---

[301] Although João das Regras uses the word 'king', this purported marriage took place when Pedro was still a prince.

Furthermore, do not think that this was done only in the towns and small places. The royal palace and the castle of Lisbon were also well watched over and guarded for three months; and the king's vassals who were inside received payment as if they were in a great war between enemies. Having done these and other such things, he says he was frightened of saying that Dona Inês had been his wife!

If someone were to ask Diogo Lopes, who is present here, what wonders Prince Pedro performed around the kingdom and how much destruction he caused to the property of Aires Gomes da Silva as well as that of Diogo Gomes de Abreu and that of many others, all of which King Afonso later paid for, that person could well say that such a son would not be afraid to tell his father that he had taken Dona Inês as his wife.

Now, supposing that it was so that, during the life of the king his father, he was afraid to declare that she was his wife, who was there to prevent him, after the king had died, from making it public as soon as he began to reign, since it pleased him so greatly that everyone should know? For he could have held an honourable funeral in Alcobaça and, by summoning the prelates and noblemen of the realm, he could have made a public declaration of how he had taken her to wife and how the whole event had taken place and people would have accepted it. But it was four years after the king [his father] had died, when no one was thinking about the matter any more, that he made public his declaration that he had done so.

Why do you think then it was done in this manner? It was because never, during the life of the king his father nor later, until that time [four years later], did he succeed in obtaining a dispensation from the Pope to make his children legitimate. This was why he made that public declaration to show that they were legitimate, for what it was worth.

Chapter 187

Concerning the impediments which the Doctor said prevented Dona Inês from being the wife of King Pedro

Having shown clearly that it was never certain that Dona Inês was King Pedro's wife, and that all his arguments were very dubious and attested great ignorance, it remains for us to look at the stronger second point, namely, if perchance she had been his legitimate wife, whether such a marriage was valid. I now submit that it was not, because of the following impediments.

It is a fact that Dona Inês was King Pedro's niece,[302] the daughter of his first cousin, as follows: King Pedro was the son of Queen Beatriz, the daughter of King Sancho [IV] of Castile. Doña Violante [Sánchez], who was the wife of Fernán Rodríguez de Castro, and Queen Beatriz were [half-]sisters, being daughters of the said King Sancho, although by different mothers. The mother of Doña Violante Sánchez was a lady called Doña Maria Alfonso, who was the wife of García de Ucero. Doña Violante Sánchez was in turn the mother of Don Pedro [Fernández] de Castro, known as 'da Guerra', who was the father of this Dona Inês. Therefore, Dona Inês was King Pedro's niece by virtue of her father being his first cousin.

Let us not occupy ourselves with what some people say, about King Pedro first having married Princess Blanca, the daughter of Prince Pedro of Castile[303] who was killed in the vale of Granada, how she was brought to this kingdom[304] and he received her as his legitimate wife in this city before he married Princess Constanza; and that therefore, King Fernando was illegitimate and unable to succeed; because, that is not how it happened, and it is of no relevance to our purpose.

But let us now come to one great impediment, beside the others, on account of which the Pope would not have granted a dispensation, whatever might come to pass, for which reason Dona Inês could in no way be his wife. Here it is: when King Pedro was still a prince and married to Princess Constanza, they had a son called Prince Luís. When he was baptised in this city, Dona Inês was made the boy's godmother and consequently became [spiritually] related to King Pedro. After that, Princess Constanza would often address her as 'cummer'[305] showing her respect, as is the custom.

[302] As previously noted (in Chapter 155, note 228 and Chapter 185, note 297 above), the term 'niece' could be more broadly applied to daughters of first cousins. See also *CKP*, Chapter 28, including note 59.

[303] Pedro of Castile, Lord of Los Cameros, and son of King Sancho IV, died in the so-called 'Disaster of La Vega de Granada', also known as the Battle of Elvira, in 1319.

[304] Blanca came to Portugal in 1328, at the age of nine, to be brought up by her future mother-in-law, until the marriage could be celebrated some four or five years hence. By 1334, serious concerns about Princess Blanca's poor health led Afonso IV of Portugal to propose to the *Cortes* at Santarém the marriage of Prince Pedro to Princess Constanza Manuel.

[305] The Portuguese term 'comadre' derives from the fact that a Catholic godmother, as a second mother whose main role was to ensure the godchild's Christian upbringing, was considered to stand in a relationship of co-parentage with the father and mother. We have opted for the English term 'cummer' when referring to the godmother in this spiritual kinship. Such spiritual ties precluded any marital relationship between the godparent and the parent of a child.

Now, how could the king be the legal husband of the cummer, the godmother to his son? Surely this could not be.

But some authorities in these matters remove this impediment thus: they say that the prince, being passionately in love with Dona Inês and wishing to sleep with her, had secretly advised her to arrive at the church with the child and to remain present at the baptism when it came to her becoming a godmother, but not to say the words that godparents use for the responses in the name of the godchild, and that she proceeded in this manner. That being so, she was not cummer to the prince, and she could marry him without committing a sin.

In support of this, the authorities mention a similar case in matrimony, where although a man may take a woman using the words ordained by the Church, doing it not with the intention of taking her to wife but because he could not otherwise sleep with her, she is not his wife in the eyes of God; thus he can later marry another woman if he never regarded the first one as his wife, afterwards doing penance for this sin. This is true, because in God's eyes he is not her husband; but the world will consider him as such and he will be constrained to lead a conjugal life.

Thus they claim that although Dona Inês was invited to be godmother and together with the other godparents she placed her hand on the child and went through the customary rituals, since it was not her will and she never consented to it, there was no spiritual relationship, and she could later marry the father of a boy who was not in truth her godson, without committing a sin. Although things may have been so, namely that before God she was not a cummer, because of this public knowledge and of the scandal it caused to everyone, the Pope would have to be notified. He would then grant them his dispensation according to the information he was given and, accepting it as true, would then leave the matter to their consciences. But this did not happen nor was the Pope ever petitioned for a dispensation.

Now you can see that it is very doubtful whether they could marry or not, but this is how the story went. Diogo Lopes, who is here, knows it well for he was present at the said baptism and was godfather to the royal child Luís together with other godparents who had been requested to fulfil that role.

But even if they could marry without a dispensation, which they could not, and their children born legitimately, which they certainly were not, the mere fact of their attacking the kingdom of their birth, in the service and company of its enemies, in order to destroy it, not once but on numerous occasions, is sufficient reason for none of them to be entitled to reign, even if they were legitimate.

The fact that they attacked these realms is well known to all; and how Prince Dinis, in the time of King Fernando came in the company of King Enrique, armed and with troops, invading the kingdom and reaching as far as Lisbon, making war with fire and plunder, killing and destroying all that they could. Likewise, Prince João, with troops and in the company of the present King of Castile, at the latter's command, came to lay siege to

Trancoso, held it under siege and assaulted it for some days. Also, when he entered the kingdom through Valle de la Mula,[306] he committed treachery when he set fire to the land with his own hands. Afterwards, he laid siege to Elvas and went through the kingdom committing many acts of war.

I know that Vasco Martins de Sousa, Diogo Lopes Pacheco, Vasco Peres Bocarro and Gil Martins Cochofel, as well as many others who are here, are well aware of this. I maintain that we would be acting insanely in electing a king who behaved as a traitor to the kingdom and who came against it to destroy it instead of giving it to one who has gone through much toil and mortal peril to defend it and is ready to go on doing so.

Chapter 188

Concerning the disagreement that there was between the noblemen and the people over the election they wanted to carry out

Despite all these reasons, as well as others which we have not mentioned here, put forward by that doctor so that everyone should be in a peaceful frame of mind to elect a king without raising any further doubt, since goodwill is deeply embedded in the minds of those who love and cannot be easily eradicated, however many reasons are given for doing so, none of those you have heard could remove the initial intention some men had in their minds and hearts, to favour the princes. Such was the case of Martim Vasques [da Cunha] and his brothers as well as all those of that alliance, who said that despite what they had heard, there was no doubt that the kingdom belonged to Prince João by right. Furthermore, they ought to go to war in his name until he was released from prison, for they found it very strange that the Master be given the title of king when someone else was entitled to rule.

So intensely did they feel this that one day Martim Vasques left the council complaining loudly: 'You can do what you like and make whoever you like king, for I am but one man and my voice counts for little. Whoever you make king, I shall help him defend the realm until I die. But, as far as I am concerned, I shall never consent to its being the Master.'

---

[306] Although bearing a Spanish name until quite recently, Valle de la Mula became Portuguese in 1297 by the Treaty of Alcañices, and lies about 5 miles (8 km) east of Almeida, virtually on the border.

Nuno Álvares, together with other noblemen as well as those town representatives [who were present], were totally against these arguments and
insisted that, to all intents and purposes, the Master should be king. They
held their own separate meetings on this matter: the noblemen in one group
and the proctors from the villages and towns in another.

Discussing this at length, one of them began by saying: 'What is the point
of talking about all this for so many days, and all this useless delay, throwing
doubt on what everyone can see clearly? God help you if you can't see what
these noblemen want to put into our heads! They are telling us to make war
in the name of Prince João, until he either dies or is released; and that we use
up our lives and worldly possessions to give the kingdom to a man who came
against it, to destroy it, and to hand it lock, stock and barrel to the King of
Castile, particularly when it is quite clear that it belongs to neither of them by
right. I tell you that you will never hear that from my mouth. Rather, I say we
elect the Master to be our king without further delay. We have more reason
to give the kingdom to him, who has risked so many dangers to defend and
protect it, rather than to someone who offered it so cheaply to its enemies.
Nor should we heed what some people say, namely that the Master should
defend it as its ruler and defender; rather, let it be as king in all respects,
because I have always heard it said, "a king for a king and the rest counts
for nothing." Since we are going to be in a war waged by a king, let a king
defend us and the realm.'

Then they all agreed with this objective and pledged themselves to remain
steadfast in its pursuit.

Likewise, the noblemen held their own separate council, at which, as we
have stated, the principal opponent to the Master becoming king and who
took the lead in this stance was Martim Vasques da Cunha.

Nuno Álvares Pereira, who was much in favour of the opposite view, was
the leader of the other group. As love and hatred cannot be really hidden,
sometimes there were such debates on this issue between the two that they
went beyond what was rational, this being something that deeply saddened
the Master. This was not because Martim Vasques and his followers wanted to
hinder the defence of the realm nor because they wished the King of Castile
to have it nor for feeling any ill will towards the Master. But because they had
great bonds of affection with and goodwill towards Prince João whom, as we
have said, they served when it behoved them to do so and they kept close to
him when he was in this kingdom. As a result, Vasco Martins da Cunha [the
Elder], his son Martim Vasques, his brothers and relatives, as well as other
allies, attracted to them a great number of the nobles.

The Master knew what was taking place between them and was greatly
troubled. He summoned Nuno Álvares and told him that he was well aware

that Martim Vasques and his brothers had many soldiers and held a number of fortresses, for which reason it was not fitting for his service that they should fall out with them at such a time. Therefore he asked Nuno Álvares not to have any quarrel with them.

'Now, my lord', said Nuno Álvares, 'you have no one else here who is against your service or opposes your being king except this braggart Martim Vasques. If you wish, I shall rid you of his opposition.'

The Master said 'God forbid that this should happen', and asked him to deal with them temperately, so that there would be no commotion, because Martim Vasques was not doing that through any ill feeling he might have towards him but because he thought it was the right thing to do. Nuno Álvares told the Master that he was pleased to obey him as long as the others were not overbearing because, surely, if they were to display haughtiness towards him, he would not have the stomach to endure it.

At this juncture, one day Martim Vasques, his brothers and other nobles together with them went to the Master's palace. While they were in the palace Nuno Álvares went there to speak to the Master, taking with him a good 300 squires wearing coats of mail and vambraces, swords belted on and carrying daggers. When Nuno Álvares entered in such company, the Master was deeply perturbed, fearing what might happen between them as he saw them in such total disagreement. However, he did not reveal anything; nor did Nuno Álvares, as he came in, display any sign of haughtiness but spoke in a modest manner to the Master and likewise to some of the latter's men.

When Martim Vasques and his brothers, as well as his relatives and other friends, saw Nuno Álvares arriving as he did, they left the palace little by little, and so Nuno Álvares was left alone speaking with the Master, later returning to his lodging.

The Master, keeping his thoughts to himself, understood Nuno Álvares's demeanour and the reason why he behaved that way, and regarded him as very courageous. He summoned Doctor João das Regras and told him all that had happened, the manner of Nuno Álvares's coming, and what he feared might be the outcome of this affair, commenting on many things about the stance of Martim Vasques.

The doctor said: 'My Lord, I have striven to show that, for obvious reasons and according to legal principles, the throne of this kingdom is totally vacant, and that the election belongs freely to the people. I have submitted much evidence from different sources which should have satisfied him and others who might be much more knowledgeable. But apparently, love and goodwill, which conquer all else, did not allow them to understand the arguments put forward by me, and they still cling to the doctrine they held. This being so, I promise you that the first day we talk about this I will expose something I wished to keep quiet about and which makes this legal process much uglier. Thereafter, let it be resolved as you deem fit.'

Chapter 189

Concerning the message that King Afonso sent to the Papal Curia in order that the prince his son might not marry Dona Inês

S peaking again in that same palace, with everybody gathered there as usual, the aforesaid great doctor began by declaring:

> My noble lords and honourable people, you know full well how I put forward at these *Cortes* certain arguments to show that the throne to these realms is vacant in every respect, and that there is no one who should or is able to inherit it through lineage, or who is entitled to inherit it. Those reasons are in themselves so clear, just as is the law that reinforces them, from which authority we should not deviate, that any rational man should be satisfied with the explanations of the issue clearly set out before you. But despite what I put forward, which should satisfy everyone, it seems that the bonds of affection which I feared at the beginning of these events still make some men hold and utterly believe that Princes João and Dinis are legitimate and can inherit, on the grounds of that public declaration in which King by Pedro said that Dona Inês had been his wife, of which we have made mention here.[307]
>
> As I thought that those arguments I gave were sufficient for everyone to see the contrary view, I had not wished to speak further about it, for the sake of discretion and to act with honesty in this case. But since everything I have put forward neither satisfies nor suffices for these men, it behoves me to show in every respect the flaw of the princes' birth without legitimacy for you all to see clearly that they were not born legitimately, nor were they ever legitimised later so that they could inherit by right of succession to any blood relative.
>
> Whoever is not satisfied with what I shall now say, and maintains his opinion, will be showing that he wants to emulate the stubbornness of the Jews, who are waiting for a Messiah who will never come. Now, my lords, in making public something I had wished to keep quiet and not talk about, the business of the princes' birth and legitimacy can be briefly summarised as follows:

---

[307] See Chapter 186 above.

When Prince Pedro had Dona Inês living with him, no one knowing for certain whether she was his wife or not, the king his father was led to understand that the prince was preparing to send an embassy to the Papal Curia to ask the Holy Father to grant his dispensation to marry Dona Inês. This was about three years before Dona Inês was put to death, King Afonso being in the town of Alenquer at the time. When he heard this, he was much displeased that this had been done. Being most unhappy with such an embassy, he made every effort to stop it and secretly wrote to the Archbishop of Braga, who at the time was at the Papal Curia, to persuade the Pope not to grant the prince's petition concerning this question, which was, for the king, greatly odious and injurious.

Now, if I were to summarise the arguments the king gave when he wrote about the matter, and of the embassy that Prince Pedro sent to the Pope after he became king and of the reply that came from the Curia and how these things happened, you would say that they were all embellished words, which is something that men do lightly, that I had used to serve my purpose, but those were not the real facts. So, in order to allay your suspicions, without detaining myself on further arguments and allegations based on other laws which might be helpful, I shall read to you the message that King Afonso sent to the Curia at that time; likewise I shall describe the embassy that King Pedro afterwards sent to the Pope as well as the reply that the latter gave him, rejecting his petition. These are all sufficient to remove an even greater doubt than the one we are dealing with and to demolish once and for all such an opinion. By this means, let us therefore put an end to this business.

Then he read a letter written in Latin, which forthwith everyone saw in Portuguese. The following was its content:

Afonso by the grace of God King of Portugal and of the Algarve, to the most honourable Father in Christ Dom Gonçalo[308] by the same grace Archbishop of Braga, good health, etc. We wish you to know that our first-born son and heir Prince Pedro is head over heels in love and is being induced by the advice of some people to marry a woman who was, according to rumour, the daughter of Don Pedro Fernández, called da Guerra, and of a mother who was not his legitimate wife. They induce him to such a marriage, despite the fact that some who are relatives of the prince to the second degree of kinship at present are acting illicitly in this regard.[309] They say that, in order to remove that impediment, the prince is minded to write to some of his

[308] The Archbishop of Braga was then Guillaume de la Garde (1349–1361), not Gonçalo.

[309] This seems to be an allusion to the conflict between the King of Castile and part of the Castilian nobility, in which Inês de Castro's brothers were deeply involved. It was believed that they planned to draw Prince Pedro into the conflict, which may

friends at the Papal Curia asking them to plead for the Pope's dispensation on the matter. If this were to be granted, there could follow forthwith a great outrage among those who live in our realms. Those who are relatives and from whom the prince my son descends have always been, until the present time, honourably married in legitimate matrimony with daughters of kings. Moreover, the said marriage, should it take place, would result in great dishonour not only to the dignity of our royal rank, to which my son expects to succeed by natural right, but also to all his honourable kindred. Therefore, we earnestly beg you in the strictest confidence on our behalf to inform the Pope of the extent to which the said marriage would be an illicit and unequal match for a prince, and to request that His Holiness be pleased not to comply with my son the prince's petition. Should the Pope need further evidence of our wishes, then show him this letter with all due secrecy. Apply yourself so diligently to this matter of our service that we shall hold ourselves duty-bound to bestow our favour on you.

Chapter 190

Concerning the message that King Pedro sent to the Pope and the reply that he received

The letter in question was sent to the Papal Curia. Pope John XXII, from whom King Pedro had been granted that general dispensation when he was still prince,[310] was no longer alive. He was succeeded by Benedict XII; after him came Clement VI and then came Innocent VI.[311]

A few years after these popes died, the death of Dona Inês took place;[312] and just over two years later, King Afonso died. King Pedro was very unsure of what was true with regard to his marriage, either because of his own understanding of it or because he was told by one of his advisers, namely whether as a consequence of that dispensation and on the strength of that union, the marriage was as it should be and his sons were legitimate, and able to inherit and succeed to the throne of the kingdom on the death of Prince Fernando his first-born son and heir, who was entitled to succeed to the throne by direct line of inheritance.

---

explain why King Afonso IV ordered Inês's death. As regards the kinship between Inês's father and Prince Pedro, see Chapter 187 above.

[310] See *CKP*, Chapter 27, including note 57, and Chapter 28. See also Chapter 186 above.

[311] Benedict XII (1334–1342); Clement VI (1342–1352; Innocent VI (1352–1362).

[312] Inês de Castro was put to death in January 1355, during Innocent VI's papacy.

Although King Pedro had received her [Dona Inês] as his legitimate wife, he had every reason to have his doubts about the validity of that marriage. That was because, through a general dispensation that was granted when he was young, he was betrothed to Princess Blanca, the daughter of Prince Pedro [of Castile], who died in the vale of Granada, whom he later did not wish to marry.[313] When the time came for him to take Princess Constanza, the daughter of Don Juan Manuel, as his lawful wife and their marriage was to be blessed in Lisbon, some people already doubted whether under the terms of such a dispensation he could marry her or not. As the king his father had ordered that all the prelates of the land should attend the marriage blessing, it happened that Dom Gonçalo [Pereira], the then Archbishop of Braga, had his doubts whether, under the terms of the dispensation, they could marry each other.

First, he wrote to Dom João,[314] the bishop of that city [Lisbon], and asked to be informed and to be sent a formal declaration as to whether he could attend the ceremony without danger to his hierarchical position. The Bishop of Lisbon replied that he had seen the said general dispensation granted by Pope John and that, having discussed the matter with certain scholars, they said they thought it sufficed for the prince to marry Princess Constanza. According to what King Pedro said, he later married Dona Inês under the same dispensation, which he should not have done, given the impediments that there were between them.

Now, regarding this doubt and other matters that were pertinent to his status, King Pedro sent his ambassadors to the Curia, at the time Geraldo Esteves[315] was there, and with them he sent to the Pope this message, which I have here.

Then the doctor exhibited a great roll of parchment, worn with age, signed by Gomes Pais de Azevedo as well as by Master Afonso and others of King Pedro's Royal Council. Included in three places on the roll, among the various things the king was requesting of the Pope, was the application for the validity of this marriage and the legitimacy of his sons, in the following words:

Likewise, you will tell the Pope in his private chamber that the king received Dona Inês de Castro, on whom God have mercy, by *verba de praesenti*, as ordained by Holy Church, by whom he had issue, who are living, and to whom he was related by blood. Moreover, the king prays that it should please His Holiness to consent to, ratify and confirm the said marriage notwithstanding the said degree of consanguinity so that legitimacy may

---

[313] See Chapter 187, note 304 above.

[314] João Afonso de Brito, Bishop of Lisbon (1326–1341).

[315] Formerly an attorney and later 'sobrejuiz', i.e. appellate court judge, to King Afonso IV of Portugal.

be conferred on the said issue living and they may have what they would have had, had the said impediment of kinship not existed. Insist on this until you have a reply on the matter.

After some petitions concerning bishoprics and other matters, it was stated elsewhere as follows:

Likewise, if you see that the Pope grants you each of the first four things, with regard to the petitions of the churches, ask him immediately for the rest, with regard to the legitimation of the marriage, and then for the other things, as they are written here. If he does not grant you each of the four things, do whatever you need to ensure that he deals with the said confirmation of the marriage, so that the young boys become legitimate. As for the other requests, do not trouble yourselves with them.

The doctor said:

Now, having seen the words of this missive, which are not mine nor are there other alleged interpretations of rulings, one should consider how much effort the emissaries must have invested at the Curia in order to gain a favourable outcome. However, leaving this aside, let us see how the Pope replied and so let us bring this discourse to an end.

He then showed a letter of reply that the Pope had sent to King Pedro, excusing himself for not granting the king's petition concerning these matters. The letter read as follows:

Innocent Bishop Servant of the Servants of God, to Pedro, our well-beloved son in Christ, most noble King of Portugal, good health and our Apostolic Blessing. May Your Royal Magnificence be assured that we have received with benevolence your honourable and prudent ambassadors.
    Among the things that the embassy transmitted to us on your behalf, the following in particular was that you, with trust and boldness, by a general dispensation [granted] in the usual form, as requested by you and the very noble King Afonso your father, from our predecessor of happy memory Pope John XXII, married and received as your wife Dona Inês, who was the daughter of Don Pedro de Castro. This Dona Inês, through a collateral line, on one side, was your relative in the second degree of kinship. On the other, through a similar line, she was your blood relative in the third degree; and in the fourth degree of affinity, she was your sister-in-law. Nevertheless, we were devoutly asked and solicited that by our apostolic and extensive power, we should graciously declare through our rescript the said marriage to have been lawfully contracted by both of you by virtue of that dispensation; and in addition the issue of this marriage to be legitimately born. Furthermore,

if we refused to grant this grace in its entirety, we were solicited on your behalf to at least be pleased, through our apostolic rescript, to legitimise your issue and that of Dona Inês, fully reintegrating it into the first principle of natural law[316] so that it would be fully qualified to succeed as if your marriage had been from its beginning valid and lawfully contracted and as if your issue had legitimately descended from it.

We can assure you, our well-beloved son, that we have thought long and hard about it and that we have considered everything that your ambassadors requested of us on your behalf; but although we very much wish to acquiesce to your wishes and to please your Royal Highness, nevertheless we are deterred by certain legitimate reasons founded in law, which we must by all means uphold, from putting into effect or even accepting your petition concerning the declaration with regard to the said marriage.

As for the second question put forward on your behalf, namely the legitimation of the issue born to you and to Dona Inês, we conclude that the Holy Apostolic See does not customarily grant such dispensations nor legitimation except to great and noble personages; and that only in the presence of clear and manifest reasons. On analysis of your request, these do not appear to have been mentioned or claimed on your behalf to the detriment of another party, who might hope to be entitled to succeed. We might accede to such a legitimation, provided that the third party concerned in the matter were to plead for and request it; or if in any other way it were clearly shown that your petition were based on the express consent of that third party. That is the necessary procedure, especially in this case, which concerns legitimation connected to the inherited succession of people who are not native to those lands subject to the temporal jurisdiction of the Church.

Therefore, our well-beloved son, the Holy Apostolic See has decided not to acquiesce to your supplication nor to grant you a favour such as you request. We beg your Royal Magnificence, and advise you with every good wish, patiently to accept our justifications by which we are moved and constrained to adopt the opposite response to your supplication, because our pastoral office does not permit us to infringe the law of Christ; rather, we must adhere to it, without deviating from its doctrine.

Given in Avignon, on the ides of July in the ninth year of our papacy [1361].

Then, the doctor said:

Now you can see here, without changing one iota, all that took place regarding Dona Inês's marriage and the legitimation of her offspring. I had

---

[316] It is possible that Fernão Lopes has in mind here St Thomas Aquinas's precept of Natural Law, which Lopes would most likely have encountered in Giles of Rome's *De regimine principum*, in the context of monarchy and hereditary succession.

wanted to avoid it for the sake of the princes' honour, despite the stage at which we are; and I believe that would have been better than forcing me to make public and broadcast forever after their incestuous birth.

Chapter 191

How all the noblemen and the people agreed to raise the Master of Avis to [the rank of] king

Having thus shown clearly how these matters developed concerning this great and weighty question, an issue which threw numerous people into doubt, everyone was very surprised at hearing things that they had known nothing about. Consequently, many who were inclined to believe this [the legal evidence against the marriage] had their previous suspicions confirmed and those who were totally against this conviction now held a new and rational belief, having all their doubts dismissed, such as Martim Vasques da Cunha and all who were of his party. Having then put forward many arguments which we shall leave aside for the sake of brevity, and since the cause of contention had been removed as a consequence of sufficiently clear evidence, they arrived, through meek and peaceful concord, at an honourable and definitive decision, namely, that they should elect their king.

The good doctor said:

> Now, my lords, since what you were so uncertain about has now been made clear, and it has pleased God that you should know that the throne of these realms is totally vacant and placed at our disposal for us to elect someone who will defend and rule them, let us not trouble ourselves any further with old tales that we might appropriate for our own ends. Moreover, since these kingdoms have always been defended and held by a king, and since we cannot do so by ourselves in an adequate manner, as demanded by our present necessity, in such circumstances we need to elect a king who will carry out all that behoves him, so that we do not fall into the subjection of our schismatic enemies, who do all they can to prejudice and ruin not only us but also the Holy Church and our lord the Pope, whose main enemies they are. As the person who is to be elected is of no less consideration than the benefit for the realm that will ensue, let us first examine the conditions that are required of him; if we find them in the one we are to elect, our election will be prudent and in no way reprehensible.

> I shall say briefly that, according to learned men, among the conditions he must fulfil are those of good lineage and great courage to defend this country. Likewise, he must love his subjects, as well as manifest righteousness and

devotion. It is clear that all these conditions are met by our great lord the Master, whom we wish to elect, as all of you are fully aware.

As for being of good lineage, consider whether being the son of a king is good enough.

As for being of great courage, he has shown it and still does inasmuch as, with only a small proportion of the realm on his side, with remarkable daring he endured the many dangers that he went through, and also in so far as he exposes himself to even greater ones that these times of ours throw upon us.

As for his love for his subjects, consider what more he could have done in the face of the King of Castile's pacts and promises, so advantageous to his honour and status at a time of dire want as was the famine and siege of Lisbon, than refusing to agree to them, to prevent his people falling under the enemy's domination.

As for his righteousness, he displayed it well when the people of Lisbon wanted to rob the Jews, as well as in the ransoming of the prisoners and in the contributions he made for that purpose, according to the rank of each one.

As for being devout and conducting his deeds in accordance with God's wishes, consider the alms he gave and his conversations with Friar João da Barroca, and you will find that all his deeds were weighty and showed prudence in judgement.

Besides this, he orders all things pertaining to the defence of this kingdom so wisely that no one else could do better. So, judging from what we have seen so far, this Dom João, the Master of Avis, who has worked and continues to work so hard for the honour and defence of this kingdom, is qualified and suitable, and deserves the honour and rank of a king.

Therefore, since it is to God's service and for the good and honour of the Holy Church, so as not to be destroyed by our enemies and to prevent it from falling into the hands of schismatics, let us agree on one desire and purpose; and in the name of God, Who is the Holy Trinity, Father, Son and Holy Spirit, let us name and choose in the best way possible this Dom João, son of King Pedro, as king and liege lord of these realms; and let us grant him the right to call himself king and to order all that is incumbent on the office of the king to be done to govern and defend them, as those who were kings up to now used to do.

Then there were many discussions on which we could spend some time, but there is no need to include them here; and by unanimous agreement among all the great men and the common people, they declared that they should promote the Master to the high dignity and rank of king, and that no one should be allowed to argue further against the decision. They also decided to go and tell him this right away.

Chapter 192

Concerning the discussions that the noblemen and the people held with the Master, and how he was raised to [the rank of] king

Having come to the agreement that we have described, the prelates, noblemen and proctors of the town communities then together made their way to the Master and begged his favour, requesting that he be pleased to assent to the election they had made and agree to take on the title, dignity and honour of king, and take charge of the defence of the realms because God had kept them for him and had so ordained.

The Master listened to this discourse and then replied, saying that he gave many thanks to God and was very grateful to Him for having instilled in their hearts and minds the desire to elect him to such an exalted rank; and he thanked the men warmly for their goodwill towards him. However, they could well see, as indeed he felt in his heart that, it was not, nor could it be, sufficient for him to receive and uphold on himself such honour and high dignity as was the royal governance. All the more because they knew that there were certain impediments, both in the defect of his birth as well as in the profession he had made to the Order of Avis, which made it impossible for him to receive such a charge and honour such as those to which they had elected him. Consequently, he could not accept.

He also said that in his heart he could not accept for another reason. They could be in no doubt that he was ready to strive, as much as he could and for as long as he lived, for the defence of the realm and to wait for the King of Castile and all his might to do battle with him. If, as the mere knight that he was, he should defeat the king, which he hoped God would allow, then it would be a great honour for him as well as for them. If, God forbid, it should happen otherwise, it would be a greater dishonour for him to be vanquished as a king than if he were defeated as a knight. Therefore, they should make decisions about levying forces, on how to raise money to pay for them, and how the kingdom should be defended, rather than dwelling on other matters.

All the prelates, noblemen and proctors of the town communities were greatly saddened and made uneasy by such a reply, thinking that, if Dom João did not accept the title and dignity of king, he would not take on the charge of the defence of the realm with the love and care that, in their opinion, was incumbent on him. For that reason people's hearts would weaken and they would not make an effort to defend themselves or make ready for their adversaries as it was necessary to do; therefore, the kingdom would be in great danger of falling into the hands of their enemies, above all as they were schismatics and rebels against the Holy Church.

Thus remaining firm in their purpose, not wishing to depart from what they had started, they told the Master again that, given the many needs confronting them, they wanted to attend to all of them with a single solution, namely by having him as their king and liege lord. With this solution they knew all the others would be provided for, so they would be less prey to the harm and perils that the King of Castile menaced them with. Since they wished to defend themselves against him and to further the honour of the Holy Father Urban VI, the true Pope of Rome, they therefore asked him to be merciful and pleaded with him in loud voices not to forsake them and leave them in such distress, but rather to graciously consent to taking the title, dignity and honour of king. He could well see how this was necessary for the kingdom, and what harm and loss would ensue if he were not to give his consent and commitment. They promised to help him with their lives and possessions, to support his rank and honour of king and to prosecute his war. In addition, they would send their most respected ambassadors to the Pope at the Curia in Rome to obtain from him all the necessary dispensations and graces to nullify all the impediments of his birth and profession as well as to confirm the rank of king that they were bestowing upon him.

When the Master heard their insistent prayers, considering the great needs of the realm and their goodwill and offers, and realising that it pleased God that he became king, since they were so insistent, although it was difficult for him to do so for the reasons he had stated, he felt he had to agree. He said that, since he could not do otherwise, he accepted their election and the name and royal dignity of king to defend the realm, with those offers they had made to him and for the honour and reverence to the Holy Father and the Apostolic See in Rome.

With this decided in full, as well as the day when he would be raised to [the rank of] king, everyone rejoiced, and Nuno Álvares was charged with preparing the palace where the ceremony was to take place. Walking through one of the halls where the king was to eat, he could not contain his joy and, although he was normally circumspect in his speech, he said to the many men accompanying him, 'This time my lord and Master will be king because it pleases God, and regardless of whether it makes anyone unhappy.'

On Thursday, 6 April in the aforesaid year of 1385, the Master, in the full bloom of his 26 years, 11 months and 25 days, was raised to the rank of king. The ceremonies, both ecclesiastical and secular, that bestowed upon him that powerful and royal status, which he well deserved, were celebrated with great festivity and merry-making, with hastilude as well as other games and tumbling, as was the custom at that time. This took place not just in the city of Coimbra, but also in other towns both big and small which supported him and his cause.

This was particularly so in Lisbon, where there took place a very noble and solemn procession which started at the cathedral and ended at [the Monastery of] São Domingos. After eating, with great merriment and joy, with many games and tumbling, the people carried a flag through the city, shouting, 'Long live King João!' In the Rua Nova, on the seaward side and so as not to block the street, they erected a huge, tall mast from a carrack to serve as a target for throwing lances.

Chapter 193

How Nuno Álvares was made constable, and concerning some aspects of his way of life

The Master having been elected and thus raised to [the rank of] king, the naming of a constable for the war was immediately discussed, as King Fernando, for the first time, had done when the English had come to Portugal during his reign. The king ordained that it be his very loyal and faithful servant Nuno Álvares Pereira, who was then twenty-four years, nine months and twelve days old and whom he knew to be of chaste habits, and very well versed in feats of chivalry.

Consequently, in view of his prudent and remarkable discernment, it could well be said of him that, although in this life blind fortune fails to reward many a deserving man, in his case it was not ungrateful, exalting him to a great and honourable office in the wars and hosts of the kingdom; and he so exercised it that, gaining stature day by day through chivalric actions, as you will see, he awakened in many the desire to emulate his greatness. That is because, if fortitude is the courageous desire, sustained by beneficial toil, to achieve great things, then this man, fearing neither rough nights of hardship nor adverse days, did not flinch at undertaking any adventurous mission in order to gain a victory over his enemies. This was not because he had the pride and temerity to despise the number of their forces but because no ancient wisdom passed down the ages could equal the acumen of this young warrior. Moreover, he was never boastful nor exalted his fortunate conquests.

He was so astute in organising his plans that no one else could understand the purpose of his strategy, other than those with whom he discussed it.

He was so endowed with astuteness and discipline, wherein lies what most matters in a war, that anyone seeking someone like him among mortals would find it a difficult task indeed. That is why it is written of him that he was a mighty and powerful rampart, and a second arm in the defence of the realm. Consequently, people said of him with great conviction that no one but he could have been chosen for a like honour who would have brought such benefit to the realm and to the king's majesty.

Just like the morning star he outshone those of his generation, with a chaste life and honourable deeds, as if the wise practices of the great heroes of antiquity seemingly glowed within him. His actions and conduct in war demonstrated such authority that none of those who accompanied him dared provoke the enemy more than he had ordered. Hence each man was ready to carry out all his orders, taking care not to disobey them in any way. Yet there always dwelled in him a discreet humility, which is the nursemaid of good habits.

No one was permitted to bring women into the camp or play dice on any of his campaigns; and whenever disagreement arose among his men which resulted in their not talking to each other, he immediately strove to reconcile them to friendship. Thus his encampment did not look like a host of warriors, but rather a virtuous community of defenders. He was judicious in all his proceedings, meting out punishment and reward equally to those [who fell] within the ambit of his justice. When he was angry with anyone, his punishment was dispensed without undue display, so that, confronted with his quiet solemnity, men felt reverence rather than fear. In his youth, he put away men's customary behaviour, and began to lay the foundation within him for all the good qualities that can be expected of an acclaimed hero, as if the wealth of all learning were hidden within him. He spent much more time than his tender age required in pondering upon virtuous things and immediately putting them into practice.

Since all such qualities were not habitual in other men, they were very highly regarded in him. Therefore, it was very difficult to imagine that any vice could be a guest where so many virtues dwelled. Nor could anyone ascribe any fault to him without being considered malicious, for although he made every effort to hide his much-praised reputation, his virtuous deeds blazoned it forth. At the great and important councils he was always the principal figure, and nothing of importance was ever done without his agreement.

His speech was elevated and prudent whenever fitting, kind and loving to those of lesser condition, and as sweet as a child's to inferiors. He was compassionate to the poor and needy, never allowing them to suffer offence and his open hands were always ready to give wherever human honour or spiritual benefit earned his generosity.

He organised his property, dispensing with lavish expenses, always to be avoided, in such a way, that on his lands he never imposed a tribute, a contribution or any other obligation of help to cover the needs of war; his house was administered by those in whom there was little or no taint of error.

His integrity being so pure, nothing was covered up or feigned in him and his word was no less trustworthy than if he had sworn it under oath. He placed his spiritual acts above everything else and was so mindful of the divine offices that he never failed to observe them on account of the visit of any personage, however important and powerful.

His conscience was so clear that, for the good of his soul, he so tempered the vehemence of anger, which appears madness in others, that even though he might be in the right, he never cut anyone short, for it is known that curtailing people's speech creates great hatred and arouses many suspicions.

He was the first to start attending Mass twice a day, saying that great lords, just as they had temporal superiority over the common people, so should they be superior in their spiritual practice.

In the main feasts of the year when the Church traditionally holds processions, he arranged for them to be held in his encampment. Sometimes people bore candles, depending on what was prescribed for the feast day, and a sermon was preached and a service performed as solemnly and devoutly as could be done in such a place. If it is said in praise of the Romans that, despite being gentiles, they did not dare to go into battle or wage war without performing the necessary rites to the god of battles, and that first of all they prayed to the gods of the lands each one had in their care, great praise should be bestowed on this man, who always gladly and fearlessly fought against his enemies, placing great trust and firm hope in God most high, having first offered his devout prayer to that Lord in whose power lie all victories. Not only of the natural gifts of grace, in themselves worthy of note, but also of the riches of good fortune, did this man garner the greatest and rarest jewels, so that from the foundation of the kingdom up until his time, one does not read of anyone like him.

Although it is said that a virtuous young man seldom gains lasting praise, this one, on the contrary, both temporally and spiritually, in life and after death, was always greatly revered by all the people, as you will hear in due course.[317]

---

[317] Thus Part 2 of the chronicle is announced in more specific terms than in the Prologue above.

BIBLIOGRAPHY OF WORKS CITED

For a comprehensive bibliography including all chronicles see volume 5.

Almeida, Jorge (ed.), *Crónica da Regência e do Reinado de D. João I* (Porto: Húmus, 2015)

Amado, Teresa, 'Belief in History', in Miguel Tamen and Helena C. Buescu (eds), *A Revisionary History of Portuguese Literature* (New York: Garland, 1999), pp. 17–29

——*Fernão Lopes, Contador de História: sobre a Crónica de D. João I* (Lisbon: Estampa, 1991)

——'Fiction as Rhetoric: A Study of Fernão Lopes's *Crónica de D. João I*', *The Medieval Chronicle*, 5 (2008), 35–46

Ayala, Pero López de, *Crónicas*, ed. José-Luis Martín (Barcelona: Planeta, 1991)

Baleiras, Isabel de Pina, 'Portugal, 1385: A people's choice or coup d'état?', in Ana Maria S. A. Rodrigues, Manuela Santos Silva, Jonathan W. Spangler (eds), *Dynastic Changes Legitimacy and Gender in Medieval and Early Modern Monarchy*, 1st Ed. (Abingdon: Routledge, 2020), pp. 43–68.

Blackmore, Josiah, '*Afeiçom* and History-Writing: The Prologue of the *Crónica de D. João I*', *Luso-Brazilian Review*, 34:2 (1997), 15–24

——'Singing the Scene of History in Fernão Lopes', in Michelle M. Hamilton and Núria Silleras-Fernández (eds), *In and Out of the Mediterranean: Medieval and Early Modern Iberian Studies* (Nashville, Tennessee: Vanderbilt University Press, 2015), pp. 143–55

Calado, Adelino de Almeida (ed.), *Estoria de Dom Nuno Alvrez Pereyra: edição crítica da 'Coronica do Condestabre'* (Coimbra: Universidade de Coimbra, 1991)

Castro, Filipe, 'In Search of Unique Iberian Ship Design Concepts', *Historical Archaeology*, 42:2 (2008), pp. 63–87

Cicero, Marcus Tullius, *De Officiis*, transl. Walter Miller, The Loeb Classical Library 30 (Cambridge, Mass: Harvard University, 1913) <https://penelope.uchicago.edu/Thayer/E/Roman/Texts/Cicero/de_Officiis/1B*.html> [Accessed 25 February 2022]

Diccionario Biografico Español online <https://dbe.rah.es/> [Accessed 14 March 2023]

Disney, A. R., *A History of Portugal and the Portuguese Empire* (Cambridge: Cambridge University Press, 2009)

Hamilton, Michelle M. and Núria Silleras-Fernández (eds), *In and Out of the Mediterranean*, (Nashville: Vanderbilt University Press, 2015)

Jensen, Frede, *The Earliest Portuguese Lyrics* (Odense: Odense University Press, 1978)

Lopes, Fernão, *Chronica Del Rey D. Ioam I De Boa Memoria E Dos Reyes De Portugal O Decimo*, Part 1, Vol. 1 (Lisbon: Printed by António Alvarez, the King's Printer, 1644)

Lopes, Luís Seabra, 'Sistemas Legais de Medidas de Peso e Capacidade, do Condado Portucalense ao Século XVI', *Portugalia*, New Series, 24 (2003), 113–64

Pedro, Duke of Coimbra (trans.), *Livro dos Ofícios de Marco Tullio Ciceram, o qual Tornou em Linguagem o Ifante D. Pedro, Duque De Coimbra*, ed. Joseph Maria Piel (Coimbra: Acta Universitatis Coimbrigensis, 1948)

Rennie, Kriston, 'The Council of Poitiers (1078) and Some Legal Considerations', *Bulletin of Medieval Canon Law* 27 (2011), 1–16 (7)

Russell, P. E., 'Archivists as Historians: The Case of the Portuguese Fifteenth-Century Royal Chroniclers', in Alan Deyermond (ed.), *Historical Literature in Medieval Iberia*: Papers of the Medieval Hispanic Research Seminar 2 (London: Dept. of Hispanic Studies, Queen Mary and Westfield College, 1996), pp. 68–83

Spiegel, Gabrielle M., *Romancing the Past: The Rise of Vernacular Prose Historiography in Thirteenth-Century France* (Berkeley: University of California Press, 1993)

.

CPSIA information can be obtained
at www.ICGtesting.com
Printed in the USA
JSHW051910110623
43011JS00001B/6

9 781855 663985